Chicana Lives and Criminal Justice

Chicana Lives and Criminal Justice
Voices from El Barrio

by Juanita Díaz-Cotto

University of Texas Press, Austin

Requests for permission to reproduce material from this work should be sent to:
   Permissions
   University of Texas Press
   P.O. Box 7819
   Austin, TX 78713-7819
   www.utexas.edu/utpress/about/bpermission.html

♾ The paper used in this book meets the minimum requirements of
ANSI/NISO Z39.48-1992 (R1997) (Permanence of Paper).

Library of Congress Cataloging-in-Publication Data

Díaz-Cotto, Juanita, 1953–
   Chicana lives and criminal justice : voices from el barrio /
by Juanita Díaz-Cotto. — 1st ed.
     p.   cm.
   Includes bibliographical references.
   ISBN 0-292-71272-3 (cl. : alk. paper) — ISBN 0-292-71316-9 (pbk. : alk. paper)
   1. Women prisoners—California.   2. Female offenders—California.
3. Mexican American women—California—Biography.   4. Mexican American
women—California—Social conditions.   I. Title.
HV9305.C2D53   2006
365ʹ.43092368720794—dc22

                                  2005029912

For Chicana/Latina prisoners everywhere.
God bless you always.

Para las presas Chicanas/Latinas en todas partes.
Que Dios las bendiga siempre.

Contents

List of Abbreviations

ABCNY	Association Bar of the City of New York
ACA	American Correctional Association
AI	Amnesty International
AIN	Andean Information Network (Cochabamba, Bolivia; also RAI)
BJS	Bureau of Justice Statistics
CANY	Correctional Association of New York
CBC	California Board of Corrections
CDC	California Department of Corrections
CDOJ	California Department of Justice
CEDIB	Centro de Documentación e Información, Bolivia
CGW	Coordination Group on Women
CIA	Central Intelligence Agency
CJC	California Judicial Council
CJP	Consultorio Jurídico Popular
CPRP	Chicano Pinto Research Project
CRPC	Critical Resistance Publications Collective
CSAT	Center for Substance Abuse Treatment
CTFJC	California Task Force on Juvenile Crime and the Juvenile Justice Response
DEA	Drug Enforcement Administration
DOD	Department of Defense
EOP	Executive Office of the President
HINTF	Hispanic Inmate Needs Task Force
HRW	Human Rights Watch
IEES	Instituto de Estudios Económicos y Sociales
ICI	Independent Commission of Inquiry on the U.S. Invasion of Panama
INS	Immigration and Naturalization Service
LACJD	Los Angeles County Jail Division

LASD   Los Angeles County Sheriff's Department
LAT   *Los Angeles Times*
LEAA   Law Enforcement Assistance Administration
LT   *Lesbian Tide*
MALDEF   Mexican American Legal Defense and Education Fund
NCCD   National Council on Crime and Delinquency
NCLOE   National Commission on Law Observance and
          Enforcement
NYCBOC   New York City Board of Corrections
NYCLA   New York County Lawyers Association
NYP   *New York Post*
NYSDOCS   New York State Department of Correctional Services
NYT   *New York Times*
RAI   Red Andina de Información (also AIN)
SBI   Sybil Brand Institute for Women
SFC   *San Francisco Chronicle*
SJMN   *San Jose Mercury News*
TNI   Transnational Institute
UN   United Nations
USC   U.S. Congress
USCB   U.S. Census Bureau
USCCR   U.S. Commission on Civil Rights
USDOJ   U.S. Department of Justice
USDOS   U.S. Department of State
USGAO   U.S. General Accounting Office
USHR   U.S. House of Representatives
WCRWC   Women's Commission for Refugee Women and Children
WOLA   Washington Office of Latin America

Glossary

barrio: A neighborhood, the territory claimed by a gang, or the gang itself
black-and-white: Police car
boosting: Shoplifting
calladita: Quiet
chismolera: Gossip
chichis: Breasts
chola/cholita: Female gang member
cholo: Male gang member
comadre: One's child's godmother
compadre: One's child's godfather
connection: Drug supplier
coyote: Smuggler of undocumented immigrants
familia: Family
gavacha: Anglo/European/white woman; pintas interviewed used these words interchangeably
kingpin: Large-scale drug smuggler
madrina: Godmother
manflora: Lesbian
mayata: African-American woman
menudo: Tripe soup
mula: Drug courier
padrino: Godfather
paño: Cloth
PCH: Pacific Coast Highway
placas: Graffiti
playadero: Mexican beach resort gigolo
PO: Parole officer
tecata: Female heroin addict
testimonio: Testimonial, life history
veterana/o: Old-timer, older homegirl/homeboy
vida loca: the "crazy life" of the gang member

Acknowledgments

It is with deep gratitude that I thank the following persons for believing in this book.

All former prisoners who granted me interviews because they wanted their stories to be heard despite experiencing intense sorrow while reliving their past with me. I will forever remember your courage and your will to survive and thrive.

All the prisoners' rights activists (including former prisoners) who gave me interviews and opened their homes and offices to me. May God continue to bless your work.

Doris Bonaparte Lee, for her spiritual support and guidance. May I be as unselfish with others as you have been with me.

Roz Calvert, for her friendship and love, her unceasing support of my political work, her research assistance, and her willingness to take responsibility for the major editing of this and my previous book. You have been the "wind beneath my wings."

Ursula B., Catherine Campbell, the Mah-Andujo family, and María Santos, her son, Alejandro, and her partner, Richard Curci, for welcoming me into their homes when I needed places to stay in California. Iris Vélez, José Morales, and their children for their hospitality while I was working in Puerto Rico.

My father, José Roberto Díaz Nieves, for his encouragement.

For reviewing all or parts of the manuscript I thank Dr. Juan Mah y Busch, Dr. Greg Thomas, Dr. Beth Richie, Dr. Ben Olguín, Rochelle Morris, and my sister María del Carmen Díaz Cotto. I particularly want to thank Dr. Leo Wilton, a former student and now cherished friend and colleague, who reviewed the manuscript several times.

Mimi Anderson, Christine Bexley, Jason Canales, Dorcas Castro, Bridget Christensen, Marjorie Coismain, Taína del Valle, Arianna Eisenson, Jahaira Estrada, Chasedy Figueroa, Olivia Flores, Asia Fogenay, Armando Freemonde, Alecia Henry, Tiffany Javier, Daisy Kim,

Klara Leybel, Amy Lucas, Joelle Martyanik, Lisa Mehmel, Shevonne McKenzie, Deborah Montes, Maija Neville, Erica Padín, Wendy Pao, Gipsy Paredes, Rachel Passaretti, Holly Peacock, Eliza Ross, Deborah Santiago, Wendy Saravia, Diana Valencia, and Xochilt Zuñiga, former SUNY-Binghamton graduate and undergraduate students who, out of a deep sense of solidarity, helped me with many aspects of this project.

Michele Sahairam and Sarah Keough, who transcribed interviews.

Yolanda Retter for some last-minute research assistance.

Nancy Hall, Nancy Scafetta, Sandra Grier, Rosemary Hinkey, Pat Keenan, Patricia Sovier-DeMario, Nancy Garlack, Lisa Fegley, and Margaret Rogers, SUNY-Binghamton staff who assisted with various administrative tasks.

Dara Silberstein, the Women's Studies Program, and the Interlibrary Loan Office for their support.

For making their files accessible to me in California I especially thank: Ellen Barry and Legal Services for Prisoners with Children; Luis Talamantez; Patty, Lisa Schnepple, and Betty Bassette at the *Chowchilla News*; the *Madera Tribune* staff; the Madera City Library; and the libraries of California State at Fullerton and Fresno and of the University of Southern California.

My mother, Juanita Cotto Torres, the Dr. Naula McGann Drescher Affirmative Action Leave Grant, the SUNY Research Foundation, and the McNair Scholars Program, for their financial support.

Theresa May and the University of Texas Press, for believing in this book.

Preface

Interviewing Chicana Pintas

She's here to document us!
—Ursula

When I arrived in Los Angeles in early 1995 my initial goal was to carry out a comparative study of Chicana and Chicano prisoners much along the lines of my book *Gender, Ethnicity, and the State: Latina and Latino Prison Politics* (1996), where I compared the experiences of Latina and Latino prisoners in New York State (Díaz-Cotto 1996). I wanted to compare and contrast the ways in which Latinas/os on the East Coast and Chicanas/os on the West Coast were affected by criminal justice policies, the manner in which they sought to change oppressive conditions, and how those of us on the outside could contribute to such efforts. As a community activist and academic, I also wanted to use the resources I have at my disposal to help give voice to Latina/o prisoners, among the most silenced members of our communities.

However, unlike New York, where the influence of Latino prisoner gangs was minimal during the 1970–1987 period I studied, in California, where Chicana/o communities have been in existence for more than 150 years and where Chicana/o gangs have been in existence since the 1920s, any serious prison study must address the impact of Chicano gangs within the prison structure (Davidson 1974; Donovan 1992; Mirandé 1987; Moore 1978). My only contacts when I arrived in California were two prisoners' rights attorneys—one I had met in New York years before, the other a stranger to whom I had been referred. I therefore questioned whether I would be able to carry out the comparative study I envisioned without developing the extensive contacts with former gang members that other students of Chicano prisoners had established (Davidson 1974; Moore 1978).

By the time I had met a significant number of Chicano former prisoners who were willing to talk to me about their experiences with the criminal justice system, I had become deeply involved in interviewing *pintas* (here understood as Chicana convicts or former convicts) about their lives.

I met the first pinta I interviewed when I accepted an invitation by an African-American former prisoner and prisoners' rights activist to visit a substance abuse recovery program near San Francisco. There he introduced me to Ursula (pseudonym),[1] who was employed by the recovery program. It was through a conversation with her that I began to compile the oral histories that are the heart of this book.

I arrived in California with a number of reservations. Mainly, I feared that being Puerto Rican, a woman, and from the East Coast would interfere with my ability to interview Chicanas/os from the West Coast. My initial concerns vanished when I overheard Ursula say to a friend over the phone, "She is here to document us!" The excitement was so clear in her voice that I was filled with joy and gratitude. From then on I knew that I could relax and enjoy meeting the various Chicanas who were going to come into my life. Within a few days I had interviewed Ursula and six other women she contacted for me. Moreover, she offered me her living room couch to sleep on whenever I was doing interviews in the area.

By the time I sat down to write this preface I had interviewed 42 former prisoners. At least 29 of them were Chicanas, and the remaining 13 were of Mexican, Puerto Rican, Anglo/European, African-American, and mixed racial/ethnic backgrounds.

The interviews took place in workplaces, homes, conference rooms, hotel rooms, coffee shops, public parks, and my car. Overall, the interviews took me to Milwaukee, Wisconsin, and 29 cities in California, from as far south as San Diego to as far north as Santa Rosa. The interviews took place between 1995 and 2001.

I met most of the pintas I interviewed through a network of other pintas who were "clean and sober," that is, were recovering from alcohol and other drug abuse. A few I met at prisoners' rights conferences or through prisoners' rights organizations. I met one Chicana, who later became my contact in her area, at California Department of Corrections (CDC) hearings in Sacramento.

The book focuses on the lives of 24 of the 29 pintas interviewed. At the time of the interviews, they were between 29 and 62 years of age, born between 1934 and 1967. Despite their differences, they shared a number of commonalities. All but one had been heroin-addicted for long periods of time. Most had combined heroin use with other drugs. At the time of the interview, 17 were recovering from drug abuse. The rest had been exposed to alcohol and drug rehabilitation programs at some point in their lives. Those "in recovery" were anywhere from four days to 18 years clean and sober.

While I did not specifically set out to interview Chicanas who were heroin addicts or who were in recovery, I soon discovered the advantages of interviewing precisely such women. Firstly, a significant proportion of incarcerated Chicanas (and non-Chicanas) in California are imprisoned for drug-related crimes such as possession, sale, and/or being under the influence of a controlled substance. Hence, although the sample interviewed is not representative of all pintas in the state, it reflects the experiences of many women who come in contact with the criminal justice system. The sample is also fairly representative of heroin-addicted Chicanas in California (Moore and Mata 1981).

Secondly, and very importantly, as with most addicts, their involvement with the criminal justice system had been extensive. The fact that in California they could be arrested for "possession" and being "under the influence" of a controlled substance made them easy targets for frequent police harassment and arrests when they were not selling drugs. They were also likely to have engaged in other types of illegal, primarily nonviolent economic activities to support themselves, their families, and their drug habits. These activities increased their chances of arrest. They included theft, burglary, robbery,[2] and prostitution.

Chicanas' histories of repeated arrests and incarcerations also allowed me to document their reports of long-term changes in the composition of the women's jail and prison population, Chicana involvement in gangs and illegal activities, and the treatment of Chicanas by police officers, court personnel, penal staff, probation, and parole officers.

Another advantage of interviewing women recovering from drug abuse was that because of the emphasis recovery programs place on honest self-appraisal, the women were able to review their lives from many perspectives with a degree of honesty and clarity that might not have been possible to most still addicted to drugs. Nonetheless, I also felt that the three Chicanas who were clearly under the influence of heroin during the interviews were extremely honest about their lives. The fact that I had a working knowledge of recovery programs proved to be a valuable asset, as the women did not feel that they had to explain or justify to me their addiction or behavior or the aims of such programs.

The pintas I interviewed came primarily from poor and working-class urban families, as I did. This also helped them feel comfortable talking with me. Additionally, two out of every three pintas had been involved in same-sex experiences or relationships at one point or another in their lives. Once again, my being an open lesbian allowed the women to speak freely about their own sexuality.

While initially my main goal was to document Chicanas' experiences in penal institutions, once they began to share their lives with me I decided to broaden the scope of the book to include topics that went beyond imprisonment. As a result, *Chicana Lives and Criminal Justice* not only addresses the experiences of Chicanas in jail[3] but also explores family histories, gang involvement, addiction to drugs, encounters with the juvenile and adult criminal justice systems, their successful and unsuccessful attempts to recover from addiction, and the impact of the war on drugs on their lives and their communities. For while imprisonment was a traumatic experience and an important turning point in the women's lives, it was only one of many experiences that have shaped their lives.

I found that Chicanas experienced violence and abuse while incarcerated, but patterns of violence and abuse began years before their imprisonment and continued years after their release. Sometimes it took place at a relative's or friend's house. At other times it took place on the street or in institutions for youths. Abusers could be family members, friends, acquaintances, strangers, lovers, law enforcement officers, jail or prison guards, probation or parole officers. The abuse was relentless. Yet, the women's will to survive and thrive was equally strong.

One experience I did not foresee was how emotionally challenging it would be to transcribe, review, and edit the interviews. The same feelings were experienced by my editor, Roz Calvert, who listened to all the interviews. I was grateful that I could share with her my feelings of sadness, indignation, and anger at the physical, sexual, and emotional violence pintas have experienced and continue to experience in their lives. But I also found great comfort in hearing how pintas repeatedly found the inner strength to overcome painful experiences. One moment they were crying, remembering some traumatic experience; the next moment they were laughing, recalling another, equally painful experience they now found humorous. It was beautiful to watch that process unfold.

Perhaps the most difficult decision I had to make was how much of what the women revealed to me should be made public. Specifically, did I, as a non-Chicana, have the right to publish their experiences of sexual, physical, and emotional abuse in their homes? My fear was that the material included here would be used to misrepresent all Chicana/o families and contribute unwillingly to the promulgation of racist stereotypes so rampant within U.S. society and reminiscent of the classic works of Oscar Lewis (1959, 1961, 1966) and Daniel P. Moynihan (1967). These, by ignoring the role of social factors, ultimately blamed Mexican, Puerto Rican, and African-American families for their own oppression.

In order to avoid any unintentional misunderstandings about Chicana/o family life I asked several Chicana/o friends and colleagues to review the manuscript and comment on my preoccupations. I also studied the available, yet scant, sources that examined the families of origin of Chicana heroin addicts and confirmed that the family histories I had gathered were representative of the population studied (Moore and Mata 1981). Ultimately, I decided to publish the data gathered because Chicanas had shared their stories with me and trusted me to tell them. I decided to remain true to that trust.

Having said this, however, it is also important to note that the interviews on which this book is based do not present pintas as being merely the *victims of* external forces. Their stories clearly show that they are women who, when faced with certain economic, political, and personal circumstances, made decisions, some more conscious than others, some healthier than others. These decisions brought them into increasing contact with the criminal justice system and contributed to the perpetuation of the cycle of violence in which they had lived since childhood. Most importantly, by the time of the interviews most of them had been able to make choices that helped them break free of their addictions and allowed them to have the opportunity to live their lives much freer of violence.

It is by looking at how women's lives are affected by their own actions as well as by larger societal forces, in this case the Family, the Barrio, and the State, that we can more fully understand the constraints they face and how these affect the decisions they make. Any strategies seeking to change oppressive social structures and empower women and people of color must, of necessity, address both issues.

In view of the above, this book provides an alternative to the perspectives offered by social scientists, mainstream mass media, and government personnel, who tend to either ignore or distort the experiences of those who come in contact with criminal justice agencies and to justify discriminatory treatment and oppressive state policies.

The victims of such policies must be heard because rarely are the illegal actions of government agencies seriously exposed and examined by the mainstream media, much less other ruling elites. Equally important, "these women are often absent from academic and social policy discussions relating to their lives" (Johnson 2003: 3).

Ultimately, the goal of this book is to let pintas, particularly heroin-addicted pintas, or *tecatas*, as they are known on the street, speak out about their own lives. They themselves provide the bulk of the analysis about their motivations and the circumstances under which they made the decisions that brought them in contact with the criminal justice system. In the end, it is the diverse yet often similar experiences in their families, in their barrios, and with the state that show us how addiction, poverty, discrimination, violence, and the war on drugs are experienced by those living in the barrio.

Chicana Lives and Criminal Justice

Introduction

Most social science, government, and private studies of women's criminality attribute the causes of women's crimes to either individual pathology or the collective pathologies said to characterize the social classes and/or racial/ethnic groups from which women "criminals" come. These explanations ignore or undermine women's interpretations of their own motivations and actions.

Such studies are overwhelmingly based on women who have been arrested and incarcerated. As a result, although most women in the United States are Anglo/European, social scientists, government personnel, and laypeople generally take it for granted that because they compose the majority of imprisoned women, women of color are more likely to be "criminals."

Most researchers ignore how discrimination based on social class, race/ethnicity, age, and gender help determine why and how certain groups are disproportionately labeled criminal, arrested, and incarcerated.

Radical and progressive social scientists and community activists have increasingly come to challenge mainstream interpretations of the causes of women's crimes and the political motivations and models on which such interpretations are based. Likewise, they seek to change not only criminal justice policies but the social, political, and economic structures on which such policies are based.

It is important for policy implementation, advocacy, and progressive organizing to debate the weight that race/ethnicity, class, gender, sexual orientation, and age play in the implementation of criminal justice and other policies. Nonetheless, the impact of the war on drugs on Latinas/os in the United States,[1] discussed in Chapter 1, and the experiences of pintas discussed throughout this book clearly demonstrate that social inequalities interact simultaneously at the personal and societal levels to produce a situation wherein people of color, primarily men but increasingly women, are disproportionately arrested and imprisoned in the United States. Moreover, the life histories on which this book is based show that the actions of pintas were not just the result of individual or collective pathology but were the outcome of the interplay of a complex set of personal and systemic factors.

Researching Women of Color and the U.S. Criminal Justice System

Within this context, a few texts have begun to address the oversights within the social science literature by offering multilevel analysis of the experiences of women of color and the criminal justice system.[2]

Moreover, during the past decade, women of color researchers, active in various progressive social movements, have examined the interrelationships among class, race, ethnicity, gender, and, although not always explicitly, sexual orientation and how they frame women's experiences with the criminal justice system (Díaz-Cotto 1996, 2004, 2006; Johnson 2003; Richie 1996; Ross 1998; Sudbury 2002, 2004a, 2004b). These researchers show how discriminatory policies lead to the criminalization and disproportionate imprisonment of women of color and influence how they are treated while incarcerated. They also analyze both the systemic causes behind the persecution of women of color by criminal justice and other state agencies and the ways these hinder women's ability to exert their agency, that is, their ability to act on their own behalf.

Most importantly, through the use of life-history interviews, or *testimonios*, conducted with incarcerated and formerly incarcerated women of color, these researchers have prioritized women's own explanations of the motivations behind their actions as well as validated women's accounts of their experiences with the criminal justice system. The testimonios illustrate how women exert their agency to free themselves from violent relationships, personally destructive behavior, economic difficulties, multiple forms of discrimination, and socially prescribed gender role expectations.

These works complement the autobiographical accounts of former prisoners such as Assata Shakur (1987) and Angela Davis (1988, 1992). Such accounts have provided significant insights into the inner workings of criminal justice and other state policies as they pertain to women of color and their communities (James 1998). Like Gilmore (1998) and Sudbury (2004a, 2004b), they expose how U.S. criminal justice policies serve to maintain the subordination of people of color within capitalist societies. Combined, these works extend to the field of criminal justice the types of multilevel analysis provided in other fields by feminists of color.[3]

Researching Latinas and the War on Drugs

Chicana Lives and Criminal Justice extends a multilevel analysis and, at the same time, expands our current knowledge of the impact of criminal justice policies on Latinas and their communities. At a time when many Latinas are being arrested and incarcerated for low-level, nonviolent, drug-related, and economic crimes (some also drug-related), it is imperative that we understand the various personal and societal factors that have contributed to this trend, particularly if we want to reverse it.

A number of studies describe the overall experience of Latinas/os with law enforcement, the courts, and incarceration.[4] A few focus on or make references to the prison experiences of Latinas.[5] Some have explored related topics such as Latinas' experience with illegal drug use[6] and participation in gangs.[7]

Much of the information available on the impact of the war on drugs on people of color tends to focus on men. Some governmental and private reports provide a general description of the women who are arrested and imprisoned for drug crimes and the types of offenses in question (BJS 1994a, 1999, 2001a; CANY 1985; HRW 1997a, 2000). A few studies make passing reference to the increasing arrests of women for drug crimes as part of their discussion of women's experiences with the U.S. criminal justice system (Bloom 1996; Mann 1993, 1995b; Turk, Owen, and Bloom 1995). Others explore the individual experiences of women impacted by drug-related and mandatory sentencing laws (CANY 1992, 1999; Johnson 2003). Díaz-Cotto (2004, 2006) and Sudbury (2004a, 2004b) draw parallels between the impact of the war on drugs on women of color in the United States and on those abroad.

As valuable as all these sources are, few make more than a passing reference to the fact that Latinas constitute a significant proportion of those arrested and, most importantly, those imprisoned for drug-related crimes in the United States. *Chicana Lives* thus seeks to complement these studies by exploring the ways Chicanas and, consequently, their communities have been affected by the war on drugs in California.

Until now few people have been interested in listening to what pintas, particularly addicts—among those most affected by the war on drugs—have to say about the effects such policies have on their lives. This book seeks to break with previous social science research both by providing an analysis of the diverse personal and systemic forces that affect the lives of pintas and by allowing them to provide the bulk of the analysis concerning their own lives and their experiences with the criminal justice system. The book also breaks with earlier social science tradition in that its targeted audience is not only social scientists, criminal justice personnel, and/or community activists, but also pintas/os and their barrios.

The life histories, in which pintas recount the stories of their lives from childhood through release from penal institutions, are based on a series of open-ended questions. They form the crux of the book because they are currently the major source of information on Chicanas' experience with the criminal justice system. The voices of pintas must be heard because their lives are seldom portrayed in the mass media or considered where criminal justice policies are framed or even in male-oriented prisoners' rights advocacy groups. At the same time, law enforcement and prison guards' unions, pro-incarceration victims' rights lobbies, and other conservative groups have ample exposure in the mass media and within governmental circles.

Chicana Lives is part of my larger political commitment to allow the voices of previously unheard Latinas/os to be heard. The ultimate goal is to encourage those who tell their stories and those who listen to them to change oppressive social structures. As with my earlier work *Compañeras: Latina Lesbians* (under Ramos 1987, 2004) and *Gender, Ethnicity, and the State* (1996), the gathering of testimonios on which *Chicana Lives* is based is itself a development of Latinas' own agency. Unlike *Gender, Ethnicity, and the State,* however, in which I focus my attention on the prison experiences of Latinas and Latinos, *Chicana Lives* follows Chicanas' experiences inside and outside the walls, drawing the parallels between them.

The Study

Chicana Lives primarily focuses on the experiences of Chicanas with the California criminal justice system. The criminal justice system as here understood includes those "organizations responsible for passing criminal laws, preventing crime, and apprehending, processing, and supervising offenders" (Kratcoski and Walker 1984: 563). It includes the legislative, executive, and judicial branches of government. When speaking about the national and/or international enforcement of drug laws, such agencies also include the CIA, the U.S. Armed Forces, the U.S. Customs Service, and the U.S. Department of Housing.

The book is based on 24 life histories with pintas, all but one of them heroin addicts. While only their jail experiences are discussed in this book, all but four also served time in *la pinta*, the penitentiary. Additional interviews were done with non-Chicana former prisoners and male former prisoners, and prisoners' rights advocates such as attorneys, family members, health care professionals, academics, and members of community organizations (some of them also former prisoners). Former employees of the Los Angeles County Sheriff's Department (LASD) and the California Department of Corrections (CDC) were also interviewed.

The information provided by non-Chicana prisoners and others interviewed was used to complement data concerning the experiences of pintas at Sybil Brand Institute for Women (SBI), the Los Angeles women's jail, between November 1963, when it opened, and 1997, when it was closed.[8]

The interviews were further complemented by extensive research of court cases, government and private documents and reports, and California newspapers. The latter included the *Fresno Bee*, the *San Francisco Chronicle*, the *Santa Ana Register*, the *Orange County Register*, the *Sacramento Bee*, the *Los Angeles Times*, the *Madera Tribune*, the *Chowchilla News*, and *La Opinión*. The years covered by the newspaper research ranged from January 1964 to March 1999. The information found in these sources about women's experience, particularly that of Chicanas, with the criminal justice system was minimal. Nonetheless, a few sources did support pintas' overall description of their experiences with law enforcement and SBI.

The attention given to SBI, which covers almost a half of the book, was motivated by the fact that incarceration is perhaps the most significant way in which criminal justice agencies seek to punish those arrested under war-on-drugs policies. Also, it was to SBI that many drug-addicted pintas returned as they lived out lives of repeated arrests and incarceration. In total, 16 of the 24 pintas whose life histories are here documented were held at SBI, all more than once.

It was at SBI that many experimented with same-sex relationships. Moreover, it was at SBI that for the first time most pintas came into close proximity with African Americans and whites. There, they learned to put aside their barrio gang rivalries in order to provide a "united front" before the overwhelmingly white female guard force and the significant African-American prisoner population. Conversely, pintas learned to set aside interracial, interethnic rivalries and joined with non-Chicana prisoners to demand changes in treatment and living conditions.

Another motivation for the attention given to SBI is that although most women imprisoned in the United States are held in jails as op-posed to prisons, few researchers have concerned themselves with documenting the personal and institutional experiences of women in such facilities (Richie 1996; Watterson 1996). In fact, I found only a few references to SBI in mainstream newspapers, grassroots feminist news-letters, government publications, and social science literature (Watter-son 1996) despite the fact that SBI was the Los Angeles County women's jail for 34 years.

In view of the above, the testimonios provided by pintas for this book are a means of helping to break the silence about the experiences of women imprisoned at SBI and the changes that took place in women's jails all over the country as a result of the war on drugs.

A look at Chicanas' experiences of incarceration at SBI also demon-strates that the patterns of abuse Chicanas encountered on the outside continued on the inside at the hands of penal staff. Once institution-alized, Chicanas were further stigmatized, now as convicts. Such stig-matization contributed further to their alienation from and rejection by society at large.

While this book focuses on experiences of pintas in the California criminal justice system, it is important to place these experiences in an international context wherein Latinas/os everywhere are targeted for arrest and incarceration under the auspices of the U.S.-led interna-tional war on drugs.[9]

While elsewhere I compare the impact of the war on drugs on women in the United States, Latin America, and Europe (Díaz-Cotto 2004, 2006),[10] Chapter 1 briefly discusses the motivations and objectives be-hind the drug war and its overall impact on Latinas in the United States, particularly New York and California. It is within this setting that we can best understand the motivations and conditions under which Chi-canas in California are repeatedly arrested and imprisoned primarily for low-level, nonviolent economic and drug-related crimes.

Other chapters illustrate how the drug war is played out in Chicana/o communities in California and in the lives of Chicanas in particular. For although drug policies were only one factor pintas contended with, these perpetuated the cycle of personal and systemic violence to which the women were exposed throughout their lives. Likewise, the drug war exacerbated discriminatory criminal justice policies based primarily on race/ethnicity, gender, and social class. Yet, the war on drugs did little to reduce pintas' addictions; rather, it increased their isolation and alienation from society at large, thus reinforcing their inclination to use drugs.

Having said this, however, the fact remains that the war on drugs was only one of the many obstacles pintas faced. As a result, Chapters 2–18 examine several major themes discussed in the life histories of the 24 pintas at the center of this book. By tracing simultaneously their individual and collective experiences with the Family, the Barrio, and the State, we arrive at a preliminary composite "biography" of the life of a pinta. (Some individual narratives are printed in extended form because they amplify particular points, demonstrate the progression of some point being made, or illustrate issues of agency that were not covered earlier.)

In order to differentiate between the experiences of pintas prior to their first adult incarceration and their experiences during and after incarceration, the book is divided into two parts. Part I (Chapters 1–9) opens with a discussion of the war on drugs, primarily its impact on Latinas/os (Chapter 1).

In Chapter 2, pintas begin to relive their most salient life experiences, particularly as they pertained to physical, emotional, and sexual abuse they experienced as youths and adults, and how these influenced decisions they made in their lives. Chapter 3 follows those pintas who came in contact with the juvenile justice system and explores the conditions under which those first encounters took place and their experiences in youth placements. Pintas' motivation for joining barrio gangs, the benefits of such membership, and the types of activities they engaged in as gang members are the subject of Chapter 4. Chapter 5 explores pintas' initiation into alcohol and other drug abuse and the circumstances under which this took place.

While Chapter 6 provides information on the legal and illegal economic activities pintas engaged in to support themselves, their children, and their drug habits, Chapter 7 reveals various types of offenses for which they were arrested as adults and the circumstances surrounding the arrests. Pintas' experiences of harassment and/or brutality at the hands of law enforcement officers are explored in Chapter 8; an underlying question guiding the chapter was whether pintas' experiences with law enforcement were significantly different from those of Chicanos. Chapter 9 reviews pintas' interactions with prosecutors, defense attorneys, and judges and the types of sentences and post-release supervision they received, particularly following their first adult arrests.

Part II (Chapters 10–17) traces Chicanas' experiences of incarceration at SBI between 1963 and 1997. The chapters pay particular attention to the conditions under which Chicanas were incarcerated, the manner in which they sought to empower themselves in relation to non-Chicana prisoners and staff.

In Chapter 18, pintas examine various dilemmas they confronted once released from jails (and prisons), including how to adequately support themselves and their families, get and stay clean and sober, and stay out of penal institutions. Chapter 19 offers some concluding observations and remarks as well as a summary of the major themes underlying the experiences of pintas interviewed. These include: violence in their lives; biological and nonbiological kinship networks; gender role expectations; racism and discriminatory criminal justice policies; economic constraints; addiction; and pintas' efforts to exert their agency through various means and in diverse settings.

PART I

PRE-INCARCERATION EXPERIENCES

1

Latinas/os and the War on Drugs

Current drug policy relies on an "enforcement" or "penal" model, emphasizing interdiction, arrest, prosecution and incarceration of both distributors and users of controlled substances as its primary "weapons" in what has often been characterized as a war on drugs.
—New York County Lawyers Association, Drug Policy Task Force, 1996

The war on drugs highlights the role that Latinas/os in the United States and Latin American nations play in the production, trafficking, and consumption of "illicit drugs" such as marijuana, heroin, and cocaine.[1] At the same time, it masks the roles that U.S. government agencies, law enforcement officers, middle- and upper-class whites, and private corporations have played in the development of the drug industry and the "multinational drug trade" (Joyce and Malamud 1998: 195).[2] It downplays the demand for such drugs among whites in the United States and Europe (Reuter 1998).

Internationally, such stereotyping criminalizes entire nations by dividing the world into producer/aggressor countries, generally in Latin America and the Third World, and consumer/victim countries in Europe and the United States (Dorado 1998). Within this context, individuals such as Latin American women drug couriers, or *mulas*, are arbitrarily transformed from "'courier' (poor, foreign, visible and vulnerable) into trafficker 'aggressor' (wealthy, powerful, manipulative, and dangerous)" (Green 1996: 3). Portraying all who transport drugs as dangerous is then justified by labeling them "narco-traffickers." The imposition of severe sentences for drug crimes, in turn, proves how dangerous they are.

In the United States, the war on drugs scapegoats groups that have historically been criminalized in various ways and are therefore easy targets for governmental repression (Churchill and Vander Wall 1988, 1989, 1992). These include Latinas/os and other people of color, immigrants, undocumented workers, non–English speakers, the poor, and those seeking social justice. In the mainstream media these groups are portrayed as wetbacks, junkies, knife-wielding Puerto Ricans, promiscuous Latinas, revolutionaries, terrorists, and Mexican thieves like the popular "Frito Bandito" commercials of the past. Latest among these images is the Latina gang member living her *vida loca* and the Latin American mula transporting drugs into the United States and Europe. Combined, these images depict Latinos, and increasingly Latinas, as immoral, criminal, and violent.

Drug-war rhetoric also justifies the manner in which law enforcement agencies have allowed informants, some of them drug kingpins themselves, to remain free while at the same time imprisoning vast numbers of people who play peripheral roles in drug trafficking.[3]

The war on drugs was initiated by Richard Nixon in 1968 on the heels of the racially charged "law and order" discourse of the "war on crime" of the late 1950s and 1960s. It was Nixon who shifted the focus from education and treatment options as ways of reducing the demand for illegal drugs to law enforcement options. He argued that it was addicts seeking to support their habits who perpetrated most street crimes and that only more convictions and imprisonment would deter them (Beckett and Sasson 2000). To achieve those goals, in 1973 he created the Drug Enforcement Administration (DEA). The war on drugs was also a response to the growing use of drugs among middle- and upper-class whites, particularly the young.

The drug war was intensified under subsequent presidential administrations with the creation of new civilian positions to enforce it, notably the "drug czar," and a redefinition of the roles of existing federal agencies now given major responsibility for drug law enforcement, including the FBI, Department of Defense (DOD), and INS (Beckett and Sasson 2000; Call 1993).

Domestically, the war on drugs was about reestablishing "order" in the wake of the various civil rights movements of the 1960s and 1970s. It allowed the federal government to save face amidst the disillusionment brought about by the disclosure that the United States played a major role in supporting and frequently establishing oppressive regimes throughout the world, but particularly in Latin America and Asia. Ultimately, the drug war sought to divert attention from the criminal actions of the U.S. government at home and abroad by scapegoating the people and movements that demanded to be heard: people of color; women; welfare rights and anti-war activists; anti-capitalists; lesbians and gays; and national liberation struggles.

At the international level, the U.S. exportation of the war on drugs sought to achieve a consensus that a common enemy threatened national, hemispheric, and international security. This enemy, so the argument went, combined drug trafficking, terrorist violence, and guerrilla warfare to produce a situation in which "narco-trafficking," spearheaded by "narco-terrorists" and "narco-guerrillas," threatened the security of the Western Hemisphere and, ultimately, of the "free world" (i.e., capitalist countries). Because of its transnational nature, this common enemy required common responses as outlined in the 1988 U.N. Vienna Convention (UN 1991). These responses included: the passage of mandatory and drug-related sentencing laws; increased arrests and imprisonment for drug crimes; the eradication of illicit crops; the militarization of enforcement efforts; and coordination of military, police, and civilian law enforcement operations under the direction of U.S. agencies (e.g., Pentagon, CIA, DEA, U.S. Customs Service).[4] Ultimately, the war on drugs became a means by which to justify the exportation to Latin America of U.S. advisors, weapons, and funding both to curb illicit drug trade and to quash revolutionary movements (Alonso 1997).

The United States' insistence that other countries implement drug-war policies according to U.S. government priorities and its disregard for human rights abroad led to its expulsion from both the U.N. Human Rights Commission and the U.N. International Narcotics Control Board[5] in May 2001 (*Australian Financial Review* 2001; Williams 2001).

In the United States, war-on-drugs policies were implemented despite the fact that what makes international drug trafficking viable is the demand for drugs, primarily from Anglo-Europeans. The demand for drugs, however, as several studies have shown, can be most effectively reduced through educational campaigns and treatment programs including "therapeutic communities, pharmacotherapies, outpatient drug-free programs, inpatient hospitalization, therapy-based (or psychiatric inpatient) programs, twelve-step programs, and multimodality programs" (EOP 1997: 47). One of the advantages of treatment is that all types of treatment reduce drug use, drug-related illness, and "criminal" activity (CSAT 1996; Gerstein et al. 1994). Equally important, "treatment can be effective for all" regardless of age, class, sex, race, or nationality (EOP 1997, 47–48).

Furthermore, drug-war policies were pursued even though it was known as early as 1977 that they were ineffective in reducing drug-related crime (ABCNY 1977). The Drug Policy Task Force of the New York County Lawyers Association (NYCLA) has argued that the drug war has been unable to significantly reduce the importation, distribution, and consumption of drugs, drug-related violent crime, or the profits generated by the illegal drug market (NYCLA 1996). The drug war has also been characterized by the "failure to provide meaningful treatment and other assistance to substance abusers and their families; and failure to provide meaningful economic opportunities to those attracted to the drug trade for the lack of other available avenues for financial advancement" (NYCLA 1996: 6).

The imprisonment rate for drug-related crimes also continued to increase despite evidence that severe sentences and imprisonment do not significantly affect the incidence of drug use or drug trafficking (Tonry 1995). During the late 1990s some states moved to make corrections and sentencing reforms that diverted low-level nonviolent drug offenders into alternatives-to-incarceration programs (King and Mauer 2002),[6] yet local, state, and federal agencies as well as politicians and the mass media have continued to exploit public fears concerning the threat posed by urban gangs, drug-related violence, and drug trafficking. Such fears have led to public demands for harsher sentences and more prison construction (Beckett and Sasson 2000), although much of the violence that takes place in the United States is neither drug- nor gang-related. Moreover, as NYCLA has argued, a significant amount of violence that is drug-related is the result of alcohol-induced violent behavior and the nature of the war on drugs itself. That is, the prohibition of controlled substances, as opposed to their decriminalization or legalization, has led to increased competition for drug markets among drug distributors, growth in the illegal weapons trade, and violent encounters between law enforcement officers and drug dealers (NYCLA 1996).

Shifting the focus from drug enforcement and prison construction to education and drug treatment programs has been strongly resisted by law enforcement unions (Dunn 1996; EOP 1990; Idelson 1995). A change in priorities would mean a cut in revenues for law enforcement agencies that, unable to secure increased funding for other anti-crime initiatives, have become increasingly dependent on funding designated for drug-related anti-crime initiatives. Two examples of these are "block grants earmarked for drug law enforcement" at the local and state levels and "forfeiture provisions authorizing law enforcement agencies to seize 'drug-related' assets" (Blumenson and Nilsen 1997: 2). These include bank accounts, cash, businesses, houses, land, cars, boats, airplanes, drugs, jewelry, and equipment used to transport, store, and manufacture drugs.

Ironically, the monies generated from forfeitures have contributed to government corruption as police departments, bent on increasing their financial resources, seize property and assets even when no crime has been committed. The funds so generated have led to the creation of "self-financing, unaccountable law enforcement agencies divorced from any meaningful legislative oversight" (Blumenson and Nilsen 1997: 3).

Forfeiture laws have proved so profitable that during the 1990s the U.S. Department of Housing and Urban Development (HUD) sought the right to conduct independent raids in HUD-subsidized housing projects in order to benefit from such laws (Damuzi 2001). In 1999 the agency won a lawsuit that allows it to evict families from HUD-subsidized housing projects even when only one family member is caught with drugs. Moreover, in New York City, for example, "the presence of a felon in a household living in public housing in the mid-1990s became legal cause for all the members of that household to be evicted, no matter their age or level of social vulnerability" (Bourgois 2003: xxii–xxiii). Because poor and working-class Latinas/os compose a significant proportion of public housing residents, they have been substantially and disproportionately affected by such laws.

Guards' unions have also benefited from the drug war and the resulting growth in the number of prisoners and penal institutions. As their ranks have swelled with the growth in the number of facilities, so too have their wages and job security. In states like New York and California (Schiraldi 1994), prison guards' unions are now among the most powerful lobbyists and campaign contributors to politicians and victims' rights organizations, supporting tougher sentencing laws and the building of more penal institutions. The increasing influence of the California Correctional Peace Officers Association was demonstrated by the rise in corrections funding from 3.9% of the state budget in 1984 to 18% in 2002. (ibid.: 3).

The continued support for punitive law enforcement solutions despite their dismal failure to achieve any of the proclaimed goals of the war on drugs clearly shows that reducing the demand for illegal drugs is not the priority of government elites. In fact, although the legislative intent behind such policies was to arrest and incapacitate major drug traffickers, instead drug kingpins and corrupt local, state, and federal officials are rarely arrested, prosecuted, or imprisoned for drug trafficking, while low-level drug offenders are severely punished.

Other consequences of the war on drugs have been the weakening of civil governments and a surge in the number of human rights violations by government agents. Such violations include the profiling of people of color and their communities as drug dealers, the discriminatory imposition of curfew and loitering laws in inner cities, and the expansion of "federal prosecutors' capacity to use illegally obtained evidence" (Beckett and Sasson 2000: 72). These have led to a surge in police searches of people of color and their homes and in confiscations of their property even when they are innocent of a crime. Likewise, innocent persons without adequate financial and legal resources have felt forced to plea bargain and accept prison terms rather than risk being found guilty at their trials and sent to prison for long periods of time (NYCLA 1996: 12). To these human rights violations have been added "unwarranted and unjustified drug testing of employees" as well as "property searches of children" (NYCLA 1996: 14).

Combined, the policies violate the First, Sixth, Seventh, Eighth, and Fourteenth Amendments of the U.S. Constitution. This is so because they deny defendants the right to counsel, due process, and a speedy trial. Moreover, defendants in civil cases often are denied the right "to a jury trial . . . in federal court," to be free from "warrantless and unreasonable searches and seizures," to bail, and to be free from "cruel and unusual" punishment (Johnson 2003: 48–49).

Soon after September 11, 2001, human and civil rights violations continued to escalate as the Department of Justice began using the provisions of the newly passed USA PATRIOT Act of October 2001 to invoke "intelligence powers . . . to conduct surveillance operations and demand access to records" not previously accessible without the authorization and strict monitoring of federal judges (Lichtblau 2003: 1A). Invoking intelligence powers, which use "differing standards of evidence" than criminal investigations, allows federal investigators to suspend habeas corpus, ignore the need to obtain grand jury subpoenas, "initiate wiretaps," "track private Internet communications," and seize bank accounts (ibid.).

In the United States, federal agents now frequently use the excuse of a terrorist threat to invoke intelligence powers that allow them to seize records and carry out surveillance and criminal investigations of suspected drug traffickers (Leone and Anrig 2003; Lichtblau 2003).

Latinas/os and Criminal Justice Policies

The study of the impact of criminal justice policies on Latinas/os in the United States within this context is imperative, as they have become the largest ethnic minority in the country (USCB 2001). In 2000, Latinas/os comprised 12.5% of the U.S. population (Hornor 1999: 7).[7] It is expected that as the Latina/o population increases, so will its arrest and incarceration rate in relation to African Americans and whites.

The overrepresentation of Latinas/os among the U.S. penal population was evident in 1997, when they composed 29.3% of prisoners in federal institutions (BJS 2001d: 517). In 1999 they were 17.0% of sentenced prisoners under state jurisdiction (BJS 2001c: 11) and 15.5% of those in local jails (BJS 2001a: 3).

In California, at least 38.5% of those held in jail on June 30, 1999, were "Hispanic" (BJS 2001a: 22),[8] although at the time Latinas/os composed 32.4% of the state's population (USCB 2001: 4). By 2002, Latinas/os comprised 35.4% of state prisoners in California.[9]

Several factors account for the increase in the Latina/o prisoner population. For one, the Latina/o population is a young population (USCB 2001). It is the young, particularly Latina/o and African-American youths, who are more likely to be arrested and incarcerated. This trend is already apparent in the overrepresentation of Latinas/os in juvenile arrests, juvenile correctional facilities, adult jails, and prisons.[10] By 2002, Latina/o youth comprised 48% of the wards and 51.3% of the parolees of the California Youth Authority (Byrnes, Macallair, and Shorter 2002: 7).

Other factors contributing to the increasing arrest and imprisonment of Latinas/os are racism, excessive police patrolling of poor and working-class neighborhoods, criminal laws that target the types of crimes committed by these social classes, inadequate legal representation, and the hardship imposed by unnecessary and sometimes excessive bail.[11] Bail also discriminates against the poor because all persons, regardless of economic status, are generally expected to pay the same.

Language barriers present at all levels of the criminal justice process also prevent Latinas/os from receiving equal treatment under the law.[12] This contributes to the overrepresentation of non-English-speaking Latinas/os within the prisoner population.

Furthermore, because Latinas/os are not as likely to be channeled into alternatives-to-incarceration programs as African Americans and whites are and few existing programs have been designed specifically for them, it is not surprising that they are overrepresented in pre-trial detention centers (Aguirre and Baker 1988; LEAA 1980). The fact that incarceration prior to the adjudication of guilt or innocence increases one's likelihood of being sentenced to jail or prison[13] means that, once arrested, Latinas/os are likely both to be sentenced to serve time in penal institutions and to receive harsher sentences.

In states including California and New York, more aggressive law enforcement practices and tougher parole board decisions have also led to an increase in Latinas/os convicted and in the length of their sentences. These trends were set into motion with the proclamation of the war on drugs at the state and federal levels, the reinstitution of the death penalty, and the passage of mandatory and drug-related sentencing laws during the 1970s, 1980s, and 1990s.[14] Examples of such legislation include second felony offender laws, violent felony offender laws, changes in consecutive-sentence provisions, the Sentencing Reform Act of 1984, the Violent Crimes Control and Law Enforcement Act of 1994, New York's Rockefeller drug laws,[15] and California's Three Strikes Law.[16] The latter, for example, mandated "that the penalty for a second felony be doubled and that a third felony result in 25 years to life. To be convicted under the law, only the first two felony convictions must be 'strikeable' (serious but not necessarily violent) offenses; the third can be any offense, no matter how minor" (Beckett and Sasson 2000: 180).

Taken as a whole, such legislation reduced defendants' ability to plea bargain, made imprisonment mandatory for certain offenses, abolished parole for some offenders, and increased the length of sentences for others. It also curtailed judges' discretion over sentencing. As the case of mandatory minimum drug laws illustrated,

mandatory minimum drug laws oblige judges to ignore information about an offender's job status, family obligations, history of victimization, and potential for rehabilitation. Moreover, because these laws punish according to the volume of the drug seized, they oblige judges to overlook even the particular details of the offense. (Beckett and Sasson 2002: 176)[17]

Ironically, in California, those most affected by the state's Three Strikes Law were convicted for nonviolent property crimes (e.g., theft and burglary) and low-level drug offenses, primarily possession (Beckett and Sasson 2002; Clark, Austin, and Henry 1997). In New York, those most affected by mandatory and drug-related sentencing laws were also low-level drug offenders mainly arrested for sales (HRW 1997a). Many did not have prior criminal records. According to Human Rights Watch (HRW), low-level offenders include "people who possess drugs for their own use, small-scale street-level dealers, or people who occupy low positions in drug operations, such as lookouts, steerers, or couriers" (HRW 1997a: 15).

Another set of laws that increased sentence lengths are truth-in-sentencing laws. These laws changed the focus from indeterminate sentences (with no fixed maximum prison term) to determinate sentences (which provide a fixed maximum).[18] These laws also mandated that persons convicted of felonies must serve most of their sentences before being eligible for parole. The 1994 Federal Crime Control Act, for example, stipulated that states applying for federal funding to build new prisons must require felony offenders to serve at least 85% of their sentences (Beckett and Sasson 2000; U.S. Sentencing Commission 1991). Because drug crimes are often processed as felonies, those arrested for violation of drug laws were more severely affected by truth-in-sentencing laws.

Likewise, federal sentencing guidelines and most state laws discriminate against the poor by legislating more severe penalties for offenses involving crack cocaine than those involving powder cocaine, which is used more frequently by middle- and upper-class whites. According to Beckett and Sasson (2000: 179), "The decision by the U.S. Congress to impose a 5-year mandatory prison term (with a statutory maximum of 20 years) for five grams of crack but for 500 grams of cocaine therefore had a racially discriminatory impact."

Beckett and Sasson (2000) also argue that "school zone" laws which impose mandatory sentences for the sale of drugs within a certain proximity of a school discriminate against people of color because schools are much more densely concentrated in inner city neighborhoods where a disproportionate number of people of color tend to live.

Overall, these crime-fighting initiatives have been supported by many well-meaning victims' rights advocates, some of whom are spurred on and backed by government leaders, law enforcement and penal elites, and corporate-controlled media campaigns that have highlighted gang and drug crimes committed by people of color and called for harsher punishments.[19] Due to the discriminatory manner in which criminal justice policies have been framed and implemented, such demands necessarily result in the increasing arrest and imprisonment of more poor and working-class whites, but particularly of more people of color.

Latinas and the War on Drugs

As a result of the interactions of the policies discussed above, it is not surprising to find that during the 1980s and 1990s the war on drugs had more severe impacts on Latinas/os and African Americans than on whites. Thus while whites in the United States compose the majority of those who traffic drugs and over 80% of those who consume them (NYCLA 1996: 12), they are less likely to be arrested and sentenced to prison for such offenses. Even when arrested for such crimes, the U.S. Sentencing Commission and the federal judiciary found that whites are more likely to receive lower minimum sentences than people of color.

Partly due to disparate treatment, in 1997 Latinas/os composed 33% of those imprisoned in federal facilities for drug offenses (BJS 2001b: 11). In 1999 they were 20.7% of those under state jurisdiction for drug crimes (BJS 2001c: 11). In New York, 46.6% of drug felons in prisons in 1996 were Latina/o, 47.6% were African-American, and 5.3% were white (HRW 1997a: 14).

In California, the increasing arrests of Latina/o youth during the 1990s was also significantly associated with drug-related crimes. In 1999, Latina/o juveniles (10 to 17 years old) composed 43.6% of juveniles arrested on misdemeanor drug charges in California and 42.5% of those arrested on felony drug charges (CDOJ 2000b: 20, 22). Police harassment of Latina/o youth as well as gang-related crimes, many of which are associated with drugs, have also contributed to this increase (Mirandé 1987; NCLOE 1977).

Men have always composed the overwhelming number of those arrested and incarcerated.[20] However, the war on drugs has more severely affected women than men. By 1991, 32.8% of women in state prisons were serving sentences for drug offenses compared to 20.7% of the men (BJS 1994a: 3). In 1998, 30% of women in jail, 34% of women in state prisons, and 72% of women in federal prisons were serving time for drug crimes (BJS 1999: 6). In New York this trend was already apparent as of the late 1970s, when "a notably higher percentage of female new commitments were sentenced for drug crimes than male new commitments" (NYSDOCS 1986a: 19). This discrepancy continued through the 1990s. In California, 43% of the female felons (up from 13.2% in 1983) and 26.7% of the male felons (up from 7% in 1983) were imprisoned for drug-related offenses as of December 31, 1999 (CDC 2000a: Table 13). In 2001, adolescent girls (7.7%) held in California Youth Authority (CYA) facilities were also more likely than boys (5.1%) to have been committed for drug offenses that year (Byrnes, Macallair, and Shorter 2002: 7).

As a result of the interaction of gender and racial/ethnic factors, Latinas in New York were more likely to be imprisoned for drug offenses than Latinos. Hence, at the end of 1987, 62.3% of Latinas and 36% of Latinos incarcerated in New York were imprisoned for drug offenses, and on December 31, 2001, 61.5% of incarcerated Latinas and 38.8% of Latinos were imprisoned for such offenses (NYSDOCS 2002: 87).

Several reasons could account for this gender discrepancy. One argument has been that as economic conditions have worsened for many as a result of sectoral job losses in the United States, drastic cuts in social services, and the increasing incarceration of men of color, Latinas and other poor and working-class women have been forced to find new ways of generating an income. Within this context the global demand for drugs has provided for some an alternative source of employment (Díaz-Cotto 2004, 2006; Sudbury 2002, 2004a, 2004b).

Another explanation offered is that more women than men are using drugs. According to Coramae Richey Mann, "studies of drug use by arrestees repeatedly show a higher percentage of female than male arrestees who test positive, particularly for multidrug use" (Mann 1995b: 120). Several government reports also indicate that women in state prisons are more likely than male prisoners to have been under the influence of drugs at the time of their arrests (BJS 1994a, 1999). Some of those supporting this explanation argue that more women are using alcohol and illegal drugs in an attempt to cover up and numb the pain resulting from the physical and sexual abuse to which they have been repeatedly exposed since childhood. The fact that an overwhelming number of women offenders, as compared to men, are survivors of incest, rape, and battering seems to partly support this argument (BJS 1999).

Others sustain that the discrepancy in drug arrest rates for Latinas and Latinos is the result of sexism. Women do not tend to occupy major roles in drug networks and therefore in drug transactions. In fact, in New York City, Bourgois (2003) found, "The male-dominated ranks of the underground economy exclude females from the more profitable, autonomous entrepreneurial niches such as dealing, mugging, and burglarizing" (279). Thus, lacking information that is most sought by law enforcement personnel and/or assets that can be forfeited, Latinas do not have the same plea-bargaining power Latinos have to secure lesser charges and sentences or no sentences at all (CANY 1999; Szalavitz 1999).

Ironically, because Latinas and other women tend to be the primary caretakers of their children, they are more vulnerable than men to threats from both drug connections and criminal justice personnel. In fact, Latinas are sometimes arrested on drug violations in an attempt to pressure them to give information concerning the illegal activities of men in their lives (e.g., mates, brothers, fathers). Women who refuse to provide such information, whether out of loyalty to men or fear of retaliation by drug associates, are often punished more severely by district attorneys (Szalavitz 1999). So too are women who are willing to cooperate but do not have the type of information district attorneys value. Moreover, when arrested in their homes, they are also more likely than men to be charged with "child endangerment" and "contributing to the delinquency of a minor," adding further charges.

Still others argue that women may actually be facing more pressure by men in their lives to provide "free or cheap labor in the drug business" (Sudbury 2002: 229). Although pintas interviewed did not offer this argument as an explanation, a number of them did say that Chicanos seem less inclined than in the past to take the blame for crimes committed jointly in order to spare Chicanas imprisonment and separation from their children. In fact, they were more likely than before to try to convince women partners to take full responsibility for joint crimes. They assumed that women, particularly those with no previous arrest records, would more easily "beat the rap," that is, win the case, or, if convicted, get a shorter sentence than men with criminal records. Nonetheless, due to mandatory and drug-related sentencing laws, Latinas and other women are at least as vulnerable as men to receiving harsh sentences for drug crimes, even when their level of participation in illegal drug enterprises is less than that of men.

Once Latinas come in contact with the criminal justice system they are more likely than white and sometimes African-American women to be sentenced to prison for drug crimes. According to BJS, in 1998, "[w]hile nearly two-thirds of women under probation supervision are white, nearly two-thirds of those confined in local jails and State and Federal prisons are minority" (BJS 1999: 7). At the time, Latinas comprised 6% of the U.S. population (Marotta and García 2003) but 15% of women in jails, 15% of women in state prisons, 32% of women in federal prisons, and 10% of women on parole (BJS 1999: 7). That is, they composed approximately 1 in 7 women in jail, "about 1 in 7 women in State prisons but nearly 1 in 3 female prisoners in Federal custody" (BJS 1999: 7).

A study conducted by Mann (1995b) comparing New York, California, and Florida found that Latinas in California were more likely to be sentenced to prison for felonies than were African-American or white women. Thus, in 1990, "23.8% of Latinas arrested for felonies in California were sentenced to prison compared with 18.3% of African-American women, [and] 16.8% of white women" (Mann 1995b: 128). White women felons in California were also less likely to be imprisoned for drug violations and theft than Latina and African-American women, even though they were the most often arrested for burglary, drugs, and theft (Mann 1995b: 128). Hence, in 1990, Latinas comprised 18.7% of women arrested for drug violations but 26.1% of those imprisoned for drug offenses. African-American women were 30.5% of women arrested on drug charges but 34.1% of those incarcerated for drug offenses (Mann 1995b: 128). White women were 48.5% of women arrested for drug violations but only 38.3% of those sentenced to prison. These discrepancies existed although, as Mann has indicated, at least one study found that female heroin and opiate use is similar among all three groups (Pettiway 1987).

In New York, 78.9% of the felonies leading to women's imprisonment in 1990 were drug violations. However, at the time, Latinas were 28.8% of women arrested but 41.2% of women sentenced to prison for such offenses (Mann 1995b: 128).[21] During the late 1990s, Latinas continued to be more likely than African-American but particularly white women to be sentenced to prison for drug offenses. Between 1997 and 2000, 71.3% to 79.5% of new court commitments for Latinas were for drug offenses, overwhelmingly for sales and secondly for possession (NYSDOCS 2000: 81).[22]

Once in the system, Latinas, particularly those with no previous arrest records, tended to reject plea-bargain offers, believing they would be found innocent. However, most did not have the financial resources to post bails[23] or hire private attorneys as did middle- and upper-class women charged with similar crimes.[24] Other Latinas, even when innocent, frequently pled guilty to a lesser offense in order to get a reduced sentence.[25]

Likewise, poor women could not afford to pay the costs of private recovery programs accessible to women with higher incomes. Thus, addicted Latinas often ended up in the criminal justice system, where treatment was usually not an option due to lack of available programs and to mandatory sentencing laws (CANY 1999).

Moreover, as noted by NYCLA (1996: 13),

[f]or those women who have substance abuse problems, a combination of mandatory reporting requirements and the child abuse and neglect laws serve to deprive them of access to medical services, pre-natal care, and even substance abuse counseling.

Hence, as Maia Szalavitz (1999) has pointed out, addicted women are less likely than non-addicts to seek medical services or treatment for their addiction for fear that they will be referred to police authorities by medical authorities. They also fear that imprisonment, particularly for those given long sentences, could result in the permanent loss of custody of their children. Likewise, 1980s and early 1990s publicity around "crack babies" promoted by the anti-abortion movement led several states to enact laws that tend to "criminalize the use of drugs by pregnant women" and subject them to prenatal incarceration and/ or prison sentences if the child is born drug-dependent (ibid.; see also Bourgois 2003).

At all times, among those most vulnerable were the non-English-speaking, particularly foreign drug couriers, who rarely had access to Spanish-speaking attorneys or translators (CANY 1992; CJC 1997).[26] Furthermore, Latinas and other women of color were more likely to be stopped for trafficking, strip searched, and arrested at airports than white women, even when they did not come from "source countries." According to the Correctional Association of New York (CANY), women more likely to be profiled as drug couriers were "Black and Hispanic women traveling alone, or with other women, from the Caribbean, Africa and South America" (CANY 1992: 11).[27]

A number of Latin American couriers interviewed by CANY spoke about how they were used as "decoys" by drug traffickers. That is, customs agents were informed about women transporting small amounts of drugs on a flight in order to detract attention from other passengers carrying larger amounts (CANY 1992).

Harsh sentences were applied in cases involving drug couriers even when many women argued that they were forced to transport drugs by dire economic conditions[28] they faced in their countries of origin or threats made on them and/or family members. Others had been asked by friends or acquaintances to deliver a bag to someone in the United States, the contents unknown to them until their arrest. Some couriers did not see the drugs even after their arrest because they were arrested in one location and federal officials took the evidence somewhere else. In fact, in New York, "[n]either the drugs, nor photographs, nor any other evidence is required as proof of the charge" during grand jury proceedings (CANY 1992: 10).

Once convicted for drug-related crimes, Latin American couriers who are not U.S. citizens, along with other noncitizens who have broken U.S. laws, are considered "criminal aliens" and subject to the sentencing stipulations provided under the Sentencing Report Act of 1984 and the Anti-Drug Abuse Act of 1986 (BJS 1996). The former requires prisoners to serve at least 85% of their sentences, and the latter stipulates that those who have been convicted of distributing or importing controlled substances must serve "a mandatory minimum of 5- or 10-year term of imprisonment depending upon the quantity of drugs involved" (BJS 1996: 8). While some criminal aliens are deported after the conclusion of criminal proceedings,[29] others are deportable once their sentences have been completed (BJS 1996: 3).[30]

Latinas and other women, whether pintas or not, have been affected by three decades of "get tough on crime" policies in yet other ways. Mona J. E. Danner has described some of these collateral effects:

A portion of the costs of prison construction and maintenance are paid for by cutting social services from which women benefit. In addition, since women are more likely to be employed in social services and men are more likely to be employed in criminal justice, the increase in the criminal justice system at the expense of the social service system places women's employment opportunities in jeopardy. Finally, the incarceration of parents leaves behind children who may be traumatized and whose emotional and economic care is left to women. (Danner 2000: 215)

Moreover, as NYCLA has indicated,

[w]hen fathers are incarcerated for drug use or sale, it is the women who are left to raise children in single parent homes. When teenage boys become involved in the drug trade, it is their mothers who are evicted when civil forfeiture laws are enforced. When men who are injection drug users share needles because of the lack of availability of clean needles, the women they sleep with risk HIV infection. (1996: 13)

Furthermore, Karlene Faith (1981) has observed, "Women are only rarely involved in armed drug deals, but they are often the victims in revenge killings between men" (99).

In summary, the war on drugs has severely affected Latinas/os because of the overemphasis on drug crimes by criminal justice agencies (Beckett and Sasson 2000); Latina/o overrepresentation in drug arrests; the fact that drug offenses are among the most harshly punished (CANY 1985, 1992, 1999; HRW 1997a); and discriminatory criminal law enforcement policies. The combined result of these policies is that Latinas/os, but particularly Latinas, are disproportionately arrested, convicted, and sentenced to jails and prisons. Due to the lack of support services during and after incarceration, their recidivism rates are among the highest.

The Prison-Industrial-Military Complex

At the close of the 20th century, the United States imprisoned more persons, both per capita and in numbers, than any other country in the world. According to the U.S. Bureau of Justice Statistics (BJS), at the end of 2000, more than 2 million persons were held in federal (6.9%), state (60.9%), and local (32.1%) facilities (BJS 2001c: 1, 2).[31] That is, "1 in every 143 U.S. residents were incarcerated in State or Federal prison or a local jail"[32] (BJS 2001c: 2). To government facilities were added privately operated jails (BJS 2001a, 2001b) and prisons (Bates 1981).[33] Many facilities became overcrowded soon after they were opened (BJS 2001c: 9).

California is one of the states that best exemplifies these trends. By June 30, 1999, there were 145 jails under 77 jail jurisdictions (BJS 2001a: 14). Since the early 1980s, the California Department of Corrections

(CDC) "has been involved in the largest prison building program in the United States," at a cost of $5.27 billion (CDC 2002: 1). This entailed expanding existing facilities and constructing new public and private institutions. On June 30, 2000, California had 86 state public and private adult prisons (BJS 2001c: 9), including the two largest women's prisons in the world. As a result of these trends, in mid-1999, California held the highest number of persons under the jurisdiction of jail authorities in the United States (BJS 2001a: 14). At year-end 2000, it also held the highest number of persons under state or federal jurisdiction in the country (BJS 2001c: 3). In 2002, it cost the state of California $26,690 to house each prisoner (CDC 2002: 1).

The number of persons under the supervision of local, state, and federal penal authorities continued to increase even after the crime rate had begun to show marked decreases for many offenses during the 1980s (Beckett and Sasson 2000; DOJ 1981–2002; Lichtblau 2000). In California, for example, the arrest rate for misdemeanors peaked during the early 1980s, while that for felonies peaked during the late 1980s (CDOJ 2000a: 26).

It was the contradiction between increasing imprisonment rates, particularly of people of color, and declining crime rates that led human rights advocates to intensify their criticism of massive prison construction during the 1980s and 1990s. They argued that imprisonment rates had little to do with crime rates and more to do with racism, economic trends, and governmental policies that target certain kinds of crime for prosecution (i.e., street crimes) and thereby certain groups for imprisonment (i.e., poor and working-class whites, but particularly people of color).[34]

Critics of the war on drugs documented the ways private corporations and government agencies benefited from continued prison construction. Companies such as Corrections Corporation of America and Wackenhut Corporation have made millions by "designing, constructing, financing, and managing prisons, jails and detention centers" (Sudbury 2004a: 224). Other businesses benefiting from such ties include energy providers, legal firms, those providing security, food delivery, and telephone services, and firms in the garment industry. To these are added companies that benefit from the labor directly performed by prisoners for and within privately run prisons.

The globalization of the drug war has also been accompanied by the exportation of U.S.-based private prison companies and their subsidiaries to other countries, including Puerto Rico and South Africa (Martin 2000; Sudbury 2002).

It was their questioning of the economic and political objectives of such policies and the ways private corporations and government agencies profit from both prison labor and prison construction that led prisoners' rights advocates to speak about the "prison-industrial complex" (PIC).[35] PIC calls to mind the concept of the "military-industrial complex" first used by Dwight Eisenhower and subsequently appropriated by the Left to describe the alliance between military and corporate interests.

PIC critics expose how ties between private corporations and state elites are safeguarded by the millions of dollars the former spend in political campaign contributions and in lobbying politicians in order to obtain lucrative prison contacts. In turn, private companies recruit lobbyists and corporate administrators from the ranks of former penal employees, politicians, and high-level bureaucrats.

The term "PIC" also calls attention to how urban but particularly rural communities, encouraged by politicians, private corporations, and the mass media, seek to rely on jails and/or prisons for solutions to economic difficulties created by the flight of industry and capital to Third World countries (Gilmore 1998). PIC critics indicate how the mass media contribute to the criminalization of people of color by encouraging the fear of crime and portraying criminals as being primarily people of color.

Notwithstanding its usefulness in describing important phenomena taking place in the United States, the term PIC only partially describes the reality of those Latinas/os living along the U.S.-Mexican border, where the military has joined forces with the INS, the DEA, and U.S. and Mexican police forces in its increasing war against undocumented immigrants under the aegis of the war on drugs (HRW 1995b).

The discriminatory enforcement of immigration policies, combined with the emphasis on stopping the trafficking of drugs, money, and people across the border, have led to a greater incarceration of foreign nationals (including children) and a host of human rights violations.[36] While such violations have been extensively documented by civil and human rights organizations, it is important to note that foreign nationals are frequently subjected to verbal, sexual, and/or physical abuse by federal agents and other law enforcement personnel during arrest and incarceration in local, state, and federal institutions and private, for-profit facilities contracted by the INS to hold adults and minors. Many are detained in overcrowded, unsanitary facilities for indefinite periods and denied access to appropriate legal counsel, translators, and adequate recreation. While adults may be released pending deportation or exclusion proceedings, minors are not granted the same rights.

Moreover, PIC does not fully describe the reality of Latin American countries where the U.S. and local military forces, along with various U.S. federal agencies (e.g., DEA, CIA), are partners in carrying out drug-war policies alongside corporate and state elites.[37] While elsewhere I compare the impact of the war on drugs on Latinas in the United States, Europe, and Latin America (Díaz-Cotto 2004, 2006), suffice it to say here that in Latin America, the growing militarization of the war on drugs has been aimed at eliminating illegal drug production and trade as well as quashing Latin American revolutionary movements (Alonso 1997), all considered national and international security threats. As in the United States, the drug war has led to increased corruption, the weakening of civil governments, and widespread human rights violations. Entire indigenous communities have been devastated and its members displaced. The number of women, men, and children arrested and imprisoned for drug crimes has drastically increased, along with the construction of more jails and prisons. Like their sisters in the United States, many women in Latin America are arrested primarily for economic and low-level, nonviolent drug crimes.

As a result of the above, the term "prison-industrial-military complex" would be more appropriate to describe the overall Latina/o experience of the war on drugs both in Latin American and significant areas of the United States.

Concluding Observations

Within this context, it becomes imperative that we understand how the lives of pintas and other Latina prisoners in the United States are intertwined with the ideological arguments sponsored by the war on drugs and the policies it engenders. For even in those cases where Chicana addicts are sent to jails or prisons for short periods of time, the fact that they are repeatedly arrested and incarcerated for "breaking the law" contributes to maintaining the ideological justification for the war on drugs and other repressive policies that target poor and working-class people. It is in poor and working-class neighborhoods where whites, Latinas/os, and other people of color live that such policies are played out on a day-to-day basis. They are the ones portrayed as being dangerous and violent, and, hence, deserving of being imprisoned for long periods of time.

It is against this backdrop that we can better understand some of the motivations behind the criminalization of Chicana addicts in California and their repeated arrests for low-level nonviolent economic and drug-related crimes.

2

Families and Early Experiences of Abuse

We get so used, . . . even by our own supposedly "loved ones" . . .
And then after they do it, they're . . . hugging you and telling you
how they're sorry because they love you so much. "Well, if you
loved me so much, why did you do this to me?" . . . And . . . after a
while, . . . the word love, it was a conjunction. It wasn't a feeling . . .
It was like, "Yeah, okay, so you love me? Okay. Now what?"
—Melinda

Much has been written about the nature and characteristics of Chi-
cana/o families (Zambrana 1995). Regardless of the political motivations behind conflicting arguments, a significant number of students of
Chicana/o families center their discussions on the extent of women's
deference to males in their families and the importance of maintaining close, often extended, family networks as well as retaining "a strong
sense of ethnic identity" (Hurtado 1995: 47).

Diverse opinions exist as to the degree to which Chicana/o families
are affected by larger social, political, and economic factors including
poverty, underemployment, and institutional racism. Also debated is
the impact that immigration, changing economic conditions, and various social movements (e.g., feminist, lesbian and gay) have on gender
roles in the family. Equally important have been the discussions concerning the effect on Chicana/o families of addiction, incarceration,
AIDS, teenage pregnancy, high school drop-out rates, and participation
in gangs.

While such discussions have been rich, little has been documented
on the families of pintas, particularly drug-addicted Chicanas (Moore
and Mata 1981), and the effects of the war on drugs on their families.
What few studies there are confirm the findings of national and California data that highlight the widespread physical and/or sexual abuse
to which incarcerated women of all racial and ethnic groups have

been exposed at some point in their lives (BJS 1994a; Turk, Owen, and Bloom 1995).

The depiction of Chicana/o families in this book is not meant to be a representative sample of all Chicana/o families or even of all families of Chicana pintas. It does, however, provide a sample of the types of families from which pintas interviewed came. When I began to interview pintas about their family histories, the questions I asked them included: Were you ever physically or sexually abused? Did you ever talk to anyone about it? How did those around you react when you told them? What impact did such experiences have on the decisions you made and the actions you took early on in life?

Because the voices of sexual and physical abuse survivors within Latina/o communities are often silenced, once I asked these questions pintas interviewed felt free, sometimes for the first time in their lives, to begin sharing their experiences openly. As it turned out, their experiences of childhood and adolescent physical and sexual abuse were among the major turning points in their lives. Hence, they are given centrality in this chapter.

However, because this chapter focuses primarily on childhood and adolescent experiences it does not give a full description of the various types of relationships pintas had with their families throughout their lives. For some, family members may have failed to meet their needs for nurturing and protection while they were youths, yet the same or other family members may have provided them support as their lives unfolded.

Family Demographics

Most of the Chicanas whose life histories are discussed throughout this book were born and raised in urban areas, two-thirds of them in Southern California, primarily Los Angeles (Appendix A). Most are also the children of parents born in Aztlán, or the southwestern United States (i.e., Arizona, California, Colorado, New Mexico, and Texas). Although few caretakers had finished high school, two out of three parents spoke Spanish and at least some English. More than half of the pintas interviewed were bilingual. All but a few came from working-class families in which there was at least one wage earner.[1] Though several spoke about having grown up in extreme poverty, few reported parents who collected welfare while their daughters were growing up (see also Moore and Mata 1981).

Pintas came from diverse types of families, including single- and two-parent households, but primarily extended family networks. Care-takers were predominantly heterosexual. While almost half were raised by both parents or a mother and a stepfather (see also Moore and Mata 1981), a handful were raised by their mothers. Only one was "state-raised," that is, raised in government institutions for children and juve-niles (10–17 years old). All but one of the remainder were raised by a combination of relatives. More than half had five or more siblings.

As youths the women preferred to remain at home with their bio-logical families. Yet at least half of those interviewed felt forced to run away from home between the ages of 13 and 16 (Appendix A). Reasons for running away included physical, emotional, and sexual abuse as well as neglect, abandonment, strict families, divorce, and parents' ad-dictions or mental illnesses. While some ran away with their "home-girls," that is, barrio or neighborhood friends, at least eight left home to live with male partners.

Although only three spent any significant amount of time in foster homes as children, one out of every four had spent time, between the ages of 11 and 17, either in county facilities for juvenile offenders (juve-nile halls) or in CYA facilities, that is, state facilities for the most seri-ous youth offenders (see Boyd 2003).[2]

Beginnings

Gina was the eldest of eight children. Her parents entrusted her early upbringing to the care of women relatives.

Who raised me? Okay . . . I guess it started with my mom and dad till I was four months. Then from there I went to my grandmother's and . . . my aunt, and stood there until I was nine. Then from there I went to my great grandmother's until I was 11, come back home . . . until I was 14. Then ran away . . . At 16 I got married, but I got pregnant at 15.

Luisa was raised by her mother and her sister, Tina, who was 24 years older than she. Considering them too strict, she began running away from home at the age of 15.

To me my parents were my mom and my sister Tina . . . the one that died . . . through alcohol 'cause she used to drink a lot . . . She was more like my role model . . . She had been a barmaid . . . all her life . . . And I used to like the way she used to dress and I used to like the money, the tips . . . I was infatuated with her, with all her doings, you know. And she was real sexy and her hairdos were high. She looked like a Mexican Liz Taylor . . . [But] they were very, very strict . . .

I don't even really remember having a childhood. I mean, . . . my parents tried . . . their best. But . . . [I] never got to go out at night, like on the weekends with your friends. Like let's say . . . on Friday nights you have like a . . . dance for . . . ninth and tenth graders, and they would go only for two or three hours, I could never go to that . . . It's like, . . . "Get your ass home!" I could never wear makeup at the age of . . . 15, nothing! So everything that I couldn't do I rebelled and I did it all and I just became my own boss at a very young age.

For Lillian, it was also her parents' strictness with her coupled with their alcoholism and emotional neglect that led her to distance herself from them and run away repeatedly.

I think because my parents were really strict with us, very, very strict . . . We had to be in by the time it got dark and there was no leniency to us. And . . . we were raised with . . . alcohol . . . yet you didn't call anybody an alcoholic. There were parties all the time . . . There was a lot of commotion and no attention. Not . . . that I know what quality time was, or nourishment, . . . it wasn't happening when I was growing up. I know they did what they . . . thought was best, but . . .

Parents' monitoring of their daughters' behavior was partly directed toward protecting them from the sexual advances of the men around them and perceived negative influences outside their homes (e.g., drugs, gangs). It was also a way to keep them from exerting their independence as young women.

As a result of her mother's addiction and arrest, Melinda was placed with a combination of relatives and in a children's shelter.

A combination of people, my mother and then my grandparents . . . Then I went to my father with my stepmother. And then . . . when I was 12 going on 13 . . . I went to a shelter . . . My little sister went to her grandmother's . . . And then I went back to my mother . . . My mother, . . . the first 10 or 11 years of my life, she was a housewife . . . Then she herself got involved with drugs.

Mercedes and her sister were placed in a combination of foster homes as a result of their mother's drug addiction until Mercedes decided to live with her grandmother.

My mother was an alcoholic and a drug addict, and my father was an alcoholic as well. They divorced when I was two and my mother was pregnant with my biological sister. As my mother's alcoholism progressed I became a product of . . . foster homes . . . I was . . . raised in the system from the age of . . . five to eight . . . I was taken to court for the last time and was asked by the judge who I wanted to go live with. My biological sister . . . chose to live with . . . my mother and I chose to live with my grandmother . . . So at the age of . . . eight I lived with my grandmother in this huge Victorian house . . . in Boyle Heights . . . And I remember my grandmother treated me like a princess . . . I was like the *niña bonita.* . . . She brought me beautiful fancy dresses and she did all these wonderful things . . . So I never really had a connection with my mother anymore . . . My mother lived behind my grandmother in a little small room with her addict husband. And I could remember like going into that room and just finding red pills and white pills and blue pills.

The separation of siblings was very traumatic for Chicanas such as Mercedes, who was temporarily placed in a shelter with her half-brother.

I had another sibling with me . . . He must have been the age of a year and a half . . . I . . . remember . . . one day running to the toddler unit, going to see my baby brother . . . And the only thing I remember of this little brother was . . . he was being pulled by a large man, which was his father, and he was reaching out for me crying . . . He was hysterical.

Sometimes it was the parents' incarceration that led to their separation from their children (Appendix A).

Yolanda: When I was little, I was raised with my mom and my stepdad . . . And then . . . my mom got arrested and then I went with my grandma.

Once their mothers were incarcerated, it was difficult for Chicana children to maintain a relationship with them.

Paula became estranged from her parents because she could not accept their divorce.

I was just going back and forth with my parents . . . They had remarried and I had to deal with stepparents and I didn't like either one of them . . . I wanted my parents . . . to . . . get back together, and that just wasn't happening . . . So . . . when my stepfather would try to tell me something then I'd get mad and then go with my daddy. When she would tell me something, my stepmother, then I'd go back home . . . So, finally, I just got tired of all of them . . . and . . . said . . . , "Fuck all of you guys!" and I ran away from home. I was gone for about five months. And that's when I started using.

Some Chicana/o families were split up temporarily as a result of immigration policies.

Linda: See, we were born here . . . in East L.A. Back in the '40s they had bad immigration stuff like they have it now, you know, where they wanted to send all the illegals back to Mexico. My parents didn't have the immigration.[3] My brother . . . said the Immigration took my dad back to Mexico and they took him to TJ[4] and my mother followed him. They left us here . . . My brother found us in an abandoned house with no food, no lights, no *nada* . . . [So] he transported us to TJ with my mom and dad . . . We lived there, I don't know how many years, but I was going to school over there. And my mother came back to the United States and we stood there with my dad . . . [Later] one of my sisters sent us back, me and my youngest sister, and my brother. I could have been about nine, 10 years old.

Deborah's Story: Coping with a Mother's Mental Illness

Deborah's story illustrates how her mother's mental illness contributed to her alienation from her family.

My father's . . . always been an alcoholic . . . We were in Palmdale and . . . there was a lot of fighting between them two. And they lost the house there . . . He ended up in jail and we ended up in the projects . . . I remember . . . living in the projects with this mentally ill mother. And, you know, I love her. She was . . . a beautiful person. But . . . we lived in the dark. She didn't let us go out. She spent hours and hours just repeatedly writing the same thing over and over . . . We didn't have no friends . . . She always felt that people were out to get us . . . She would talk to herself throughout the house, you know.

Deborah's mother eventually tried to kill herself and her children.

I was the oldest and I got up in the middle of the night and I smelled the gas . . . She turned the gas on in the house . . . Then I tried to wake my mother up and, of course, she took some pills on top of that and she wouldn't wake up . . . So I let a neighbor know . . . I carried my little brother down from the stairs. The people I could carry, I carried them out . . . There was five of us then at that time . . . I was probably about 12 . . . My dad . . . was in jail . . . something . . . related to alcoholism, DUIs . . . She was probably in there for about . . . three years, Camarillo State Hospital[5] . . . We were all split up.

Feeling that her relatives were not supportive of her mother led Deborah to distance herself emotionally from them.

I mean, they never even told us what happened to my mom . . . I would learn, but it was being in another room and hearing the aunts and uncles discuss how "Connie's crazy." . . . I'd always hear that so I grew up hating my family members . . . I resented them talking about her, and I was angry about that too.

Released from the state hospital, Deborah's mother regained custody of her children. Once reunited, however, the emotional gap between Deborah and her parents widened.

She moved to . . . South Gate . . . I used to have a brother that lived there and he . . . got her an apartment in front of his house . . . My dad was out of jail at this time, had kind of went from place to place picking up my sister in San Diego and I had another sister in foster care . . . My brother was the only one that didn't come back 'cause he didn't want to. And, you know, my dad would drink . . . It was just the same old thing . . . You know, I didn't learn how to cook by my mother . . . We didn't like sit at the table together. It was like . . . just no direction, no nothing from her . . . We . . . were poor . . . She was on AFDC[6] . . . She still talked to herself and, you know, I just didn't wanna be there . . . When . . . they gave us all back to her that's when I went on my own.

Deborah looked to her peers in the gangs for support.

I ditched school a lot, you know. I . . . was already using alcohol, reds, weed . . . Most of my friends were people that . . . were fighting. I found my place in . . . the gangs, you know, and I had fit very well there.

At 15, Deborah ran away from home.

I lived with a . . . friend of mine that I had. She was . . . probably about three years older than me but she already had kids . . . I . . . would kick it at her house . . . She used to get loaded. She . . . worked. I watched her little kid.

Sexual Abuse

A recurrent theme throughout the interviews was the sexual abuse pintas experienced while growing up. Twenty-one of the 24 interviewed were sexually abused as children and/or adolescents. In this sense they were representative of women imprisoned in California and throughout the United States (BJS 1994a; Turk, Owen, and Bloom 1995). Sexual abuse included fondling and rape. While some spoke about having been abused one time, others shared how they had been repeatedly abused until they were in their early teens. Regardless of how frequently the abuse took place, it left deep emotional scars apparent in the pain that came up for the women as they retold their stories.

Pintas were abused primarily by Chicano relatives and acquaintances, a few by strangers (Appendix A). One was sexually abused by a woman.

Luisa: My real dad, yes . . . I was like maybe five or six years old. And I had some . . . male cousins. I was about seven, six . . . They were 19, 20, 25.

Gina: Relatives . . . friends . . . There was a big house and . . . everybody lived in different areas . . . And my uncle . . . used to molest me. That's when I was real young too. We lived there and he was an alcoholic . . . After my father died I had a nightmare he was molesting me and I never remember him molesting me. But that nightmare kept coming and kept coming, you know, and I'd just . . . wake up screaming, . . . man.

Paula: My parents were still married . . . It was their *compadre* . . . My parents left me over there one night to spend the night . . . I was asleep with my cousins in the room and he came in, you know . . . And . . . he was touching me and . . . I just laid there. I didn't know what to do . . . I cried the whole time . . . There was no words spoken at all, none . . . And my aunt was in the other room . . . I was his victim, you know. It wasn't his own children. It was . . . me that he chose . . . I was about five . . . And I didn't tell nobody until I was 30 years old.

Mercedes: Through the interim of my mother's drinking and using I was molested . . . by the neighbor, touching, feeling, no penetration . . . I was also molested by my mother's husband's brother . . . That was a traumatization point for me. I remember running away. Going to the window and always going to grandma's 'cause that was a safe place for me.

Victoria: It happened a lot as a child . . . It was always . . . at the babysitter's . . . either a son or someone they knew . . . Every single one of my mother's boyfriends always came on to me, always.

Deborah: I had an uncle that . . . tried to molest me when I was asleep . . . I was probably about 12 . . . He was my mother's brother and I was placed with him through the system because my mother had tried to kill the whole family and was sent to a mental hospital . . . His wife was upstairs asleep, pregnant . . . They were newly married. And when I was asleep in a den downstairs, he tried to molest me . . . To like buy me . . . he says, "I'll buy you a watch if . . . you just let me, you know, touch you." And . . . he really probably messed with the wrong person because . . . I was real angry about what had happened to us, splitting up. And . . . my anger was . . . real powerful . . . And I hit him with an ash tray. You know, back in the . . . '60s like the ash trays were like heavy glass, you know, and I picked up one of those and I had hit him and I took off.

In an attempt to keep her quiet, Deborah's uncle sent her to live with relatives out of state.

I got picked up walking in the middle of the morning . . . and I was in juvenile hall . . . for a couple of days . . . The police officer . . . couldn't understand what was going on . . . He knew something had happened to me but I wouldn't talk . . . So he [the uncle] just got me out of juvenile hall and had me . . . sent to Michigan, to an aunt over there.

Lillian's sexual assault took place outside her home when she was raped by three strangers at the age of 14.

I wasn't molested as a child but I was raped at . . . 14 years old [by] three Black men . . . I went . . . to the store to pick up something . . . and they took me out to a creek out in Stockton area, and that's where they raped me. And they beat me with a crow bar.

Melinda's Story: Love Is Just a Word

Melinda's story, although extreme, illustrates the devastating impact sexual and other forms of abuse have on a child's self-esteem and ability to love and trust others.

I've been molested since I was four years old . . . Go down the line . . . Because not only my grandfather raped me, my uncles raped me, my father jumped me.

As is common with victims of sexual abuse, the memory of her rape by her grandfather was still vivid in Melinda's memory at the time of the interview.

I mean, I was four years old and I remember when I got raped. It was like a monster was on top of me and it was melting and turning ugly and ugly and ugly. All of the sudden I felt this burning sensation. And (crying) . . . I found out it was my own grandfather, a man I admired 'cause he took care of me.

During her late teens Melinda was raped once again when her mother pimped her out to a drug connection.

I was sound asleep . . . And when I went like this [moving her hand to the side] there was a hand like that. And it was because my mother was sick . . . and she wanted some dope . . . This guy liked me and . . . it was like she sold me. And . . . all of a sudden I had this man on top of me and my mother was getting fixed up.

For Melinda, the rapes did not end in her home. As a teenager she was also gang-raped . . . When she sought the help of the police they blamed her for the assault.

I was gang-banged in William Street Park . . . I don't even remember if it was four guys, five guys. But all I know is . . . I went to this party and they slipped . . . something in my drink . . . I was at a house . . . with a friend. All of a sudden . . . my friend disappeared . . . And next thing I know I don't have a drink in front of me, I have like all these faces in my face and . . . being thrown backwards, forwards . . . I remember trying to claw something. And I had to go back to that park to find out what was I clawing . . . I was probably rolled down that creek and I was trying to claw out and somebody was pulling me from behind . . . I was thrown partially naked with shit and cum and mud in my face, my clothes. I was ripped apart and . . . you could tell I was raped. What did the cops do? Said I had no business being where I was.

Melinda cried as she shared her feelings about the abuse and the constant betrayal she experienced at the hands of loved ones.

I mean, it sounds like a motion picture, I know. (crying) But you know what? . . . We get so used, . . . even by our own supposedly "loved ones." . . . And then after they do it, they're . . . hugging you and telling you how they're sorry because they love you so much. "Well, if you loved me so much, why did you do this to me?" And to still grow up with the idea in your head . . . to find so much forgiveness because they're your parents. 'Cause religion has put in our heads that . . . if you turn away from your parents or you hit your parents, . . . that part that you used to hit 'em would . . . shrivel up and dry up. If you hated your parents, that your kids were gonna grow up to hate you, you know. These things are . . . put in your head that you . . . grow up so messed up. And . . . after a while, . . . the word love, it was a conjunction. It wasn't a feeling . . . It was like, "Yeah, okay, so you love me? Okay. Now what?" . . . It's like that little motto . . . , "Spread your legs, I think I love you." . . . It was a true saying 'cause . . . if I didn't spread 'em, I didn't love you. I said, "Oh, oh, there's gotta be a different concept to this, you know."

Physical Abuse

A third of pintas interviewed said they had been physically abused as children by parents or other family members (Appendix A). In this sense they were also representative of incarcerated women throughout the United States (BJS 1994a; Turk, Owen, Bloom 1995).

Lucy: My mom . . . was the kind that broke brooms over your back, threw frying pans at you, yelled, and screamed . . . She was addicted to heroin, and like reds and rainbows.[7]

Victoria: My mother has a very violent temper . . . She . . . really had a bad habit of just back-handing, whoop! . . . And . . . I just remember her being very nervous . . . She'd start shaking and she'd stretch her hand and she'd grit her teeth and . . . she would get the belt. She put a belt to us all the time, you know. And, I mean, I . . . was one of these children that was always into everything . . . I was very, very, as they say, *traviesa*, mischievous . . . I was just constantly crying for attention . . . I . . . got a lot of negative attention, I know that much.

Linda: My dad . . . was alcoholic and he was the type that . . . whenever he was out of the house I never knew what condition he was going to come back in. But it was like I was always very defensive because he was going to hit us, you know, and every day, if not twice a day, over nothing . . . I mean, . . . it's not that you did anything.

Linda finally resisted by hitting her father back.

I wasn't typical of the Chicanas, no. I mean, what Chicana is going to hit her father with a baseball bat? . . . I got tired of him beating on me. And . . . I almost seen him where he was going to hit my mom . . . And I knew he was gonna get her by the hair, so I turned around, picked up a bat and let him have it, and then took off . . . I came back. I guess I got hungry . . . But I knew he was gonna get me, you know. So your typical Chicanas from my generation didn't do stuff like that.

Linda and her siblings were also severely beaten by one of their older sisters.

She was very much like my dad . . . She was very abusive . . . She was the type that . . . she sent you up to take a bath and . . . if she thought you didn't wash your ears, I mean, you got a beating for it. If . . . you weren't chewing your food like she thought it should be chewed, you'd get a beating for it. I mean, it's like you couldn't do nothing to satisfy this woman.

Psychological Abuse

In Victoria's case, the complexities of sexual and physical abuse were compounded by the psychological trauma she suffered watching her father physically abuse other women in his life.

And although I never seen my father be violent towards me, my father was very violent. That's one of the reasons why my mother left him . . . And even into his second marriage, you know, I lived with him for about a year, and I'd see him slap around . . . my stepmother.

The fact that their parents and other adults did not always protect them from abuse intensified the deep feelings of abandonment and betrayal Chicanas felt.

Melinda: My mother was always too busy trying to make other people happy and patting us on the head and telling us she loved us. And she loved us awful (crying). How could she have kept us where people were hurting us?

Melinda, whose mother was an addict, was also emotionally traumatized by the frequent raids on her home by white police officers.

When I was . . . nine . . . my mother was living in a . . . little shack house and . . . my mother was wheeling and dealing . . . And it was early, early in the morning . . . My mother had just had my . . . baby sister. And the baby was in the crib and I was getting ready to change her. My mother was sleeping, nodding, or something. And there was a tap on the door and I went to go see who it was, you know, quietly 'cause everybody was sleeping . . . And as I opened the door . . . that man just kicked that door and broke it down and had a gun, "Don't move!" How . . . you expect me to move, there's a gun in my head? . . . (laugh) I . . . froze . . . All I could say, "Mommy! Mommy!" . . . And then they wouldn't let me touch my . . . baby sister. She was crying . . . And we had all these people just storming in like a SWAT team and grabbing everybody . . . My mom had some people over and they were laying on the floor sleeping, passed out. And all of a sudden you see these people . . . , when they say, "Raid!" everybody jumping up. And . . . I seen them grabbing things and trying to flush them . . . And all the running, . . . the commotion . . . You know, nine years old you don't know what the hell's happening . . . And you're just scared because here this man has you by the throat . . . It was a nightmare. But after a while it's like that was a way of life . . . As a child I think I've been in about six or seven raids.

Reactions to the Abuse

How Chicana children and the adults around them responded to the abuse and the frequent post-traumatic stress disorder (PTSD) that accompanied it was almost as significant as the abuse itself. For the response could either help them begin the road to emotional recovery or further add to their sense of betrayal, isolation, and abandonment. PTSD was a reaction to severe trauma characterized by hypervigilance, sleep disorders, flashbacks and other intrusive thoughts, and emotionality (Bass and Davis 1988; Herman 1992; Tome 1992). Despite such severe symptoms, fear kept many Chicana children from revealing the abuse.

Paula: Back at that time I didn't tell anybody . . . because I was scared and I didn't think anybody would believe me . . . I thought . . . maybe he would try to hurt me . . . if I told.

Deborah: I mean, here I was angry with the system already . . . We were taken away from my mother. You know, my mother had a . . . breakdown . . . I see the police haul her off and . . . these people are supposed to put me in a safe place . . . And then . . . the system . . . puts me in a home where this guy can molest me. Now, who am I supposed to tell? . . . You know, I was like, "Screw you!" . . . So . . . everything was in here (pointing to her heart). I didn't talk about how I felt . . . Not [any] people in the school system, not [any] people in Social Services, nobody ever asked me how I felt, nobody.

Gina: When I was five years old . . . I walked in on . . . my mother and my father . . . and I went outside to tell the kids . . . that I'd seen them doing something, you know. So she busted my ear where I couldn't eat or anything and she told me, "Don't you ever tell anyone what happens in this house!" So when I got molested I was scared to say anything 'cause I was gonna get hit again. So I didn't tell nobody . . . My mother was a very cold woman, very cold. I would try to kiss her in the cheek but she'd turn her face . . . And I think also she came from a sexually abused [background]. That's why she won't talk about nothing . . . Like some mothers sit down and talk to you when you're getting to be a little older, you know, . . . talk to you about your period, talk to you about different things. She wouldn't do it . . . My father wouldn't do it with my brothers. I used to do it with my brothers.

Victoria: I know now I was just really afraid and part of me didn't want her to be disappointed in me . . . And my mother . . . always had . . . a way of being very demeaning, you know. I remember trying to explain to her a couple of times, "I don't wanna go to that babysitter's house." She was like, "Well, I gotta work. That's too bad." . . . And . . . she just . . . didn't hear me. And for many years . . . I was very resentful towards my mother . . . You know, for a nine-year-old to tell their mom, "I hate you, you fucking bitch!" . . . something has to be going on with that little kid . . . I just never comprehended, "How come you didn't know, Ma?" . . . I asked her . . . when I was working through these issues and got into therapy.

Victoria also blamed herself for the abuse.

I . . . kind of blamed myself because I always have looked older than what I was . . . I blossomed very early. I mean, I started my period at nine years old . . . And . . . I was one of those children that were . . . all over the place. And . . . being at the babysitter, you know, there was certain rooms I knew not to go into but I would go into them anyway . . . And being a little girl and . . . being without my father, you know, there was a part of me that kind of liked that attention I'm thinking . . . And, yeah, I blamed myself because of the way I looked and . . . the way I carried myself.

Melinda: It was like we were brought up that . . . you couldn't talk about it. It was like we'd get pacified . . . When they'd hurt us, they'd throw us . . . a candy bar or something. You know, "To soothe the child's mind, just soothe the child's pain." So we were becoming addicts at an early age, but candy addicts. They wondered why I was getting so big. You know, mistreat me, beat me, then throw me, no, not the doll, throw me a candy bar, you know, and I won't say anything. And if I do I might get beat up. Yeah, I was always being done like that.

When Chicanas told of the abuse, however, they had no assurance that they would be believed or, if believed, protected from further abuse.

While in Rosa's case, her mother left her father partly as a result of his having molested Rosa at the age of three, Diana's mother continued to live with her father while her daughter was growing up.

Diana: My mom . . . was always fighting with my father about the way that he acted out because of the . . . molestation . . . She knew . . . Those issues were like years before, like when I was . . . four.

Sometimes Chicanas told of the abuse but were not believed by their caretakers. Those who believed them were often other women in the family who had been sexually abused, sometimes by the same perpetrator.

Yolanda: The only one that believed me was my mom. Shit, 'cause he did it to my mom . . . My mom was in . . . and out of prison. She'd come home and she'd stay out for about a month and she'll go back 'cause she was using drugs . . . At the time I was living with my grandma and she didn't believe me. I was a child and she would never believe me.

In only three cases (one of them a gang rape) was the sexual abuse reported to criminal justice agencies. However, in none of the cases did the authorities' solution address the needs of the victim. Melinda, who had been raped by her grandfather, and Carmen, abused by her father, explained.

Melinda: The law all they did to him? Gave him . . . a year probation and put him right smack back into our house to hurt me some more!

Carmen: I was raised in the judicial system . . . since I was six years old . . . till I was 18 years old . . . I was made a ward of the state because my dad was molesting me when I was a child. Because my mom was in denial for the fact that it was happening and she said I was . . . making stories up.

Yet, even when they remained silent, Chicanas' reactions to the abuse made it apparent that something was wrong.

Paula: And I . . . didn't understand about killing yourself . . . but . . . a few days after . . . it happened . . . I took . . . Drano . . . I was doing it to hurt myself 'cause my mom kept telling me all the time to stay away from it. And when that happened . . . I didn't comprehend then that I wanted to kill myself, but I know that . . . what I wanted to do was hurt myself . . . And they took me to the hospital and they had to pump my stomach.

Melinda: Once my relatives abused me I started putting shields. I wouldn't trust nobody . . . It was like I was growing up really fast . . . I didn't realize I was learning a lesson. But the lesson of distrust . . . Distrust was a big, major thing for me . . . And I sometimes . . . slip into that a lot.

Melinda's pain and humiliation were intensified by the cruelty of schoolmates who found out about the abuse.

Kids would find out in school. I had one in particular that when she found out that my grandfather abused me, she'd use it in school to get back at me. Like if . . . I was comfortably eating lunch in a bench and there was nowhere to sit, she'd actually go over there and ride my ass and tell me, "If you don't get off of the bench . . . , I'm gonna tell everybody you let your grandfather fuck you." . . . If I was with someone I'd say, "Let's go sit in the grass or something," and I'd give it to her.

Melinda eventually learned to stand up for herself.

I would stand up for my rights after a while . . . I used to get in fights in school for my rights . . . (laughs).

Despite the abuse Melinda experienced in and outside of her home she managed to do well in school.

As dysfunctional as my family was, it just seemed like I was the good seed. I was a straight-A student. I . . . wanted to be loved so bad . . . I was always carrying a book or something, . . . very studious . . . I was so active in school. You know, I was in the basketball.

Other Chicana children reacted to abuse by misbehaving in school.

Gina: I just would act bad . . . I would break things. I would scream . . . Try to beat 'em up . . . I used to steal the . . . community chest money and miss the bus . . . I would run away . . . I could go to El Rey and eat tacos . . . What I think is why I acted so bad is that's the only way I got attention, you know . . . They hit you but you get attention.

The situation was complicated further by the racism many Chicanas encountered at school.

Linda: I remember going to school and if you were a Mexican that nurse would come in automatically and stand you outside of the classroom . . . and she'd start searching for knives . . . They were very prejudiced . . . This was in East L.A. . . . The other . . . part of why I didn't like school is because as I was brought up at home, Spanish was my primary language. And coming from Tijuana over here, Spanish was my primary language. The teachers could not understand why I couldn't understand certain words in English . . . I mean, they just insisted that I should have been speaking English, but they never asked why I didn't . . . The schoolteachers were very, very prejudiced . . . They were all white teachers . . . I think I got turned off to school that first day I went.

Physical abuse at the hands of teachers added to Chicanas' sense of betrayal and abandonment.

Linda: [One] white teacher was six foot or more and would go out there and swat you and bend you over and make you stand up straight.

While some Chicana girls responded to the racism and physical abuse by submitting to the will of school authorities, others fought back.

Linda: My sister would just go along with whatever it was they wanted her to go along with. And I was the opposite . . . I mean, after a while it's like I . . . just fought back . . . I could have gotten physical, yeah. I remember that man that used to swat . . . me . . . Mr. Hogan was his name. I'll never forget him. He was the arts and crafts. And he had a trailer where the kids would go make plastic ashtrays, candle holders, little wallets. It was interesting . . . One day he swat me and I . . . looked at him straight in the eye and I said, "This is it!" . . . So I remember I went home and . . . I came back in the evening and I broke into his trailer and I stole everything he had in that trailer and what I couldn't steal I destroyed. And when I went back to school he looked at me and he knew that I had done it, but he couldn't prove it. And I looked at him, inside . . . I was saying to myself, "Prove it!"

Linda bullied other children at school in response to the anger she felt at her family's poverty, the physical abuse at home, and the discrimination she faced at school.

If . . . I thought they didn't look at me right or I thought she was thinking she looked cute or something, *yo peleaba con ella*[8] . . . I . . . just bump into them and it started . . . I didn't discriminate . . . I wasn't afraid of Black, white, or Latinas . . . I wasn't a very large kid. I was just a very daring kid . . . I would take away their lunch money. I didn't get no cafeteria money so I would go to the restroom and I knew which girls had it and I would take it away from them, you know? And not that I was going to eat in the cafeteria anyway. I'd go somewhere else. Walk out of school and go . . . buy my own food . . . You know what it was? Bottom line, I think it was a lot of envy that I had, you know, the nice clothes, the nice clean-cut girls.

She also stole food and clothing.

I started providing for myself at a early age . . . I'd say about between 11 and 12 . . . If I was hungry, then I'd go and steal food and eat . . . If I needed a pair of shoes, I'd go steal a pair of shoes. Whatever I needed as far as my . . . clothing, was, I'd just go and steal it . . . But I never got caught.

Ditching became part of the school experience of many young Chicanas.

Linda: I used go to the movies whenever I ditched school . . . I used to see the truant officers . . . It's like I learned to recognize their feet so that every time I went to a movie I'd go under the seat and I could see their feet coming down and I could see their feet going up. So, I knew when it was safe for me to get up so they wouldn't pick me up . . . I'm the type of a kid that I would check in and out of schools. The last grade I remember that I checked out of was . . . fifth grade.

Gina: I only went to like . . . grammar school. But they threw me out of grammar school . . . [for] fights in school and not . . . behaving right . . . I must have been about 10 . . . Put me in a special school for girls . . . You could go home and all that but it was like they didn't teach you how to read or anything. All they would teach is how to quilt, sew . . . I guess they figured what's the sense in teaching them anything, you know . . . And from there they graduate you to junior high because of your age, I guess . . . And I never really finished junior high. I was never there . . . [I'd] go out with the girls and drink.

Frequently, it was while ditching school that Chicanas began to experiment with alcohol and other drugs. Drugs quickly became the means of coping with the anger and emotional pain.

Victoria: My mother had a credenza full of liquor . . . I think she just had the credenza like for company or for looks . . . And . . . for some reason, I was always attracted to . . . the Chivas Regal bottle . . . And . . . by age 11 I knew how much to drink and how much water I had to put back because I knew she was marking it . . . And because of the lack of supervision my house was always the house where everybody went to party, to get high . . . My house was the . . . ditching party house. So we would all go up there and . . . just get stoned out of our minds.

Chicana juveniles also sought to take care of themselves by running away from home.

Lillian: I was raised in Los Gatos with white people. I'd go to the East Side to get some action . . . A 25-year-old was involved. We used to stay at her house when we used to run away and we used to baby-sit her kids for her. And there was me and my best friend and two other girls and my sister.

Yolanda: I stayed with my grandma until I was 13. That's when I ran away . . . Because of that [abuse] I ran away. Mainly because nobody believed me . . . The girl that ran away with me, she just ran away with me because . . . I didn't want to be by myself . . . We just started junior high school . . . When . . . I left my grandma's house, we had slept right here in Lincoln Heights in front of a doctor's office on a porch . . . [Then] one of my . . . real dad's sisters, her . . . boyfriend, husband, or whatever he was, . . . they had like split up, he had a house and I asked him if I could stay there. And there was like about eight men living in that house but they never touched me or nothing. So I stayed there for a few months. Then, I had met this connection . . . the man that I ended up with . . . for about 10 years. I ended up with him at 14 . . . He was 25.

While the families of most Chicana runaways did look for them, Yolanda's did not.

Nobody even looked for me . . . I mean, . . . I have a lot of brothers and sisters. I have my aunts and uncles. I have cousins. And nobody even looked for me. My grandmother didn't even look for me.

Lillian's reaction to being raped by three strangers was to run away from her home in Stockton to a friend's house in San Jose.

And then my parents were contacted by a family friend . . . My mother . . . came down here, took me to the doctor . . . here in San Jose . . . He did a pap, but it's not to say that you got raped, you could of had sex, you know? And . . . I didn't have sex at that age, not willingly.

Although Lillian's parents were supportive of her after the rape, her father dropped the rape case he had initiated against the perpetrators. He wanted to spare his daughter exposure to a criminal justice process that, because of its insensitivity to rape victims, often victimizes them further. In spite of the violent experience, however, Lillian never received counseling. Her response was to drop out of school, run away from home, and anesthetize her feelings with alcohol and other drugs.

I never went back to school . . . I took off from home again. I met this older lady and I started baby-sitting for her. And then she started dressing me up and I started going to nightclubs with her, and that was all at 15 . . . I just started drinking and using.

At the age of 14 and with her parents' consent, Gina began dating a 22-year-old Chicano who had already served time in prison.

You know, when you're a kid and you watch TV and . . . you see all these gangsters, "Man, they're all right." . . . So . . . my husband came out of prison. He was one of them gangsters . . . And I was young. I didn't know no better . . . and I . . . got infatuated . . . I was 14 when I met him. He was, what? Twenty-two . . . That was my first boyfriend too that they allowed me to have.

By 15, Gina was pregnant with her first child. Her parents reacted by kicking her out of the house.

I had been living there in the backyard, in a little room back there. They had him living there [too]. When I got pregnant . . . I came over here to my aunt's house, the one that had raised me . . . And I was scared and then she called my parents and told 'em. My father said he didn't want me in the house, that I was a whore, . . . but they kept him there.

Sometimes the parents of Chicanas were able to free their daughters from destructive relationships and friendships.

Lillian: I met a biker. He was 35 at the time. I was working in bars, serving beer and wine with a fake ID, riding with bikers for about a year and a half . . . My parents found out that I was with him. It was an older man . . . and my . . . dad threatened to . . . put him to jail . . . so he left me.

At least one pinta married her rapist and had his children rather than bear the shame of telling her family about the rape.

Linda: I got raped in the projects at the age of 15 . . . He was a gang member also, but I didn't know him . . . He had just got out of juvenile hall . . . And then, of course, because . . . at that time if anything happened to you, it was too shameful to talk to anybody, I felt I couldn't talk to my family . . . I felt that I had . . . nowhere to go, so, therefore, this guy had to be my husband . . . So I ran away from home at the age of 15 . . . After I ran away I wanted to go back home and . . . my mom . . . said, "No. You made your bed, now you lay on it." . . . So I felt trapped . . . And out of that came two children . . . I stood there till I was 18 and I couldn't . . . deal with . . . our relationship . . . anymore . . . Because I guess in a sense I was prostituting myself . . . with him, . . . you know, exchanging sex for a roof . . . I wasn't there 'cause I loved him or because I wanted to be there, I was there because I had nowhere else to go . . . What was so bad about being with him? . . . I had a lot of anger. The other part that was so bad was that that's not the person that I had planned to marry . . . But because of my involvement with a gang and involvement with the alcohol and the drugs, I was in a place where I shouldn't have been.

Whether still at home or on the run, Chicanas like Victoria adopted the image of the *chola*, or Chicana gang member (see Harris 1988: 144–145; Vigil 1988), as a shield against further abuse.

I . . . picked up the ways of the other teenage girls . . . Like I said, I always looked older than what I was so I was able to . . . wear the big hair and . . . the makeup . . . And then I got into the *cholita* sort of stereotype . . . The clothing was, you know, the arched Levis and the baggy, baggy pants and the little push-up bras, you know, to . . . squeeze your *chichis* so when you wear your little tank tops you look real sexy . . . The black band. Those used to be real popular . . . Black lipstick. Dark burgundy nail polish, as burgundy as you can get it. Much later I was expelled from my school for wearing burgundy lipstick and nails. . . . And I . . . stuck with that . . . image for many years . . . I think that image kept me safe. It . . . intimidated and . . . that's what I wanted to do. And I believe it stems from childhood, always feeling so powerless. So it was safe for me. And it was like, I . . . believe now a defense mechanism.

Victoria also adopted the image of the chola because she was attracted by the closeness that existed between gang members in her barrio.

I remember admiring the older girls, you know, the . . . cholas and the cholos. And . . . I just wanted so, so badly to be a part of that. And they seemed like such a . . . network. It's just a family. And . . . I think it's something I never really had a taste of. And . . . that's what I did like. And so I would . . . hang around with those kind of kids.

However, according to Victoria, "along with that came the drinking beer and smoking weed."

Battering

For at least half of the pintas interviewed, the physical abuse did not end when they were young. As teenagers or adults they found themselves involved in abusive relationships with partners. While nine were battered by male partners (see also Moore and Mata 1981), three were battered by female partners. Two were battered by both. By the time of the interview, all had been able to leave their abusers.

Cristina: He broke my nose when I was three months pregnant with my son. And then he beat me up when I was three months pregnant with my daughter.

Dulce: I'd always got beat up . . . I took a lot of stuff and I always thought it was my fault because I thought I wasn't doing what I was supposed to do. And I thought I deserved a lot of that. And . . . she beat me up so bad one time that my shoulder was dislocated. She's left me beat up on the street . . . But . . . still to this day, I care for her but I don't . . . love her . . . I feel bad for her. I get angry with me today because . . . I miss talking to her . . . 'cause . . . for 10 years we had good times, you know . . . I was finally able to stand up to her and tell her that she needs to stay away and stop calling me . . . And you would think I would have seen it when we were in jail. And I didn't because I . . . thought that that was love and all I wanted was someone to like me and love me.

Melinda: It's like . . . I was taught, "You got to get beat up or . . . they don't love you" type thing . . . It seems like the men I picked . . . wanted to be so macho with me they forget about the loving thing. "You're a woman and you're . . . supposed to be barefoot and pregnant." They beat the shit out of me if I burned a tortilla. These are Chicano dudes . . . And the last . . . one tried to . . . hit me and I turned around, ¡Ya estuvo!⁹ and boom! I jammed him, you know (laughs). I said, "And don't move from there 'cause if you get up I guarantee you, you ain't gonna get up for the rest of your life . . . Don't throw me in bed, . . . toss me this way, toss me this way . . . and then say, "¡Ya estuvo!" and then tell me that . . . your eggs . . . are burned 'cause I know I'm a damn good cook!"

It was their determination to escape physical and/or sexual abuse, and for some the confines of strict gender roles, that made at least half of the pintas interviewed begin to run away from home during childhood and adolescence. Others who had been equally abused, however, chose to stay at home with their families.

Their loyalty to their families and the need for emotional and cultural support, particularly at such an early age, led even those who had moved out of their homes to stay in touch with family members, particularly their mothers and siblings. For in the end, what they wanted and needed was to love and be loved both as young women and as Chicanas growing up in a hostile social environment.

Although the stories disclosed here highlight the physical and sexual abuse pintas interviewed experienced, it was clear from remarks they made at diverse points during the interviews and documented in subsequent chapters that their mothers, sisters, grandmothers, and most male relatives continued to be active participants in their lives.

Ironically, the resistance of young Chicanas was a reflection of the resilience shown by other women around them who managed to survive and thrive amidst multiple oppressive personal, economic, and social conditions confronting them. For while some women in their lives prioritized the demands of men and/or were caught up in addiction, incarceration, or mental illness, pintas also had examples of women in their families and barrios who clearly exerted their agency. The decisions young Chicanas made, however, simultaneously reproduced both the healthy and unhealthy behaviors they saw around them.

3

Youth Arrests and Placements

From the age of 15 to 17 . . . I was in and out of . . . juvenile hall . . .
five or six [times] . . . because of . . . being incorrigible. Didn't want
to go to school . . . I just never went home . . . I was . . . a runaway.
I used to party. I used to steal clothes to put on . . . I didn't care
about life . . . My parents couldn't handle me . . . I felt like I was
treated like shit so I'm gonna just continue treating myself like shit.
—Luisa

As their stories in the previous chapter show, Chicanas became more
and more alienated from their parents and other adults as a result of the
sexual, physical, and emotional abuse and neglect they experienced.
Feelings of betrayal, abandonment, and anger were reinforced by the
discriminatory treatment and/or indifference of adults around them—
schoolteachers, social service workers, and law enforcement officers.

While at least one pinta interviewed had tried to commit suicide as
a child, others confronted their parents angrily at home, cut school,
bullied other children, ran away from home, experimented with alcohol and illegal drugs, and/or joined barrio youth gangs (see Chapter 4).
Those who repeatedly ran away from home eventually stayed away altogether, moving in with homegirls or homeboys who used alcohol and
other drugs. Their male partners tended to be older, and most had been
exposed to the juvenile and/or adult criminal justice systems.

To support themselves financially and assert their independence,
Chicanas participated in a number of activities with peers in their barrios. These activities, coupled at times with parental neglect, brought
them into contact with law enforcement agencies. Such contacts led
one in four pintas interviewed to be placed in juvenile hall and/or other
institutions for youths for significant periods of time.

In this section Chicanas recount the experiences and actions that first brought them into contact with the juvenile justice system. They talk about the treatment accorded them by law enforcement officers, the conditions they encountered in youth facilities, and their experiences with staff and non-Chicana/o youth in such placements. An underlying question was whether such placements allowed Chicanas to begin recovering from previous traumatic childhood experiences.

Status and Delinquent Offenses

Ten of the 24 pintas interviewed had encounters with law enforcement officers while they were still under 18 years of age. Most of them were first arrested between the ages of 13 and 15. Another was taken out of her home by police when her home was raided and her caretakers arrested.

Four of the 10 were first arrested for status offenses, that is, actions for which adults would not be arrested. These included running away, incorrigibility, curfew violations, and truancy. The other six were first arrested for delinquent offenses or a combination of delinquent and status offenses. Initial delinquent offenses included grand theft auto (GTA), vandalism, burglary, possession of drugs and/or paraphernalia, and, in one case, transporting people across the U.S.-Mexican border.

Status offenses were generally committed as a response to difficulties at home. Delinquent offenses were already a sign that Chicanas interviewed had begun to experiment with illegal drugs and were trying to find ways to support themselves and their incipient drug habit. Many were under the influence of alcohol or other drugs when they were arrested.

Doris was first arrested for running away and GTA.

My home seemed insane to me . . . [My parents] took speed . . . and . . . my friend's home was easier to live [in]. It was more comfortable there . . . Someone left their keys in the ignition and I took it . . . When I ran away [I was] probably 14 . . . I'd smoke weed . . . I went to juvenile hall . . . and they . . . released me to my parents' custody . . . I couldn't get over on why they let me go . . . But they just dropped the charges . . . I . . . thought it would be nice to stay there.

Diana's first arrest illustrates the vulnerability of young Chicanas/os to police harassment in white neighborhoods.

The . . . neighborhood I grew up in was [an] . . . upper-middle-class Anglo neighborhood. So I think we were the . . . first Mexicans in this area . . . The first time I . . . was arrested, I was arrested for curfew . . . I was . . . just parked on a street . . . I was with a couple of friends, and I guess we looked suspicious sitting there . . . At the time . . . they were in the process of developing this area, and so there was a lot of construction . . . And I remember turning and . . . pulling the car over. And like . . . the minute that we were there they pulled in front of us . . . And . . . they came to the window and they started questioning Saul . . . They started asking for IDs, and he had a warrant for an outstanding ticket . . . And they took him and because I was within hours of being 18 they took me too 'cause they couldn't leave me there . . . And I remember I was on a diet . . . I had a . . . container and it had those little . . . tablets of like sweeteners and they took it when they . . . arrested me . . . They thought they were drugs . . . I didn't use at that time . . . They had a . . . juvenile hearing . . . It wasn't like . . . a formal . . . court procedure . . . They put me on a summary probation.

Linda's repeated arrests for curfew violations during the 1940s and 1950s while growing up in East Los Angeles demonstrated the long-standing pattern of arrest and harassment of Chicana/o youths by law enforcement personnel (see also Chapter 8).

Back then, they used to have curfews. Anything over 10 o'clock you were breaking the curfew. And . . . it was like a joke . . . They would pick you up, take you to the substation, turn you loose, pick you up, take you to the substation. I mean, I did that I don't know how many times . . . They wouldn't put handcuffs. They would just put everybody . . . in the back seat and take you to the little Hollenbeck Police Station.

Both in the patrol cars and at the police station officers tried to scare Chicana youths by sexually harassing them.

Linda: And they put you in a room and . . . a lot of times you'd get sexual remarks from the officers, whoever would pick us up, "Which one of you am I taking to the motel?" or "Which one of you am I gonna take home?" . . . And then they'd let you go . . . "Go home." . . . They turned you loose after about maybe two hours . . . I don't remember my parents ever being called.

While some Chicanas were scared by the arrests and sexual harassment, others like Linda refused to feel intimidated.

The first time they picked me up, we were in the projects, Eliso projects, and we were all drinking . . . I thought it was a joke. I laughed . . . at them. And every time they did it I would laugh at them.

Other youths came into contact with law enforcement officers as a result of their parents' actions.

Lucy: My mom had a boyfriend . . . in Long Beach . . . And my mother had a gun and he was real scared that my mother was going to shoot him and he smacked my mother. And my mom was real mad and she . . . taught us how to make those . . . cocktail bombs . . . They were done . . . with . . . gasoline. And you put a cloth in there and then you light it . . . She drove us . . . And then we threw it at the door . . . I was . . . 13, my sister was 12, and my brother was 11. And they arrested us because we blew down the door . . . They didn't do nothing to my mom . . . No one told on my mom . . . I just knew I hated it and I hated my mom.

At the age of 13, Victoria was arrested for the first time for a burglary.

What had happened was that we were up at my mother's house, and . . . we were drinking Old English 800 malt liquor and we were smoking weed. And I had the wonderful idea of breaking into my neighbor's house . . . I think I was just looking for some money, just to have. You know, I always remember wanting money when I was younger . . . We were pretty poor . . . And always, just always wanting something that I didn't have . . . It was me, my brother, a friend of mine . . . She was African-American and white . . . And [an] African-American guy.

While it was Victoria's first arrest, LASD considered the burglary serious.

They were a white gay couple . . . I . . . thought they were really cool too. But . . . we . . . were getting stoned and . . . we just . . . didn't care about who we stepped on . . . And we even stole food out of that house 'cause I remember we were hungry . . . I believe the sheriffs made such a big deal out of it because I ended up with a little baggy of . . . green emeralds and he had another baggy of . . . miscellaneous jewelry.

When Victoria was arrested and taken to juvenile hall her mother, who frequently worked two jobs to support her children, felt relief.

My mother was like very glad to see me go to jail[1] 'cause by that time I was . . . constantly in trouble . . . I think just for a little bit before that happened I had gotten kicked out of school 'cause I tried to sell a teacher marijuana . . . So I couldn't go to school in Altadena anymore. And I was like, basically, . . . kicked out of Altadena at the age of 13. They labeled me a "menace to society."

While not many officers seemed to take an interest in young Chicanas, some did.

Victoria: Sheriff Udell . . . He was a . . . wonderful huge . . . Black sheriff . . . Mean as hell, but he took a liking to me for some reason . . . I . . . think I loved him because he was really cool . . . After that he tried so hard to get me away from those people and into programs. And he would always, once in a while, come up to my mother's house and check up on me.

Victoria felt both fear and pride when first arrested.

I remember . . . my first time like getting arrested. And because I was so much into the image I thought that, "Yeah . . . I'm . . . finally cool," you know. Like I finally reached the Big Time. And I said, "Okay, yeah. Yeah, I'm going to jail . . . I don't give a shit . . . Call my mom. Go ahead!" You know . . . I . . . put on such a great front in front of my friends and . . . in front of all the people there . . . but . . . deep down . . . I was really frightened . . . You know, I'm still a kid and . . . I just tried so hard to be so grown.

Paula's history of juvenile arrests began with running away from home at the age of 15 and her initiation into heroin use.

My oldest brother, Tony, was . . . a dope fiend and I remember he had all his stuff wrapped in a *paño* [cloth]. And . . . he put it in between his towels in his room and he told me, "If mom comes in here . . . get it and hide it. Hold it for me." . . . So everybody left and I packed my little bag and I got his stash and I took it to one of his friends . . . I told him I wanted to know what it was . . . 'cause I was around my brother and all his dope friends . . . So . . . I wanted to see what it was all about . . . So the dude showed me . . . how to do everything, how to register, how to hit yourself, how to cook it up . . . And that was at 15 . . . and I've been using ever since.

Months later Paula was arrested and taken to juvenile hall.

So my brother found out where we were and he was on his way. And they got word to us by another homeboy and the dude got scared . . . of my brother, so he took off . . . And I was lost really without him 'cause I . . . had been with him for five months . . . I was scared . . . and I was tired . . . and I wanted to go home . . . I called my biological father and I asked him if I could come home and he said, "Yes." So I came home and I had four balloons[2] with me and I had two syringes . . . So when I went in the bathroom I took two balloons with me and I took one syringe. And I left the rest of it in . . . those duffle bags. And they searched my duffle bag.

And so when I got out of the shower there was two cops sitting in the bedroom. And they told me to take the towel off and . . . put my [clothes and] shoes on. And they handcuffed me and they took me to juvenile hall.

Although it was Paula's first offense, she was sentenced to juvenile hall for a year. Her addiction, however, continued unaddressed.

They give you like a . . . public defender for juveniles . . . He used to come see me before court dates . . . He would explain to me what was going on . . . And, you know, the proof was right there . . . And then I had marks, you know . . . I had bruises . . . And so it was an open-and-shut case . . . So they gave me a year for . . . all of it . . . And then when I was there . . . I tried to escape. And then I went back to court and they gave me six more months.

Deborah's Story: Smuggling for Money

Deborah first came into contact with law enforcement personnel for ditching school at the age of 14. At 15, she was arrested for her first delinquent offense. By then, she had a child, and her 24-four-year-old Chicano partner had introduced her to snorting heroin.

I was going through a lot with him, and I always felt like, "God, man, I rather . . . be loaded than to think that I would crack up like my mom." . . . I couldn't take care of the baby if I was drunk, you know, so . . . he introduced me to snorting . . . heroin.

Within the next year she married her partner and joined him and his family in smuggling both people and money across the Mexican-U.S. border. On several occasions Deborah was arrested in Mexico.

His whole family was into criminal activity. His mother was involved. When I'd get busted over there [Mexico] I would tell them that she was my mother and she would always get me out. My mom never was involved in any of it . . . I got out and just went right back . . . I spent from the age of 15 all the way up until [17] doing that.

Deborah's experiences demonstrated how Chicana youths learned to use the resources and opportunities available to them to achieve desired goals. In Deborah's case, working as a *coyote*, a smuggler of undocumented immigrants, required her to be daring, organized, and responsible in order to work effectively with an extensive network of accomplices, both Chicana/o and Mexican.

Back then, the borders were really lax . . . What we did is that we had a contact person over there that would gather people . . . that were trying to come over. And I literally put these people in the trunk of my car and crossed the border with them . . . A lot of times we'd bring them over through the fence . . . In Tijuana . . . they'd cut the fence and they'd run in the middle of the night. Our work was done like always early morning . . . You know, like 12 midnight . . . They'd go over and I'd meet 'em right in San Ysidro, right on the other side . . . There was another checkpoint in San Clemente . . . We'd get them to San Clemente . . . Or . . . I would drive through . . . You know, I'd put somebody with me in the car like he would look like my husband. We'd carry a child with us. We'd look like we're on vacation, and we'd have people in the trunk.

Deborah's motivations for engaging in smuggling were both economic and drug-related.

And like I made a lot of money doing that . . . At that time it was like $350 a person . . . It was a job . . . I bought me a car. I had me an apartment . . . Me and my husband, we're partying out there in Tijuana . . . We did a lot of drinking . . . and we took a lot of pills . . . I would . . . like smoke, take acid.

At 17, Deborah was arrested along with her husband and the undocumented immigrants they had just brought into the United States.

There's like checkpoints right in the middle of the highway . . . and . . . they're all different . . . The person that went ahead of us, they called us in the motel and they said . . . that they [INS] were off [duty] so we came. And . . . when we were coming through the checkpoint they were going back on. And . . . we had people in the trunk, we had people . . . just on the back seat on the floor so you couldn't see their heads . . . So we ran for it . . . When we made a run for it the immigration officer got in front of the car trying to tell us to stop and we just pressed the pedal and we went, oosh! You know, and he [the driver] . . . didn't mean to run him over but he went over his foot. Well, they chased us . . . and when we were getting off on the ramp the car tipped over with all these people. So we got busted . . . Nobody got killed . . . I was probably going on 17.

Deborah and her husband were held for a year in the San Diego County Jail while they were fighting their case.

I was always using different names. I was under another name so I just said, "Well, you know what? Here I am. I'm stuck . . ." I was like . . . close to 17. "I'm just gonna tell them I'm 18." . . . I never got my mom involved in anything . . . and to say that I was 17 would mean to get her involved . . . So I just decided to ride this thing and I did. And I was . . . incarcerated for a whole year before they found out how old I was . . . At that time they didn't have like the Federal Detention Center. They had the San Diego County Jail . . . but I was housed with federal prisoners.

On the brink of being sentenced to a federal penitentiary, Deborah was released as a result of her mother's intervention.

We were gonna go to sentencing and . . . I called my sister in South Gate . . . and I told her, ". . . I don't want you to tell Moms but I'm gonna tell you where I'm at." . . . Eventually she told my mom . . . and . . . my mom . . . went to that court hearing. And she brought this little suitcase. It was all full of old medical cards, stickers, and . . . baby pictures . . . I was going under Pacheco at that time, and . . . [when] she heard them calling me by that name she blew it . . . "That is not her name!" She started yelling . . . "And how dare you have my daughter. And I demand that you release her . . . or I'm going to sue you . . . She is only 17 years old!" . . . And the judge . . . goes, "I order you to sit down or I'm gonna . . . arrest you for contempt of court." . . . She told him, "I don't give a . . . shit who you are. I'm her mother and if you don't release her right now I'm gonna bomb this court!" "Arrest that lady!" The bailiff went after her. She started hitting him and . . . they arrested her. And then I got all upset and . . . it was like all way out of control . . . And she had my birth certificate . . . and they had forwarded it to the judge's chambers. "And why would you lie about your age? You could of been out of here a long time ago." And I . . . told him . . . "You know, I've been on my own . . . My mother is mentally ill and . . . she doesn't know what she's saying." And . . . they released her that day . . . I got out the day of my . . . 18th birthday. And my mom was sitting in the back there . . . My husband . . . got five years.

Juvenile Hall and Other Placements

Not all Chicanas arrested went to juvenile hall or CYA facilities.[3] Of the 10 who were arrested for status and/or delinquent offenses, eight were sent to juvenile hall. Only six of these spent any significant time there. One of the six was state-raised from the age of six.

Which Chicanas were sent to juvenile hall and how long they stayed there depended partly on the reasons for arrest and parents' willingness to take them back home. The California Judicial Council (CJC) Advisory Committee on Racial and Ethnic Bias in the courts also concluded that racial and ethnic discrimination influenced which youths were institutionalized.

[E]ven though White children account for approximately 75% of all children arrested . . . Latino and African American young people are more likely to be arrested, less likely to make bail, less likely to be released while awaiting trial, less likely to be represented, more likely to be convicted, and more likely to be sentenced to secure detention. . . . (CJC 1997: 14)

Studies have shown that young women are more likely to be institutionalized than boys for status offenses (CGW 1998; Chesney-Lind and Shelden 1998; LEAA 1975). They are also more likely than boys to be institutionalized "if there was any evidence of sexual activity, regardless of the offense for which these females had been initially convicted" (CGW 1998: 19).

First Impressions

Lillian was first sent to juvenile hall in San Jose at the age of 11 for running away from home. Between the ages of 11 and 13 she was arrested for running away, uncontrollable, petty theft, and grand theft.

I would say the first couple of times I was scared . . . I think because they scared me, the way they talked, you know. And I was gonna end up . . . being taken away from my parents. And I was gonna end up being in a foster home and I wasn't gonna know anybody there. And I was gonna be alone. I wasn't gonna see my sisters and brothers anymore. And that would scare me for a while . . . I missed my mom a lot but I wasn't . . . willing to show that.

Victoria remembered how upon being sentenced to juvenile hall at the age of 13 for burglary and being under the influence, she was forced to shed the physical image of the chola she had so carefully adopted to protect herself from abuse.

We got taken to the . . . sheriff's . . . substation . . . And . . . there, you know, I think I ate a cold sandwich and an apple and a cookie and some milk. And it was late at night when they transported me to . . . East Lake Juvenile Hall . . . It was . . . terrible. I remember being . . . homesick . . . I remember missing cigarettes and . . . the drugs, the getting high . . . At juvenile hall . . . they used to make you take a shower before you went in. You had to wash your hair and . . . wash your whole face and just your whole body . . . It really killed me to be without my makeup or my blow dryer and . . . hair spray . . . I couldn't fix my hair . . . I had to throw it in a ponytail and I didn't feel so tough like that . . . And . . . for the first time . . . in my life, I had a feeling that maybe I wasn't so bad, you know, so tough.

Paula's introduction to juvenile hall at the age of 15 for running away and possession of heroin and paraphernalia was marked by being forced to withdraw from heroin for the first time.

So then they dropped me off and strip-searched me, booked me in . . . Then they just put me in population . . . What I went through when I kicked? The experience? Sweating, you know, the night sweats. And you're real cold and the next minute you're real hot. Your bones ache. Your nose . . . waters a lot. Your eyes water. You're yawning a lot. You don't sleep. You take . . . cat naps . . . You sleep for maybe a few minutes and you just toss and turn a lot. And it's . . . a constant ache . . . in your bones . . . Hot showers helps . . . but . . . it's real painful. You throw up a lot . . . You got cramps . . . It's . . . a constant ache, you know, 24 hours of every day until . . . you sweat it all out of your system . . . And . . . then your body starts coming back to normal. You start getting your . . . sleeping . . . pattern back . . . And you start . . . getting hungry and . . . you could sleep. And then the sweats finally go away, you know. And then your bones don't ache anymore . . . Usually, it takes about a good week to two weeks . . . It depends on how long your run is, you know . . . They didn't give me nothing. I had to just sweat it out.

Though nurses and doctors at the institution knew that Paula was detoxing from heroin, they gave her no medication to ease the symptoms. After kicking heroin, Paula had a difficult time settling into the institution and accepting the rules and regulations.

It was all new to me being locked up . . . I was in a . . . two-woman cell . . . And there was no privacy and . . . the toilet in your room. If you had to . . . go, your roommate's right there . . . And you had to shower with everybody . . . And you could only come out at certain hours . . . And then you had to . . . abide by all the rules . . . So I was real rebellious . . . and I was in Lockdown a lot . . . And at the time it seemed safer to me to just be in Lockdown . . . because I was scared my first time . . . to go in there.

While some Chicanas initially felt safer when placed in lockdown, the condition ultimately deepened their sense of depression, frustration, and anger.

Lillian: Solitaire. You're locked in a room with a mirror, with a window in front of you . . . There was . . . a metal bunk with a real thin, thin mattress and a sink and a toilet. And the sink was like one of those little tiny faucets like you get in . . . elementary school, that you had to almost put your mouth over the top of it to get any water out of . . . Your trays were brought to you. Your shoes stayed outside the door. That's how they did count when they went through. You sat there and you vegetated . . . They . . . took you out for a half-hour . . . each day . . . on the . . . open blacktop . . . to get air or . . . sunshine. But you got so depressed in there that you didn't even want to be out there. You didn't care after a while . . . And I was real angry in there . . . I remember at one time staying in there for 22 days and another time staying in there for close to 30 . . . because I was given . . . one of my meals, and I threw it back at the counselor . . . I used to hit the walls . . . Or I'd get the pillow and just scream in the pillow . . . I used to put the pillow over my head and try to suffocate myself . . . I never went that far with it. It wasn't something I wanted to do. It was thoughts that came in my mind and left . . . when I was angry . . . I used to bruise my hands. At . . . one time I hit my head on the wall because they wouldn't come and open the door. And I remember slamming my head on the . . . door. And I remember the counselor going over there and saying, "That's good. That's really good." Like intimidating me and telling me . . . "Now you'll stay in there another three days . . ." So pretty soon I just stopped and I just . . . waited to get out. And when I got out I tried to stab somebody in the cafeteria with a fork . . . They gave me two weeks in Solitaire because I didn't touch her but it was a threat.

Eventually, even the most rebellious Chicanas decided to face their fears about being in the General Population rather than deal with constant isolation.

Paula: I got tired of being in Lockdown. And I got to know my roommate better and . . . you become friends . . . And you feel safer . . . once you know who your cellmate is . . . and what they're about . . . So . . . after a while I stopped fighting back . . . and I started going with the program, you know, instead of fighting against it. And it got easier . . . And I went to school and . . . I had a little bit more freedom.

Conditions

Despite the good intentions of some adults in their lives, the living conditions encountered by Chicana juveniles in many placements were just as damaging as the conditions they faced on the outside.

Lillian: It was filthy. The bunks weren't even metal, they were blocks of cement. There was cockroaches and crickets coming out of the . . . blocks of cement at night . . . I was petrified. I couldn't sleep in there. I used to sit . . . holding onto my knees in the corner of the bunk because I used to be so afraid . . . And cockroaches in the jelly . . . for breakfast. They served you like bowls of jelly, big quantities of everything on the table but you were only allowed to have one serving. I remember drinking a lot of milk in there . . . I remember somebody . . . making or bringing something in, some type of wine . . . And I remember drinking some of that to go to sleep one night.

During the 1980s and 1990s, the number of Chicanas sent to juvenile halls continued to increase (CGW 1998). The staff, however, remained predominantly white and secondly African-American. Though some Chicanas found staff to be respectful, others found them to be aloof or verbally abusive.

Lillian: I felt they were authority figures. I never . . . had anybody to talk to in there. Nobody ever introduced anything to me as far as research or help or counselors or Big Brother system, nothing like that.

Victoria: I know there was a lot of verbal abuse from . . . staff . . . They'd say things like, "Little fast-ass girl. You don't even know what . . . sex is." And . . . "You don't even know why you're here" sort of thing. You know, just really demeaning stuff like that to . . . a young girl.

At times, siblings and cousins were incarcerated together. Sometimes it was because the children had been taken away due to parental incarceration, abuse, and/or neglect. In other cases, juvenile family members were arrested for offenses committed jointly. Furthermore, the fact that many Chicana/o extended families tended to live within the same barrios and that criminal justice policies targeted entire Chicana/o neighborhoods for surveillance and harassment made relatives more susceptible to being arrested together.

Luisa: They liked me and my sister and my brother, the one that's dead now. They . . . already knew us . . . We were in and out . . . My mom used to go and see all three of us.

Lillian: We all rotated. It was a rotating door. And . . . my sister went in and out with me. She's a year older than I am. She was involved with . . . like . . . purse snatching and . . . theft.

For some Chicanas, their placement in juvenile hall was only a temporary stop on the way to other child placements.

Melinda: I went to juvenile hall, but it wasn't because of me . . . Our parents got arrested in a raid, and they didn't know where to take . . . my sister and I . . . And my sister was in one cell like, one cubby hole, and I was in the other cubby hole. Had these big old spoons and we kept hitting the walls so we could let each other know that we hear each other. And the officers kept telling us to be quiet and we kept crying, . . . "I want my sister! I want my sister!" . . . I don't know if it was an hour or two, but to us, we were kids, it seemed like forever . . . before they took us to the shelter.

After spending a few hours in juvenile hall, Melinda and her sister were transferred to the children's shelter. There they were cruelly treated by peers.

I went through a lot of embarrassment in the . . . children's shelter . . . because by that time I was like 13 years old . . . I had just began high school. And in the gymnasium I'd be wearing "Property of the County," you know, Santa Clara. . . . And now I was being humiliated . . . by the kids . . . They were making us feel like we were the . . . bad people. Not our parents, we were . . . And the kids in school would push us and . . . , "Nobody wants you. You guys are gonna grown up trampies . . ." And my sister and I would just start crying . . . We'd just run. . . It wasn't that we were cutting school, it was that we . . . couldn't take it no more.

In hindsight, Melinda remembered the children's shelter and county jail seeming very similar.

In fact, . . . the first time I . . . fell into jail, it seemed like a similarity. 'Cause . . . it was like . . . when we'd come from school the bus would drop us right in front of the door. Then they'd lock us behind there . . . We'd line up and go to . . . eat. Then we were assigned . . . duties and jobs. It seemed I always ended up in the . . . dishwashing area (laughs) . . . Everybody cried there, you know. And then we'd . . . go back and have a little TV. We would take our . . . shower . . . and go to bed, wake up. It's a routine. So when I got to jail it seemed like, "I've done this trip before," you know.

Unlike most Chicana youths, Melinda and her sister were not taken in by relatives. In fact, it was only when their half-brother's grandparents agreed to take them in that they were able to leave the children's shelter.

It was months before anybody took us out of there . . . None of our . . . relatives wanted us because of our parents . . . It's like after a while some things like died, you know, like, "Nobody loves us and nobody cares about us." I started growing real lonely inside . . . (crying). My stepfather's parents, they're . . . middle-class people . . . They're Polish people . . . They took a liking to us . . . They . . . took us out and gave us a room . . . They put me to high school again . . . and I shared a room with the baby and my sister . . . They were real good to me. I was going to the team . . . I was in catechism. I was doing routine stuff that . . . I enjoyed.

Nonetheless, the children's lives were disrupted once again when they were returned to their mother after her release from prison.

Melinda: Then I was pulled out of there . . . As soon as she got released out of prison . . . I had just gotten stable . . . It was . . . like heaven had come to me and then it was taken from me. So I just felt really like maybe it wasn't meant for me, you know . . . That's the . . . feeling that I ended up [with], that I wasn't worthy of the good things in life.

While some Chicanas/os spent only a few days or weeks in juvenile hall, others like Victoria spent months there.

And my brother went to jail too. My mom didn't come and pick us up. She basically told them, "Keep . . . them for a while, you know . . . I can't control them."

Victoria's mother did, nonetheless, visit her children.

Some youths who complied with institutional regulations were allowed to go home on weekend passes.

Paula: Back then in my days . . . if you were real good you could leave for the weekend . . . And I wanted to go home. I wanted to visit . . . But it didn't happen no time soon . . . maybe 10 months . . . Eventually, after I stopped being an ass . . . I was getting those privileges where I could go home.

Alliances and Hostilities

Once settled into the general population, juveniles were kept busy through a series of educational and recreational programs.

Victoria: They'd have an alternating list where . . . whenever your . . . turn came on you'd have to clean and sweep the "day room" . . . where we ate and watched TV and stuff like that . . . They had general education from sixth grade on up . . . They had soccer and . . . baseball outside and football. And then, I, myself, liked to go into the gym . . . 'cause they had a radio. And so we used to play oldies songs and . . . listen to . . . good funk music. We would be in there dancing and . . . laughing and messing around . . . And at that time it was coed so . . . we'd be hanging out with the guys.

Luisa, who was reported to authorities by her mother for being incorrigible, running away, and truancy, explained that the way Chicanas carried themselves in juvenile hall also determined whether they were accepted or rejected by their peers.

But I knew one thing—to keep my mouth shut and to not gossip. And I did that for a whole lot of years. I never got in shit. My identity was a fool . . . "She's a nut and if you pick on her, she might not kick your ass but she's gonna fight with you."

Overall, Chicana youths did not have much difficulty making friends in juvenile hall.

Victoria: They basically came and talked to me . . . and I would like introduce myself too . . . And somebody looked at me too long and it'd be like, "What are you looking at?" . . . "I'm looking at you" . . . "Is that right?" "Where you from?" You know. "Altadena. Where *you* from?" . . . And then we'd start talking and then before you know it we had a . . . relationship.

Although Victoria interacted with African-American and white girls, like other young Chicanas she gravitated toward Chicanas.

I think it was because we . . . felt a little bit more comfortable because we knew each other's culture.

Non-English-speaking Latinas had the hardest time fitting in.

Victoria: If they were just Spanish-speaking, kind of like they were treated almost as if they were outcasts because they didn't know the language . . . They'd be kind of like . . . the "nobodies" in jail.

Staff members depended on bilingual Chicanas to translate for them. The lack of bilingual staff and translation services for Spanish-monolingual youths in county and state facilities made the isolation of Spanish monolinguals even more severe (Boyd 2003; Byrnes, Macallair, and Shorter 2002).

Ethnic/Racial Solidarity and Conflict

Despite the conflicts between rival Chicana/o gangs on the outside (see Chapter 4), once in juvenile hall, Chicanas from rival barrios tended to bond with one another as *Raza,* meaning the Chicana/o "race" or people. The immediate motivation for such bonding was that they were forced to present a "united front" before African-American and white youths and adults, groups with whom most had not previously closely associated.

Luisa: We'd click all together at juvenile hall even if we were from different gangs.

Lillian: We talked about . . . what we did, crimes, ways of doing it, ways of getting money, you know, not liking our parents' rules, you know, deciding to rebel and do what we wanted to do . . . I mean, that was our goal. And . . . we talked a lot about . . . what we could do when we came out, you know. Sometimes it was in humor . . . that . . . it would be like more of . . . trying to . . . get into more trouble, having more contacts, more runaway spots.

Although Chicanas preferred to socialize with peers from their own racial or ethnic group, staff discouraged such bonding.

Lillian: In juvenile hall . . . the groups always had to be mixed . . . specially at dinnertime . . . It had to be unsegregated . . . So they . . . had to sit one African-American, one white, one Latina, and, you know, if there were Asian, Asian . . . So you couldn't really sit with your friends.

The conflicts between Chicana and African-American youths were generally less intense inside juvenile hall, though, than they were on the street or even later on in jail (see Chapter 14).

Paula: Everybody got along, basically. You know, there was a few fights every now and then but everybody really got along back then.

Luisa: In juvie hall, I hung around with Blacks and Mexicans . . . The whites were very little accepted, and the Blacks were more accepted . . . They were fun . . . We used to love to dance . . . I learned a lot from the Blacks.

Despite the support systems juvenile girls created among themselves, some vented their frustration and anger on peers.

Lillian: Sometimes just pulling chairs out from underneath people . . . and piss them off. Antagonizing people, threatening people, taking cigarettes from 'em, taking shirts from 'em . . . fighting over the boys in the next unit . . . I would throw . . . silverware, utensils, across the cafeteria while we were eating and be locked up.

According to Lillian, white youths were easily intimidated by Chicanas' solidarity. Thus, they quickly surrendered their money and goods.

I . . . always remember hearing, I mean, even from the first day I ever went into juvenile hall that, you know, "The Raza stick together . . ." I felt that the Latinas were closer-knit. They were more structured. They were a stronger group. I think we were more of . . . the type that were . . . given more by the . . . white girls because they . . . were . . . intimidated by us.

Chicanas coerced white youths into giving them their cigarettes, food, and clothing.

Lillian: If we liked their shoes and they were in better condition, we'd take that . . . Cigarettes, you know, candy, whatever they had.

African Americans were less likely to be targeted because they were not as easy to intimidate and Chicana youths felt closer to them.

Lillian: I think the Blacks . . . were more so on our side than the whites were . . . as a whole.

Sexuality and Same-sex Relationships

It was in juvenile hall that some Chicanas first discovered their sexual feelings for other women. For Victoria it happened the first time she went to juvenile hall at the age of 13.

They used to throw dances like every other Saturday in the gym. So they were having like a dance and . . . some girls were dancing with some of the boys from the other side. And I'd seen two girls dancing together, like slow dance, and it just kind of like stirred something in me. And . . . then . . . someone asked me to dance . . . And we were slow dancing and . . . it just felt really cool, you know . . . I was like 13 going on 14 . . . I . . . didn't know what to do or anything but we just . . . danced . . . for a long time.

The experience made a deep emotional impact on Victoria.

And then . . . I was kissed . . . I just really liked it . . . I . . . never forgot about . . . that experience . . . It just always stayed with me . . . And I . . . grew up really wild. I was with a lot of guys . . . but I always thought about that, you know . . . I'd think about the girls because it was something like real new and . . . it's something like totally exciting to me . . . I'd been with boys . . . so that was like no big deal . . . Seeing other girls . . . was just a little bit more special.

Expressions of affection of a sexual nature were quite common between girls in juvenile facilities.

Paula: When our cells were open . . . and the day room was open, . . . in what they'd call "free time," you could come out . . . Some of the girls used to just kick back in their cells . . . And the doors used to be open . . . and you could see 'em kissing and . . . laying with each other . . . on the same bed . . . They had their clothes on, but, I mean, they'd be laying on the same bed . . . just kissing and playing with each other's hair.

While staff members tolerated girls dancing together, they did not tolerate other expressions of affection between them.

Paula: If they got caught . . . they wouldn't put them in Lockdown for it. They would just separate them . . . If they were roommates they would move 'em, you know.

For many Chicanas, their sexual experiences with other girls in juvenile hall never went beyond writing love notes to one another and kissing.

Victoria: We would like write little notes and . . . see each other. And it was just . . . special . . . something really pure about it.

Luisa was perplexed that youths who on the outside acted heterosexual engaged in same-sex encounters or relationships while in juvenile hall.

And . . . the thing there in juvenile hall is that . . . I don't think no one was really lesbian. I think maybe one or two out of the whole crowd were lesbian, but all of a sudden everyone there is a lesbian, you know.

Despite their feelings for women, most pintas adopted a heterosexual lifestyle upon their release from juvenile hall. Such feelings, however, did resurface for most once they were sentenced to jail (see Chapter 15) and/or prison. And at the time of the interviews, two out of three identified either as lesbian or bisexual.

Revolving Door

The friendships Chicanas made with other girls inside the institutions sometimes continued on the outside.

Lillian: When we got out we exchanged phone numbers, called each other . . . God, probably about five that I used to hang with all the time, consistently . . . We used to sneak and meet each other at the malls . . . We'd meet guys there . . . And then, my best friend . . . didn't have a mother . . . so we had a lot of freedom at her house because the father worked all the time.

Released from juvenile hall, some Chicanas changed their friends and stopped doing drugs. Others picked up their drug use where they had left off.

Paula: It was the same old thing, you know . . . I went right back to drugs . . . And . . . I was in and out . . . for . . . violating probation from 16 all the way up to . . . when I turned 18 . . . I went home . . . I was good maybe for the first three weeks . . . and then I went right back to . . . the barrio. So I was back with my friends again doing the same old thing . . . They all were [Chicanos], except for a few . . . white.

Luisa: From the age of 15 to 17 . . . I was in and out of . . . juvenile hall . . . five or six [times] . . . because of . . . being incorrigible. Didn't want to go to school . . . I just never went home . . . I was . . . a runaway. I used to party. I used to steal clothes to put on . . . I didn't care about life . . . My parents couldn't handle me . . . I felt like I was treated like shit so I'm gonna just continue treating myself like shit.

Juvenile court tried to discipline Lillian, who was repeatedly arrested for status and delinquent offenses, by sending her to juvenile hall in San Jose and putting her under house arrest when her family moved to Stockton.

I did like four months in the juvenile hall. I'd get out. I would be on probation. I'd run away again. I would do a six-month sentence in juvenile hall, and then I'd be in for violation of probation. And then . . . I picked up the "grand theft," which was the purse snatching . . . Grand theft is because you take it bodily off a human being . . . I did nine months in . . . the juvenile hall and probation until they moved me out of the county . . . And then I was put on house arrest in Stockton . . . I had to stay inside the house or be with my parents outside of the home.

Lillian's parents had relocated their family to Stockton in order to remove their daughter from what they perceived to be a destructive environment.

And then I went to another juvenile home in Stockton. This is before the rape happened. I went in there for a violation, a "leaving the grounds," when I was on . . . house arrest . . . I took off with the girls that I met at school. And there was three Black women and then some low-riders, you know, some Mexican guys . . . And we went to a park and we drank T.J. Swan. And I got picked up by the cops there for drinking out in the park area and went to the juvenile hall in Stockton.

For Luisa, periods in juvenile hall were sometimes preceded or followed by periods in other types of institutions for youths.

I would get out of juvenile hall and get in trouble and they sent me [some] place. Get out of that place, get in trouble, and they sent me to another place. Yeah, for about . . . two and a half years. Then at 16 . . . I went into this home and it was called Lathrop Hall. And that was like a 90-day observation . . . So I completed that program . . . But I would always go back to the same thing . . . And then

I . . . got arrested again and . . . I was in this convent . . . It was called Maryville, in Rosemead . . . And it was a really nice place 'cause they had some staff and we used to called them "The Godmothers." And I remember being there for a whole year and I did good, you know . . . I used to tutor little kids. And the teacher was nice. I used to go to school. [But] I used to take off on the weekends, always go out and party. Like . . . me and my sister . . . would tell my mom, "Mom, I'm just gonna go and see a friend" . . . and we'd go out and get loaded and laid and, you know, just party.

Luisa eventually ran away from her placement, was arrested, put on probation, and sent to juvenile hall once again.

So then I left from that place, and they had a warrant out for my arrest and I got arrested . . . because I was on probation by then . . . I went to juvenile hall and I met this guy there and I got pregnant from him when he got out. I was 16 years old . . . The courts released me because my moms said, "You know, my daughter has a home she could go to. *De hambre no se va morir.*"[4] So my mom took me in her home and I had the baby. And I was doing good for about a year, and then I just started messing up bad, real bad. I have a brother that died at the age of 21 of an overdose. They found him dead with the outfit still in his arm. And I guess I hadn't processed my brother's death . . . you know, and I think I just piggy-backed . . . on his death . . . I had my daughter. I left her with my mom.

Carmen's case of repeated institutionalization from the age of six until she was 18 demonstrated most clearly the destructive impact that untreated sexual abuse and addiction, coupled with punitive criminal justice policies, had on Chicana children and adolescents. While most Chicanas interviewed did not come into contact with child welfare agencies and the juvenile justice system until their early teens (Appendix A), Carmen was removed from her home at the age of six due to her father's sexual abuse of her and her mother's continued denial of it. Carmen became a ward of the court and was shuffled from one placement to another, partly as a result of her actions and partly due to her family's and the system's inability to address her particular needs.

Well, first they started with open placements . . . For a while I did the foster home thing . . . I . . . didn't stay too long in these foster homes due to the fact that I was real rebellious. And some of the foster homes have kids and I would beat up the kids . . . I'm very incorrigible, very angry. I'm very, you know, spiteful and a troublemaker as a child . . . Then . . . they started putting me in like girls homes with a bunch of girls. There it was structured . . . where you had to do things but you could go to school in the streets and . . . you'd . . . go to the show . . . You had access to the outside world . . . But then after eight . . . that's when I started getting really bad . . . The first time I . . . got arrested for [being] affiliated with . . . drugs . . . I was eight years old, you know . . . And at 12 years old I landed up in closed placement . . . We were locked in there and you had to do your time in there . . . You couldn't leave anywhere, but it wasn't like Youth Authority . . . But then what happened was I still kept on fighting . . . and I would find a way to escape . . . I always went with a couple of other people and we would go to their . . . barrios and, you know, . . . party with the homeboys, the homegirls . . . But then what happened was I started getting involved with gangs. I started getting involved . . . with drugs and alcohol and smoking weed and sniffing paint . . . And I started getting arrested . . . And this happened for . . . about three years. And then when I was 15 they finally . . . sentenced . . . me . . . to Youth Authority. And I stayed there from when I was 15 to 18 . . . And then I graduated from Youth Authority and came out to the real world . . . just knowing how to party. It was real hard for me to function, and going back to a dysfunctional family and a family that I had a lot of anger toward, . . . it was real hard to find myself. So I went right back into drugs and, of course, now I started doing adult time, which . . . ended up to be county time.

Institutional Comforts

After repeated placement in juvenile hall, some Chicanas came to feel comfortable in the institutions.

Lillian: I would say after the third or fourth time it was a slumber party for me . . . That's where the girls were . . . I think the probation officers and being on house arrest . . . was more intimidating to me at that time than the juvenile itself was.

Luisa: It was like home away from home. The food was good and . . . we used to do things like watch TV. And . . . if you cleaned the hall . . . you'd get extra points and they'd give you candy and . . . little incentives . . . And then sometimes the women that used to take care of us they used to talk to us real nice . . . And I still missed home. I still missed my mom. I still wanted to be with them, but there was something about juvenile hall that was comfortable for me.

The comfort some Chicanas felt while detained in juvenile hall might be interpreted by some to mean that they had become institutionalized, that is, that they neither functioned effectively outside of the institution nor desired to do so. However, some Chicanas interviewed were attracted to juvenile hall because while in the institution they enjoyed a temporary reprieve from drugs, street life, and abusive or chaotic living situations. Another attraction was that in juvenile hall, as in their barrios, Chicanas found peers who were undergoing similar experiences and could offer them support, friendship, and understanding. Moreover, a few were able to establish rapport with sympathetic staff members. None of the Chicanas interviewed, however, claimed that they really wanted to remain in juvenile hall for long or that they needed the structure of juvenile institutions to survive.

The actions Chicana youths took to numb their feelings, protect themselves from abuse, and become financially independent were their survival tools. However, once they started to medicate their feelings with alcohol and illegal drugs and began to break the law to support themselves and their addictions, they were punished by being placed in youth facilities. Yet, this incarceration did little to address the core issues of physical and sexual abuse, family disruption, and addiction.

Even in the few cases where supportive staff was available, Chicana youths were not offered services specifically targeted to meet their needs. None of the Chicanas interviewed spoke about receiving counseling or therapy to help them heal from physical and/or sexual abuse and mitigate the symptoms of PTSD. Likewise, while some Chicanas were arrested for drug-related crimes, none spoke about having been referred to drug and/or alcohol recovery treatment programs while juveniles.

Few of those in placements had access to Chicana/o, bilingual, or culturally sensitive staff. None had access to programs specifically designed to address the needs and concerns of barrio youths or their families. While they were offered educational and vocational programs, these were not designed to make them financially self-sufficient and independent young women.

In short, rather than locking them up, juvenile authorities could have provided a holistic approach that included family counseling, counseling for sexual and physical abuse and PTSD, drug and alcohol counseling, and adequate educational and job training programs that would allow older youths who opted for economic self-sufficiency to adequately support themselves. Furthermore, the adults in their lives should have been held more accountable for the abuse and neglect.

Ultimately, Chicanas did not prefer to live in youth facilities. But they were more vulnerable to arrest and incarceration due to the actions they took to support themselves and their budding addictions, the prejudices of criminal justice personnel, and the misguided policies of the war on drugs.

The continued overincarceration of Chicana youth showed how the juvenile justice system was vested in controlling the behavior of young Chicanas who challenged diverse socially prescribed roles based on race/ethnicity, gender, sexual orientation, class, and age. It was much easier to incarcerate victimized youths than to help them empower themselves or try to change their home environments, the criminal justice system, and society at large.

4

Barrios and Gangs

Being in the neighborhood it becomes a family. The . . . family
you don't have at home . . . Like the homeboys . . . and the
homegirls . . . become like a brother and sister to you . . . We're
bonded . . . And that becomes our neighborhood . . . It becomes
like . . . our house. You know, that's were we live. That's where we
hang at . . . And we take care of that neighborhood and we don't
allow nobody to come in and destroy it or come in our area.
—Sonia

Often alienated from their parents and other adults in their lives and
discriminated against as poor and working-class women of color, Chicana youths developed closer ties in their barrios with their homegirls and homeboys, many of whom were gang-affiliated. "Homies" included siblings and male and female peers and partners. Their peers,
however, were only partially able to meet the emotional and economic
needs of Chicanas. In some cases, the abuse Chicanas experienced in
their homes was reproduced in their relationships with homies, particularly sexual partners.

For a significant number of Chicanas/os, barrio associations did not
lead to involvement in illegal activities (Yolanda). For pintas interviewed, however, such ties, combined with their addiction to drugs
and limited economic and educational opportunities, eventually led
them to break the law. Those who joined barrio gangs were more likely
to come in contact with already biased law enforcement officers. Although some lawbreaking was sponsored by gangs, other activities
took place with gang members but were not gang-sponsored (Jankowski 1991; Vigil 1988).

Several assumptions underlie the discussion of gang activities in
this chapter. Chicana/o youth groups, including gangs, challenge mainstream society in multiple ways and exhibit symbols of ethnic pride
(Mirandé 1987). Likewise, they demand an end to the discriminatory

implementation of criminal justice policies, such as police brutality and harassment of Chicana/o communities. As a result, they play political functions of various sorts in communities besieged by poverty, racism, and discriminatory criminal justice policies.[1]

Nonetheless, the existence of Chicana/o gangs has been used by the media, social scientists, and government agencies to successfully criminalize Chicana/o youths by portraying them, in general, as "dangerous 'gang members' or 'gangsters'" (Mirandé and López 1992: 17). The fact that some gangs and individual gang members victimize others does not take away the potential for many of them to play positive political roles in their communities (Brotherton and Barrios 2004; Jankowski 1991; Mirandé 1987).

It is within this context that a few studies have explored Latina participation in barrio gangs.[2] This chapter provides brief sketches of Chicana involvement in gangs during the 1970s, 1980s, and 1990s. Two of my primary concerns were to identify the motivations Chicana youths had for joining gangs and how these were related to earlier childhood experiences. Other key questions were: What types of support did Chicanas receive from homies, primarily those who were gang-affiliated? How different was the participation of Chicanas and Chicanos in gangs and gang activities? How did gang activities expose them to come in contact with criminal justice agencies? What impact did Chicanas' drug addiction have on gang membership?

Joining Barrio Youth Gangs

Chicana/o gangs have existed in Southern California since the 1920s (Harris 1988). Most are divided into subgroups or cliques (*klikas*), usually based on age, sex, and/or geographic lines.[3] Chicanas have formed part of mixed Chicana/o gangs from the beginning (Moore and Hagedorn 2001), either integrated with men or forming all-female cliques within them. Chicanas have also formed separate women's gangs, some of which are affiliated with male gangs through alliances (Harris 1988; Miranda 2003; Moore 1991). All the former Chicana gang members interviewed for this book had been members of female cliques within mixed gangs.

Although most gang-affiliated Chicanas limited themselves to barrio youth gangs, a few participated in actions sponsored by larger organized Chicano gangs such as the Mexican Mafia (EME).[4] EME, nonetheless, included many members of barrio youth gangs from Los Angeles.

At least 10 of the 24 pintas interviewed joined gangs as teenagers.

At the time of the interviews, some were still considered gang members by homies although they had withdrawn from active gang participation years before. Joining gangs fulfilled multiple needs.

Sonia: You drift away from your parents . . . especially if . . . you're with young parents . . . I mean, they're . . . into their own thing, you know. My mother and father . . . worked all day long, but when they came home they drank and weekend parties and playing cards, dancing. And . . . we're taught children are to be quiet . . . And . . . you just listen and let the parents do the talking, you know, or the decisions. So it's kind of hard trying to grow [up].

Sonia also found in gang membership a degree of freedom from traditional gender roles she did not enjoy at home (see Moore 1991). Reconciling the conflicting expectations of family and peers was nonetheless difficult.

I was living like two lives, trying to please my friends, trying . . . to please the neighborhood, and still trying to please my parents. 'Cause I was . . . my daddy's little girl . . . so he wouldn't allow me to go out or anything . . . Like my brother was allowed to go and do whatever he wanted, but he's a man . . . So I took it upon myself to do it my way . . . I was like really living two lives because I was not permitted to be in no gang. It was all behind my mother's and father's backs. You know, I was going to school with the Oxfords and the pleated skirts and the bubble hairdo back then . . . So when my mother and father used to go to work . . . I'd change clothes . . . and then by the time they came home I changed to my clothes that they knew I wore . . . Here my mother and father training me or teaching me go the right road, go to school and give me everything I need, but I ditched and I took those pills . . . You know . . . going to parties . . . hanging out at somebody's house . . . They didn't know 'cause they were at work.

Sonia's dilemma reflected what Moore and Mata (1981) have pointed out, that Chicana "girls have stepped further from the community expectations when they join the gang than do boys" (49). That is, gang lifestyles took them further away from gender role expectations that sought to restrict them to the home, the family, and the church (although economic conditions also forced many Chicanas to work outside the home). Hence, for most Chicanas/os, "the norms of the gang were in direct conflict with the wishes and desires of their parents" (Harris 1988: 155) and the larger Chicana/o community (Moore 1991; Torres 1979).

Gang membership satisfied the need of Chicana adolescents to belong and feel socially recognized and respected.

Graciela: They made you feel like . . . you're somebody, you know. Because you're recognized wherever you go. When you're in a gang people know you.

For others it was the desire to share gang activities with male partners or gain more personal power that attracted them to the gang.

Paula: A lot of 'em . . . it's because their man is in it . . . And, off the top, you know, they follow the old man . . . But . . . it's still like it is back then, you know, to make a name for yourself, to . . . look like you're the "big somebody."

Sonia: I used to go with a boyfriend . . . I was sneaking around, seeing him at the age of 12 years old . . . He had already been in to YA . . . He was from the same neighborhood and he was well-known . . . He just was one to do crimes all the time even if we didn't use drugs at the time . . . And I got fascinated by that fast . . . kind of lifestyle. And I used to run away from home . . . and go stay with him . . . And then, finally, at the age of 16 I . . . left home.

Furthermore, in the gang, Chicanas could demonstrate that they, like the men, were courageous and trustworthy, that they too were leaders.

Paula: I knew that my family loved me, you know, but I . . . didn't like anybody telling me what to do . . . And I . . . liked being on the streets and I knew how to survive the street . . . And the respect, you know, it wasn't handed to me, I earned it . . . by . . . showing that I wasn't no punk . . . that I can go do what you want me to do . . . And I wasn't a follower because a lot of things that . . . we did . . . I would come up with the idea . . . And I had respect from my own age group, you know, along with my brother Tony . . . And then I started criming with them.

For Chicanas who had been victims of repeated sexual and physical abuse while growing up, gang-banging, or fighting with rival gangs, was a means of getting attention, acceptance, and respect as well as releasing their pent-up anger.

Luisa: It was very attracting to me . . . And I wanted to be so much accepted. I . . . wanted to be known. Being that I went through so much when I was a little kid, you know, being a victim at a very young age . . . all I wanted was attention and I got it in the wrong way. So . . . growing up I . . . did a lot of . . . very negative . . . stuff, by beating people . . . upside the head, just jumping women. And I loved it. I got the credit . . . I got praised.

Nonetheless, while many Chicanas felt safer in their gangs than in their homes or school, the violence associated with some of the gangs' activities (Jankowski 1991) frequently exacerbated the symptoms of post-traumatic stress disorder Chicanas lived with as the result of earlier abuse.[5]

Not all Chicanas who joined gangs came from gang-affiliated families. In fact, none of those interviewed said their parents were gang-affiliated, though other family members and even some of their children were. Luisa commented on the difference between herself and her sisters.

They were totally different . . . They're from Mexico. They married their husbands and being with their husbands from day one to this day . . . And not me . . . I was the only fuck-up. Me and my little sister, but she changed at the age of 16. I continued for about another 17 years.

Relationships Chicanas built with their peers in gangs were sometimes much closer than those with siblings.

Luisa: We used to all sit in crowds . . . you know, music, partying, dancing, crying. You know, some people would be getting tattoos. It was . . . scandalous . . . *la vida loca*. I loved it. At that time, they'd back me up. "That's my homegirl. Don't be talking about my homegirl." We'd share each other's clothes. We put each other's makeup on . . . And we'd get busted and go to jail together . . . That to me, that was like more like a sister than the sisters I had.

Frequently, however, siblings were part of a Chicana's homie network.

Carmen: I was raised in gangs . . . When I was at placements that's all it was, ex-gang members in placement . . . I met them through the system . . . basically. They were . . . from . . . my hometown . . . All my brothers and sisters were [also] gang members . . . So when I got out of Youth Authority I went back to where I knew was my family . . . And . . . we kind of stuck together and that was *la familia*. We went . . . through a lot of hard times together.

While many of those who have written about Chicana/o gangs emphasize how gang involvement leads to criminal activity and imprisonment, several pintas pointed out that the overwhelming number of gang members were not, in fact, incarcerated.

Yolanda: It was like only like a third of us went to prison and the rest . . . , you know, life has . . . been good to them, you know . . . Some of them got good backgrounds, different families. I mean, . . . their life is better than mine, you know, the way I was brought up, you know.

Most who write about Chicana/o gangs emphasize how gang members came from broken homes, but Yolanda argued that was not always the case.

Some of them just did it to do it, just like I did it. You know, some of them had good families, you know. They just wanted to be out there.

The fact that gangs were multigenerational, including *veteranas/os,* or old-timers, who were the siblings, aunts, uncles, cousins, parents, and sometimes grandparents of gang members, gave members a sense of continuity. It also illustrated how the gang had formed part of the history of the barrio and had sought to protect it from outsiders throughout the years (Jankowski 1991).

Luisa: We would . . . be partying with the ones that were veteranos already, like 45, 50 years old, from Florence. So . . . we're following that generation. Now . . . I'm grown and my daughter went through the same experience I did and got loaded in the same spot where I got loaded.

Gang Activities

Many of the legal and illegal activities associated with Chicana gang members were pursued by non-Chicana/o teenagers as well, gang members or not.

Luisa: And we used to just dance and make out, you know. Meet somebody and maybe going in . . . somebody's car and have sex. It was crazy! (laughs) . . . Dancing, messing around, crying a lot when I was loaded. I would reminisce about . . . home.

Sonia: I was from a gang called Hoyo Maravilla, you know . . . And there we drank, we partied, took pills, smoked weed, and eventually got introduced to heroin, you know.

Stealing cars was an activity Paula and some of her homeboys did together.

Paula: We'd go to just [steal] cars parked on the side of the street, you know, . . . parking lots . . . We'd use them to go crime 'cause none of us had cars . . . I used to steal my mother's car . . . But we would use it just to crime, ride around, you know, get us from one place to the next . . . and then, we'd let it go.

Some gang members also committed robberies together. Paula and her homies targeted well-off Chicana/o, but primarily white, neighborhoods.

I would just pick any neighborhood . . . It was all white people and some of the better areas . . . where white people that have money . . . and some upper-class Chicanos, you know, some that were well-off . . . We'd hang out at the park and . . . like . . . when I'd go criming, you know, like . . . stealing their purses or their wallets, . . . if they wouldn't give it up right away, . . . then I would hold the point of the gun in my hand, which would be that back end sticking out, . . . and I would just hit 'em with it and keep hitting them until they would give it up . . . And if I didn't have my gun on me or if . . . I had a partner with me doing the crime . . . then I would just sock them with my fist . . . until they would give it up . . . And then I would take off running . . . I never hit no Chicanos . . . They were all white.

Sometimes, through targeting white neighborhoods, Chicanas/os sought to retaliate for the discriminatory treatment they received from whites.

Paula: It's got a lot to do with . . . the white people and the way they . . . treat you . . . Back in my day there was a lot of prejudice . . . And I feel this is where they [Chicanos] get a lot of their . . . control or they feel they have a lot of power . . . Like . . . to get into maybe certain places . . . because . . . the white man will fear 'em, you know.

Cities like Los Angeles, from which almost half of the 24 pintas interviewed came, contained within them many barrios. The barrio or territory claimed by a gang could cover a few blocks or a few miles. Gangs were "generally named after the street, housing project, or barrio from which the gang" originated (Harris 1988: 95). Once a barrio's borders were delineated by gang members, fights ensued when gangs tried to encroach upon each other's territory.

A large part of gang activity during the 1970s and 1980s involved gang-banging, that is, fighting. Such fights were a way of both "protecting" their barrios and releasing the accumulated anger many Chicana/o youths felt when confronted with limited economic opportunities and/or neglect and abuse inside and outside the home. The latter included police harassment, brutality, arrest, and incarceration (Mirande 1987; Torres 1979).

Which rival gangs were targeted for gang-banging generally depended upon which neighborhoods bordered Chicana/o barrios. Chicanas discussed what gang-banging entailed.

Graciela: We used to go to different neighborhoods just to fight with the other . . . people. We used to go drive to the different neighborhoods and yell out our neighborhood. And we used to . . . jump off the car if we see somebody, and we'd fight 'em. Came back to our neighborhood and somebody from out of town was here we used to fight with them, make 'em leave . . . Just to let them know that we were for our own neighborhood . . . Back then it was just [with] your hands.

During the 1950s and 1960s, Linda's gang in Flats fought primarily with other Chicanas/os.

I've been in physical fights . . . among Chicano . . . Sometimes it was just go somewhere and start a fight. But it was against Mexicans because that's all there was around here . . . Well, if they came down to where we hung around, yeah, we'd fight the whites. But they didn't come . . . And we had . . . some Blacks at Eliso Village . . . There was only one time that they fought that I can remember . . . The Blacks didn't come over here. The Chicanos didn't go to South Central. So basically everybody stood in their own territory . . . We knew not to travel out of your territory because that was trouble.

Paula, on the other hand, remembers how her gang, the Santos, fought rival white gangs.

We would go like away from our barrio and we'd go into places that we shouldn't of been . . . and we would just make trouble. You know, break windows in buildings and . . . just fight with the . . . white people . . . And back in . . . those days when I was real young . . . they didn't have guns . . . Some carried knives but it wasn't even . . . where they would use it, you know. It was all about boxing.

Cristina discussed what Chicana/o gangs fought about during the 1990s.

Drugs is one of 'em. Or sometimes one might get jealous 'cause one makes more money than the other . . . Gang territory. It's just, "I'm from Wilmas, you're from Pedro. I'm better than you." Which is stupid because they . . . don't even own it. It's not like they bought it, you know. You just rent a house somewhere . . . It's just like if their family couldn't afford living in Pedro they'd move to Wilmington. And then . . . if . . . I'm from Pedro and that person's from Wilmington they're gonna fight . . . And nobody owns this land . . . Whoever got in a fight on the streets we took it from there. Like if I got jumped . . . we going back to . . . get whoever we get. And then they'll retaliate back and it's just a volleyball.

Fights between gangs most frequently took place in isolated areas not easily spotted by police officers.

Paula: They would fight in the park . . . But . . . I'd say **98** percent of the time . . . the fights would take place in the alley.

As the years passed, Chicana/o gangs throughout California underwent other significant changes. Paula described the changes that took place in the Santos gang as its members became more immersed in heroin use, other illegal activities, and violence.

Well, as the . . . years went on . . . we started carrying guns and . . . pistol whipping . . . a lot of our victims. Then everybody was using heroin . . . It just wasn't me anymore . . . And, you know, stealing cars and breaking into houses . . . and . . . fighting with the West Side, you know, . . . the Diablos . . . That's another gang that . . . formed . . . You know, that was the West Side and we were the South Side . . . It was all a big . . . control . . . thing . . . Who's to get the customer . . . and . . . what side had better dope, and fighting for their turf . . . I've seen a lot of people killed . . . It still has to do with . . . power . . . And they're not united. They were more united. It . . . was two different turfs and two different *gangas* but . . . there was a little bit more respect . . . Now it's just like totally out of control, you know . . . They can't come to terms about nothing.

Pintas interviewed agreed that until the 1970s, gang fights did not generally involve guns, though they could involve fists, chains, bats, and knives (Moore 1991; Moore, Vigil, and Levy 1995). While some male gang members did carry guns "'cause that was the man thing to do," (Linda), they fought with their fists for the same reason. During the 1970s and into the early 1980s, gang violence escalated as guns were introduced into gang warfare and drive-by shootings became common (Moore 1991). While the violence waned during much of the 1980s, by the end of the 1980s it had begun to rise again. Chicana gang members participated in the violence, although to a lesser extent than Chicanos.

Deborah: The gangs I think have changed quite a bit from when we grew up, from the '60s, '70s . . . Back then . . . gang members didn't fight with guns . . . It was like with your fist. You know, it was like straight toe-to-toe fighting . . . Get a bat, whatever . . . The worst weapon we might of had was a knife . . . But generally, it was the guys that were using those. The women you might have heard way back when they had razors up here in their hairpieces . . . It's none of this cowardly stuff that we got today. It's easy to pick up a gun and shoot somebody that's going down the street that doesn't even know you got a gun pointing at 'em!

Graciela: Like I said, in nowadays they all carry guns and there's no more fighting. They just shoot now. You can't even walk down the street. I remember when I was living on Wilmington Boulevard and D Street, every night a group from out of town would come in and shoot right there on Wilmington Boulevard. All the sudden, at a certain time of night, you just hear shooting. And Wilmington started firing back . . . It was like a war going on and just bullets flying everywhere . . . Yes, there's a few women in there.

Paula commented on how in her gang the focus of gang-banging switched from whites to other Chicana/o gangs.

Back in those days when I was young . . . we never hurt our own Raza . . . There seemed to be more . . . understanding, you know. "You stay on your side. We stay on our side . . . You don't do nothing . . . to try to take over . . . like our customers or the women," you know . . . It was all about respect . . . Every once in a while . . . that would be broken . . . and then they would . . . box . . . There was more . . . peace . . . even though it was two separate *gangas* . . . I'd say about the . . . early 70s, that's when it started getting ugly . . . It's not even focused on white people like it was back then . . . You still have it but as not as much as it used to be . . . Once they started going at each other and really killing each other off . . . the white people just phased out. I mean, . . . they weren't the targets anymore.

In a few cases, Chicana/o gangs have been able to put aside their differences and sign peace treaties or truces. The treaties, which became more prominent during the 1990s, were generally made by male gang members, although some current and former Chicana gang members were involved.

Cristina: There's a truce now. Before the truce we fought big-time. Wilmington was against Harbor City, Pedro, Carson, and Long Beach. We're the middle so we gotta be the strongest. You got all these other cities around us like a circle. So, anywhere we go, we're in another neighborhood. It's not like we can go to the store and it's in our neighborhood. We'd have to go to Pedro if we wanted something, to the show or whatever. And so, yeah, we're fighting big-time. Then they started the truces.

Values, Codes, and Rituals

Another salient feature of gangs were the values, codes, and rituals associated with them. These regulated members' relationships with one another as well as with non–gang members. They helped develop a collective identity that insured the group's continued survival (Jankowski 1991). For Chicanas/os who experienced disconnection from their families and public and private institutions such as schools and churches, gangs provided a sense of continuity and stability. Gang codes included trustworthiness, honesty, courage, loyalty to one's homies and the barrio, honoring the veteranas/os, and no snitching, that is, informing.

Along with the codes were the rituals of being "jumped in" the gang and adopting a style of dress and speech that differentiated cholas/os from other Chicanas/os. Tattoos became the trademark of individual gang members who generally had the names of their barrios or partners marked on their skin. *Placas*, or graffiti, were most often the trademark of a barrio. "Hand signs for the letters of the gang's initials were used as a greeting among members of the same gang and as a way to diss a rival gang" (Christensen 1999: 76). While nicknames were also clever and important ways of identifying and describing individual gang members, they were not included here because they make those interviewed too easily identifiable.

Being jumped into the gang reflected that gang members had come to trust Chicanas who, through their previous participation in various gang activities, had already demonstrated their loyalty to the gang and the barrio. Being jumped in was, thus, a formality.

Luisa: You kind of run around with them. Go to school with them. You get in trouble. You get suspended . . . You go to ditching parties. You drink. You know, you smoke your little pot. You do your little transactions together and they see that you're down . . . to getting in trouble and getting into shit. And then they just say, "You know, if you want to get in the barrio we're going to have to kick your ass." So I said, ¿Dónde? . . . So that's how I got in. That's the way they do it when you get . . . initiated . . . into a neighborhood.

Luisa: I got my ass kicked from about three older women . . . They were very popular women in the barrio . . . One of them was . . . like . . . 15 years older than me . . . These are the women that initiated me to the neighborhood . . . I was in a room and they cornered me in . . . They told me not to, but I was fighting back. Shit, they were pounding my head and beating the shit out of me . . . Got my ass kicked and then I was proud 'cause I was involved.

Being jumped into the gang was also a way to prove how much one could take if attacked by others. Once jumped in Chicanas became members.

Luisa: Automatically. Like putting the straw on a soda and drink out of it.

Once identified as being from a certain barrio, the label of homegirl/boy was jealously guarded by Chicanas/os.

Luisa: See . . . you have to be very careful of who you call homegirl because people are very, "What do you mean you're my homegirl? You ain't from my hood!"

Not all Chicanas/os had to get jumped into the gang to be members. Some were considered part of the gang because they had been born in that barrio or because their siblings were already respected gang members.

Luisa: You don't have to get cornered in. You can hang around. You could be a . . . sympathizer. But you don't have to get your ass kicked in it. And I did, like a dummy. But at the time it was fun.

Paula: I was welcome wherever I went . . . I didn't have to prove myself, you know . . . It had a lot to do with my . . . brother's popularity . . . You know, "That's Tony's sister . . ." At that time they called us the Santos. That was over there on the South Side of Escondido.

Linda: I didn't have an initiation. I just walked into it . . . Don't forget my brothers . . . And we were all born down there . . . Flats . . . People didn't get beat up to belong to the gang.

For many Chicanas, being part of a gang involved bragging about membership and being a visible gang member. Adopting the chola image fulfilled these functions and allowed Chicanas to simultaneously show off their femininity and their toughness. Not all Chicanas, however, adopted the dress and lingo (Galindo 1993) associated with gang members. Some, in fact, dressed quite tomboyishly (Miranda 2003).

Deborah: I wore T-shirts and Levis and tennis shoes . . . That was my wardrobe up until probably, till I . . . started holding a . . . decent job in recovery . . . It's like there's some gang members that will go out there and they are very visible . . . But I couldn't afford the . . . clothes, you know, . . . Everybody . . . talks about, you know, "I'm from so-and-so." I never really got into that.

One of the most important gang codes was "no snitching." Thus, even when Luisa was cut by a rival gang member during a fight, she refused to talk to the police about the incident.

Luisa: And then, when the cops came that night they asked me who had done it and I says, "I don't know. It was just a crowd of people that just jumped me." And the two females were right there . . . one from Mexico . . . and one Chicana . . . I guess they thought I was going to tell on them, but I never told.

The all-important code of no snitching eventually followed pintas into jails (see Chapter 14) and prisons.

Another gang code was respecting the veteranas/os, who, because of their age, willingness to fight for their barrio throughout the years, and ability to survive inside the barrio and/or in penal institutions, had earned respect. Veteranas/os helped keep track of the gang's history.

Cristina: She's older than me. I give her the respect 'cause she's been around and back . . . She's lived that life . . . She knows the . . . good points and bad points of being there . . . They earn the . . . respect. Because if you're a gang member you know . . . a lot [about] life, in general, giving birth, watching them disappear from you . . . Like, for my age I've seen too many of them die in front of me, you know.

Respecting their elders and valuing the veteranas/os was one of the ways Chicana/o gang members maintained a sense of continuity with traditional Chicana/o family values that emphasized respect for elders. For gang members, veteranas/os were part of the extended family system that both the gang and the barrio represented.

Gender and Sexuality

While Chicana gang members have generally been portrayed as playing merely supportive roles to male members, Chicanas assumed a variety of roles depending on their personalities and the gang they belonged to. Moreover, women's cliques of mixed gangs often enjoyed a certain degree of autonomy from male cliques (Moore 1991, 1994). According to Rita, Chicanas played three main roles in mixed gangs: sexual partners, friends, and fighting partners.

Fighting partners, buddies. Either they're being with each other or they just hung out. Everybody just hung out and partied, got high.

Graciela, a member of one of Wilmington's West Side gangs, saw the relationship between male and female gang members as one of camaraderie but not always free of tensions. While some of the tensions were caused by Chicanas dating boys from other gangs, at times it was the opposite (Vigil 1988).

Just friends, homegirl, homeboy . . . They'd get mad at us sometimes 'cause we messed up their play with their blonde girlfriends they used to bring in from out of town. We used to chase them out. But other than that they respected us. They were there for us if we needed them . . . If they asked us to do something, if we couldn't do it, we couldn't do it. But most of the time that they asked us to do something we'd do it for 'em.

A common observation is that women gang members are frequently considered the property of the men (Brotherton and Barrios 2004; Jankowski 1991; Moore 1991). A second assumption is that to be accepted in a mixed gang Chicanas must have sex with multiple male partners. None of the pintas interviewed claimed to have been pressured to have sex with male gang members. However, they spoke of Chicanas who they considered to be quite promiscuous (see Harris 1988).

Deborah: In Los Angeles County, there's a lot of gangs and there's a lot of women . . . There are a lot of girls that . . . I would see would sleep with a whole bunch of different guys.

While some Chicanas opted to play a secondary role vis-à-vis male gang members, others, like Paula, preferred to crime with homeboys in the gang.

I ran with nothing but my homeboys . . . They were all boys except for maybe . . . five girls . . . There was a lot of . . . males. There must have been about . . . 15 . . . Now there's more women, you know, that . . . are claiming Santos . . . But back then . . . women were about a handful, and it remained like that for years . . . On the West Side they didn't have any females . . . in the . . . other gang that they formed, the Diablos. They do now.

Sometimes there was at least one identifiable lesbian in a gang. However, they were seen as the exceptions rather than the rule and accepted "in spite of" the fact that they were lesbians (see Miranda 2003).[6]

Luisa: One of the ones that cornered me . . . she was a . . . butch. A lot of women were scared of her because she was like real aggressive and she was older . . . She used to threaten them . . . Those homeboys, they really never did nothing because this family was real big . . . so a lot of people respected them . . . I don't even think they knew she was a lesbian but we knew, me and the girls.

Paula: Just the way that they would talk . . . about gay people . . . I don't think they would of accepted 'em . . . You know . . . how it was a disgrace . . . to your Raza . . . But it was different with me . . . because I was . . . raised with these people . . . In fact, they knew before my parents did . . . because . . . I was afraid to tell my family and I was afraid to tell my brothers. So . . . I confided in . . . some of the homeboys . . . And it didn't make a difference . . . that I was gay, you know. I never flaunted in their face . . . but they knew . . . And it was strange, there just wasn't any . . . gay people in my barrio. I was the only one that I know of.

With the advent of the lesbian and gay civil rights movement during the late 1960s and early 1970s, more Chicanas became willing to come out to their peers in the gangs, and at least one group of lesbians in California had formed their own gang.

Deborah: I know a lot of women that are . . . gays and I have a daughter that's [gay] . . . When I was growing up . . . people didn't come out with that way back then as they do today . . . Patricia had a sister that was stone . . . stud . . . and she was from . . . Florence . . . She was accepted . . . I know that there are gangs that are gay . . . I have run into women that do have this group . . . I think you find . . . those groups now more so because everybody's . . . just out of the closet . . . They were not openly like that . . . at that time . . . In jail they are, and when they're out here they're not.

While in some gangs open lesbians were accepted by their peers, some female gangs tried to protect themselves from being labeled lesbians by both prohibiting lesbians from joining their gangs and monitoring closely "inappropriate love" between members (Miranda 2003: 98). Notwithstanding such public declarations, however, Victoria pointed out that some publicly heterosexual-identified homegirls did engage in sexual interchanges with one another both in the barrio and while they were incarcerated together (see Chapter 15).

While most pintas interviewed enjoyed being in mixed gangs, some enjoyed the freedom of hanging out only with the homegirls.

Graciela: There was a boys' and girls' gang, but I hung around nothing but girls. We were all from the West Side around Morehall Park.

Pintas described some of the illegal activities women in gangs did together.

Yolanda: I did a lot of stupid things with a bunch of other girls . . . A lot of tagging . . . spray painting . . . A lot of . . . theft-related things, car stealing . . . I mean, I would beat up people just because I didn't like the way they looked or the way they talked or for a lot of stupid reasons.

Luisa: I kicked a whole lot of ass . . . And I must have cut maybe four or five people. Then the last time it backfired on me. The knife, it bent on me and . . . a girl that must have weighed like 250 pounds sat on me while the other one was slicing me . . . I must have been like maybe 20 at the time, 21 . . . And I remember my daughter . . . like four years old . . . waking up and . . . saying, "My mommy, my mommy, don't cut my mommy. My mommy is bleeding! Oh, my God!"

Cristina was part of a larger West Side gang in Wilmington that broke down into smaller cliques, including, among others, the Tic Toc Locas and the Tic Toc Locos.

There was Tic Toc Locas . . . Tic Toc Locos . . . It was a corner store and it was called Tic Toc. . . . Everyone kicked back at Tic Toc . . . My sister and them had club jackets . . . A lot of them got their tattoos of 'em . . . We'd have meetings on my mom's block. The girls would be kicking in one corner and the guys in the other.

Cristina described what women gang members discussed.

Boys, the girls that we couldn't stand. "Oh, so-and-so had a baby. She dropped out of school." Or "So-and-so got beat up by so-and-so." Or "Armando got a brand new car." Or "Delimar's getting married." And "Oh, did you know so-and-so went to jail?" It was basically that.

While pintas interviewed generally described their relationships with homegirls as being positive, Linda, who preferred the company of homeboys, described how she used other Chicanas.

I would use women . . . I would use them to go to places that I wanted to go because maybe something interesting like a connection was there and I didn't want to go by myself. Then I would hook up with the women and we'd both go together.

Linda added that distrust among homegirls was based on their competing for men who have access to drugs.

Yeah, there were a lot of us . . . There was no trust among us. We just didn't trust each other . . . because of the dope . . . So there was no way we could have been friends . . . I didn't trust them [Chicanos] either, but they had something I wanted.

Pintas commented on some of the changes that have taken place since the 1980s with respect to the types of activities performed by Chicana gang members and the expectations placed on them by male gang members and male partners. With the passage of California's Three Strikes Law, Chicanos increasingly sought to avoid further arrests that could lead to lengthy mandatory sentence terms. Thus, some Chicanos became more willing to let women deal drugs.

Deborah: I think that they let the women take on these roles . . . as far as the drug dealings because . . . they're not as easy on time anymore. You know, California has really been impacted by . . . the Three Strikes thing.

Additionally, as more and more Chicanos were sent to prison for drug-related crimes, more Chicanas were forced by economic circumstances and their own drug addictions to engage in illegal activities previously performed by the men in their lives.

Paula: Well, the women, when their old man would get busted . . . they stay in the gang and they continue doing whatever it was that they were doing, . . . crime, you know, whatever . . . to support their . . . own habit.

Moreover, some Chicanas took over drug businesses previously controlled by their male partners (Moore and Mata 1981).

During the 1980s and 1990s, Chicanas became even more willing to form both women's subsidiaries in mixed gangs and independent women's gangs (Miranda 2003). Some of these were also more likely than in the past to deal in drugs.

Paula: Now . . . women got their own little gangs . . . and . . . they'd be going out for the same thing the men are, you know, and that's the big old power trip, you know, control. Who can sell more drugs. Who had better drugs. Weapons, now, you know.

Chicanas like Deborah who were active in gangs during the 1960s and 1970s also saw changes take place in the ages at which Chicanas started participating in gangs.

I think there's much more expected of the women than there were way back then. These women today, they're getting involved in gang activity at the age of II, you know, 10 years old. You wouldn't hear of that back in the '70s or the '60s . . . Those are children.

Despite the increasing willingness of Chicanas to participate in illegal gang activities generally associated with men, female gangs and subsidiaries continued to make up a small number of the existing gangs. Likewise, Chicanos continued to dominate the largest aspects of such business. This was most evident in the barriers to women's membership in the Mexican Mafia.

The Mexican Mafia, EME

Linda joined the Flats gang during the mid-1950s while growing up in Boyle Heights in Los Angeles. One of the most significant aspects of Flats was that some of its members were also members of EME. Some Chicanas became involved with the organization through male relatives.

Linda: As a teenager, I was involved with a gang here on . . . Boyle Heights . . . They used to call them Flats . . . And I used to do a lot of association . . . with some of them and they were in the Mexican Mafia . . . Brothers and nephews . . . because they've gone through the prison system . . . so that's how the associations comes around.

Despite her association with EME members, Linda said her involvement with them was about using drugs and not trafficking.

Paula's gang-related activities did not end with her barrio youth gang. Eventually, she hooked up with EME-affiliated homeboys and began trafficking drugs across the U.S.-Mexican border with them.

Originally how we all started out was from the border brothers that were bringing it across . . . the border right here . . . in Tijuana . . . you know, that were here illegally . . . They would bring it with them . . . And then once you get in good with them then they . . . tip you off on who you can go to across the border, and you just make the *mero*[7] over there . . . Back then . . . you could . . . cross the border, go do your thing, and bring it right across, you know, no problem . . . You didn't have that back then where people are snitching you off . . . You had a few here and there . . . But now . . . they'd just buy everybody off and they know everything because everybody is being tipped off . . . They know when, where, who . . . And . . . they got dogs and . . . if you even look suspicious . . . they searching you.

While only men were allowed to join EME, a few women such as Paula were allowed to participate in EME-related enterprises, primarily transporting drugs across the Mexican-U.S. border. Asked if Chicanas were allowed to have guns, steal, and/or kill other people, Paula answered, "Yes."

According to Paula, Chicanas ran with EME-affiliated men for the same reason Chicanos did: "They just have more power." Paula described how she became involved in EME-related activities alongside some of her homeboys. She illustrated the acceptable level of involvement for Chicanas and what was expected of both women and men.

I started running around with homeboys that were affiliated . . . It's all male . . . Women can't join . . . But when you run with 'em . . . they let you in a little bit here and there, you know, certain places, things, people . . . Certain places you couldn't go into . . . Certain people you couldn't meet . . . You have to be able to not rat, just go down, you know, even if you . . . only participated so much and the rest is on the other person . . . You have to be real strong. You have to be able to do what they do.

The seriousness of being involved with EME was demonstrated by the scale of the drugs, money, and weapons involved.

Paula: From what I've seen, the involvement I've had, . . . it's a lot of drugs, a lot of big people, big money, artillery . . . They used to have grenades, AK-47s, 9-millimeters, bullet-proof vests.

Despite the different scale of involvement in drug enterprises, some of the goals of barrio gangs and EME were the same: to achieve power, control, respect, and greater independence from mainstream economic activities. The money earned from large-scale drug trafficking allowed EME-affiliated Chicanas/os to have a greater freedom of movement and enjoy a higher standard of living.

Paula: Power, money, just living real, real proper . . . Just being able to buy what you wanna buy whenever . . . you see it . . . Yeah, being able to get up and go where you wanna go. If you feel like going to Disneyland or on vacation somewhere in Méjico . . . Things that we can't normally do . . . because we don't have . . . the funds.

Though Paula had earned a substantial amount of money as a result of her involvement with EME, she spent all the proceeds on her addiction.

I used it all on . . . drugs. Every bit of it went on drugs, you know.

Likewise, none of the pintas who had access to diverse sources of income generated by illegal activities were ultimately able to accumulate enough income to support themselves, their families, and/or their drug habits for long periods of time.

Leaving the Gang

While for most Chicanas being in a gang was something they did while they were in their teens and early twenties, for others it became a permanent way of life.

Deborah: I think it's just a thing that we do when we're young . . . There's some people that never mature and stay in that madness. They . . . grow up and turn their houses into party houses. I know a woman like that, 50 years old! You know, ¡Viva la Raza! and still holds it down for the neighborhood and lets . . . all these youngsters party in her home . . . There's a lot of people still out there in the barrio that do that.

Some pintas felt it was easy for members to leave the gang. Others claimed membership was for life and those trying to get out were penalized (Harris 1988).

Sonia: They jump you into the gang . . . And the same way if you want to get out of that gang you get jumped . . . out, you know.

Luisa: Because if you get in by getting your ass kicked you stay in. You can't get out. That's just . . . a code.

Pintas noted that there were many motivations for Chicanas to leave the gang.

Cristina: I was having kids at 16 and everybody's out there gang-banging. I was doing that when I was 13. By the time I was 15 I was having my kids. So by the time my kids were old enough and I was like 23 then that's when I started to go back out. And, at that age, everybody else is having their kids . . . I was in the same gang all the way through. I just got to a point where I said, "No, no more." I had to think of my kids. I guess everything changes. I mean, from me going back and forth to jail and then I'm seeing my brothers back and forth, and they're all getting prison time and now my sister-in-law is getting prison time . . . I can't afford prison time . . . My boyfriend I have now did eight years. His mom and dad died . . . while he was in there. What if my dad dies and my brother's away? And that's my heart, you know, I can't afford that.

Deborah: A lot of these women are either dead, or married, have kids, or [are] church people now. I mean, I'm 4I years old. Florencia's in prison . . . Iliana is out there. She's still abusing. Marcela . . . is infected . . . You know, AIDS has . . . infected many of the people that I know.

Paula: The thing with it now is that . . . we're all old now, you know . . . We're all pushing 50 . . . A lot of 'em turned their life around . . . Some of 'em are married and have families . . . Some of them are with Victory Outreach Church . . . They're Christian now . . . But most of my friends, you know, they're dead. They either got killed or they killed themselves or they're doing life in prison . . . And it just . . . faded out. The name and the gang hasn't . . . The new generation has it . . . but they're old-timers . . . most of 'em are dead . . . It's just something of our past . . . that we were all once in.

When Paula was released on parole in 1996, she did not resume her gang involvement for a number of reasons.

I didn't leave it . . . but I'm not . . . claiming it no more . . . Well, . . . now that I'm in recovery I'm not in it. But it wasn't up until a . . . little over a year ago . . . How did recovery make a difference? Because it's something that I couldn't be a part of anymore. You know, because it's still gots to do with drugs, criming, and I don't wanna be there anymore.

Parole conditions also kept Paula from resuming her relationship with her former associates on the streets. Ironically, EME's policy that women cannot join the gang made it easier for Paula to break her ties to it.

Paula: Because you're not . . . actually committed to them, you know . . . It's not to say like for a male that actually joins . . . And there is no way for a male . . . that . . . you can ever leave, it's just something that you . . . either die or you grow old, you know.

Despite strong ties Chicanas had with their barrios and their gangs, once pintas became addicted to heroin, such ties were severely disrupted or severed though they continued to associate with some of their homies (Harris 1988; Moore and Mata 1981). Out of necessity they became more likely to venture into other Chicana/o and non-Chicana/o neighborhoods to buy drugs and develop new drug-related associations.

Deborah: When I started using heroin . . . there were no boundaries for me . . . You didn't have to be from Florence for me to use. You could be from Maravilla.

You could of been from The Avenue. You could be a wino in the street. I'll use with you if you had it . . . It was like, you know, wherever the drugs are at, that's where you belong.

Sonia: You get involved in drugs and then it's not about the . . . neighborhood. Because when you get involved in drugs you . . . go everywhere to score. So you don't really hang with the neighborhood no more . . . Once I became a heroin addict it . . . wasn't all about the gang, it was all about the money that I can make to support my habit . . . Eventually your . . . mentality changes 'cause all you're thinking about is . . . not the gang so much, although you claim that neighborhood, but you're not there, because you're going different places to do crimes. You move to different areas . . . away from the cops so they won't know you. So you don't . . . think of the gang that much until you're busted and you go to prison and you start telling people where you're from, you know. Or . . . you hang around with the homegirls that are in prison.

Asked if they had to face any retaliation for leaving the gang, several Chicanas responded that they had not.

Cristina: As far as a lot of 'em, they still see me in it. It's not like I faded away. To them, "Yeah, you still . . . from the West Side. You'll always be from the West Side." But they know I'm trying to get away from it. They know, "I don't want my kids involved. So don't tell my kids about it." . . . I throw it back to them at another way, "Would you want your kids killed? . . . Okay, well, I don't want mine either. That's why I do what I do." And they just leave me alone.

Deborah: I know a lot of the people still but . . . I've matured . . . And a lot of the people that I grew up with and . . . partied with . . . are very happy for me.

The fact that one stopped being an active gang member, however, did not mean that Chicanas shunned their barrios or their former associates. It meant that they stopped engaging in gang activities.

Deborah: I would say that, you know . . . you could take the girl out of the neighborhood but you can't take the neighborhood out of her . . . I will never forget where I came from. I will never forget my life. I live in Pasadena. I have a nice little house, but I will never forget my people over there. And anything that I can ever do for them I will do, in the sense that it's good for them and not harmful to me . . . And I will help anybody that wants to get off the street and . . . find a better life for themselves . . . And they know this . . . I'm not involved in any illegal activity . . . I live it through a straight and narrow arrow here . . . I don't associate myself in that way any more. I'm just a married recovery person now.

5

Addiction

I . . . tied myself off with a paño, and your veins pops up. They come to the surface, you know. And you find one good one that's popping up on the top of your skin pretty, pretty good, you know, and then you just stick the needle in. But you have to get a register, you know. And if you don't get it, you gotta keep poking it until you get it . . . Because if some of the veins are too shallow, you're . . . more than likely . . . not gonna get it, you know. So you have to sometimes go deeper . . . And when you pull the top of the . . . syringe up . . . the blood pops . . . into the . . . syringe . . . So that lets you know that . . . it's clear for you to inject whatever . . . you're gonna inject . . . And then that's when you know that you have a register and you can shoot the heroin in. And if you don't get that then you can't do it. Because if you push it in anyway what it's gonna do is it's gonna bubble and it's gonna stay on the top. It's like skin-popping. Then that's how you . . . get a lot of abscesses.
—Paula

This chapter reveals how Chicanas became addicted to alcohol, heroin, and other drugs at an early age. It identifies their motivations for using drugs, who introduced them to drug use, and the conditions under which they first started using. Moreover, it shows the impact addiction had on their health, lives, and relationships with those around them.

An overwhelming number of pintas interviewed were introduced to alcohol, marijuana, and the sniffing of several substances like glue and paint during their preteen and early teenage years (11–14).[1] In this sense they were similar to the sample of Chicana heroin addicts first studied during 1980 and 1981 by Moore and Mata (1981). Chicanas' introduction to PCP (also called angel dust, sherm, embalming fluid) tended to occur between the ages of 14 and 16. These were combined with several types of pills, the most common of which were "reds," tuinol, valium (all downers or depressants), and codeine.[2] Chicanas most often used these drugs prior to becoming heroin addicts.

With few exceptions, pintas interviewed began to use heroin and powder cocaine beginning in their late teens (17–19) and early 20s. A few were eventually introduced to crack cocaine. Again, as in the case of Moore and Mata's (1981) sample, most Chicanas had made heroin their "drug of choice," that is, their preferred drug, by the time they were 20.

One-third tried to substitute methadone for heroin at some point in their lives through government-sponsored rehabilitation programs. For none did methadone become a means to recover from addiction.

Introduction to Alcohol and Illegal Drugs

Pintas interviewed were, with few exceptions, introduced to alcohol and illegal drugs by other Chicanas/os. Most commonly, they began drinking alcohol with parents and other relatives at home.

Linda: Well, my dad used to get me to drink when I was a little kid. I don't know how old I was. He used to make that homemade [liquor] out of cactus plant. And that I can remember on my own, I started maybe 12, 13, somewhere around there.

Lucy: My mom co-signed a lot of our stuff, you know . . . I remember . . . where my mom okayed us to drink. Not to do weed . . . but she would like buy us little bottles of Bacardi and Coke . . . I remember going to the show, and we would take people with us and my mom would buy us alcohol . . . I was 13, my sister was 12.

Gina: When I first . . . drank, I was little. I remember . . . we used to steal it from . . . the family when they had parties . . . But I drank in school because I had trouble in school behind drinking. You know, the teacher wanted to know what I had in the cup and I wouldn't tell her and so she kept on, so I threw it in her face. I was about nine.

Experimentation with other drugs generally took place in the company of homegirls/boys (partners, friends, relatives), many of whom were gang-affiliated (Moore and Mata 1981).

Graciela: I was the first one out of the five that my mom has to use heroin and to use any kind of drugs. I was the one that brought it in to the home . . . I was using PCP at the time.

Mercedes: I was sniffing glue by the age of 12. There was like . . . five of us . . . that used to ditch school and sniff glue all day, all night . . . That was like the thing to do. And we sniffed Tester's Glue. No one ever found out.

Linda: I was heavily into . . . what they call nowadays "low-riding" . . . This is at the age of 13, 14 . . . At . . . 15 . . . I was getting high . . . with the same people that I was involved with in a gang.

Introduced to their first drug, pintas soon began experimenting with others.

Diana: My gateway drug was alcohol . . . I grew up with an alcoholic father. So it was there in the house. I started drinking . . . at 11 . . . That's all it took me before I started popping pills, seconals, reds, yellow jackets, downers, lots of them. And then some speed too, little bennies, cross tops. And it was pills and . . . then weed [age 11], and then the LSD [age 12], all of the '60s and '70s drugs. And it was only a year that I used all the pills and all that stuff before I started injecting heroin.

Carmen: I started off . . . using PCP . . . which is a Kool cigarette dipped in PCP. And then from there I went on to shoot heroin. And from heroin I went on to shooting cocaine. And from cocaine I went to smoking rock . . . So I went from one addiction to the other . . . I was like 18 years old [1975] when I first started shooting heroin. The last time I used was three years ago [1993].

All but one of the pintas interviewed used heroin. All but a few of them were intravenous drug users. And though a lot of women preferred to sniff cocaine, others preferred to shoot it or smoke it in the form of crack. The drugs pintas used at any one time depended on the type of high they wanted, the duration of each high, their preferred method for taking the drug, and how functional they could be while on it.

Rosa: I remember when I learned how to smoke [cocaine] you got the effect real quick. Like you would with a needle almost, except that the . . . effect was short-lived. And so you had to continue, you know. Where with the needle you . . . can do it and wait a few hours before doing it again. But the crack it was continuous, continuous.

Once introduced to heroin, however, it quickly became pintas' drug of choice.

Heroin

For many pintas what attracted them to heroin were the effects they had seen the drug have on those close to them. This stimulated their curiosity about the drug (Moore and Mata 1981).

Paula: I stole it from my brother and I had no idea what it was . . . But I used to watch him and his friends, you know. When my mom was going to work . . . they would come and . . . they'd be sick . . . And then they'd go in the bathroom and do their thing, and then come back out, and they'd be all happy . . . But I didn't know what they were doing.

Luisa: I was already living with a man that was 40 years old . . . I remember him shooting dope all the time, you know . . . I always wondered . . . what it feels like. So I started shooting dope at the age of 19 . . . At the end of my using I did nothing but heroin and . . . alcohol.

Yolanda became curious about heroin when she started living and selling drugs with her Chicano partner after running away from home.

I met him at a party . . . He used to sell a lot of drugs and . . . I was just interested in the money . . . And I was young . . . I didn't have nowhere to go and I stayed with him . . . Heroin and cocaine he used to sell. And then I started selling when I was like 15, 16. Started using at 17 . . . And that's how I started using because I'd seen it. I mean, I was around it all my life . . . Even with my parents . . . 'cause they used to sell it too. That's why my grandma took us. And . . . the father of my kids . . . I asked him for it because . . . I was getting curious and I wanted to see . . . what . . . my mom felt, what my dad felt, what he felt.

Marta first came into contact with heroin at the age of 17. She was initiated into heroin use by Delia, an older Chicana heroin addict and the mother of one of her high school friends.

Marta: This guy I used to see was the dealer. And I always used to see him bag it, cut it, and balloon it. So I would . . . help him. So I knew that was money. So I'd balloon two for him, one for me . . . as I'm doing it . . . I'm . . . taking some under my knees, you know. So when I'm ready to get up I grab 'em . . . with a tissue in hand, go in the bathroom, stick 'em in my pocket . . . And I used to take 'em to her [Delia] and I go, "Look what I found." . . . And she goes, "I could get rid of them for you . . . and I could give you a little taste to see, you know, what it's like." . . . I didn't like it at first because I threw up every time I drank water or soda . . . It didn't agree with me. But as . . . days went by . . . I would do it and see . . . that my stomach was settling . . . And pretty soon I was strung out.

For Linda, part of the attraction of heroin and other drugs was that they were easily accessible.

My oldest brother and my brother that was . . . three years younger than I am . . . were very well known among the drug community . . . They were dealers. They were money-making men. And being the younger sister and being 18, 19, 20, 21, and knowing the right people because of my brothers, I always got turned on.

Some pintas also preferred heroin because the heroin high lasted longer than with other drugs.

Marta: On some people, it might last three hours, four hours. Other people, it could last six hours to nine hours.

Heroin was also less expensive than powder cocaine and easily accessible in Chicana/o barrios because a significant number of dealers were Latinas/os (Dulce). Accessibility of the drug in the barrio also meant residents could find employment in the drug trade. Most importantly, many pintas interviewed preferred heroin because of its calming effect and the fact that it allowed them to continue carrying out day-to-day responsibilities such as cleaning their homes and taking care of their partners and children (Moore and Mata 1981). Asked what she did after she got high on heroin Matilde responded:

I either go home if I'm not at home and finish doing what I gotta do like clean the house or finish washing, take care of my son.

The preference for heroin and other depressants, as opposed to uppers, among pintas interviewed might also signify that they were seeking "some form of release from life, rather than deeper engagement with it" (Faith 1981: 84).

Kicking Heroin

Once pintas were addicted to heroin, their desire for the heroin high, coupled with the painful withdrawal symptoms, kept them chasing the heroin, in some cases, for more than 30 years.

The withdrawal symptoms would begin as soon as the high had worn off. At that point addicts had to make a quick decision about how to get the next fix.

Marta: Let's say, like me now, okay, . . . I'm loaded . . . I got loaded earlier so I'll be fine. I'll go to sleep and let's say I wake up, oh, maybe three hours later, I'm sick because I wore it off by sleeping . . . And it's either I have to have it right there and then, or, fuck, I'm gonna suffer, you know. And, you don't know what to do . . . "Should I go out there and try to sell my body? Or should I take the chance of going boosting?" . . . Because you have to have it 'cause without that you don't function . . . And I went through some problems, I mean, kicking, the chills, you know, the runny nose, the runny eyes . . . And then you get the onsets where you just wanna hit somebody, pull your hair . . . 'cause you can't take that pain, you know . . . You're in pain . . . and everything aches you . . . And it's like, "Oh, God, when is this pain gonna go away?" . . . But the minute you get your needle and pick up your stuff and you shoot up, oh, you're great.

While Chicana addicts were forced to withdraw from heroin whenever they could not get the drug, there were times when they kicked heroin deliberately. Gina, who at the time of the interview was four days clean and sober, shared how she had sometimes forced herself to kick heroin.

Gina: Okay, when I kicked on heroin, I don't go to no recovery house. I don't go nowhere. Like this last time that I kicked . . . I was out there for 10 years using and I got fed up . . . I locked my door. I . . . took the phone off . . . I put a bucket there and I laid there and kicked and kicked and kicked. And I had money to go get stuff but I was just sick and tired of being sick and tired.

The severity of the withdrawal depended on the type of drug being kicked.

Rita: I've spent from either two weeks to two months until your body feels . . . normal, as normal as it's gonna get . . . People are different. Some people they smoke a lot of coke. They go into cocaine comas. All they wanna do is eat and sleep . . . You know, it's different.

Overdosing and Abscesses

Like kicking heroin, overdosing was something most Chicana heroin addicts had to contend with at one time or another, either because they overdosed themselves or because someone they were with overdosed on one drug or more.

Mercedes: An overdose is when you . . . inject too much heroin into you and you just . . . go into a coma sort of thing, like a blackout.

Overdosing could also result from mixing heroin with other drugs or chemicals or from dirty needles (Faith 1981: 74). Generally overdosing was not fatal. It depended on the quantity of drug consumed, its quality, and/or the combination of drugs used. Because seeking medical care could lead to arrest for being "under the influence of a controlled substance," help was not frequently sought. Hence, it was generally other addicts who took care of their sick friends, relatives, lovers, and customers.

Mercedes: I overdosed one time . . . I was at a gas station on Washington Boulevard [with] my boyfriend. And . . . we went in and . . . we shot up some drugs. And we walked out and I went, Whack! and ended up on the floor. And he told everybody that I had a seizure. So he got me out of it . . . I've overdosed a few times but nothing where I had to end up in the hospital.

Abscesses were another of the liabilities of injecting drugs.

Mercedes: Once I was arrested . . . , well they check you for marks. And the first place they check you is . . . your arms. And they wanted me to pull up my sleeve and I remember I had an army-green khaki dress . . . with some tight stretchy pants on, and I couldn't even pull up my sleeve 'cause my arm was so fat and . . . it was so inflamed and it was so infected . . . I had . . . a large abscess in my arm . . . Immediately they took me to the emergency. They have a special floor for only inmates, people that have been arrested. And they had to drain my . . . abscess. An abscess is something that you get from using heroin, either a dirty needle or . . . your arm just gets infected. And it becomes a hard ball and it . . . fills with pus and it's just a real icky thing to get . . . I was in total pain and . . . crying. But they had to . . . clean it out and stuff it with gauze. So I had this hole in my arm to . . . continue to drain it. And that's the way I had to go . . . back to SBI, with my arm bandaged up and, you know, like I'd come out of the war.

Most pintas interviewed chose to mainline heroin (inject it into their veins). Others preferred snorting it or skin-popping it (injecting it directly beneath the skin surface), neither of which left needle marks (see Moore and Mata 1981). Moreover, while skin-popping did not involve going into a vein, the effects were similar to shooting heroin. It also gave pintas a faster high than mainlining. One of its disadvantages, however, was that they could still get abscesses.

The Methadone "Cure"

A number of pintas tried to kick heroin by substituting it with methadone, a synthetic narcotic administered under medical supervision mostly in methadone maintenance centers (Faith 1981). The advantages of methadone were that it could be obtained for free and there was less chance of infection because it was medically administered.

Marta voluntarily sought out methadone treatment. Gina was given the option by the court of going to jail or participating in a methadone maintenance program while awaiting sentencing. Methadone, however, had serious side effects and was more addictive and therefore harder and more painful to kick than heroin (Moore 1991). This was especially true for pintas who took methadone during its early experimental stages. For none of the pintas interviewed was methadone a stepping stone to recovery.

Marta: You . . . go to any methadone clinic, you go to a rehab, you know, and you're gonna suffer the three days you're there anyway . . . It's like being in jail where you're gonna have to suffer 'cause . . . you . . . can't get it . . . But in a clinic or in a hospital you're gonna suffer but you also know you can get it . . . I ain't gonna stay sick . . . [But] then, you know, you're only getting strung out from one drug to another 'cause the methadone gets you strung out too. And the minute you leave that methadone . . . your body starts aching because you don't have the methadone in your system . . . And . . . the first thing that you're gonna think of is getting a fix to . . . stop that body from aching . . . So it's really . . . one drug to another, except one drug's legal and the other one's not.

Gina: At the time, they were giving us 120 milligrams . . . of methadone . . . It hadn't been in practice that long . . . They had us like fucking vegetables, man! I would go like this [leaning over] to give the baby the bottle and I'd stay right there, you know. I'd go to the bathroom, I laid [down], go to sleep . . . I'd be right there in the bathroom, you know . . . It was ugly . . . the way they had us . . . I was only out six months on bail with that 120 milligrams of methadone . . . I don't know how the government has all these people on methadone maintenance . . . I got a girlfriend right now, she was in the joint with me before, but behind the methadone she's . . . been in a coma two years.

While pintas interviewed were not specifically asked about other types of health problems associated with either heroin or methadone use, heroin addicts interviewed by Moore and Mata (1981) associated heroin with anxiety, hepatitis, weight loss, and malnutrition. They associated methadone with weight loss, anxiety, constipation, and loss of memory. Methadone could also cause respiratory depression (Faith 1981). To these symptoms were added the physical effects of legal drugs such as alcohol, which, according to the National Council on Alcoholism, affects the liver, the kidneys, the central nervous system, the heart, the brain, and every other major organ in the body. All three drugs led to problems in pregnancy.

Dulce's Story: Heroin Becomes Family

Dulce's story illustrates how the progression of drug addiction led many Chicanas to lose not only their legal employment and material possessions but also their self-esteem and ties to loved ones. Her addiction to drugs began in her late 20s when she was introduced to heroin in San Jose.

A cousin of mine . . . had . . . committed suicide. I couldn't deal with it . . . One of his brothers came to me . . . [He] told me, "I'm going to give you something to relax." And my lover at the time said, ". . . It's up to you . . . Yeah, you're gonna feel relaxed. It's gonna be good and okay." . . . For a minute I was [scared] . . . but it was like, "Go ahead, do it! and I turned away. And I just felt real warm all over. It was like, "Wow, this is nice! . . . It was a real warm, warm feeling, relaxed . . . I could talk . . . And if there was a hundred people in there . . . I knew every conversation that was going on . . . I loved it. And it was like, "Wow, this is it! This is it!" . . . And . . . after I didn't feel it, I'm like, "What's . . . going on?" "Oh, you already came down." "Oh, well I want some more." "We'll let's go get some . . ." . . . And we got more . . . But . . . no one ever told me that you could be addicted to it . . . And it went on like that for a few days. And when I didn't have the money, I was getting sick and I didn't understand it. I didn't know what it was from. I was dying to throw up . . . and I was in bed shivering and I said, "What is wrong?" I thought it was . . . the flu. But then I was told by my partner that's what it was and she told me, "If you get some you won't feel like that no more." I didn't have the money. I didn't know what to do. So . . . I called a friend of mine in Sacramento, had her wire me some money. She wired me $500 and I got well, got my girlfriend well, and we partied. And before you know it, that $500 was gone . . . But see at that time, everybody still believed that I was still the same person. They didn't know that this person Dulce isn't Dulce no more, but a whole different person. And . . . they . . . didn't think twice to lend me money . . . I had no idea that this was going to take me on like the way it did until after it happened. And then it was like,

"Yeah, I'm gonna stop." . . . Before you knew it, I started getting into the register box at work . . . It got to where my partner had to come and fix me at work. It got so bad that I couldn't do it in my arms anymore because I couldn't hide it. I started going into my neck. Then we started finding other places to go because I'd scar real easy . . . I lost the job behind it. I ended up quitting voluntarily before they would fire me. Because when they were questioning $50 missing from each register, I knew I had to do something . . . And so I . . . just said, "Forget it, I'm going," and I quit. And I think I was real lucky 'cause . . . charges were never pressed on me. After that happened . . . I lost the apartment, got into a smaller place. Wasn't there very long and lost that place. And couldn't show my face anymore because nobody believed me. Everybody knew that something was wrong. They didn't know how bad it was. I was no longer just doing heroin, I was doing speed balls—heroin and cocaine—you mix them together . . . They're known as "The Belushis." . . . I started selling everything I had. I had crystal galore. A lot of Princess House. I sold it all, piece by piece. I would go to the jewelry store, buy jewelry on credit to go take it to the dealer because this is what they wanted. They'd ask, "If you can get me this, I'll give you this much dope," because I didn't have the cash. So . . . I'd charge everything and took 'em watches, rings, bracelets, necklaces, the things that they wanted . . . for just maybe a dime bag, which is a $10 or $20 bag of dope . . . It just got real bad . . . I remember selling my stereo. I had an '83 Grand Prix, fully loaded, brand-new off the show floor . . . I sold it for a thousand dollars after I paid it off . . . My family, everybody said, "That's it, we know you're gone." I sold everything. I remember selling some stuff that . . . belonged to my brothers, my sisters. I didn't care. I became real scandalous because it wasn't only me anymore, it was me and my partner. And before I knew it I was in East Palo Alto 'cause that's where I would go and get it 'cause . . . I found out it was cheaper over there. You can get more. And I said, "Forget it. Why even go back? I have nowhere to go over there anyway. We'll just stay here." And that's where we stayed, in East Palo Alto. We didn't know people . . . We got to know people real quick, learned the hustle there. I was on the streets. I didn't have a place to live . . . For me, "on the streets" was in the . . . bushes. In East Palo Alto . . . right off the 101 Freeway there was a bunch of bushes there . . . They don't have them anymore . . . We used to go get some cardboard because we knew that there's a big old freeway lamp there and it would light up for the cars . . . But because . . . those bushes were so close . . . you could get this cardboard and you could just get whatever you can, find clothes . . . blankets and just huddle up in there. And you had that . . . light that would brighten up the street. You had somewhere that you could fix in the dark and you wouldn't have to worry about the cops. And so it was okay in the summertime. In the wintertime it was freezing. But I slept in abandoned cars, abandoned houses . . . Or didn't sleep at all because I wasn't sure if I was going to get a wake-up [fix]. So you didn't want to fall asleep to not wake up hurting. Walk all night because you . . . didn't have nowhere to go. Or sit at the park all night. And if you were lucky enough that day, you'd make enough money to go get a room . . . Before I cleaned up, I had a $500 habit of heroin a day. And about maybe $50 of coke that I would mix throughout the day with the heroin.

6

Staying Alive
Hustling and Other Jobs

*I'd promise you the stars and the moon. They used to call me
"Betty Crocker Talker" because I could get you to give me 20
bucks and make you believe that you were going to have it in
the next 10 minutes, 'cause I was going to . . . turn it around and
do something . . . The dealers, they got to the point where . . .
they'd . . . tell me, "Here go sell this." I'd sell it. I'd come back with
their money. So I knew that if I did that they wouldn't only give
me some money to eat or to get a room, but they would give me
dope on top of that. And I knew I had a wake-up in the morning, I
wasn't going to be sick. Not to mention the person I got it for was
going to kick me down because I got 'em a good deal, or so they
thought . . . 'cause I was already in the bag before they got the bag.
And they thought they were getting a real good deal so they'd kick
me down a dollar or two to buy a new outfit plus they'd give me a
little bit of their dope. So either way, I got it all the way around.*
—Dulce

Throughout their lives, pintas used diverse legal and illegal means to
support themselves, their drug habits, and their loved ones. Those who
were able to secure legal employment did so (see Chapter 18). However,
because most had limited educational backgrounds it was difficult to
secure the type of employment that would allow them to adequately
support themselves. For those who left home as juveniles with little
education, the economic difficulties were compounded.

A few at some point in their lives had access to government sub-
sidies such as Aid to Families with Dependent Children (AFDC) and
General Relief (GR), a county subsidy not available after the latter 1990s
to those convicted of drug cases. With a few exceptions, the income
they generated from such sources was not enough to cover both living
expenses and a growing drug habit.

Having a male partner who could amply provide both money and drugs sometimes kept Chicanas from having to engage in illegal activities. Other Chicanas depended on female partners for such support. However, as they began to have children, particularly at an early age, they found that even two incomes were rarely enough to support a family and two drug habits. Moreover, partners, particularly when addicted or dealers, were frequently arrested and incarcerated, leaving Chicanas to fend for themselves. At least one pinta interviewed took over her partner's drug business ("held the bag") while he was strung out on drugs. It was not uncommon for Chicanas to hold the bag at some point during their addiction.

As their own drug habits worsened and they were unable to maintain legal work or support the escalating costs of the drugs, pintas interviewed found themselves engaging in illegal activities more often to secure quick cash and expenses.

Those without partners engaged in illegal activities on their own. Most Chicanas preferred to work with others, whether partners, homies, or "road dogs" (running partners). Whether they preferred to work alone or with others, however, Chicanas sought to exert some measure of "independence and/or autonomy" in their drug dealings (Moore and Mata 1981: 88), with some holding the bag at some point in their lives.[1]

The priorities of pintas were clear. When engaged in illegal activities they did everything possible to stay out of jail or prison, keep custody of their children, support their habit, and—given the dangerous nature of some of their activities—stay alive. In order to do this they had to learn to negotiate with partners, clients, dealers, and law enforcement officers.

It is the nature of the illegal activities pintas engaged in that is the subject of this chapter. For such endeavors made them more susceptible to coming into contact with law enforcement personnel and being arrested and incarcerated. Such activities also showed how creative, daring, courageous, desperate, and rash pintas could be.

Matilde: I was on GR, so I had money from there, General Relief. And . . . we used to go boost, stealing, like shampoos and lotions . . . We would . . . have to go to the store every day . . . One time I had a bunch of ham and then the other time I had shampoos.

Sonia: I committed . . . every crime there was. I've done burglaries. I've done robberies, grand thefts, petty thefts. Eventually, as time went on I became a prostitute. And at the time that I became a prostitute it wasn't the tensions of being a prostitute, it was the tensions of robbing these tricks, getting 'em and taking them for whatever they had.

Luisa: I was robbing *mejicanos* from . . . Tijuana . . . I would set them up . . . They were desperate for sex . . . They'd pay you any money to get you. So it was an easy catch . . . because they were vulnerable . . . I would tell them that I would give them my body for $10 and then I had my signals of how to get the homeboys inside. They'd come in with their gun, they'd lay him flat, and then I'd take all their money, jewelry, everything they had . . . One time I took a turkey . . . from . . . one of the guys that we robbed 'cause it was Thanksgiving and I wanted to have a turkey . . . At Disneyland in the parking lot . . . we'd rob the "Europeans," as you call them today, . . . Europeans and mejicanos, but more the *mejicanitos*.

Marta's way of hustling for drug money included sex work, larceny-theft, forgery, and robbery. Sometimes she committed her offenses alone. At other times she joined family members or Chicana/o friends to rob "johns" or "tricks" (male customers). Marta described the actions that led her to serve seven years at Terminal Island, a federal penitentiary.

I robbed the stores after I would cash my checks, my mini-markets. I would rob them [with] a vent brush . . . those round ones . . . for when you roll your hair . . . They thought it was a gun . . . 'cause I had it in my trench coat. I would tell 'em it is. "Don't move because I got people in back of me."

Marta bluffed about having people backing her up.

Lillian recounted how in a matter of hours she robbed both an individual and a house.

I went to my mom's house . . . and I was loaded and my dad told me to leave . . . I . . . asked . . . somebody . . . for a ride. I didn't know her . . . She . . . asked me for directions to get to this place and I took her . . . to this apartment complex that she was looking for. And she went outside and left me in the car. She was gonna take me back. And she had a cigarette packet, you know, like by the ashtray. But . . . the ashtray was real clean so I opened it up and it was just . . . rolled with money. So I took the money and I ran. I . . . jammed around the corner and took a taxicab, went to the connection's, scored a gram of PCP, and got loaded there. And then I ended up going back to my mom's house because I was waiting for my welfare check . . . I was getting welfare for my son . . . She wasn't there at the house, so I didn't have a key to get in. So I went to the neighbor's house . . .

I asked the kids, "Can I use the phone?" . . . Their parents weren't there . . . So they told me to go ahead and go inside the house and use the phone . . . And then they directed me in . . . their parents' bedroom where the jewelry . . . was all out on the dresser, you know, the pearl rings and 14-karat gold writing pens . . . Her wedding set was in there. The man's wedding set with diamonds on it, watches, Rolex watches, diamond watches, dressy watches . . . And I was using the phone trying to find out where my mother was. I seen all this stuff there and I thought, "You know, I could trade it for drugs." So I just loaded my purse and . . . I split out the back door . . . And then, that night I came back . . . I was loaded. Well, I had hocked all the jewelry, you know . . . $5,000 worth of diamond and gold . . . I mean, a Rolex watch for one joint for $20, to anybody on the streets. And when I went back the kids told their parents that I was the one that went into the house to use the phone. And there's where the cops came at my mom's door and arrested me [for] under the influence and possession, . . . first-degree burglary.

Carmen was the only pinta interviewed who claimed to have been a pimp for sex workers.

I lived in a lot of hard-core gang-violence . . . I lived . . . the drug scene. I lived a life . . . of pimping where . . . I'm a lesbian and I had my, what you call my "old ladies." And for . . . drugs . . . they would prostitute and I'd watch their backs and I carried a gun and . . . we made money that way.

To commit armed robberies and burglaries, however, Carmen sought out her Chicano homeboys.

We were into professional boosting or . . . shoplifting, going in stores and lifting stuff, selling it in the . . . black market for half the price . . . I did a lot of armed robberies . . . And, you know, burglaries, breaking into houses and . . . robbing gas stations . . . different stores . . . Those were with my homeboys.

Diana's Story: Trick or Trade?

Diana engaged in sex work, for which she was arrested numerous times.

They would pull over and ask if I were dating, or if I was working. And it would depend on how I felt about that person, if I thought that I . . . could trust them . . . or how sick I was. You know, how desperate I was would depend if I went with them . . . I mean, I made a lot of bad choices.

While other sex workers had pimps, Diana preferred to work the streets alone.

I'm out there selling . . . myself to give my money to a man, for what? . . . So they can take my money? . . . I never saw any protection out there . . . I was out there mostly by myself. I lived in a motel.

Pimps also frequently encouraged addiction in order to keep sex workers dependent on them.

The price Diana charged johns varied.

Forty dollars, sometimes more, it just depends on the service . . . If I was doing like half and half . . . like oral sex and . . . [intercourse] . . . maybe 60, 70 dollars. But if each one separate, $40. And then . . . like anything like out of the ordinary . . . I mean . . . during the periods of time that I've had a lover out there and we were both working, we would do threesomes, 100 bucks, 150.

Diana learned the trade from other sex workers.

I learned out there, you know, [from] girls . . . I mean, when you live in that kind of element in the motels . . . that's all it is, you know . . . it's prostitution, drugs . . . So it doesn't take much to hook up . . . when you're that active in the streets because most of the people hanging out in the streets are up to something.

Sometimes Diana would lure tricks to a hotel, where she would rob them.

I got that money however I could get it . . . If I had to rob somebody I would . . . It just would depend on what was convenient at that time . . . If I was too sick to turn a trick . . . I would pick somebody up like I was . . . gonna turn a trick and . . . take him to a room and . . . make him go in and take a shower . . . Leave while they were in the shower with all of their clothes and their money and everything else.

A few times Diana robbed Mexican drug connections, either alone, or in the company of Chicano homeboys.

I've been involved in a couple of situations . . . that were . . . drug-related. You know, . . . I've taken another person to a connection's house with a . . . pistol and they've been robbed . . . Me, personally . . . no, but I've been with somebody that has robbed somebody like that . . . I mean, these things happen. And in the little neighborhood that I ran around in it happened a lot . . . Usually it was the . . . homeboys . . . robbing the wetbacks, you know, and it was never the wetbacks robbing the homeboys . . . I robbed that connection another time alone . . . And what happened that time was . . . I went over there to the house to . . . pick up . . . [drugs]. And I went around to the back of the house and the door was open and nobody was answering. And I went into the house and . . . he was laid out on the floor and I didn't . . . know what was going on . . . The house was trashed . . . And I tried to wake him up and he wouldn't wake up. And . . . when I looked up on the . . . mantel he had . . . one of those big freezer storage baggies, piled, filled . . . He used to deal in pounds and pounds of cocaine . . . And I looked at it and I looked at him . . . And . . . that time I was scared and I started to walk out . . . And I said, "No, I can't do that. It's calling my name." So I went back into the house and . . . I robbed him and . . . I left . . . And I . . . locked myself up in a room and I stayed loaded for a couple of days . . . And then I called somebody to come and get me. And I . . . left and went into a recovery house.

Lucy's Story: Dangerous Liaisons

Lucy also engaged in sex work to support her habit, although at first she shunned the idea.

Even before I actually was doing anything, you would walk down the street and people would stop you. "Do you want a ride?" . . . And I didn't know then what was going on, you know . . . And one time, I took a ride and someone told me did I want to make some money and I told them, "I ain't no fucking whore!" . . . But afterwards, when I started doing more heroin and . . . started knowing more girls, you know, they'll tell you where to go. You know . . . just out there . . . on the boulevard, Anaheim, Wilmington, PCH . . . PCH, you know, it's kind of open ground . . . A car would stop, ask if I want a date.

Sometimes Lucy shared her room with her addicted sister.

At the same time my sister was out there working the streets and we were . . . sharing the same room.

Like Diana, Lucy's fees varied.

Lucy: It wasn't something that was a flat fee . . . Okay . . . Depending on . . . what they wanted and what the person was driving . . . If it was head . . . , it was between 20 and 40 . . . But, you know, a lay, . . . depending what the person . . . look like. You know . . . sometimes 20, sometimes 50. Depending on who it was . . . and what they offered. Some people wanna . . . kick it in a motel for awhile and it was $150 . . . The least I would accept was $20 . . . The most I've ever got . . . was, I think, $150.

Sex work, however, was a dangerous occupation. Lucy described a rape and an attempted rape she experienced.

The first time that it happened to me . . . the guy . . . took me to a deserted place . . . It was in Riverside . . . Had a gun and put it to . . . my chest . . . And told me to take . . . my . . . pants down and . . . I did. And he started talking crazy. You know, that kind of bitch stuff, and loud. And I told him, "You don't have to talk like that . . . You are gonna get what you want . . . Just get it over with." . . . And . . . I started praying . . . I asked Jesus for help. He says Jesus wasn't gonna help me. And the sucker couldn't get a hard-on. So it sounds like I got help. He kicked me out of the car . . . Then he went ahead and drove off. You know, and he was cussing me out . . . The other time I was in L.A. County. This one was a cute Puerto Rican. That's the reason why I even got in the car . . . And we started talking and everything and then he pulled me off into . . . this place where the rakes go into. Then . . . just pulled off a knife and he started cussing at me . . . And more or less did the same kind of thing but this time I just kept my mouth shut and just went ahead and let him. And he just left me dumped there. But how I handle it is . . . cry (crying) . . . And I figured if I wouldn't have been out there doing my thing, I wouldn't have . . . been subjected to it . . . I put myself in that predicament . . . I started in '89 . . . The last time I prostituted was . . . December 1993.

While Lucy partly blamed herself for putting herself in such situations, it was clear to her that the violence from johns was intended to control and terrorize sex workers.

I've been raped . . . But . . . I wasn't a fighter or anything like that so it wasn't necessary, all that kind of stuff. If you want it, I'll give it to you. It was their control thing. I wasn't an arguer or a fighter at that point because I knew who was stronger and who had the upper hand.

Linda's Story: It's a Family Affair

Linda worked for her brothers trafficking both money and drugs across the Mexican-U.S. border.

I have two brothers that were in the system and two sisters that were in the system . . . I was used by my brothers as far as holding their money bags or those stashes that they had whenever they felt the police were getting too close to them. They would run into my house . . . I was used by my family as far as transporting drugs from Mexico into the United States . . . I was their mule . . . I'd go anytime, any day . . . All my transportation is connected with my family. It has nothing to do with outsiders.

For Linda, transporting drugs from Mexico became a routine affair.

I got pretty good at that damn border . . . I never got caught, and I used to cross at anytime between 3 o'clock in the morning. And . . . the guards would ask me . . . "What are you doing out here?" And you know what used to throw them off? . . . When I used to tell them, ". . . You know, this is where they got all the male whores. I came to get me a male whore . . . or a prostitute . . . Let it be male or female" . . . They'd laugh and they'd laugh and they thought it was cute . . . And I'm gone! . . . All they asked me, where was I born, and I'd say L.A. That was it.

Although Linda was entrusted with drugs and money, she felt discriminated against by male connections, including her brothers, who did not trust known women heroin addicts.[2] A few dealers refused to sell drugs to women because they felt women were more likely to snitch than men, or they feared getting into conflicts with boyfriends or family members (see Moore and Mata 1981).[3] Others felt that if arrested, women's fear of losing their children might make them more susceptible to police intimidation. Chicanas generally rejected such stereotypes.

Linda: I've always sniffed heroin, and I've always skin-popped heroin. And the reason I did that is because the connections back then, if they were money-making connections, would not touch a woman who was a heroin addict, needle user . . . They didn't trust them. And if anything happened they always said they would turn on them. By that they meant that the women would put the finger on them and they'd wind up going to jail. And, of course, coming from that with my brothers . . . I knew that. So what I used to do is to skin-pop or I used to snort . . . I'd say more sniffing than anything else because . . . if my brothers would have known that I was doing that they probably would have never trusted me.

Linda's motivations for dealing—economic gain and to support her brothers—reinforced one another.

I started doing that with my brother when I was 18. And that was because of . . . finances. He asked me if I wanted a loan, he'd give me so much money, and I said yes. I jumped in the car with him and we went. I crossed, he drove. Or sometimes we would both be in the same car and we'd both cross . . . The last time I did that kind of trafficking was when I picked up a sale in . . . '63. And that's 'cause I went to jail.

Another of Linda's hustles was to get sexually involved with drug connections.

I was a pretty good little thief as a kid, you know. I gave up my stealing career 'cause I . . . didn't have to steal anymore. Then I'd go and fall in love . . . I used to say I was never a prostitute . . . because I'd never stand on the . . . street, but I'd fall in love every 30 days. And usually the men that I would fall in love with were the men that were the connection. As long as they were a connection and they were making money and they had drugs, I'd fall in love . . . But it was real easy when he ran out of the drugs for me to say, "Well." If they didn't run out, they'd be in jail because he was the man so he'd take care of it, you know . . . And if they didn't wind up in jail and the drugs ran out it was like, it was no big deal. I'd set it up until they were just out of the picture. I mean, I had to survive. I was surviving since I was a very young kid.

Yolanda's Story: Holding the Bag—A Full-time Job

While pintas interviewed did not generally play the leading role in large drug enterprises, Yolanda did.

I was the one that's doing . . . everything . . . I was this dumb one that was taking the stuff and delivering it or getting phone calls . . . I'm the one that went to get the drugs, delivered the drugs and sold the drugs, while he kicked back . . . He didn't work . . . He was always home . . . I'm the one that paid the bills . . . took care of my daughter . . . He didn't force it on me. I just . . . seen that he was . . . already strung out . . . All he cared was, you know, getting well . . . He'd seen me doing everything so he just left it like that . . . I'm the one that kept everything up . . . because I liked the money.

Yolanda described her introduction to drug dealing before she became an addict.

I got the drugs from these Colombian people that I used to sell for . . . I met him through the . . . father of my kids . . . He asked me if I wanted to make some money so I tell him, "Yeah, well, what do you want me to do?" And . . . he says, "I want you to sell . . . for me." He says, "I'll send you the people . . ." He showed me how to . . . cut it . . . how to bag it up . . . putting the heroin in a balloon . . . At that time it was $25 . . . And then he brought me customers . . . The customers told the others . . . Next thing you know I had a gang of people calling me and it was just . . . like on the hour . . . that I was doing this, constantly dealing, making . . . a lot of money . . . At the time I wasn't using drugs.

She also found ways to make additional money.

The people that I sold for it's like he was getting . . . half of everything of what I make . . . We'd . . . cut it, bag it up. He goes like, "You gonna make this much and . . . you gonna give me this much." So when . . . I paid him that's when he gave me mine, you know. I . . . gave him $200, I kept $200 . . . But when he was gone . . . I would cut all the bags up and I'll redo them and make more.

Before becoming an addict, Yolanda used the money to fulfill a number of personal needs and desires.

Whenever I wanted something I had the money to buy it, things that I didn't have when I was young, you know, like clothes. If I wanted another car I could get another car. If I . . . liked this ring at the store I could buy it whenever I wanted to, you know, food. I didn't . . . need for nothing.

The business of drug dealing took up much more time than most legal full-time jobs. Pintas spent the remainder of their time taking care of their children and partners. They were left with little time to spend on recreation, though they now could afford it.

Yolanda: I was so busy into selling that I didn't care about going nowhere. I was worried about my business 'cause I supplied this one community.

Asked if she knew any pintas who went on vacation with the money they made from drug sales, Cristina responded that most Chicana addicts rarely left their barrios. Those who did not spend all their money on getting high tended to spend money on their families.

Most women . . . did the drugs . . . They'll buy cars. Or . . . if they have an old man in prison, send him the money to survive in there . . . Some of them put their kids in, like, baseball, which costs, that's 40 bucks right there. Oh, send their kids off on . . . the school trips that they have in the summer here. But as for themselves, no, they stay here.

Mercedes' Story

Mercedes described how she moved temporarily to Mexico to pursue a lucrative credit card fraud enterprise with her Chicano boyfriend after she served her first jail sentence.

When I got out I was still on probation. I met this guy . . . and he talked me into moving to . . . Puerto Vallarta, Mexico. Girl, I sold everything, bought a van, moved . . . and I fit perfect. I was bilingual. I had the long hair . . . I worked in a restaurant bar and I ran credit cards throughout Mexico because I was very connected . . . My partner taught me all of this. He was there like two years prior to me . . . but he . . . couldn't run female credit cards without a female, you know.

Puerto Vallarta is a tourist town and it's all beach . . . The *playaderos* . . . lived in Puerto Vallarta . . . Caucasians or Canadians would be attracted to the playaderos. The playaderos would rip them off. And for the most part, it was always credit cards. So they would give me the credit cards and only expect like shoes or a pair or pants . . . They weren't . . . addicts. They were thieves. That was their survival. So it wasn't like they wanted a lot . . . So I used to go to Guadalajara and get them whatever they wanted . . . Nobody ever questioned it . . . Remember, these are tourist ports that want their merchandise bought. So it's not like they were going to question that . . . They wanted a sale and they knew that . . . they were "hot" credit cards . . . I mean, I would even do deals with some of the . . . stores there . . . I had a whole setup. I did this for about four years . . . My boyfriend left me because it was tourist season and . . . he had a lot of contact with rich . . . white women that were attracted to Latinos . . . That was appalling to me. It's like, "What? You bring me to another country and what are you talking about? You gonna see this woman for you and *me*?" . . . I didn't know that . . . when you're partners with an addict . . . the female [or male] could make money for the both of you and it didn't matter as long as it was money for the both of you. And I couldn't understand that . . . So he left me for this other woman. So I felt betrayed and abandoned . . . And by that time the *federales* were after me . . . So immediately I was informed and I flew out of Vallarta.

Upon returning to Los Angeles, Mercedes soon began boosting for a living.

I started using drugs again . . . Now I was using locally, like in my community. And that same house that my grandmother told me not to look at . . . I now started using drugs there. And now I didn't . . . have a job . . . I didn't know anything about GR or AFDC . . . I didn't even know how to be an addict, let alone what I was going to do about getting money. So there was other women that were around me that were boosters, and they would just ask me to go with them, you know, to be a . . . lookout . . . They were boosting clothes . . . And, of course, they exposed me to their fences that were buying the clothing. So . . . not only did I learn the skill, but I also developed a system with the fences . . . You know, basically these fences were just people that were in the community, basically *mejicana* women or Chicana women that were like 50, 60 years old, that bought hot merchandise . . . and actually went out into the community and sold these clothes for . . . a higher price. And we [addicts] were very . . . exploited because . . . I believe that they knew what it was for, you know, and whatever price that they came up with . . . we pretty much went with that price.

Prior to her first arrest and moving to Mexico, Mercedes had worked in various types of legal white collar jobs. It was her ability to adopt a middle-class appearance and demeanor that had allowed her to run a credit card fraud in Mexico and boost from department stores in Los Angeles.

I would say I was a heroin addict in silk because I knew I had to play the part. And because I had been exposed to the corporate world I knew . . . what the attire was for women that had credit cards, for women that have a job . . . And, basically, I was always dressed either in a suit, a dress, high heels . . . I knew I had to look like I had money. And, basically, I would go into . . . the clothing department [of] . . . all the major stores . . . There was times when I took a . . . large trash bag. And there was times that I took large bags from the store. You know, store bags, that you could just . . . throw the clothes in and just walk out with the store bag . . . I would steal silk . . . I'd roll them up in balls and stuff them in my purse and stuff them on me. You know, I'd wear a girdle and I would fit all the dresses in me . . . The easiest part about silk is that they would put the alarm on the seam so all you had to do was pull the seam and just pull the lock out . . . I used to steal Levis too before they started putting alarms on . . . Levis . . . I've hit every mall there is . . . from here to Orange County, from Orange County to San Fernando Valley . . . I've been arrested quite a few times for shoplifting. But, for the most part, I didn't get caught.

Mercedes used her Chicano boyfriend to drive her to the malls, act as a lookout, and hold the stolen merchandise while she boosted from different department stores.

Eventually, Mercedes' heroin addiction progressed to the point that she was unable to boost from stores and was reduced to selling drugs in the streets to support her habit.

'Cause at this point in time I was already using 15 spoons. And it was good stuff . . . I was pregnant and I was running around downtown . . . The whole scenario would be I'd get up early morning and go hit the streets and sell drugs . . . all afternoon. And then I'd go back and fix in between . . . I had a little Black friend named Little Bit. She was gorgeous. She was from out of state. And she . . . was a heroin addict too . . . Basically, Black women downtown were crack smokers. They weren't heroin addicts. But she was my old heroin addict friend. But she'd sell crack to make money for heroin. I'd sell heroin to make money for coke. So I was like, "What a combination!" . . . Basically, I'd go to her room and we'd get loaded. We'd shoot dope all night, smoke rock, slam cocaine, you know.

Dulce's Story: Do or Die

Dulce shared the difficulties she and her lover had breaking into a new turf to deal drugs after they became homeless in East Palo Alto.

It was hard at first because you're new on the block and they want to know if you're taking their territory . . . Because, you know, you're out there hustling for business . . . People come up and, "Where can I get this? Where can I get that?" You'd go and you'd take them to the dealer . . . Or sometimes they have to wait . . . "Okay, give me your money and I'll get it for you." . . . And if you do it for them a few times, you don't mess with them . . . they come back to you . . . And then, because I knew Spanish so well I could get it for them . . . So a lot of people there would get upset 'cause . . . they'd say we're taking their customers.

Dulce's customers were local residents of East Palo Alto as well as women and men who would drive in from other cities to buy drugs from dealers who stood near the freeway.

All we had to do was just stand there, 'cause they'd come off of the Freeway 101 and they knew what we were there for . . . A lot of people come from Santa Cruz, from Hayward . . . And . . . you got in there with them real quick . . . 'cause what they want to do is go in and get out because of the cops . . . So I get stuff for them from the connection . . . Boom! Make a few dollars . . . add some dope for myself.

One of the advantages Dulce had was the fact that she was bilingual and could communicate easily with the Latina/o dealers in East Palo Alto.

A lot of . . . the . . . dealers . . . have a hard time talking with the . . . people out there 'cause in East Palo Alto there are a lot of Black people and a lot of dealers are . . . Latinos. Basically, your heroin dealers are Latino . . . a good 90 percent of them . . . The Black people are usually your . . . coke dealers . . . Latinos . . . they dealt powdered coke but not the crack.

Dulce's lover provided her protection while she was dealing.

And my partner would watch my back . . . She couldn't talk good Spanish . . . A good majority of the people, they used to think she was a guy, the way she talked, the way she would carry herself. So I was pretty secure there.

Dulce also worked hard because she was supporting two drug habits. But eventually addiction pushed the relationship with her partner to the limit.

I was on it because I knew that it wasn't just for me . . . I was taking care of her habit . . . And me, . . . I thought I . . . had this greatest love . . . I remember a lot of times going without to make sure my partner was fixed . . . I remember us fighting and practically killing each other for it. It was no longer the partner I thought I had . . . I thought it was real glamorous at first. [She] wasn't the same person. I wasn't the same person.

Dulce found the danger and fear that accompanied drug dealing exhilarating.

And it was all new to me. So I thought, "Wow, this is cool!" . . . Not only was [it] . . . the fear, but it was the adrenaline that came with it, you know, the excitement . . . the, "Yeah, let's go do it!" thing. And, "Okay, you watch my back. I'm going to run up there. I'm gonna run back down." And the thing about it for me was . . . the adrenaline of beating the cops . . . And I can remember telling . . . my PO, "Catch me if you can." . . . And they told me, "Within time, . . . you'll hang yourself." And it happened that way. But . . . you couldn't survive in East Palo Alto without picking up quick if you wanted to survive. It was "Do or die."

Dulce's illegal activities also included driving the car for her lover and other Latino associates while they stole from department stores.

I remember that I got so brave and bold to say, "Yeah, I'll go and drive for you." We'd go to different stores, Mervin's, what have you, I would be the driver. These guys would go in and just get racks of stuff. Throw 'em in the back of the truck. Go to East Palo Alto, a certain area. Open it up. "Okay, what do you want? You want Bugles? . . . Bugle Boy pants, Bugle Boy shirts, sweaters" . . . All the Latinos, they'd always play volleyball at a certain time and a certain place and we would go there. That was like their cover. Like you know, no one knew, but everybody knew.

With one exception, all the men involved in the robberies were parolees. They taught Dulce new ways of breaking the law.

Matter of fact, everybody that was there, with the exception of me and my girlfriend, were all parolees . . . A lot of the stuff I learned too was from the parolees. They showed me how to use credit cards. They showed me how to rob a connection . . . Especially being a woman, how I can get in and out. I can distract them by going in there 'cause, you know . . . I'm a real trustworthy person with them. They see me and you wouldn't think I'd do that. And as I'm talking to you . . . I can see the bag of dope there . . . And we're talking and I'm taking it.

Robbing a connection, however, was a particularly dangerous enterprise.

I remember robbing a connection of . . . I'd say a good eight grams of heroin and five of cocaine . . . They found out afterwards. I had a shotgun to my head . . . I got beat up . . . real big-time . . . One guy and two girls . . . The guy was a Black guy. He's the one that had the gun to my head. And the girls, Latinas. And they did [it] mainly because they wanted . . . dope. "You do this. I'll give you some dope." So, "Yeah, why not?" . . . And they left me just there lying on the park.

While Dulce engaged in illegal activities primarily with Latinas/os, when her lover went to jail, an older African-American man became Dulce's road dog. It was he who took care of her injuries after the beating.

One person, Benny, he helped me out. He was my road dog. He was a Black guy, an older man. He used to work for the city of Palo Alto. He became a heroin addict. And he and I were always cool together. He would . . . say, "I'll take care of you" . . . and he did. He'd fixed me up some medications . . . He helped me out with a lot of cuts and sores and . . . bruises. And he fixed me doing heroin . . . I didn't have to do nothing for him . . . After I got well, . . . just to pay him back, I went out and got me a few customers.

As shown above, pintas' addiction and illegal activities were intertwined with periods of legal employment, incarcerations, attempts to get clean and sober, childbearing and child raising, and relationships with partners, other family members, and barrio connections. Ultimately, their lifestyles contributed to their involvement with the criminal justice system.

7

Adult Arrests

All the reasons that I've gone to Sybil Brand have been drug-related charges . . . I had "possessions." I had . . . a couple of burglaries. I had "receiving stolen property," "forgeries," some "under the influence." . . . I mean, I was just a dope fiend.
—Deborah

Chicanas understood that their addiction to legal drugs such as alcohol and nicotine could be lethal to their health. They were also aware that their abuse of alcohol often led them into conflict with others around them, including law enforcement officers. Nevertheless, it was their addiction to illegal drugs, primarily heroin, cocaine, and pills, that was penalized severely even when they were merely "under the influence of" or in "possession of" these substances for personal use and were not breaking the law in other ways.

Pintas interviewed had been arrested for at least 26 different offenses as adults, not including arrests for violation of probation and parole (Appendix B). They were arrested most often for low-level nonviolent economic and drug-related crimes. Most economic crimes were also drug-related in that Chicanas were breaking the law to support their drug habits. Drug crimes included being under the influence and possession of a controlled substance, the two most frequent causes of arrests for pintas interviewed. Other drug-related offenses were possession with intent to sell, sales, public intoxication, driving under the influence (DUI), transporting drugs, and possession of paraphernalia. Economic crimes for which Chicanas interviewed were arrested included larceny, burglary, robbery, forgery, grand theft, fraud, bribery, receiving stolen property, prostitution, and transporting people across the Mexican-U.S. border.

These distinctions resemble those made by pintas interviewed and differ from those of the Bureau of Justice Statistics (BJS), which divides offenses into five major categories: violent offenses, property offenses, drug offenses, public-order offenses, and other offenses (BJS 2000). Thus, while the BJS classifies driving while intoxicated as a public-order offense, I consider it a drug-related offense because alcohol is a drug. And while the BJS classifies larceny-theft and burglary as property offenses, robbery as a violent offense, and prostitution as a public-order offense, I consider them economic crimes because the motivations behind them are clearly economic in nature.

In only a few cases were pintas interviewed arrested for violent crimes (i.e., assaulting a police officer, DUI with bodily injury, and murder). All assaults on officers as well as resisting arrest were committed while Chicanas were under the influence and were either trying to defend themselves or loved ones from police assault and brutality. The three murder charges, all dropped, concerned cases in which pintas were being pressured to testify against someone else. The cases involving child endangerment and contributing to the delinquency of a minor concerned pintas whose children were present when their homes were raided.

Probation or parole violations were frequent and included being under the influence, turning in a "dirty" (positive) urine analysis (UA), not reporting to parole officers (POs), moving without notifying POs, failing to report to mandated programs, associating with known felons, and getting arrested for new crimes. Such violations were considered grounds to return Chicanas to jail or prison.

It is important to note that some pintas were arrested repeatedly for the same offense although it is listed here as occurring only once per person. Thus, for example, while 15 of the pintas had been arrested for being under the influence, some were arrested for that offense alone more than 15 times.

While some offenses were classified as misdemeanors punishable with up to one year in jail, others were classified as felonies and were punishable with up to life in state prison. In California, drug offenses are divided into four felony and two misdemeanor categories. Felony categories include: "narcotics (heroin, cocaine, etc.), dangerous drugs (barbiturates, phencyclidine, methamphetamine, etc.), marijuana, and all other offenses (manufacturing of a controlled substance, forging/altering of a narcotic prescription, etc.)" (CDOJ 2000: 6). Misdemeanors are divided into two categories: "marijuana and other drugs (possession of paraphernalia, etc.)" (ibid.).

All pintas interviewed served time in county jails (Appendix A). Twenty of the 24 had also served time in state prisons. A few served time in state prison camps and federal institutions. This chapter reveals some of the immediate circumstances surrounding their adult arrests.

First Adult Arrests and Dispositions

Two of every three pintas interviewed were first arrested as adults between the ages of 18 and 21, and another six were arrested between the ages of 22 and 25 (see Appendix A). At least 15 pintas were first arrested as adults for drug-related offenses and another six for drug-related economic crimes (Appendices A, B).

Rosa: The first time I got arrested I got arrested for a DUI, and I was . . . 21 . . . I was drunk and I ran into a fence . . . I was trying to run away and they kept me there until the police came. And then the police took me down to the . . . station and I stayed overnight. And I had to go to court in Beverly Hills . . . I had community service and [a] fine.

Luisa: I went to Sybil Brand [at 18] because I was . . . under the influence of . . . alcohol. And it's like everything I always did, it was always under the influence of alcohol . . . A highway patrol had to bump my car in front of another highway patrol car because I was so loaded . . . And I was going in the opposite direction . . . I was in a stolen car . . . My theme was stealing cars . . . The cop came and took the key from the ignition and I got arrested.

Matilde: The first time . . . I got arrested . . . I think it was in 1983 . . . I was with some friends and we were smoking some PCP . . . at . . . Wilhall Park . . . They took us all out of the car, and then they started searching the car. That's when they found that PCP. It was in my purse . . . The LAPD . . . got me for sales . . . because I had . . . a bottle . . . but it was mine, it was for me.

Melinda: My first arrest I was 19 years old . . . I had "possession with the intent to sell" . . . I had a shirt on and . . . my mother had put some drugs in the pouch because she was wearing the shirt before I was. I didn't even know it was in there. They brought out this white powder at the time. Later . . . I found out it was cocaine.

Gina: They finally found out I was a user and I used to deal . . . They . . . got me for . . . under the influence. They gave me a year . . . At that time you just served half . . . I was off for one month and went back with another year. Same thing . . . 15, 20 times.

Yolanda: I didn't get arrested until I was 18 years old, for selling drugs . . . I was in my house . . . This white man came and got some drugs from me . . . I sold to an informant . . . an ounce . . . And like a few hours later they came back and raided my house.

Mercedes: I started using heroin and I started drinking and I started using . . . a lot of Quaaludes . . . I met this girl that lived around the corner from my house, and she used to do heroin . . . And this woman would tell me, "You know what, let's go burglarize this house. It's all set up. This guy knows that we're going to burglarize it 'cause it's for insurance purposes." . . . I was . . . like, "You're nuts! I would never do something like that, ever." And . . . as I continued to hear this scenario of . . . what we can get and why we should do this I [said] *¡Pues vamos! Fuimos*[1] . . . in my Volkswagen. We were getting stupid stuff out of that house. And I was . . . getting the blender . . . and . . . the police got there . . . So I now had a burglary . . . charge . . . And I went to jail. I got bailed out. That was my first offense.

Dulce: The very first time I went to jail I was 31 years old . . . Someone on a . . . residential street had called the cops. They said we looked suspicious because we were taking the license plates off my truck, which was true . . . It was me, my partner, we were in the front seat and . . . the other two people were in the back of the camper. And [I] didn't know there was anything back there . . . And so when I was asked whose vehicle it was I said, "It's mine." They said, "Can we search it?" "Sure." I had nothing to hide. And, sure enough, they found all this stolen property . . . I cried and cried and cried because my partner told me, "No matter what you do or say, you do not snitch." . . . So . . . I went and I took the rap for other people that wasn't even mine . . . But because it was my vehicle and these people were with me, they said it was mine . . . And I ended up doing three months . . . in Santa Clara County.

Estela's first arrest at the age of 24 was among the most serious discussed.

March of 1983, I got arrested for a "DUI, with bodily injury" . . . I totaled seven cars and injured three people . . . They arrested me right here at the scene of the crime . . . I had split open my whole chin, all my fingers, my head, my back . . . And . . . the cop, he . . . was real nice to me . . . He was a Chicano dude . . . He took me to Harbor General.

The Arrest Cycle

Once drug-addicted Chicanas were arrested for the first time, law enforcement officers continued to monitor their actions. Such surveillance, and the fact that being under the influence and possession of a controlled substance were crimes, made Chicana addicts in California more vulnerable to arrest than nonaddicts.

Chicanas who had been arrested as youths were frequently arrested in the same barrios as adults.

Linda: At the age of 18 . . . when I started getting involved with the dealers . . . I got picked up right there at Brooklyn Avenue, César Chávez now, . . . right here at Hollenbeck Police Station . . . By this time they were not black-and-whites like when I was a teenager. Now I'm into the narcotics officers, the detectives. "Narcos," as they used to call them.

Linda was often arrested along with sexual partners who were also her drug connections.

So then I started getting arrested with these men . . . I'd wind up in Hollenbeck Police Station. I hit just about every police station there is in L.A. County, all the way to the border. (laughs)

Joint possession was a frequent charge used when Chicanas were arrested along with others.

Gina: When they got more than one person they bounced up with "joint possession" until somebody took the rap. When somebody takes the rap, then they cut the rest loose.

In 1979 Luisa was arrested with her Chicano boyfriend for robbing undocumented Mexicans.

I got arrested in '79. I have 14 counts of robberies, and they only charged me with seven. The man that I was involved with had already been in and out of prison. He had a gun. They charged me and him with the gun . . . I was robbing mejicanos, from . . . Tijuana.

Victoria was arrested six times between 1987 and 1992.

The first time was "under the influence of PCP." The second time was . . . "DUI, driving under the influence of a controlled substance." The third time was "suspicion of burglary." The fourth time was "under the influence of PCP." The fifth time was another DUI. . . . And . . . this last time was GTA, . . . grand theft auto. We were in a stolen car.

Released from jail after her first sentence, Yolanda was soon rearrested on "possession for sale" charges.

They arrested me, and I got caught with drugs again. But this time I got caught for sales and transportation . . . I was taking the drugs somewhere and . . . I got pulled over . . . on 39th and National . . . because I had a busted tail light . . . They search my . . . car, asked me for a license. I didn't have one. They asked for a registration. I didn't have one . . . And my truck was full of . . . heroin and cocaine, and a lot of money, about three grand . . . And I . . . just had everything out there and not hiding it . . . They took me to jail . . . and I was . . . thinking, "I'm going to prison." At that time I . . . didn't care that I was going, it's that I . . . got caught again for being sloppy.

Sonia and a friend were once arrested on multiple felonies.

At that time I had . . . five felonies . . . I had a robbery, burglary, grand theft, receiving, and assault . . . [I] had been going into the stores boosting . . . Well, [one] lady manager and the box boys surrounded the car. I mean, they wouldn't let us go . . . unless we gave her the merchandise. So I gave her the merchandise and she still called the cops. So we drove the car and we tried to run her over . . . She ended up trying to sit on the side of the . . . driver . . . She was trying to hold the steering wheel and step on the brakes so we couldn't go nowhere. And she bit my girlfriend on the arm . . . I turned around and . . . put my arm . . . behind my . . . friend's neck to grab hold of the lady manager. Grabbed her from her hair and pulled her back and kept on looking at her so she could leave the steering wheel. Well, our car hit a partition and the car died out and all the cops came and they arrested us. So at the time they were giving us just "under the influence" and a "petty theft." But then they opened . . . the car and they found all the merchandise I had . . . I had $400 of meat from markets . . . about $500 of liquor . . . and I had like about five women's suits and they were like $200 suits. So that's why they got the grand theft and the . . . robbery . . . The assault was on the manager.

From time to time, Chicanas like Gina were snitched on by other addicts. Snitching was a common hazard Chicana addicts had to contend with (Moore and Mata 1981).

Gina: We used to give this dude a credit while he went and boost . . . okay, for a whole year. And then he got popped and he gave us up . . . He called the . . . house . . . I didn't know he was at the fucking police station. So he calls . . . "Bring me two spoons over here to the park." . . . I sent my old man to take them . . . and they followed him. And they seen where we lived and went and got a search warrant and came to the house and knocked the door down, man. It was scary, shit! 'Cause you already know what's happening when they knock, the doors come down . . . There was a bunch of them, man . . . That time, it must have been about eight. They looked white. They all had long hair and all that like hippie-like looking . . . You know what? I thought they were the fucking hippies that lived upstairs from us that were robbing us, man. And it was the fucking police!

On one occasion Gina was arrested after she was set up by other Chicanas to take the fall.

See, it was not even my house. It wasn't my gun. And it wasn't my stuff. But like I went there to go get down, and I used to stay there sometimes because them people baptized my baby . . . And . . . informers, they snitched on them . . . They was a bunch of Chicanas . . . These people would score from him, and when they'd go score from him, they would see me there. And they knew me from the joint. And . . . they told 'em that I'm the one that taught them how to cut it, I'm the one that was testing the stuff. So when they walked in . . . the . . . kid that's cutting the stuff and I was fixing. So what does that look like? I'm testing it, you know. So they gave me . . . five to 15, but I did five . . . When I went back to the joint they told me, "They railroaded you, Gina. They railroaded you good." Yeah, because of my past record. And they didn't have a record and they weren't users, see . . . So they had to put it on somebody. The . . . guy got two years . . . The lady got nine months probation. The son got probation . . . I got the five. And . . . that wasn't even my house.

Gina was also arrested after her daughter, an addict, snitched on her in order to get a more lenient sentence herself. The feelings of resentment and hatred that already existed between the two women deepened as a result of that incident.

And one time my daughter gave me up. She snitched on me . . . 'cause she got busted on something, so I guess she didn't have nobody to give up but she gave me up . . . And the narcs came to the house and they searched my house . . . And I found out it was her. I hated her . . . I wanted to pay somebody to kill her . . . I knew if I gave them stuff they would do it. I couldn't find her.

Arrests for prostitution were among the most insidious.

Diana: Any of those . . . under the influences or . . . the prostitution, usually I would just get jacked up in the street . . . If I was walking down the street usually they would stop me, you know, if they suspected that I was out there working . . . [Or] if . . . they pulled over right after they picked me up . . . then I know I'm being arrested for soliciting.

On one occasion Diana was arrested but was subsequently released by the officer after they had sex.

I had an incident where . . . I did end up going with the [white] cop and he had already . . . placed me under arrest. He didn't put any handcuffs on me but he kept driving . . . I asked him to give me a break and I told him I was on my way to prison if he arrested me. And he pulled over and we talked . . . And in this area there's a lot of motels and . . . he drove to a motel and he got a room and we talked . . . And he ended up not arresting me and I ended up turning a trick. And he took me back and he told me to stay off the streets . . . He told me I didn't belong out there.

While as a result of her long arrest history Diana could not remember during the interview if she had been a sex worker for eight or 10 years, she vividly remembered the first time she was arrested for sex work.

The first time I got arrested for prostitution . . . I remember it was like the second day, maybe the third day that I'd ever been out there. And . . . I was strung out. And my connection's sister used to work and . . . she turned me out to the street. And . . . this might have been the first time that I'd gone out by myself, because the first couple of times I went out with her. And I . . . was just walking and this . . . white . . . man pulled over and he asked me if I was . . . working . . . and I told him, "Yeah." And I got in the car with him and . . . I started showing him where to go. And . . . then the next thing I knew . . . he stopped the car and he told me I was under arrest, then he pulled out his badge . . . And there was a . . . black-and-white, and they got out and they put the handcuffs and they took me to jail.

Diana discussed the difference in how she felt the first time she was arrested for sex work as opposed to other offenses.

I was trying to get high. I was trying to get well. I was strung out . . . It was probably about nine o'clock in the morning and I got arrested . . . All of my arrests before that were . . . drug-related, you know, under the influence or drunk driving . . . So I didn't feel so bad about those . . . I was always loaded . . . I think that . . . was the first time that I had realized that I had compromised any part of my value system . . . I'd been in jail before. It was the way I felt about . . . being out there selling myself . . . I felt shameful and I felt dirty, dirty . . . And then [to] have . . . to call my lover and tell her, "You know what? You need to come and get me." And then I'll have to lie to her . . . She didn't know that I was using. I mean . . . I had two separate lives.

Julia served seven years of a 12-year sentence at a federal prison for transporting drugs across state borders. Once released, she was soon arrested in California.

What happened was that . . . I left . . . some dope with my sister . . . And somebody came over . . . with a lot of people and . . . ended up taking the drugs . . . And . . . I get . . . home and she told me about it. I went over the girl's house, and there was like six and I had done time with all of them. And I . . . said, "I want my drugs back!" . . . and . . . they all laughed. So I went into my Montecarlo . . . I'd put a gun in there. And I came up and I started shooting all the windows . . . all their garage. I shot all their sliding doors . . . And I shot all in the house. And everybody . . . jumped under the bed and I took off . . . And by the time I got home the whole house was surrounded . . . And they had like six agents there, 12 undercovers on a van, and I didn't know . . . And I already had . . . stopped at the . . . corner and . . . something told me, "Hide the gun." And I put the gun down the sewer pipe . . . and I went home . . . So . . . I opened the door and there was my sister, my dad, and my brothers were all cuffed, sitting on the . . . couch 'cause they're all parolees themselves . . . They were searching the whole house . . . I walk in and immediately this police officer gets me and puts my hands in the back. And . . . I pushed her and she fell on the couch . . . And then they stuck me in . . . my room and they made me take off all my clothes . . . Just regular procedure. You know, they . . . make you bend down, squat, cough, like that . . . And she's telling my parole agent, "She ain't loaded." . . . She was giving me . . . the eye test and everything else with the lighter . . . to see if I had narcotics on me . . . And I didn't have any narcotics on me that day. And they . . . tore my whole room up. They found . . . a syringe . . . about three of them . . . So that's the only thing they can get me with . . . But they had an eye witness across the street, pedestrian that said that "they seen you with a gun and shooting." So they tried me for that and I got a whole year . . . They got my dad for "under the influence." . . . They took my dad and gave him a 30-day dry-out.

Julia's arrest along with that of her father shows how generations of Chicana/o families were swept up by the war on drugs.

Like some of the other pintas interviewed, Julia was able to stay clean and sober for periods of time. During these times, she was able to avoid run-ins with the law. However, once she started using drugs again, she was arrested.

And then there was a gap there. The gap was that I got clean and sober. I got tired of the system. I got serious in my recovery, and I led a clean and sober life from 1990 to '93 . . . [Then] I relapsed. And when I had relapsed I . . . was at a girlfriend's house and she . . . OD'd. And I was giving her CPR . . . And when I revived her I was trying to pull her outside, and it happened to be that two officers that knew me were . . . patrolling the area and they seen me. And immediately the woman officer came out and approached me and did not read me my rights and told me to stop. And I told her I wasn't gonna go down that easy this time . . . If she was gonna take me, she would have to take me down. And, of course, I was under the influence of sherm, PCP. And she ran after me and I . . . used self-defense on her. I used martial arts. That's what got me the "assaulting a police officer." I damaged her knee cap, damaged her wrist, and gave her a . . . broken nose.

Once arrested, Chicanas were booked. That is, they were photographed and fingerprinted, and a record was made of their names, addresses, and the charges against them. Following booking, pintas were strip-searched and put in cells pending their first court appearances on the charges. However, there were times when Chicanas were taken to booking after having been beaten severely by officers. The following chapter discusses specific cases of police harassment and brutality against Chicanas.

8

Police Harassment and Brutality

*There used to be some shopping stores on Brooklyn Avenue that I
used to come to . . . I'm coming from the store with a menudo and . . .
here comes a car. They jump out the car and I'm told to put my
menudo down. And, "Let me look at your arms." . . . They would
look more to see if you had any type of mark on the body . . . and
they wanted to see if I was high . . . Then they say, "Put your hands
to the back." They handcuff me, put me in the car, and take me
in . . . And my menudo still on the corner . . . Why? I had a menudo?
(laughs) . . . I was never caught with anything in my possession,
but I was always being stopped . . . I'd say . . . more than 30 times.
I mean, it's like every time I turned around they were there.*
—Linda

The overall experiences of Chicana/o communities in California, but
particularly of Chicanos, with law enforcement personnel have been
well-documented.[1] However, the distinctive experiences of Chicanas
have not been given much attention to date. This chapter, by including firsthand accounts of the impact of the war on drugs on Chicanas,
seeks to complement the existing literature, thus allowing us to understand more fully the experiences of barrio residents with law enforcement agencies.

The chapter focuses on police harassment and brutality against Chicanas by the predominantly white male local, county, state, and federal
law enforcement officers with whom they came in contact.[2] It shows
how the community-wide surveillance of Chicana/o barrios intensified
under the war on drugs and made it virtually impossible for Chicanas/
os to escape police harassment and brutality. This was so regardless of
Chicanas'/os' gender, age, sexual orientation, where they lived or so-
cialized, and whether or not they engaged in illegal activities.

Chicanas were frequently harassed by officers because they were profiled as criminals, notably if they lived in Chicana/o barrios or were found in neighborhoods where they did not "belong" (i.e., white, middle to upper class, suburban).

Sex workers and addicts were especially vulnerable to arrests and mistreatment because their activities were highly visible.[3] Chicana addicts, who were overwhelmingly users but not traffickers, were also targeted because officers assumed they were dealers and/or knew Latino drug kingpins. Such assumptions led officers to try to intimidate or bribe Chicanas into informing on drug connections, who often were the men in their lives.

As a result, pintas interviewed experienced routine surveillance, harassment, arrests, and excessive use of force in the streets, at police stations, and/or during raids of their homes. Almost half (10) were brutally beaten at least once, and sometimes by more than one officer. Such beatings always resulted in psychological damage and, for some, permanent physical damage. In one case, the beating and subsequent denial of medical care led to a miscarriage.

In spite of the documented continued excessive use of force and murder of unarmed Chicanas/os in California, particularly in Los Angeles, throughout the 1970s, 1980s, and 1990s, rarely have officers been prosecuted for their crimes (AI 1992; Chemerinsky 2000; Christopher Commission 1991; Kolts 1992).

Experiences with Police Officers and Deputy Sheriffs

Pintas interviewed were most likely to come in contact with officers from the LAPD and deputies from the LASD (AI 1992: 5). The LAPD "polices the city of Los Angeles," while the LASD "polices all the unincorporated areas of Los Angeles County as well as, by contract, 42 cities in the county" (AI 1992: 5).[4] The LASD also runs the county jail system. Those Chicanas/os who lived in or visited public housing projects also had frequent contact with Project Patrol (PP). They also came in contact with officers from the State Highway Patrol, FBI agents, and in one case, the military police. The vast majority of officers, sheriffs, and agents who composed these agencies were white males.

Linda: It seems like . . . through my whole arrest history . . . they were all white . . . Except when I was in Hollenbeck . . . I remember . . . Chicanos . . . and white. There wasn't too many Black officers in East L.A. years ago . . . That's what we used to say . . . that the white people [that] used to come into East L.A., they were narcos . . . And they'd be . . . ran out of East L.A. . . . 'cause . . . everybody was used to white people being cops.

The type of relationships Chicanas/os had with officers differed depending on the agency involved.

Luisa: You have LAPD and you have the sheriffs. And LAPD is in East Los Angeles . . . And they would treat us a lot nicer than the sheriffs would. The sheriffs were really, really pigs. They were very, very prejudiced.

Rarely did pintas interviewed remember officers (henceforth including sheriff's deputies) reading them their rights.

Linda: I don't think they ever read them to anybody in East L.A. at that time. I don't think anybody knew what their rights were . . . Back then . . . I don't think any of us knew we had any . . . I mean, not unless you . . . have those jailhouse lawyers that . . . start educating you and telling you that "yeah, you do have rights and they shouldn't have done this." But you couldn't do that because automatic . . . then they would turn on you . . . What they do is pick you up for nothing . . . and start beating you. Because you weren't supposed to ask questions . . . As a teenager they . . . thought it was cute, me . . . asking, "Why am I here?" They'd come up with a smart remark. As an adult . . . I guess it was something that was known in the streets that you just didn't ask why they picked you up . . . I think there was a lot of stuff they used to do with the Hispanics. And I think they used to treat the women just like they treated the men.

Diana: They put the handcuffs on you and throw you in the black-and-white and take you to the station . . . I don't think I've ever been read my rights.

Most physical assaults of Chicanas/os by officers took place within the victims' barrios.

Luisa: We used to have a lot of parties and there was always somebody . . . getting their ass kicked in the neighborhood . . . They were white . . . sheriffs. They were mean.

Luisa: The cops would come in . . . when someone was fighting . . . They would come and they would . . . either bust us or kick our ass a little. I never really got hit by the cops. Got kind of shoved around a little but never beat . . . But I would see the way they would beat my homeboys.

Linda: I seen them beat the hell out of them kids, literally . . . They got 'em stomach down, laying on the floor with handcuffs, hands in the back, and they're beating them with . . . the sticks they carry. Yeah, or they're kicking them. I have seen that done to young women. I have seen it done to young men.

Once officers started beating Chicanas/os, there was always the danger that they would murder somebody.

Luisa: And they killed a homeboy in front of us . . . You know how they ask you to stand with your hands on the wall, turned around? Well, he did that. And I don't know what they thought but they just shot him . . . two or three times . . . And his guts were hanging and everything . . . That was devastating.

The physical abuse took other forms as well.

Linda: The twisting of the arms when your arms go back for you to be handcuffed, the tightness of the handcuffs, pushing into the cars, the grabbing of the hair . . . Handcuffed, thrown on the floor . . . Back was slammed against the wall . . . so they could handcuff you. Your . . . head . . . would hit the wall.

Arrests were also frequently accompanied by racial, ethnic, and sexist slurs.

Linda: And there's a lot of harassment . . . And it was there with the women also. I mean, to hear a cop call you a bitch or a whore it was no big deal. It's like you just got used to it. I mean, that's what . . . you grew up with . . . In Norwalk . . . whenever you got arrested . . . you could hear words like "fucking Mexicans," "dirty Mexicans" . . . "fucking whore" . . . "bitch," "slut." . . . That was routine . . . I mean, we're talking about angry men.

Chicanas who were more difficult for officers to handle were more severely abused.

Luisa: One time . . . in Long Beach . . . I was going on a drunk, on a . . . DUI. He got me from my neck so hard . . . that he left his fingerprints in my neck . . . I had purple prints like that of his . . . hand where he . . . caught me and was choking me. Because I was drunk, I guess, and he couldn't control me. So he . . . goes, "You fucking bitch! If you don't shut up I'm going to stick this . . . billy club up . . . your ass or up your throat." And he had me by my neck when he was telling me that, and I spit in his face . . . I was a nut, huh? . . . He just got very upset, red . . . He didn't do nothing . . . The door . . . to the elevator . . . had opened.

In August 1994, eight months before my interview with Julia, she had been severely beaten by several, mostly Latino, San Jose officers for resisting arrest and assaulting a police officer while under the influence of PCP. At the time of the interview Julia was still emotionally and physically traumatized by the experience.

I have an . . . incident when I got arrested this last time . . . by San Jose PD . . . They physically harmed me . . . for resisting arrest . . . They broke my front teeth, and there's a fractured disk . . . And they broke my nose. And they hit me with billy clubs. They kicked me and banged my head against the concrete and jabbed by face into the dirt . . . It looked like I had a pinball on my eye, like right here on my cheek. And it was cracked in the middle. And it . . . was like black and blue really bad . . . And . . . I couldn't see. My both eyes were black and blue. I had bruises all over my legs, you know, all over my . . . arms, my face. And they broke out my teeth really bad. They didn't give me no . . . kind of dental assistance on 'em, you know, and they just left 'em like that . . . 'Cause I hurt that . . . lady cop, their buddy. I injured her really bad so I guess they took it out on me . . . Six, all male, one female . . . They were all Hispanics, one white.

The several stories below demonstrate diverse ways Chicanas responded to police officers they felt were targeting them for arrest and incarceration.

Cristina's Story: "Arrest me or let me go!"

Cristina's arrest history began with her first GTA charge at the age of 23. Unlike the other pintas interviewed, Cristina is not an addict. However, because of her associates and the barrio she lived in, the officers kept a close watch on her. Thus, Cristina was bound to be arrested sooner or later. The arrests, however, were sometimes carried out on trumped-up charges.

At the age of 23, Cristina, along with a homegirl and eight of their homeboys, was arrested by the LAPD for murder. They were arrested during a weapons raid in a housing complex where one of her friends lived. During the raid officers confiscated weapons and shot one of Cristina's friends. The initial charge of murder was designed to intimidate the group into providing information about the gun running. Officers also tried to intimidate Cristina and her friends by holding them at the police station longer than necessary and asking them about their suspected gang affiliations.

We . . . got busted about three o'clock. So by eight we should have had a detective there and there wasn't one . . . They say, "Oh, we're sending 'em from L.A." I go, "Well, . . . you got your own right here." ". . . Well, we got to talk to a special one." . . . Came down asking us questions. "Where you from?" See I have a "W" [tattoo] here, so they always say, "Wilmas." But . . . it was . . . for . . . a nickname for another guy. So I always get hassled for it. I said, "No. I'm not a gang member" . . . I've never admitted that I was, never, on none of my records 'cause you get more time in jail if . . . you're a gang member, an extra year . . . The people out here know, yeah; but as far as the police . . . they didn't know. You know, I'm not one with all these tattoos. I've got only so many, you know.

Ultimately, Cristina and her friends were released because of the lack of evidence against them.

We got released about 11:30 . . . They didn't have nothing on us. There was nobody murdered. They just seen all the guns. They figured they catch one that was dirty and all the guns were clean.

Harbor Division Police Department was responsible for patrolling Wilmington, among other cities. Cristina described ways in which Harbor officers, encouraged by the war on drugs, profiled and targeted all barrio residents as gang members and drug dealers.

Curfew sometimes . . . "gang gathering" . . . Or they'll say, "Oh, we know there's narcotics being sold here. You're a known dope dealer so I'm gonna stop you." "You're wearing baggy clothes." . . . So it's automatically, "You're a gang member." . . . Anything can single you out.

Sometimes they'll play stupid on you. Okay, a lot of 'em do carry dope. I'm not saying they're innocent . . . They'll [cops] see you on the corner. They'll go straight, come around the corner and see who runs . . . But if you still stay there they'll flashlight . . . If they know you by name, "Hey . . . Grumpy, what are you doing here on the corner?" . . . "Oh, I'm talking to my lady on the phone." "Well, why don't you hang up and go now."

They run their names . . . More than likely they'll pull their guns to see if they have any weapons. Search 'em down. Pat 'em down. If they're in a vehicle, they'll search the whole vehicle, give 'em a reason to impound it. "Who's driving it? Driving without a license, I'm taking it from you now." . . . And if you got warrants they take you to the station. You go to court the next day and then they ship you to the county . . . Or if they think you're somebody else, they'll take you in.

Asked how often such random shakedowns occurred, Cristina replied, "Every day they drive the boulevard, every day."

While community members were not, in principle, opposed to curfew sweeps or the monitoring of gang activity and drug dealing in their barrios, they did object to the arbitrary and frequently abusive manner in which officers treated barrio residents. Officers also showed up in barrios asking questions about people they were looking for and arrested residents when they refused to answer their questions.

Cristina: Like . . . say everybody in this complex building . . . was to kick it on the balcony and a cop was to go by, . . . they're gonna stop, ask questions, "What are you doing? Who lives there?" . . . But if you don't answer, "Well, we'll take you to the station then you'll have to answer us." . . . Or I've even had them come up with pictures asking me who people were.

According to Cristina, while officers were more likely to stop Chicanos on the streets, women who were stopped along with men were treated similarly.

They don't stop girls as much as they do the . . . guys. [But] if the girls are there with the guys they just stuck like a duck. Like they . . . can't go nowhere. It could be like say five females and one guy. They will stop all the females to talk to that one guy, see? . . . They're treated basically the same, handcuffed along and gone just like they are . . . If they got anything on 'em, it could be like say . . . you got a knife in your purse or it could be a roach clip, which is usually a ticket. If they want to be an asshole they'll take you to the station. If you're a minor they gonna take you and just call your parents anyway.

Chicanas were also patted down on the street by male officers, although they were not supposed to pat down women.

Cristina: And like one time, they tried to search me and I told 'em, "Don't you touch me!" 'Cause . . . a male cop . . . cannot search a female . . . They had searched me on the street before.

While the stated objective of such searches was to see if suspects were hiding drugs or weapons on them, those of women by male officers were also frequently part of a pattern of sexual harassment and intimidation to which women suspects were routinely subjected. This was especially true in cases where male officers had the option of taking those arrested to SBI or to a substation where women officers could conduct the searches.[5] Still, regardless of who conducted the searches and where, they were always invasive and humiliating.

Cristina: Okay, she'll come behind you . . . They'll go underneath your bra, shake it out . . . They'll tell you, "Pull your bra and just shake it." . . . They'll go between your legs, all the way.

Cristina sought to protect herself from being pat-searched in different ways.

'Cause see I . . . wear clothes . . . not tight but enough where you can see I don't got no weapons. I don't even carry a purse. I don't carry my ID . . . I don't like things hanging from me or nothing, give them the reasons to say, "Oh, you got this. Oh, you got that." . . . They could be a little asshole, "Why you don't carry your ID? We're taking you in."

Once at the police station, women could be strip- and cavity-searched, even when menstruating, to make sure they were not hiding drugs inside their bodies.

Cristina: If you have a Kotex on . . . if they want, they'll take you to the station and strip-search you there . . . and make sure you have nothing, like dope.

Street harassment by officers was relentless, and it affected not only those directly targeted but their families as well.

Cristina: I was waiting at the phone booth 'cause I called my dad to come get me, 'cause as soon as they see me they pulled up on me . . . They said, "Hang up the phone." I said, "No, I'm talking to my dad." . . . They said, "Hang it up!" I said, "Dad, come get me." Which was only three, four blocks around the corner . . . And they go, "Well, we're gonna take you to jail." I said, "For what?" They said, "For loitering." I go, ". . . I just went into the store and bought me a juice. You can't say I'm loitering." . . . They go, "Well, we'll get you for trespassing." "It's a liquor store! How can you get me for trespassing? They didn't complain." . . . So we're . . . there arguing when mom pulls up and they ask my mom, "Well, who's this?" "Oh, that's my daughter." "What's her name?" You know, told them my name. And they go, "How old is she?" Told 'em my age. "Oh, well, we're gonna take her to jail. She don't have her ID with her." "Well, I gave birth to her, I know." My dad's over there talking, "Shut up . . . old man, because we'll take you in too!" I said, "You ain't taking my dad in." And he goes, "Oh, do you want me to tell your mom what you do? . . . Did you tell your mom you got arrested last week? . . . Yeah, we busted her in a dope house," . . . which they never did . . . I said, "Yeah, did you tell my mom I went to jail for . . . murder and there was no body?" . . . He shut it up. "Oh, I'm only letting you go because your mom was here." He made my dad park the car and get the hell out of there. And he told her, "You know what, Miss? . . . We're gonna release her to you, but if we see her again we gonna . . . take her in if she don't have her ID."

Chicanas who, like Cristina, lived in projects were also routinely harassed at home. The excuses given for such visits varied. On one occasion, officers showed up at Cristina's home on the complaint of her jealous ex-husband.

He was so high he went and told the police . . . that my [new] boyfriend shot someone. So they came to my house . . . and I . . . [had] swept everything . . . in one pile and left it there. Okay, so I'm sitting outside . . . eating my sunflower seeds and my Cherry Seven-Up soda. One of the homeboys came . . . The cops roll up and they put the lights on. They just, "Santos!" "What?" "Well, we got a complaint." . . . "Oh, yeah, well, why don't you come on in . . ." "Who's this?" "Oh, a friend." . . . They start harassing him but they let him go. They came in my house and they started turning on all the lights in the house and I go, "Well, when you go upstairs to one bedroom . . . watch the light because my baby is sleeping." They said, ". . . Oh, we can get you for neglect." I go, "Neglect? How you figure neglect? My baby's asleep, well-fed, ain't nothing wrong with her." . . . "Oh, you got a dirty house." I said, "Here, take me to jail . . . for a dirty house."

Cristina allowed officers to come into her house repeatedly without a warrant for several reasons. She did not know her rights. She felt she had nothing to hide. She did not want officers to think she was intimidated by them. Such home visits continued until her father put a stop to them.

So the cops would always come to my house and wanna look in . . . But one time they came my dad was there, they're knocking at the door. ". . . Could we come in?" ". . . You got a search warrant?" "No, but we can get one." "Go get one 'cause you ain't coming to my daughter's house no more unless you have a search warrant." That stopped them from coming and bugging me.

Project Patrol was a distinct force within the California public housing system. Its officers worked closely with local police departments, exchanging information about and monitoring project residents.

Cristina: They . . . supervise the projects . . . I think they have the authority to detain until an officer comes. I'm not too sure how that works. But they're the ones that give out all the tickets and everything now . . . Then Project Patrol got the authority to stop anybody on the boulevard. There was real, real bad drug trafficking back then, real bad.

At one point, PP officers spread rumors that Cristina had cocaine stored in her refrigerator.

So Project Patrol . . . I can't even think of his name. He used to tell me, ". . . There's a rumor going on that you keep coke in your freezer." . . . I . . . brought him to my house, said, "Open my freezer. What do you see?" And he . . . looked and there was nothing but foods . . . And he used to tell them, "Lay off of her."

While at least one PP officer tried to protect Cristina from unfounded accusations, another went out of his way to make her life difficult.

Officer Scott . . . He used to sit there and literally put the flashlight in my house. "Santos, I know what you doing!" He used to irritate me . . . He used to always yell and stand in the corner making noise . . . He'd say, . . . "These are Scott's streets . . . These . . . projects are mine!" . . . One day I was going to Compton . . . I got my money and I ran out the house. Scott stopped me. He goes, "Come here, . . . you can't go nowhere." "Shit, you can't tell me I can't leave!" He put my hands on the car, started going through my stuff. My . . . brother comes out. "Hey, Scott, why don't you let her go, man?" . . . "No, I ain't gonna let her go. I'm gonna take her to the station. I told her she couldn't leave." "Hey, Scott, . . . I'll keep her in the house. You just cut her loose." . . . So he cut me loose to my brother . . . Shit, I was 23, 24 . . . That's when they were real bad on people even walking to the store. Hell, I'm not in lockdown.

Despite officers' suspicion that Cristina was involved in the sale of drugs, at the time of the interview she had never been arrested for any drug-related offense. In 1993, Cristina was charged with resisting arrest and obstructing justice when she sought to stop officers who were beating her boyfriend.

I was just standing on the street corner with my boyfriend, but he was under the influence and he was on parole . . . A patrol car . . . stopped . . . They were white . . . He goes, "Can we talk to you?" I go, "I guess . . ." And it was Highway Patrol . . . And that's when they noticed his eyes . . . "Oh, you're under the influence." . . . And they tried to arrest him . . . but he gonna be like a rabbit and try to run . . . Okay, they put me in the . . . cop car . . . Well, the cop that had me was a big old cop. Well, he had went to go help his partner beat up my so-called boyfriend . . . And the guy was already down. I could see two cops jumping him . . . So I undid the seatbelt, then I opened up the door, and I got out the cop car . . . and I started to take my handcuffs from the . . . back to the front. That's when he'd seen me. So he didn't want to throw me on the ground . . . Another white cop came. The white cop says, "This is all you gotta do," and he kicked my feet and I fell on the floor.

On one occasion, California Highway Patrol repeatedly harassed Cristina's parents at home while looking for her. They also refiled a pending misdemeanor charge as a felony in order to send her to jail.

And they kept going to my mom's, . . . bugging my mom. This is Highway Patrol at that . . . So I went to the station . . . They're asking me questions . . . They rebooked me . . . The cop lady said, "Why are they refiling on you as a . . . felony?" . . . I said, "I don't know." But what I found out was because the guy I was with . . . his rap sheet was bad . . . so behind him they put me felony . . . All I ever had on my record was a GTAs . . . and just because I was with an ex-convict they put felony charges on me . . . Well, they gave me six months . . . And then I was on summary probation for three years.

On another occasion, Lomita sheriffs arrested Cristina and denied her permission to call home to notify her family.

And another time they arrested me I didn't make a phone call for the whole three-day weekend I was gone . . . the Lomita sheriffs took me and . . . since they didn't have a female officer, instead of taking me to Sybil Brand they took me all the way to Lennox . . . And I go, "Well, can I use the phone to call?" "No." And you're supposed to have three phone calls . . . My mom didn't know where I was at. Then, finally, on the third day they let me call, right before I was coming back to go to court 'cause I . . . went on a Friday, they let me call on a Sunday night before I went Monday to court.

For Chicanas, even a trip to the beach could lead to police harassment. Cristina described an incident of racial prejudice that occurred in Redondo Beach, a white neighborhood patrolled by Torrance police and nicknamed "Little Mississippi" by people of color.

A cop came up to me and [I have] an ID that says Wilmington. "Oh, you're the ones from . . . Wilmington. We can't stand you guys 'cause you shot one of our officers and we're like family . . ." and started harassing us . . . And it was . . . a Blood gang that . . . shot the cops out here . . . So they started bugging me. I said, "You either arrest me or let me go . . . I'm just walking the beach like everybody else walking this beach." So they let us go.

Linda's Story: "Catch me when, if you can."

Linda's case illustrated how, during the 1950s and 1960s, officers were already targeting addicts for harassment. Linda was repeatedly stopped and pat-searched on the street by male officers in East L.A. from her first adult arrest at 18.

I don't remember ever seeing a woman police officer to search a woman . . . The only time I remember women police was in Sybil Brand.

On occasion, the harassment continued on the street after Linda was pat-searched.

Sometimes I had to sit on the sidewalk . . . One time they had me sitting down on the sidewalk for over 45 minutes on Wilshire Boulevard . . . handcuffed . . . in the back . . . And after 45 minutes, everybody going by looking at Linda, the cops in and out . . . "Sorry, but the one we're looking for has a snake tattoo on her arm and you don't. We made a mistake."

Linda was sometimes released after being pat-searched. At other times she was taken to the station to be questioned.

The LAPD and federal agents also targeted Linda because they wanted her to inform on the men in her life.

But . . . the whole harassment thing . . . that went on was because of my brothers and because of tough people I used to associate with . . . Wanting me to be an informant . . . They wanted you to give up a connection . . . They would take me in to see . . . if they could break me . . . Threatening me with the loss of my kids. Threatening me with the . . . jail time they were capable of giving me. Saying . . . , "We know about your family . . . and we know all about you." . . . And I looked at him and I said, "Well, that's fine." . . . And I'm scared . . . but I wouldn't show it . . . And they would get pissed . . . and cuss me out. Some of them would . . . kick me in the leg.

Asked how long she would be held in jail, Linda responded:

A few days, a week, depending on whatever they felt. Because there was nothing they charged me with other than hearsay . . . I was never caught with anything in my possession, but I was always being stopped.

Linda's home was also raided often during the day or night.

Did anybody have warning? Even the federal didn't do that . . . If I was asleep, you could hear them from away. You know, . . . if you're dreaming you can hear a voice calling you and you can hear pounding. But if you hear that kind of pounding you know it's the cops . . . Then you just hear something go slam and the doors went down . . . Then they start searching the house and then they handcuff you . . . Your hands to the back . . . Then they start running around, searching . . . There's never been . . . less than two . . . The state could have had as much as four—men, no women.

Rarely did officers show pintas either warrants or identification.

Linda: If I think back, I never seen a warrant. I never seen a . . . police badge. The only ones that I remember seeing their badges being flashed in front of me were from the federal, narcotics. But from the state, never, never a warrant. At least them damned feds told you, "Well we got an indictment." . . . But the other ones didn't show nothing.

In spite of the raids, officers never found drugs in Linda's home. And with time, Linda grew accustomed to the raids.

With the police, I mean, it's like, after so many times it's like, "Oh, fuck, here we go again!" It's like you get to know the routine, you know? The crashing down of the doors, the searches, the cursing. Hoping, "Maybe this time I'll get a nice one who's not gonna kick me."

The raids continued to be terrifying for Linda's children, who were always in the home and were not allowed to communicate with their mother once the ordeal began.

My kids always had a bedroom. They wouldn't budge. They would never come out of their room . . . They never screamed. They never cried . . . They didn't panic . . . But you could feel that they were scared . . . It's like, they would stay in the room and from there they'd disappear . . . I don't know if they went first or if I went first.

At times, officers tried to intimidate the children of pintas into providing information about their relatives.

Linda: I did see a police officer one time . . . threaten my daughter . . . It was in Norwalk . . . He was looking for one of my sons. And my daughter was only . . . nine years old . . . and my daughter said, "He's not home." . . . So he had his hand on her cheek and he was going . . . , "You wouldn't lie to me?" you know. I guess she got scared . . . She just stood still . . . And that's when I came out and I told him, "You keep your hands on her and I'm going to put a rape charge on you right now . . . I'll start screaming rape. She's a minor!"

While Linda's female relatives frequently got immediate temporary custody of the children, sometimes officers took the children to county facilities. They then used Linda's fear of losing custody of her children to try to intimidate her.

They would hide my kids in order to break me . . . I'm assuming that they put them in that McClaren Hall or one of them homes. And when I tried to . . . locate my kids, it's like I couldn't get an answer from anybody . . . And so I had to get an attorney, and the attorney . . . would have to throw a writ on them so my kids would pop up again. And that was their way of trying to break me.

The fact that Linda's Chicano partners were willing to take the rap when they were jointly arrested was one of the reasons Linda was able to come out of jail quickly and rejoin her children.

They used to come back to me, home. 'Cause I would always live with men who would always go to jail instead of me because he was the man. Except for the last one.

Eventually, Linda was sentenced to serve five years in a federal penitentiary after federal agents arranged for an informant to buy drugs from her. Although Linda was never caught with drugs in her possession, she was sentenced for possession, transportation, and sale. While on bail and even after her sentencing, federal officers continued to threaten her with a 30-year prison term.

Got threatened, reporting to the last day to that same . . . cops . . . I didn't get the time that they wanted to give . . . me . . . 30 years. The judge turned around and gave me five. And on my way out . . . when I was getting the elevator, their words to me were, "If it's the last thing we do, we're gonna get you." My words to them was, "Catch me when, if you can." What they did is they turned around and refiled on the same case and the judge threw it out because you can't . . . do that. So when I stood with the five years, they were there again . . . and one more time I was being threatened about how they were gonna get me.

Graciela's Story: Buy and Bust

In Graciela's case, a Chicana undercover officer set her up for a "buy and bust" drug operation and raid of her home.

I was living . . . in the projects . . . I was selling PCP at the time . . . The reason I was selling was to keep my heroin addiction up . . . A friend of mine . . . knocked at my door and told me that there was a girl that wanted to buy a . . . $10 sherm stick . . . It's PCP. It's . . . a liquid, you dip the cigarette in it. And they call 'em sherm cigarettes . . . So she came . . . She was a Chicana . . . So I dipped it for her . . . And then . . . I didn't really pay attention that she was just standing there listening to my conversation with the younger guy . . . And my brother happened to walk in at the house . . . It was my brother, my mother, and myself at home at the time . . . About 15 minutes after that, that's when the cops came in from the front and back door . . . There was about 10, 15 of them . . . a lot of white and Chicanos . . . They threw my brother to the ground and stepped on his neck and had a gun to his head . . . And they pushed my mother on the couch. And then they put me in the middle of the floor . . . 'cause I kept yelling to leave my brother alone. And that's when the girl came in with . . . this police jacket . . . I think she was the only female . . . And she . . . told me to "Shut the fuck up!" . . . They found two little vials of PCP, $50. It's called a "$50 pour." . . . And they went to my room and they found a shoe box, I had outfits and syringes . . . They found . . . a .38 handgun. And they found some powder cocaine . . . So they arrested . . . me . . . for "direct sales to a police officer." . . . And they arrested my brother and mother . . . too . . . My mother and brother were charged with "possession for sale."

Once at the police station officers tried to coerce Graciela into turning in a drug connection.

But when we got down to the Harbor Division they kept telling me that if I would give up a connection that they would cut my brother and cut my mother loose. But I kept telling them I didn't know nobody. So they . . . made my mom go to . . . SBI with me . . . And then they came back and said that my brother had a "parole hold." . . . And then . . . after the 72 hours were up they cut my brother loose on the charge and they cut my mom loose . . . because it . . . wasn't theirs and there was no way they could charge them for "possession of sales" and charge me for "direct sales" and I was admitting to it being mine . . . I told them she had no knowledge of . . . anything that was going on . . . But my brother got a violation. He ended up doing a year behind it . . . And then the . . . detectives . . . wanted me to give somebody up. 'Cause they told me, "I know you know a connection for heroin 'cause you're a heroin addict. I know you have a PCP connection 'cause you're selling it. And you have cocaine in your house so there's three connections. Give up one of 'em and I'll let you go." I told 'em I didn't know nobody. "Well, how do you buy your drugs?" "I . . . just go out in the street, if I see someone that looks like a drug addict to me then I go up to him and ask him to buy it for me." So he goes, "So you think I'm playing with you. I want you to know that I'm real and that I'll do this for you." . . . He was a Chicano . . . He goes, "I think we could have you work for us, pay you big money. We can send you on planes to go to different states, different countries, and set up people." . . . And I told him I didn't know nobody so he gave me his card. He said, "Here, think about it. I'll prove to you that . . . I'm real." So I went to SBI. When they cut my mom loose within 72 hours, that night they called me for release and I couldn't understand why I was being released. So this was his way of letting me know that he was . . . willing to work with me if I was willing to work with him. So I guess that I was supposed to contact him . . . I didn't, I just stood at home. And a week later they came and they knocked my doors down again. And they took me back to jail and said if I would of do what . . . he asked me to do then I wouldn't be going back. And they refiled on me.

One of the reasons Graciela refused to become an informant was because veteranas/os in her barrio had warned her of the repercussions for being a snitch.

When I . . . started using heroin I used to hang around with a lot of older . . . people because they were heroin addicts and that's who I hung around with . . . Most of 'em . . . Chicanos . . . So . . . I got taught from the old school, you know, and that was one thing you don't do. You don't snitch on nobody 'cause eventually it'll catch up with you and you get killed.

Lucy's Story: Entrapment and Humiliation

For Lucy, who was a heroin addict and a sex worker for several years, police harassment began on the street and continued inside the substation with further humiliation and physical abuse.

Everything they did was like entrapment . . . When I was prostituting, I would sit there and ask them, "Are you a police officer?" and "Could you please identify yourself?" . . . They'd say they weren't. And then . . . they would go ahead and told me what they wanted and quote a price. And as soon as I would say, "Okay," . . . before I'd know it they'd park a certain way and then their backup, you know, their partner, would be with them.

Undercover officers were generally paired off with a backup officer who would be called for the arrest. The race and the ethnicity of the officers varied depending where the arrest took place.

Lucy: In Riverside, . . . like one was a Black and white dude, and another one was a Mexican and a white guy. Over here they were basically . . . all white guys, in L.A. County.

Lucy remembered how in Riverside County, white male and female officers joined together to verbally ridicule Chicanas being booked for prostitution.

Oh, my God, how they'd treat me? Belittling. They would sit there and laugh and keep you handcuffed in front of them. And . . . make remarks and about how, I call it entrapment, went . . . And some would make fun of you . . . Like laughing and talking about you as if you . . . are not there, while they're booking you, while you're up sitting there . . . Like . . . how the arrest came down . . . Like, "Stupid bitch. She did this and that," you know . . . Humiliating stuff where you just keep your mouth shut and act like nothing is going on. Like, "This isn't me. This isn't what . . . I did."

Physical abuse would frequently accompany verbal humiliation.

Lucy: Some creeps, they would sit there and some would put the handcuffs tighter on you and leave it like that. You know, "That's what you get." . . . And you keep saying, "This is tight . . . It's cutting me." You know . . . And some would leave it on.

After being humiliated and abused by officers, sex workers were released if they had no outstanding warrants.

Police Substations

The physical conditions at the police substations were equally dehumanizing, exposing pintas to humiliation and sexual harassment.

Linda: Police substations don't have showers . . . Those places are filthy, smelly, urine smell . . . I am thinking back to Hollenbeck Station . . . Sometimes they don't even have toilet paper there . . . Substations . . . all male employees . . . No bathroom doors . . . Exposed to the world . . . It was like a . . . holding cell . . . I mean, the toilet bowl is right there . . . You know, anybody can be passing by. I felt sometimes they'd watch, yeah.

Marta's Story: "I'm losing my baby!"

For Marta, the harassment and brutality she experienced at the hands of the Torrance police took place in her own barrio of La Rana. During the late 1960s, when Marta was growing up, La Rana was a strongly united Chicana/o community assailed by poverty, drugs, racism, and police brutality. At times, barrio residents responded to officers' actions by rioting. Officers, in turn, heightened their harassment and abuse of La Rana residents.

I lived in that street [Delano Boulevard]. It's one barrio . . . It's just one long road and there's houses on . . . your left side and there's houses on your right side . . . And everybody's related to everybody, you know. And . . . back then, the . . . neighborhood, La Rana, had the baddest reputation . . . So we were constantly having cops there 'cause we even fought with the cops, you know, [them] trying to arrest somebody . . . So we would like riot with them to let them go.

All the pintas interviewed who were ever exposed to the Torrance police described them as exceedingly racist toward Chicanas/os. At the time of the interview, the Torrance police force was still overwhelmingly white and male.

Marta: I mean, you couldn't even walk down the street, they'd take a look at you and . . . they'd start, "RRRR!" and . . . come and make a U Turn. "All right, put your hands behinds behind you neck, your head." They'd start searching you . . . and, "Let me see your arms," you know.

The first time Marta got arrested was during the summer of 1968 at the age of 18.

I was hanging out with Dulcinea's daughters . . . I was in front of their house . . . And I told my friends, "I gotta go home." . . . And then . . . Teresa, she goes, "Well, come on, I'll walk you halfways . . . up the street." . . . So she walked me. And then that's when the cop came up and pulled up. "Heys, what you doing, young lady?" Then he turned around, looked at me he goes, "Oh, Marta! Come here," you know. And then . . . he lifted the flashlight in my eyes and he says, "Book her, 'under the influence.'"

Officers recognized Marta because of her brother's suspected involvement with drugs and because they made it their business to know who La Rana residents were.

When barrio residents refused to answer officers' questions, they were frequently verbally assaulted.

Marta: Like they would say, "Well, . . . who's selling the drugs over here?" "I don't know." . . . If you didn't wanna talk to 'em . . . , "You fucking liar!" you know. "Shit, you're mother's a liar!" I used to tell him . . . 'cause I have a smart mouth to the cops anyway.

Both Chicanas and Chicanos would be given harsh treatment.

Marta: Even put us on the street, faced down, spread eagles. They didn't care if you had a dress . . . They didn't care if you were pregnant . . . That's just the way they're gonna treat you.

In January 1969, officers "crashed" a party in La Rana looking for Marta's brother. When they began beating her brother, Marta assaulted one of the officers. The officers responded by beating her severely.

Torrance beat me up bad. That was in . . . January 1969 . . . I was 6½ [months] . . . pregnant . . . I lost my daughter . . . We were . . . having a party in the neighborhood and I don't know who called the cops, but anyway, the cops came and they seen us . . . And they seen my brother coming out and they go, "Oh, Juan, just the motherfucker we wanna see." . . . And I look at 'em, I says, "I know you didn't call my brother no name." And my brother goes, "Oh, ¡trucha carna!" . . . And that's all he said and they started beating him up. Well, then . . . I jumped on one of the cops, started hitting him. And they turned around and I had two cops, one hitting me and the other one holding me down . . . because the other one was handcuffing . . . I kept telling 'em, "I'm pregnant!" "You lying bitch. You ain't pregnant." . . . And I go, "Fuck you! . . . If I lose my baby you're in trouble." . . . "Bitch, you wish you could be pregnant," they told me . . . They threw me on the floor and . . . hit me with the billy club . . . I had my jaw wired, my nose busted . . . I had bruises on my ribs. And . . . one rib . . . it healed wrong is what it did, you know, and sometimes I have a problem breathing behind it. But, yeah, they beat the shit out of me bad.

Once arrested and taken to the Torrance substation, Marta was denied bail and the right to arraignment for six days.

So, they took me and they put me in a . . . cell. And my mom went over there to bail me out and they told my mom I didn't have a bail yet 'cause I wasn't booked in. And I had called my mom and I told her, "Mom, I'm booked in, I am. Why did they say I don't have a bail? I'm only in here for 'under the influence.'" . . . So . . . my mom went to talk to . . . Jerry, the bail bondsman in San Pedro, . . . and he went up there . . . to the substation . . . to see what was happening . . . They told him, "Yeah, we have her but she's not booked . . . You gotta . . . wait until she goes to court." . . . I was in there six days, okay. And . . . in them six days that I was in there they didn't have a bail on me . . . And what they were trying to do is to get my bruises rid of, you know, but not knowing that my jaw was . . . supposed to be wired. It was cracked.

Despite her multiple injuries, being pregnant, and complaining of abdominal pain, Marta was denied medical care.

I yelled out, "Jailor!" "What?" "I need to talk to you please. I'm bleeding . . . I'm losing my baby." And he goes, "It's probably just your period, I'll give you some Kotex." . . . "Please, I need to see a doctor." He says, "Well, I have to talk to the . . . watch commander . . . to see if we can get you to the hospital, if they got any officers that can transport you over there. If not, you have to wait until the morning." You know. "Don't you understand?" I started crying, "I'm losing my baby!" You know. "Okay." . . . And then after I go, "Look, all I ask of you is please, I'm crying, I'm begging you, take me to the hospital. I'm losing my baby. If I lose

my baby you guys are in trouble." . . . "Are you threatening me?" he tells me . . .
"No, I'm not threatening you. I'm just telling you . . . anything happens to my baby,
you will find out that I wasn't just saying and I wasn't asking, I was begging."

Marta did lose her baby,

in the substation, . . . in my holding tank, on that bed . . . And when I got out they
took me to the hospital. They had to clean me out and then suck . . . whatever was
left, out . . . When they found out I . . . had a miscarriage, they were scared.

Marta was bailed out with the help of her white male public defender
(PD) and her white bail bondsman, Jerry, who had taken pictures of
her injuries. Although the officers were never reprimanded, the judge
dropped the charges against her.

And as soon as they bailed me out on the sixth day, okay, my mom rushed me to
the hospital . . . So I had papers . . . showing [me] leaving Torrance substation . . .
I had the papers of what was wrong with me . . . and the wires on my jaw . . .
And . . . another reason why the judge dismissed my case . . . was . . . because of
the fact they held me too long and . . . without even seeing a judge . . . They're
supposed to take you to court in 72 hours.

Marta described the pain she went through after the beating and
loss of her baby and shared why she did not sue the Torrance Police
Department.

And I went through some hell 'cause I never . . . knew what it felt like to lose a
baby. I don't believe in abortions, you know, and that hurted . . . And I have more
hate for cops behind my baby, you know. I didn't wanna bother with them. I never
wanted to see them . . . I knew I could have sued them, you know, but I didn't
even wanna do that . . . All I wanted was out of there . . . Because they had took
something that I wanted, you know . . . And yes, it made me hate cops more . . .
And to this day I hate 'em.

9

Courts and Consequences

Once arrested as adults for the first time, pintas repeatedly came in contact with prosecutors, defense attorneys, judges, and other court officers. These were overwhelmingly white and male (Appendix C). The lack of respect and discriminatory treatment such officers in California and elsewhere accord Latina/o and African-American defendants (and their attorneys) have been well documented.[1]

In addition to discriminatory treatment on the basis of their race/ethnicity, pintas, like other poor and working-class people, were at a disadvantage relative to middle- and upper-class defendants. Meeker, Dombrink, and Mallett (2000) note that members of poor and even moderate-income households, including single-parent and two-parent families in which both partners earned minimum wages or worked at low-paying jobs, found it difficult to hire competent attorneys to represent them. Those with little education, few or no English language skills, and scant knowledge of the workings of the criminal justice system were at an even greater disadvantage (CJC 1997).

In this chapter, pintas describe their experiences with defense attorneys, prosecutors, judges, and parole officers. They also speak about their experiences with bail, sentencing, probation, and parole. Most importantly, they reveal some of the ways in which they advocated on their own behalf.

Defense Attorneys

Once arrested, Chicanas had to be arraigned within 48–72 hours, depending on whether the arrest took place on a weekday or the weekend. Because of their limited financial resources, Chicanas, with few exceptions, depended on the services of usually white male public defenders. While on occasion judges ordered private attorneys to represent defendants, this was rarely the experience of pintas interviewed.

Estela: I had PDs all the time . . . Most of 'em white. Never had Chicanos . . . Mostly I had men, one woman.

Cristina: We usually get a lot of the white ones. We hardly get stuck with Mexicans.

The overall quality of the PDs was so poor that whenever I asked Chicanas if an attorney had represented them, the answer was invariably "No."

Cristina: No, I had a PD.

Luisa: No, never did. I had one of those dumb trucks. You know, . . . the county provides you . . . one of . . . their attorneys. And we used to call them "dumb trucks" . . . because . . . they weren't like the real lawyers.

Estela: I never had attorneys, couldn't afford 'em . . . I had PDs all the time.

While those interviewed knew that PDs were lawyers, they distinguished PDs from "real attorneys," that is, private attorneys, based on the quality of work done for clients.

Cristina: You have your regular PDs, and when they get full with their cases, they call the attorneys to handle [cases] . . . They're all attorneys but . . . the attorneys work harder than a PD would . . . PDs, they have so many cases it's like, you know, out the door. And the attorneys . . . work harder at finding loopholes 'cause they're trying to make a name for themselves.

Julia: I had two [private] attorneys on . . . the case . . . One was Latino and one was Italian . . . They were . . . really well-known in Santa Clara County . . . I did numerous interviews before trial with them . . . And it was like, they were on it . . . My mom and my dad . . . paid 'em really good money.

In contrast to private attorneys, PDs had large numbers of cases assigned to them and, thus, rarely had the time to prepare their cases, get to know the defendants personally, or meet with them prior to their arraignments. This particularly had repercussions when Latinas were Spanish-monolingual and had PDs who did not speak Spanish. PDs also overwhelmingly tended to recommended plea bargaining over trial (CJC 1997). As a result, most Chicanas felt that their PDs had not gone out of their way to get them the best deal possible, even on their first adult arrest (CJC 1997).

Chicanas generally accepted the terms of the plea bargaining, even when they thought they were severe, partly because they believed that if they chose to fight their cases in court, the judges would penalize them for taking the court's time. They feared they would get harsher sentences or lose time already served in jail while awaiting sentencing.

Chicanas recalled their experiences with PDs.

Lillian: One woman I remember, when I first started going in. And I remember two men, assholes. All white people . . . They don't even talk to you before the court . . . And then you go to court and you tell them if you're guilty or you're not guilty. And if you're not happy with whatever they wanna give you . . . your public defender will tell you, "They wanna give you six months and you can fight it but you're just gonna prolong your sentence term." Because you have to keep going back to court and plea bargaining with the judge. So nobody wants to do that . . . because sometimes the judge will say, "You don't get credit for time served." And if you get six months and you gotta start all over again, who wants to do that?

Paula: My first commitment . . . as an adult . . . was in . . . '80 . . . I got caught and sentenced . . . [for] "receiving stolen property," a radio . . . It was about $200 and something . . . It was a felony . . . I had a public defender. He was white . . . I'd seen him before court dates and on court dates . . . He told me . . . that . . . since I was a first-termer that we should try for CRC,[2] which is a . . . rehabilitation center . . . And he says, "They have a lot to offer you there." . . . And that was my first case as an adult and they gave me two years off the top . . . I always say that I got railroaded on that because I did not know nothing about the . . . law, you know, the rights that the criminals have.

Dulce: I had a public defender, . . . some lady, a *gringa* . . . I'd seen her one time at the jail. When she came she says, "I'm gonna be representing you . . . I want you to plead this way and plead that way." And I . . . said, "But I didn't do it." . . . She said, "It doesn't matter . . . It's going to be the officers' word against yours so just plead guilty to this and this and you'll get a lesser sentence." And I did . . . I'd seen her the second time at the courthouse in Sunnyville.

Yolanda: It went so fast . . . When I was in court I didn't know . . . what they said or how much time I got . . . All I knew was that I was going to prison for four years. Yeah, I had an attorney but he didn't explain nothing to me. They . . . appointed him to me . . . He was a white man. Public defender . . . Every time I went to court I'd seen him . . . He went to Las Colinas to see me and . . . told me that the probation department recommended state prison. So I'm sitting there and I'm like, "Okay, you know, I can handle this." . . . And I went . . . straight to prison after that . . . They sentenced me to . . . four years. I did . . . two and a half.

In Cristina's case, her PD told her to plead "no contest" but failed to inform her that it was basically equivalent to pleading guilty, something she would not have done had she been duly informed of its meaning.

As Chicanas became more knowledgeable about the workings of the system, some began to challenge their own PDs even during court proceedings.

Marta: The PDs . . . they're supposed to help you, but if you really . . . sit in court and see it for yourself, they fuck you, you know. I mean, to where they can help you get less time or maybe even get community service, you know, you end up with either two years in prison or 270 days in county . . . Because when . . . they arrest you for possession, okay, . . . like mine was .005, . . . which that ain't shit, and I was sent to prison for it . . . And I tell 'em, "First you . . . got me thinking I'm gonna get 90 days and . . . I'm gonna get probation and I'm gonna walk in court . . . with the 90 days I've been fighting this case. So when I get you to court . . . you tell them, 'Your Honor, she's been in custody 47 days . . . Probation was denied . . . If . . . you're gonna give Ms. Losada time . . . we can take 16 months.'" . . . "I ain't takin' no 16 months. In a prison? You're crazy! . . . I just got off doing time in prison . . . I've been in prison all my life . . . If any kind of time give me county time. Let me go on my kids . . . I've been away from my kids all their life, you know." ". . . Ms. Losada, slow down, you know." "What do you mean 'slow down'? It's not you that's doing the time . . . so you're not worried about it . . . You just wanna get me . . . out of the way . . . But if you do give me the 16 months I hope you . . . take care of my kids and make sure they get to school on time . . . You say you're here to help us. No, you fuck us!"

On another occasion Marta found herself coaching her inexperienced Chicano PD through the plea bargaining process.

At first I had to kick him in the leg to open his mouth because he was quiet the whole time. I was looking at . . . maximum 40 years. And they're going on and on . . . and I . . . looked at him, . . . "Talk to the judge . . . I ain't going up for no 40 years, not even 16 . . ." "Losada, slow down. I'll talk to the judge right now. Your Honor, I would like to talk to you in chambers." . . . I mean, *el pobrecito*, he . . . must have argued with that . . . judge for I don't know how long. And finally he comes back with a smile but he's red, right, . . . and he goes, "The lowest the judge will go is 13 years . . . If you fight it, you'll get the maximum 40 years." And I look at my brother and he tells me, "Take it." . . . I did . . . seven out of 13. I pleaded guilty to the charges on the condition that I would get good time/work time[3] . . . If I got in trouble I do the whole 13 years. Well, I'm not a troublemaker, you know.

Paula, who felt she had been railroaded on her first offense, later learned that she could fire a PD and request a new one. Subsequently, she was one of the few pintas interviewed who was able to get the assistance of qualified PDs.

I learned after my first case . . . that I could fire a public defender and ask for another one . . . I've been lucky enough in that department to have good public defenders where, you know, they schooled me very well . . . They even left it up to me . . . if I wanted to take that or . . . did we wanna take it all the way. And he would advise me if we should or shouldn't, but the final decision was still mine and he would support me either way . . . They schooled me on the years for each one. You know, how . . . just the slightest little thing which might not mean nothing to us, like . . . how many feet were you away . . . could change your whole sentence . . . and the crime that you actually did.

PDs assigned to Paula were also easily accessible. Asked how often she would see her attorneys, Paula replied:

Before court dates, you know, on my court dates. I could call 'em collect. They'd come if I needed to talk to 'em, you know, if I forgot something. Or if . . . I just needed to talk, you know, they would come and they would see me.

Asked if she felt that her PDs paid close attention to her case because she was involved in a highly publicized EME–related case, Paula was unsure of the answer.

During the 1990s, the financial burdens placed on poor defendants increased as California passed laws requiring them to pay some of their court fees. While some Chicanas learned to maneuver their way through the new laws, most did not.

Julia: They just recently started doing that in 1993, where . . . you also have to pay . . . your lab fees, attorney fees . . . If you have no kind of source of income and no skills to go by, it goes by a rating scale . . . You worked it out with the judge where you can make payments, but I didn't. I just told him, "I don't have no money. I don't have no kind of a skills when I get out. I'm . . . for sure gonna be working at Jack-in-the-Box or somewhere like that." I lied. So he dismissed my fine so where I didn't have to pay and he put in the paperwork.

As Chicanas acquired more knowledge of the law, through experience and information obtained from other prisoners, they were sometimes able to negotiate more favorable sentencing terms.

Sonia: You commit a crime and you go to court and you know . . . you're facing 13 years, but then they turn around and offer you four years, then you jump on it . . . I get busted for one burglary and they wanna give me four years and I jump it. And they say, ". . . You could of . . . got it dropped down to two." I go, "No, because I got 20 burglaries that I . . . didn't get caught and it might catch up on me. So I rather just close the books up." 'Cause, you know, fingerprints and all that it could catch up on you, or if they look at my record. I got a bad record. I could be facing life instead of 13 years, you know. So I . . . take a plea bargain. That's beating the system to a certain extent.

Julia: They give you an offer before you can go to jury trial 'cause they don't want to waste taxpayers money, . . . not unless it's a . . . really big client . . . I bargained myself . . . I asked the PD to set up an appointment for me to go into . . . Judge Thomas' chambers . . . And I got down to the point and I says, "Your Honor . . . I'll plead guilty to that possession of the gun . . . I'll take the plea bargain for a year." . . . 'Cause I had other charges of assaulting an officer . . . He goes, "If you plead guilty I'll give you the year with the violation run concurrent." So I took it . . . I'm glad I took the year because I . . . could have got five years. Instead I took the year and got five years enhancement if I got arrested again . . . They couldn't find the weapon but . . . there was neighbors that seen me that I had it . . . I'm a parolee. I have priors, you see, and they're gonna . . . believe . . . that person because that person was like a teacher, over me . . . So I didn't wanna take it to jury trial . . . You know, why play with the system and then . . . they give you more? . . . Like if you play with the system and they offer you something, they're giving you a break even if you're . . . guilty . . . You could at the plea bargain but it might get you more time. Like, you know, they'll get pissed off.

Nevertheless, even for Chicanas who felt confident about their ability to plea bargain, there were conditions, such as being taken to court in shackles, which they felt reduced their ability to negotiate favorable terms with the judge and added to their sense of humiliation.

Lillian: You're nothing in there. You go in there shackled. You go in there . . . with handcuffs. When I was in felony . . . ,[4] I was shackled by the ankles and the wrists all the way to court. I mean, yeah, you look real presentable in the courtroom. You know what I mean? No matter what you've done, you know, you look . . . pretty bad.

Bail

Only a handful of pintas interviewed were ever "released on their own recognizance" (OR'd). Neither OR nor bail were available to Chicanas who were homeless prior to arrest, arrested for parole violations, or considered flight risks. Only 'Cristina, who was not an addict, was repeatedly OR'd partly because she had a stable address, was never arrested for drug crimes, and was not on parole.

Less than half of the pintas interviewed ever came out on bail prior to plea bargaining or trial. Most did not have the resources to cover the bail. Some were fortunate that relatives, often their mothers, were able to raise money to bail them out at least at their first arrest.

Graciela: My mother bailed me out . . . I think it cost her $250 and . . . she had to put up my grandmother's house.

Estela: My mom bailed me. My bail was $25,000 and my mom put up her house . . . and she had to put up so much money. I think it was like $500.

Lillian: I didn't ask nobody to ever take me out of jail except for one time I asked my aunt and uncle . . . They put me out on bail.

Occasionally, Chicanas were able to use their own collateral, such as a car, to put up bail. Even in these cases, the assistance of a relative and/ or a bondsman was needed. Such was the case with Lucy, whose first arrest was for disorderly conduct and assaulting a police office while intoxicated.

Lucy: I stood in jail . . . maybe about 10 hours . . . I got bailed out . . . My Uncle Steve, he had a friend who had a bail bondsman. Just gave him my pink slip to my car and they got me out . . . I just had to pay a fine . . . I think it was something like $200.

In one rare case, an employer put up the bail and hired an attorney to represent Melinda.

Melinda: The guy that I was working for in the apartments there . . . he came out and paid the . . . full bail . . . $25,000 . . . cash . . . 'Cause all this time I've always worked . . . I managed a lot of the low-income projects . . . He put up bail and he got me a great attorney.

Once Chicanas started getting arrested repeatedly, however, even the most supportive relatives generally stopped bailing them out. This was especially the case when more than one family member was repeatedly arrested.

Estela: They never bailed me out . . . They just didn't wanna be bothered . . . because they felt it was my fault. So I stayed there.

Lucy: I always stood in there. By this time I was already separated with the kids' father, okay, and I just didn't have nobody there. My family cut me loose. My sister was in the same boat. My brothers were out there.

Lillian: I tried to get out on supervised OR . . . but I didn't have a job. I didn't have nowhere to go . . . Nobody would bail me . . . My parents didn't want me back to the house because I had already . . . been . . . so much trouble for them. You know, my mother had . . . a lot of miserable nights . . . behind us . . . She aged a lot. My dad . . . told me, "You wanna be a smart-ass? You wanna be out there on your own? Do it on your own."

Rarely could Chicanas depend on their partners, most drug-addicted themselves, to put up bail.

Frequently, if they knew they would be found guilty, Chicanas would not let their families put up bail. Sometimes, they felt too ashamed to ask for help. At other times, they feared being denied the help, so they did not ask. Without bail, Chicanas spent weeks, sometimes months in jail until their cases were heard or settled. For those sentenced to jail or prison, the time spent awaiting the verdict and/or sentencing was generally credited toward their final sentences. However, how the time served would be disposed of, was at the judge's discretion. For those who were found innocent or sentenced to alternatives-to-incarceration programs, the time spent in jail was "dead time."

Sentences

A Chicana convicted on her first nonviolent, low-level drug offense in California, simple possession for example, could be sentenced to "jail and/or probation, with or without a stipulation that she participate in a community drug program, or sentencing her to state prison" (Faith 1981: 101). In 1980 it was common to sentence first-time drug offenders to jail and/or probation or to CRC (ibid.: 102). CRC, run by CDC, held "civil narcotic addicts" and other felons. Hence, while the sentences for Chicanas convicted of their first low-level drug offenses were not necessarily always discriminatory compared to non-Chicanas convicted at the time, they were nonetheless severe. Additionally, as discussed in Chapter 1, in 1990 Chicanas in California and New York were more likely than white and sometimes African-American women to be sentenced to prison for drug violations (Mann 1995b).

Overall, the sentences given pintas interviewed varied from fines and community service to probation with three to six years joint suspended, from drug diversion to residential and methadone treatment programs, and from 14 days in jail to 13 years in a federal penitentiary.

Drug diversion programs allowed first-time offenders to avoid record of conviction by diverting them away from the criminal justice system into work, educational, or rehabilitation programs. Criminal charges were dismissed if participants completed the programs successfully. However, drug diversion programs were used less frequently in the case of Latinas/os and African Americans (CJC 1997; Faith 1981). Moreover, while low-income defendants in California were eligible to pay fines or participate in work-service programs if they paid the required fees, many could not afford to pay either and ended up doing jail time instead (CJC 1997).

One of the findings of this research was the low incidence of sentencing Chicanas to alternative-to-incarceration programs, particularly for first offenses. Alternatives to incarceration included fines, probation, community service, and drug rehabilitation programs. Turk, Owen, and Bloom (1995) also found that in California "probation prior to incarceration" was "underutilized" even in the case of first-time women offenders (47). Such programs allowed women to stay in their communities, where they could go to school, work, participate in drug rehabilitation programs, and maintain or rekindle their relationships with loved ones.

Only four of the 24 pintas interviewed were sentenced to alternatives-to-incarceration programs on their first offenses, although none of the offenses were violent.[5] The other 20 were sentenced to serve anywhere from 14 days in jail to 13 years in a federal penitentiary. Four of the 20 also received sentences that combined jail time with probation and/or joint suspended sentences of various lengths. Three years joint suspended, for example, meant that if Chicanas violated the terms of their probation, they could be sent to prison for up to three years. When that occurred, Chicanas referred to it as having been "violated." Pintas also used the term when they were sent to prison on a parole violation. That is, when their parole had been revoked. Mercedes described what the judge meant by joint-suspended.

That was my first offense. He gave me weekends and three years joint suspended and probation . . . Initially I should have gotten . . . three years prison time. But [he said], "I'm going to do a plea bargain and I'm going to give you weekends in . . . the county jail. And I'm going to give you formal probation. And I'm going to take this prison time and put it aside. And if you do any violations, . . . when you come in front of me again, I'm going to give you those three years." That's what that meant.

While Chicanas who got joint suspended sentences appeared to be better off than those sentenced to serve jail time, in reality, joint suspended sentences set up Chicana addicts to serve prison time. This was so because addicts could rarely meet the conditions imposed by sentencing provisions. For example, as soon as they were picked up for being under the influence, which addicts often were, they could be sent to prison.

Furthermore, while Chicanas interviewed were overwhelmingly arrested for crimes related to their drug habits, only one was referred to a rehabilitation program as an alternative to jail on her first offense. Nine of the 24 pintas interviewed were eventually sentenced to CRC. However, for five of the nine, the criminal justice system addressed their addiction only after years of going in and out of jail. While a number of Chicanas interviewed were still in denial of their addiction years into their incarceration histories, it is clear that a significant number might have opted to go to rehabilitation programs had the option been presented to them earlier on.

Commitment Histories

It was difficult to trace the exact commitment history of most pintas interviewed for a number of reasons. They could not remember all the times they had been arrested, much less all the sentences and actual time served on each offense. This information was accessible only from those who had a copy of their "rap sheet," or conviction record, which has to be officially requested from county, state, and/or federal authorities. Few had copies of their records at the time of the interview. A review of Graciela's arrest history, while complicated and confusing, illustrates not only why it was difficult for Chicanas interviewed to keep track of their own arrest history, but also how extensive was their contact with the criminal justice system.

Graciela: Every year since 1984 I have been in Sybil Brand [or] waiting to catch the chain[6] . . . to the . . . joint . . . November of 1984 was my first time getting incarcerated, direct sales to a police officer, sales of PCP . . . I went to Sybil Brand. I did my year . . . I got released . . . December '85 . . . I went back like four months later . . . to Sybil Brand . . . I was there for about three months . . . From Sybil Brand I got shipped to prison. I went to CIW.[7] That was the receiving center then.[8] And I stood at CIW . . . for like 20 months . . . That was my first time going . . . I got out . . . the middle of the year [and] I went right back in '87 to SBI. I sat there for another three months . . . I [had] picked up a new case, so I . . . got . . . sentenced to . . . another three years and I did the 18 months . . . So then I went to CIW . . . for eight months . . . CIW . . . shipped me to CRC to do my time 'cause at that time [at] CRC . . . they were housing "W" [CDC] numbers there . . . I did . . . the last seven months of my time . . . in CRC . . . I paroled from CRC . . . September of '88 . . . End of '89 . . . they picked me up for three armed robberies and I stood in the county jail for . . . seven . . . months fighting it . . . And then got shipped to CIW . . . for like two months . . . for violation. And I went to the board.[9] Board . . . dismissed the robberies and gave me seven months for that time served . . . By this time it was already . . . the end of 1990 . . . '91 is when I picked up the GTA robbery. I got three years on that . . . I went to Sybil Brand and I sat there for . . . like another five months 'cause I was going back and forth to court . . . I got three years and . . . that's when they were . . . already shipping to Madera.[10] I went to Madera . . . I did 27 months in Chowchilla and I paroled in December of '93 . . . This is the first time that I have stayed out this long.

Graciela paroled out in December 1993 and had not been sent to jail or prison again. However, at the time of the interview in May 1995, she had failed to report to her PO, and hence, her arrest for parole violation was imminent. In fact, during the interview, she interrupted our session and left the apartment through the first-floor bedroom window. She was hiding from her PO, who had shown up unexpectedly looking for other parolees he supervised in the building. Once he left she returned through the front door to finish the interview.

Length of Time Served

While the sentences for Chicanas interviewed varied from two weeks in jail to 13 years in a federal penitentiary, the actual time served on them varied from 10 days in SBI to seven years at a federal penitentiary or CRC.

The time actually served depended on drug-related and mandatory sentencing laws, whether prisoners were given credit for time served in jail prior to sentencing, whether they were given the minimum or maximum sentence, the number of times they had been sentenced for the same offense, their behavior while incarcerated, staff attitudes toward individual prisoners, and their POs' recommendations.

Estela and Lillian described the types of sentences and actual time served for various offenses.

Estela: Well, they'd take me to jail, I'd violate, and I go to prison. And maybe I get violated for six months, eight months . . . maybe 30 days, 60 days . . . You know, whatever the parole officer recommended for me, I got.

Lillian: I would say I did three misdemeanor charges before I got a felony with the possession . . . I did six months on the [second] one because it was . . . under the influence with a prior. . . . The . . . third time I went in it was . . . a misdemeanor for the under the influence and a violation of probation. . . . [I did] nine months . . . The . . . fourth time I went . . . it was for an under the influence, a possession, and assault on an officer. . . . I . . . picked up . . . a year . . . Actually, the time I would of spent in there I think was a year and I would of done eight months. I ended up doing 9½ months 'cause I got into another fight in there with another Black [prisoner].

Probation and Parole

In California, eligibility for release on parole was determined by whether prisoners had been sentenced under the state's determinate sentencing laws or the indeterminate sentencing laws adopted in 1978. Under indeterminate sentencing laws, pintas and other prisoners were sentenced to prison for a specified maximum period of time (e.g., three years, five years). Prisoners could, nonetheless, be released before their maximum sentences expired if they were eligible to earn "Good Time" or day-for-day credits under the Inmate Work Training Incentive Program (CDC 2002). The latter allowed prisoners to participate in vocation, educational, or work programs.

Once released from prison they were automatically placed under parole supervision, regardless of whether they had completed all or part of their maximum sentences. Parole terms were generally set for three years, although a fourth year could be added. If pintas violated the terms of their parole within that period of time, their parole could be revoked and they could be repeatedly incarcerated for terms of up to one year as recommended by their POs and imposed by the Board of Prison Terms.

Those prisoners sentenced under California's indeterminate sentencing laws were given maximums of "life" in prison (e.g., 15-to-life sentence). Not all were automatically eligible for parole. Those who were granted parole could be repeatedly returned to prison on parole violations for the rest of their lives.

Some Chicanas, like Lillian, remained on probation while going in and out of jail for a number of years. Generally, as long as they were arrested for misdemeanors, Chicanas were not sentenced to state prison. However, once they had violated probation a certain number of times or committed a felony, they were sentenced to a state penitentiary. Once released from prison, they were routinely placed on parole. Once on parole they were repeatedly arrested for parole violations of various sorts and sent to prison, even if they had not committed any new offenses.

Sonia: I had been running on parole I think three years at that time, yeah, not reporting . . . Meaning that I have to report . . . to a parole officer, . . . have . . . urine tests to see if I'm using drugs . . . and they don't know my whereabouts, where I live . . . I'll maybe come home and . . . go see her that one day and then I don't see her no more and I just go on about my business using drugs until they catch me.

One of the most common ways Chicanas violated probation or parole was through giving dirty UAs.

Estela: They took urine tests and . . . after . . . three dirties, they . . . violate you.

However, there were times where POs repeatedly violated Chicanas arbitrarily. Melinda's three years on parole took her six to seven years to complete, in part due to the obstacles put in her path by an obsessive PO. Her case illustrates the amount of power given to parole officers by criminal justice agencies.

I needed to get out of the state of California because I was getting railroaded every time. I mean, I kept going back to the joint, back to the joint. Half of the time it was just . . . this parole officer I had . . . He was a Latino . . . He didn't want me with anybody . . . He didn't like the idea I was gay . . . I got with Danny and it's like he didn't like that situation either . . . Each parole officer has a region . . . And I don't care . . . how far out of town I moved . . . it seemed he had every region wherever my name was. Every time I came out of the joint he was still my parole officer . . . I had him . . . from . . . '85 until '91 . . . I was doing a three-year parole and it took me . . . seven years to get off of it . . . I went to Arizona . . . in

'92 . . . And as soon as I got to Arizona I . . . reported over there. It is *suerte*[11] I got me a Chicano parole officer . . . My parole officer over there told him, "You know what? Forget this number. She's my property, not yours. So get off her ass!" And once . . . I cut that . . . string between me and that parole officer, it seems I did my parole really good . . . Ten months later, I was off parole.

Sometimes Chicanas found creative ways to avoid being arrested on parole violations.

Julia: They put a hold on you when you're . . . on parole and . . . there's no way you can bail. Not unless you go under another a.k.a.

Estela: When I used to go in the bathroom I used to give them pure water . . . They dip it in the toilet . . . I got away with it . . . But a couple of times I couldn't, I'd have to give 'em my urine.

Gina, on the other hand, agreed to participate in a methadone maintenance program in order to avoid a parole hold.

Gina: They told me, "The only way . . . we're gonna drop your parole hold is because you just had a baby and we want you to find someone who's gonna . . . keep the baby and . . . [on] conditions that you get on methadone."

Some Chicanas moved to a different barrio or city to avoid being arrested on parole violations.

Yolanda's story demonstrates how difficult parole stipulations, including the get-tough-on-crime policies of California's Three Strikes Law, have made it for Chicana addicts and other pintas to avoid incarceration even when arrested for the most insignificant infractions.

My last case. That was '90, '92, around there . . . I got 16 months . . . And I got out. I did good for two years and got off parole . . . in 13 months 'cause I did it clean. I . . . didn't turn in no dirties and I did what I was supposed to do. Then . . . me and my son . . . went to Target to go buy his school clothes . . . He had got . . . one of them king-size Snickers and he asked me, "Mom, could I eat this?" And I told him, "Yeah, go ahead." So I kept the wrapper after he was finished and I put it in the basket 'cause I was gonna pay for it. And when I went to . . . pay for the kid's clothes . . . I couldn't find the wrapper no more so I didn't think about it, you know . . . When I walked out the store security surrounded me and told me that I was going to jail and I asked them, "For what?" And they had me on . . . camera, saying that my son ate a candy bar. And I went . . . back to prison for it. I got a whole new number and I went back to prison with a two-year term.

The stories discussed here illustrate how pintas interviewed were at a disadvantage relative to white middle- and upper-class defendants who came in contact with criminal justice agencies. This was partly the result of criminal justice policies that targeted poor and working-class people, particularly Latinas and other people of color, for arrest and incarceration. Addicted pintas were at a further disadvantage because drug laws criminalized their illness.

Nonetheless, the actions pintas took in response to the war on drugs and other discriminatory policies clearly demonstrated that they continually exerted their agency in numerous ways. One of these was to become more knowledgeable about the inner workings of the criminal justice system in order to negotiate more favorable sentencing terms.

PART II

SYBIL BRAND INSTITUTE
FOR WOMEN AND BEYOND

Sybil Brand Institute for Women
The Institutional Setting

*It's . . . in . . . Monterey Park in L.A. . . . . It's right up the . . . Long
Beach Freeway . . . They have . . . regular buses that go up there.*
—Rita

Sybil Brand Institute for Women (SBI) was the Los Angeles County jail
for women from November 1963 until 1997, when it closed. A four-
story building located in Monterey Park, it was administered by the
LASD. Prior to its opening, women were held on the 13th floor of the
Hall of Justice in downtown Los Angeles[1] and, for a short time, in an
old Navy brig in Terminal Island (*LAT* 10/6/79, 5/15/86). Prisoners were
taken to SBI for booking from police stations, from other jails, and directly from the streets (Watterson 1996).

SBI fulfilled diverse functions including that of serving as a reception center for detainees arrested within Los Angeles County. In such
capacity the facility was responsible for "booking, processing, property
storage, record maintenance, court appearances, work release, classification, collection of bails and fines, [and] managing female inmate trust
accounts and releases" (LASD 2002).

SBI's rated capacity was 950 prisoners. While in March 1973 SBI held
800 prisoners, by July 1986 there were more than 2,000 (*LAT* 3/16/73,
7/13/86). The population fluctuated between 2,000 and 2,300 until the
transfer of most of SBI's prisoner population to the newly opened Twin
Towers jail in downtown Los Angeles (*LAT* 6/9/1997).[2] In an effort to relieve overcrowding, between October 1986 and May 1993, "model" prisoners from SBI were transferred to Mira Loma Detention Center in Lan-
caster.[3] Such transfers did little to ease SBI's overcrowding, which was
due to the impact of mandatory and drug-related sentencing laws.

Two of every three pintas interviewed served time at both SBI and
other county jails located between Sacramento and San Diego. Chapters 10–17 provide information about the history of SBI and the experi-

ences of Chicanas sentenced there during its 34-year history. They explore the treatment accorded pintas and other prisoners by institutional staff, the ways pintas responded to staff and non-Chicana prisoners, and the conditions they encountered.

The major questions this chapter asks are: What was the processing of new prisoners like? What were pintas' initial fears and impressions of jail? Did guards and other prisoners try to relieve such fears? What were the living conditions like?

Before answering these questions, a clarification must be made. Because SBI was under the jurisdiction of LASD, the guards were technically classified as sheriff's deputies. However, to distinguish between those deputies working inside from those working outside jails, I refer to those working in jails as guards throughout. Pintas, however, used the term "deputy" to mean guards at SBI.

Initial Fears and Impressions

Chicanas shared a number of fears when entering jail the first time.

Rosa: The first time I went in . . . I heard the bars clanging. And it wasn't the way it is now [dorms], it was cell block. And I was afraid of being in jail and I was afraid of . . . what was gonna happen to me . . . as far as kicking.

Luisa: So they took me to Sybil Brand. That was real scary for me . . . I didn't know what was going to happen 'cause I knew that Sybil Brand was huge . . . Then I used to hear, . . . "You know, there's a lot of women there that they'll just rape you." . . . You know, . . . war stories . . . like, "You'd better be careful because they'll just take advantage of you." And, "There's women that will steal your candy so you have to be careful." "Your money, you have to kind of keester it, you know, hide it in your breast."

Marta: Like the girls were saying, "Oh, Marta, when you go to sleep make sure . . . you tuck yourself in because if they want you they'll take it." "What you mean, 'They'll take *it*?'" . . . "You know, if they want your body, they're gonna take your body." . . . I mean, they had me all scared.

For Chicanas like Mercedes, fears about incarceration were accompanied by feelings of guilt and shame.

And just being exposed to jail. I mean, . . . in my culture . . . those are not the places that women go to, let alone, being a woman and being a heroin addict. You know, I . . . think for me that just being fearful of the unknown and being put with *those people*, you know . . . Growing up I was not exposed to . . . lesbian women . . . And remember, I went in a PCP user so it's like, "Oh, my God, all these heroin addicts and these murderers!" . . . So yes, I was very fearful.

While most first-timers were intimidated by SBI, others were not.

Deborah: When I first went there, you know, I was pretty young . . . I was probably about 21 . . . It was like the thing to do. It was like cool.

Once newcomers were released from the receiving dorm into General Population, where most prisoners were housed, they found that their fears of being sexually victimized by other prisoners were largely unfounded.

Marta: I never seen people that were gay . . . I didn't know anything of that . . . And then, I slept in the middle of two of 'em, you know, a bunk bed here, my bunk bed, and a bunk bed here . . . And I didn't know how to go to sleep because . . . I . . . heard so much about 'em . . . And I mean, they made 'em sound really bad . . . But after I talked to 'em I think different about 'em, you know. I got close to 'em and I was even with one.

Their fears of being victimized in nonsexual ways proved to be more realistic. Many, like Marta, protected themselves by adopting an aggressive stance when approached.

I didn't talk to nobody, no . . . A lot of people tried to fuck with me and they would tell me, "Hey, Do you have any shampoo I could have?" And I'd look at 'em. I said, "If I had shampoo I'd be washing my hair . . ." "Oh, yeah, I'm sorry . . . If you need anything, I got it." . . . 'Cause it's just to see who they could take from.

Graciela followed the advice veteranas/os gave her prior to her incarceration.

They just told me, ". . . You don't step on nobody's toes. You don't steal. And keep your . . . business to yourself. Don't get in other people's business and everything will be all right. Don't let no one see you're scared . . . Never let nobody get over on you even if you have to fight and you lose a fight. You just get up with your head up high. You don't walk away from nothing and you don't let nobody do nothing to you . . . You always stand up for yourself 'cause if you let them get over on you once, they'll always do it." So that's what I did.

Some pintas were surprised at how tough prisoners had to act in order to protect themselves from peers.

Luisa: In jail you had to be careful. In jail you can't cry. You can't snivel. You have to be hard-core. Because that's the only way that people will look up to you . . . If you go in there weak-minded, they're gonna kick . . . your ass, rob you. They're gonna take advantage of you . . . There were two things you had to do, either . . . just be yourself, which . . . that was me, or be real hard-core.

Incarceration was more difficult if pintas stayed focused on life outside.

Graciela: I remember when I first got . . . to Sybil Brand and the gates closed behind I just put on my mind that, "You're not going home. This is your home. So . . . just block the outside out." That way it wasn't hard time . . . Because when you're in there and you start thinking about out here you just . . . have a hard time.

Processing

Introduction to SBI began in the jail's two holding tanks, one of which had a toilet but in full view of both prisoners and guards (Watterson 1996: 68). Drunk or violent prisoners were first placed in an observation room and subsequently transferred to a holding tank.

Rosa: I remember when I got there they put us in a tank and we waited to be called and to sign papers and to be fingerprinted and put back into the tank. And then we went through a little hall, towards the back, and were showered and Kwelled and checked to see if we had any . . . drugs on us, you know, body searched. And then after that, we ended up seeing a nurse and going upstairs.

The initial treatment foreshadowed the dehumanizing manner in which prisoners would be treated throughout their stay in jail. It also echoed the physical and sexual abuse pintas had experienced prior to their incarceration. The most frightening and humiliating part of the initial screening was the "narco search" for "weapons, contraband, or narcotics" that prisoners were subjected to following the initial pat-search during booking (Watterson 1996: 67).

Linda: I could never get used to that part, you know, to have . . . to strip you down totally . . . and have you with your arms crossed . . . in the back of your head, totally naked in the front of someone you have never seen . . . And they make you bend over . . . and "Spread 'em," like they say, . . . because somebody wants to look at your rectum . . . People going back and forth, turning around and looking at you . . . There was always other women there and there was always more than two and three police officers there. There was never, never anything such as privacy in Sybil Brand.

Luisa: The cops were very, very rude. You know, . . . just the feeling of going in there and having to get naked and split your ass and let the cops see your ass. And telling you, "I want to see pink . . . Spread that ass . . . I need you to cough," in a very ugly-toned voice . . . "Okay, move!" You know, real rude. And when you're scared and they treat you rude it's . . . awful . . . It was very devastating for me.

During the searches, guards sometimes used flashlights to look inside women's bodies (Watterson 1996) or made prisoners hold a mirror beneath their vaginas (Estela). During the more invasive cavity searches, guards would make prisoners lie on a bed while they used their fingers to check inside women's bodies (Linda). Sometimes the cavity-searches were conducted in the infirmary with the assistance of medical staff (Estela).

While male guards were not allowed to conduct such searches, they were allowed to pat-search prisoners at any time. Moreover, male guards were sometimes used to help women guards disrobe violent or seriously disturbed prisoners (*Inmates of Sybil Brand Institute for Women et al. v. The County of Los Angeles et al.* App., 181 Cal. Rptr. 599 [1982a]; *LAT* 2/16/77).[4]

Clothing

Upon entering SBI, prisoners were allowed to keep their own underwear, and outsiders were allowed to mail them underwear and shoes. All other clothing was provided by the county. Through the 34-year period studied, prisoners wore either blue uniforms or uniforms color-coded to match their housing dorms.

Rita: When I first went in there . . . every dorm had different colors . . . Brown and . . . lime green . . . was misdemeanors, . . . and that's non-sentenced dorms too . . . Working Dorm was purple . . . Red was Working Dorm. The orange was Working Dorm . . . Dark blue was felony . . . The blue dresses with red stripes was state prisoners . . . That means you were going to prison . . . Then they had . . . like a tan color but that was like . . . mentally off people, . . . We called them MOs . . . [Pink] was a working dorm and pregos, when you're pregnant . . . The . . . last time I was in there, 1993, everybody was wearing . . . dark blues . . . They changed it from time to time.

Linda: They used to give you thongs, you know, . . . those rubber shoes that you slip in. One size too small, the other one would be like four sizes too big.

No makeup . . . They gave you a little blue dress that looks like those . . . county hospital gowns.

The Dorms

Sybil Brand had 12 dorms, 6 cell blocks, and a 41-bed infirmary (LASD). The jail contained a county side and a state side. The county side housed pretrial detainees and prisoners sentenced for misdemeanors. This group composed the institution's general population. The state side held prisoners on a "contractual basis" (LASD 2002). These include parole violators and other prisoners serving their sentences at SBI and state prisoners awaiting transfer to a state prison.

As in jails throughout the country, more than half the prisoners on the county side had not been convicted of any crime (*LAT* 4/10/73, 11/18/87; *Inmates of SBI* 1982a). Most were being held in jail because they could not afford to post bail.

Deborah: There's like six dorms on a floor. And . . . that is including lockup and mental lock . . . A dorm setting . . . Unless you . . . go to . . . lockup. That's a one-man cell . . . On one side of the tier's probably 15 on one side and 15 on the other . . . That's the structure of the building. Has always been the same. It's just more overcrowded now . . . The population stays around probably 1,800 to 2,000 a month.

The daily guard supervision of the dorms was minimal. Generally, there was one guard working inside the dorm at any time. Guards tended to stay inside "the cop shop," particularly at night.

Rita: It's like a booth that the cop sits in there all night long while you sleep . . . They make sure that there's no sexual activities going on at night . . . They make sure that everybody's in their bed, not walking around stealing stuff.

While male guards were required to announce their presence when entering the dorms, they frequently did not.

Cristina: You're supposed to say, "Officer on the floor," 'cause you change in there . . . "Male on the floor. Man coming in." Well, . . . they weren't even announced. He'd just walk through.

Overcrowding

In 1977, 10% of SBI prisoners were housed in cell blocks, 90% in dorms (*Inmates of SBI* 1982a). During the late 1980s, in response to severe overcrowding, single beds gave way to bunk beds. Triple bunking was introduced during the 1990s. In triple bunking, another bed was added between the two original bunks.

Graciela: Back then [1985] it was only about maybe . . . 40-something girls to a dorm . . . No more than 50 . . . And . . . it was only one bed, cot-like, . . . and you had a locker in between you and the other person. So there's . . . two rows on one side, and then there was a wall to divide it and two rows on the other side . . . If it was 50, like 25 and 25 . . . And then it has a . . . cop shop in front. And then to the right there's a bathroom with the showers and the toilets. There's four stalls in . . . each dorm . . . And there's a day room with a TV, washer, and dryer.

Rita: They don't have lockers no more . . . They had to take 'em out 'cause they had to make the room for more beds . . . [double bunks] . . . That must have been . . . like in the . . . late '80s . . . Now they got triple beds and . . . they . . . house women in the day room . . . That used to just be a recreation room where the women played cards, watched TV, talked on the phone, do laundry.

Graciela: There's about 187 girls to a dorm now . . . [1995] It's so crowded . . . sometimes they have girls sleeping . . . in the day room, on the floor.

Receiving Dorm

The dorm least preferred by prisoners at SBI was the receiving dorm. It was a nonworking dorm, thus prisoners were idle.

Cristina: I spent my time in the worst dorm, which was the receiving dorm, people coming back and forth to Mira Loma, . . . going to court. It was like a court dorm. You're there today, gone tomorrow . . . It was worse than being in a regular dorm because receiving dorms you . . . don't have the same company. I won't . . . have the same bunky . . . They steal from you. You gotta keep everything on you . . . 'cause you'd have busloads every day.

In 1982 the jails turnover rate was between 70 and 100 prisoners a day (*Inmates of SBI* 1982a). Despite such conditions Chicanas managed to give and receive some support from other prisoners in the dorm.

Cristina: They talked their cases over or, "What case you going to?" or "Do . . . you want me to hold your stuff . . . 'cause I'm not going to court today. You know, I'll sit and watch the house . . . You go do what you gotta do. I'll be back by the time you come home at 10." Like me, I always . . . held everybody's stuff.

State Dorms

Overcrowding also affected the quality of life of state prisoners.

Graciela: There's three dorms that consist of state girls . . . I remember before . . . it wasn't too many people so you . . . weren't locked down. Now you're locked down 24-7 . . . You cannot go out nowhere . . . And you were considered "high power." It's either high bail or no bail . . . The only time you get out is when you walk to meals and back . . . And we got the TV room . . . We're allowed to go on Sunday to church. They walk us from our dorm to the church . . . I mean, you got your school . . . As far as any other program, there's nothing . . . We can't go to NA, AA. And if we do I think it's allowed once a week.

The state side was searched more often, and its dorms were raided more often for contraband than county-side dorms. To escape these conditions pintas sometimes requested a "speedy removal," which forced authorities to transfer them immediately to a penitentiary.

General Population and the Honor Dorm

One of the ways prison administrators sought to encourage compliance from prisoners was by using a small number of them as "model" prisoners. These were then housed in an "honor" dorm where conditions were significantly different from those of General Population dorms.

Unlike General Population, where many prisoners remained idle due to the lack of work assignments, prisoners were assigned to the Honor Dorm on the recommendation of their work supervisors whose confidence they had earned. As a result, the dorm was also known as the "Trustie Dorm."

General Population prisoners believed that trusties had earned the trust of staff by snitching on their peers. Hence, they distrusted Honor Dorm prisoners.

Estela: Trusties are picked . . . They just pick 'em at random. No criteria, no nothing . . . If they like you or whatever, you know, then they'll pick you . . . You don't have no work references or nothing . . . It's if they like you or . . . you kiss ass, for them.

Regardless of the criteria used to select Honor Dorm prisoners, the fact was that staff expected them to act differently from other prisoners. For example, they had to wear white collars and, at one point, makeup to work. This led to the dorm being dubbed the "white collar" dorm by General Population.

Other characteristics differentiated the dorms. General Population prisoners had to ask for permission to leave their units and be escorted by guards to their destinations. Honor Dorm was not locked down during the day, and trusties could roam the facility without having to be escorted by guards.

The day room in the Honor Dorm could be used until 11 P.M., and the phones until 3 A.M. Prisoners in General Population had their lights turned off at 9 P.M. Moreover, Honor Dorm prisoners had access to soda and ice cream machines, movies, a large TV and VCR and had carpet and curtains in their dorm (Cristina).

In further contrast, stealing was kept to a minimum in the Honor Dorm because when it occurred the entire dorm would be searched. In General Population stealing was rampant, and the guards took no particular interest in preventing it.

Honor Dorm prisoners also had easier access to washing machines and bleach to wash their clothes. Those in General Population had to sign up on a first-come, first-served basis to use the washers and were not allowed the use of bleach.

Both the Honor Dorm and General Population dorms had six showers and six toilets to be shared by all the prisoners housed there. But there were fewer prisoners in the Honor Dorm to share the showers, and the showers were accessible throughout the day. Prisoners in General Population had to wait until guards escorted them to their showers. Moreover, guards denied prisoners showers arbitrarily despite state laws that mandated as of July 1973 that prisoners be taken out for a shower every other day (*LAT* 4/1/73).

Honor Dorm prisoners were required to shower regularly, look neat and clean, and keep their dorm tidy. In General Population this was harder because the dorms, toilets, showers, and recreation areas were frequently filthy. Moreover, administrators sometimes let weeks go by without making physical plant repairs.

Estela: Very unsanitary . . . They got rats living in the . . . cushion in your mattresses! And then at night you can lay down and you see 'em running on the floors . . . The . . . plumbing in there is very, very rotten . . . The water tastes rotten . . . You would taste the pipes on it . . . The bathrooms are dirty. The toilet's always clogged. They overflowed. And they used to leave it for like weeks at a time . . . and it would smell.

Rita: And they don't . . . have no cleanup crew where they go clean bathrooms and stuff. They just . . . get people those jobs, you know, "Who wants to clean up the bathroom? I want the bathroom cleaned." If the bathroom's not clean, the TV don't get turned on, the phones don't get turned on. So you have to . . . keep your room area clean. How is it dirty? Because in the morning and the night people just throw stuff all over. Towels thrown all over the floor. Trash all over. And . . . some women just smell and they don't take baths.

Overcrowding also affected prisoners' access to basic hygiene products.

Estela: They'd put out maybe six rolls in the morning of toilet paper for . . . 170-something women . . . and then maybe six at night, okay.

Estela: They didn't care if you had sanitary napkins or not. I mean, there was times when . . . they didn't have sanitary napkins for like a week, and we have to get toilet paper and roll it up and put it in there, you know.

All dorms, however, had to deal with the lack of privacy when using the toilets.

Estela: They were little stalls . . . Say like I . . . came inside the stall. There's . . . two walls right here and then the door. You sit down. Whoever's walking by can see over . . . There's a gap . . . on the bottom and then on the top, the whole thing's open.

Overcrowding gradually affected the Honor Dorm too, but for a time guards were able to keep the number of prisoners to 60, the capacity set for dorms throughout the institution. By the mid-1980s, however, when other dorms throughout the facility had more than 100 prisoners each, even the Honor Dorm gave way to double bunks (*LAT* 5/15/86).

Food

Most county prisoners complain about the food. SBI was no exception.

Marta: Well, the food was cold, for one thing. Because when they had breakfast, lunch, and dinner . . . either 8100 is gonna go first and then 3200 . . . And by the time they get to 7000 or 8000, you know, that food's cold . . . and . . . nobody wants to eat it . . . I could tell you the . . . meals they have up to now . . . SOS on Mondays, "Shit on the Shingle," which is potatoes and hamburger meat. It's like a gravy with that . . . Tuesday mornings, we'd always have pancakes . . . and Tuesdays at . . . lunchtime we'd have soup and sandwiches . . . It's the same thing over and over . . . Thursdays was fried chicken . . . or BBQ chicken, which is chicken looked so fucking old and green, you know, disgusting . . . Even the . . . lunch meat was always funny. It's . . . got a little bit of green in it . . . And . . . I had worked at kitchen from the day I went in . . . and let me tell you, I wouldn't even give that food to my dogs.

Rita: They don't put no salt, no pepper, no seasoning . . . Sometimes they give you black-eyed peas with ham in it and white rice . . . Sometimes they'd have fish . . . But you know what? After a while you get used to the food. You have to. You can't starve yourself to death.

As overcrowding increased, hot lunches were replaced with sandwiches (Graciela). Even Chicanas who could afford to buy additional items from the jail's commissary or the vending machines that were eventually placed in all the dorms had access to a limited selection of goods.

Graciela: They have vending machines now, and commissary comes around and you can buy soups, "Cup-a-Noodles." And I buy a lot of beef sticks out of the vending machine, potato chips, and I put soup and stuff together . . . We have a hot water coffee pot so everything's made with the hot water . . . 'Cause I can't eat out of the cafeteria.

The best way for pintas to have access to better-quality food was by working in the Officer's Dining Room (ODR).

Marta: I was working ODR, like cooking for the officers, which has better food for me because I was eating hamburgers. I was eating fried chicken, you know, grilled cheese sandwiches with bacon . . . And so I ate good because I wasn't stupid to . . . work for the inmates . . . I mean, who wants to eat dried-up spaghetti . . . with so-called . . . corn bread that looks half-raw . . . I mean, the bread is all old and dried and wrinkled, you know, that even got some of those green spots in it sometimes.

In response to these conditions, on February 22, 1973, the American Civil Liberties Union of Southern California filed a class action suit on behalf of sentenced prisoners and pretrial detainees at SBI (*Inmates of SBI* 1982a; *LAT* 4/10/73, 2/16/77). The suit, the trial for which did not begin until November 5, 1975, challenged "the legality of numerous conditions of confinement and practices at SBI" (*Inmates of SBI* 1982a). Prisoner complaints covered overcrowding, training of guards and supervisors, disciplinary procedures, the quality of dental and medical care, and restrictions on the receipt and use of magazines. To these were added the segregation of prisoners labeled homosexuals, the use of male guards to disrobe unstable and violent prisoners, limited access to the law library and the general library, and inadequate attorney room facilities.

Pretrial detainees also challenged booking and court transportation procedures that kept those going to and from court in transit from 4:30 A.M. to 9 P.M. They also challenged rules that denied them the use of forks and knives during meals.

Moreover, the suit argued that women prisoners were denied services and programs available to male prisoners at various county jails. These included work furlough programs, contact visits, and various educational and vocational programs. Likewise, while male prisoners had access to outside recreation time on a daily basis, SBI prisoners were only allowed to go out two (sentenced) to four (pretrial) times a week. And while women at SBI had to ask guards for written permission to use the phone, male prisoners in various county jails had free access to them (*Inmates of SBI* 1982b). The fact that in 1982 there were only five phones available to SBI prisoners and that none of them were located in General Population housing dorms made it very difficult for prisoners to maintain contact with their loved ones on the outside.

Between the time the suit was filed in 1973 until the judge's tentative ruling was issued on February 14, 1977 (*Inmates of SBI* 1982b), LASD made a number of changes in its policies (discussed in subsequent chapters). These reforms were partly designed to avoid having to make even more extensive legally binding changes that might have resulted from an adverse court decision. While the court's final decision of December 1, 1978 (*Inmates of SBI* 1982b) mandated LASD to make some changes, these were almost negligible.

II

The Keepers
Regime and Rule Enforcement

Up until the 20th century, incarcerated women were held primarily in jails and prisons for men. The rampant verbal, physical, and sexual abuse they experienced at the hands of male guards and male prisoners in these facilities has been well documented (Freedman 1981; Rafter 1985). During the 1800s, women prison reformers argued that these abuses could be eliminated through the creation of separate women's prisons (and jails) run and staffed by women (meaning white women). Once the abuse was eliminated, female prisoners could be reformed under the compassionate, yet firm, guidance of female staff (Freedman 1981).

As separate women's institutions were gradually established, beginning in 1873, it became clear that women "caretakers" were just as capable as men of verbally and physically abusing female prisoners. Female staff also have the capacity to sexually harass and assault large numbers of women prisoners through the rampant use of pat-searches, strip-searches, and cavity-searches. Having said this, however, it is important to note that the level of sexual harassment and assault experienced by female prisoners in a given facility is directly related to the number of male staff working in the institution and their access to women prisoners.

According to a 1996 Human Rights Watch report, sexual harassment and abuse of women in state prisons in California has taken multiple forms. Male staff have denied or provided "goods and privileges to prisoners to compel them to have sex, or in other cases, to reward them for having done so" (2). Male guards have used "mandatory pat-frisks or room searches" to grope prisoners. Guards frequently stood by as prisoners were undressing in bathrooms and housing units or undergoing strip searches by female guards. To this was added the rape of prisoners and the use of "threat of force, punishment or retaliation" to force prisoners to grant them sexual favors (ibid.: 75). In addition, some prisoners felt forced to "barter" sexual favors in exchange for desired goods and fair treatment. Female prisoners used all the resources at their disposal to secure better treatment and living conditions, in this case, even their bodies.

While not all staff or supervisors condoned such actions, rarely were staff members penalized by institutional, county, state, or federal authorities (HRW 1996). Even the few guards charged with violating California law had access to the legal resources provided by the powerful California Correctional Peace Officers Association, the guards' union, and the CDC. Female prisoners who complained of such abuses were, on the other hand, frequently ignored by staff supervisors and threatened and harassed by staffs' coworkers. In some cases they were harassed by guards' superiors and/or transferred to solitary confinement by prison administrators. Also placed in solitary confinement were prisoners who were impregnated by male staff and refused to reveal the identity of the father.

While some women prisoners filed both individual and class action suits challenging these conditions, others have accepted the status quo for fear of retaliation or because they felt complaints would be ignored. Moreover, many prisoners and guards did not want to stop "the most pervasive form of this abuse—the exchange of favors for preferential treatment, money, or goods"—because they profited from it (HRW 1996: 97).

It is clear from the above that the verbal, physical, and sexual abuse to which women prisoners are exposed and the manner in which it is, in practice, condoned by penal authorities reproduces the conditions of abuse experienced by prisoners prior to their incarceration (Owen and Bloom 1995b). Given the history of prior abuse of women prisoners and the PTSD many of them suffered as a result, such violations also constituted "cruel and unusual" punishment (HRW 1996).

The fact that such treatment was "business as usual" in California institutions showed that abusive treatment was one of the means by which penal authorities sought to control women who had broken cultural norms, social taboos, and civil and criminal laws to get what they needed and/or wanted.

For women of color and prisoners perceived as being "homosexuals" by penal authorities, the verbal, physical, and sexual abuse was compounded by further discriminatory treatment and abuse at the hands of the overwhelmingly white heterosexual staff.[1]

In view of the above, some of the questions explored in this chapter are: What was the extent of verbal, physical, and sexual harassment and abuse of women prisoners at SBI? Did the treatment received by lesbians and pintas differ from that given other prisoners? How did pintas respond to these conditions?

The interviews with pintas discussed in Chapters 10–17, but particularly in this chapter, reveal that the types of verbal, physical, and sexual abuse documented in women's penitentiaries were also rampant at SBI. While none of the pintas interviewed spoke about having been raped while in jail, non-Chicana prisoners interviewed did verify that such incidents had occurred. Pintas, nonetheless, observed that incidents of sexual harassment and abuse became more common as the number of male guards increased.

The interviews with pintas also revealed numerous ways they responded to abusive treatment and refused to obey institutional rules and regulations they perceived as unnecessary or harmful.

Staff and Guards

At its opening in 1963, SBI employed 102 guards, only 13 of whom were men (*LAT* 1/26/64). While by 1974 the guard force had grown to 155 in an attempt to keep up with the growing prisoner population, between 1974 and 1986 the number of guards stayed the same. Moreover, while the guard force remained overwhelmingly young and female and the wardens were overwhelmingly female in 1986, male officers were over-represented within supervisory positions.

Sybil Brand is staffed by 155 deputies, all but 14 of whom are women; 14 sergeants, half of whom are women, and six lieutenants, two of whom are women. (*LAT* 7/13/86)

As the number of employees increased to 260 in 1992 (Kolts 1992: 195), so did the number of male guards.

The composition of the civilian staff at SBI was overwhelmingly white. Chicanas/os and African Americans were concentrated in certain areas of the facility, primarily in the kitchen and maintenance areas. The relationship between the civilian staff and prisoners was closely monitored.

Graciela: They're not allowed to speak to us. Not unless it's the school that you're . . . talking to the teacher. But other than that, if it's somebody that's coming in to work electronics or plumbing, you're not allowed to speak to them.

During SBI's history, pintas noted, the guard force was also over-whelmingly white, but the number of African-American guards increased as the years went by, making them the second largest group employed at the facility. The number of Chicana/o guards remained small. While statistics were not available for the actual number of Latina/os or bilingual guards at SBI during the period studied, figures available for June 30, 1999, show that only 16.3% of jail guards in California for whom racial/ethnic data were available were classified as "Hispanic." Another 52.4% were classified as white and 9.1% as African-American (BJS 2001a: 27).[2]

During the early 1970s all guards had to undergo a 16-week training course at the Sheriff's Academy (Watterson 1996: 121). Those who wanted to work on the street as law enforcement officers had to do a two-year jail duty tour (*LAT* 7/13/86). This meant that even when there were Chicana/o officers assigned to SBI, the turnover rate among them was high.

A report on the LASD published in 1992 held that eight hours of cultural diversity training given at the Academy was not enough to sensitize white guards to the needs of the county's overwhelmingly Chicana/o and African-American prisoner populations.

[I]t also seems patently clear that after several years in a custody facility, the deputies will adopt negative, stereotyped views towards African-Americans and Hispanics because of their over-representation in the jail population. And these views will carry over and influence deputies throughout their law enforcement careers. (Kolts 1992: 238)

Good Guards, Bad Guards

Pintas mentioned a few guards who treated prisoners in a respectful manner.

Rosa: I remember . . . one white officer, he was real, real kind to me. And there was another . . . [white] lady . . . that was real kind to me . . . I was in solitary confinement for about four months and . . . they knew it was stressful for me.

Marta: You see, you got some officers that . . . know how to treat you like human beings . . . 'Cause there's a few cops there that talk to me with respect . . . And I'll ask them the question and they'll . . . get right back to me whatever the question is.

Estela: Ms. Jara, the gang lady . . . She was an officer there . . . She's . . . for the . . . people that go in and they are gang-affiliated . . . She pulls them and talks to 'em . . . She was a Chicana. Like she grew up like us . . . She knew the street life and . . . she was hip to all the . . . drug scene and . . . the low-rider and stuff . . . And she used to . . . kid around with us . . . You could always talk to her about anything . . . She's been there for years.

Some pintas, like Rita, who found herself in constant verbal and physical confrontation with guards particularly during the earlier part of her incarceration history, felt that their own behavior contributed to the type of treatment they received from guards.

Rita: I went in there . . . blaming the system . . . I couldn't see myself doing wrong . . . So . . . when they would take me to jail . . . I would have a real bad attitude . . . Like just talking shit to them . . . "You can't just tell me where I can go and when I can go." . . . I remember this one lady that worked classification . . . and she would tell me, "This is our jail. This is not your jail." . . . And you . . . roll your eyes at 'em like, "Yeah, right . . ." And I guess here I thought, "I have to be this way," 'cause I didn't want nobody to think I was weak . . . When you're in jail, to me, you're not the person you really are . . . 'cause they don't want nobody to know that they're weak. They don't want nobody to know that they're scared . . . so they hide all these feelings . . . So I . . . ended up doing a lot of time in . . . the cell block, because I . . . would always act smart with the cops and always like act like my shit didn't stink.

Eventually, however, even some of the most defiant pintas found ways to adapt to the jail routine and avoid retaliation at the hands of guards.

Rita: But as time went on I realized, "You know what? This is their system. This is their jail. Nothing's gonna change." . . . So . . . what I did was . . . as soon as I . . . knew I was gonna be there for a while, I . . . got to know some of the officers there, . . . so when I would see 'em I'd say, "Hey, you know, I'm gonna be here for a while . . . Pull me out to job . . . I don't wanna sit in the dorm."

Notwithstanding the ways in which pintas felt they contributed to their own victimization, the fact was that even the most obedient and passive prisoners found themselves continually assaulted emotionally, verbally, and physically by guards. Most felt that at times guards deliberately provoked certain prisoners they deemed to be particularly angry or vulnerable in order to set them up for physical abuse and lockup.

The assault of prisoners by guards took various forms. All the pintas interviewed complained of dehumanizing treatment, including verbal abuse and threats from guards from the moment they entered SBI.

Rosa: The ones down in the booking area . . . were very curt, very disrespectful . . . If you would ask for something, they would ignore you . . . I seen a woman that was really sick in the tank and they laughed . . . They treated you as if you were an animal. I mean, with an animal sometimes you pet an animal. And there they wanted . . . you to know that you had no power whatsoever, that when they told you to do something, you had to do it or else.

Graciela: In the county jail the staff . . . they're real assholes. They have no respect for you. Because we're in jail we get treated like we're nothing. They talk to you mean and . . . you can't say a word back to 'em. And they make you feel like you're nothing because we're . . . in jail . . . They tell you, "You ain't' nothing. Look where you're at." "Shut up, bitch!"

Most guards were dismissive of prisoners' needs.

Marta: "Excuse me officer." "What? . . . I ain't got time. I'm busy right now!" . . . I said, "I just wanna ask you one little question . . ." He says, "Well, hurry up, you catch up to me." "Well, I can't . . . I gotta get permission from my staff . . . Let them know that I'm with you . . . I mean, I'll . . . get thrown in Lockup if I don't have a reason why I was out of the dorm, you know." And he said, "Well . . . that's the chance you gotta take." [I said], "Oh, fuck you then!"

Some pintas felt that female guards were more abusive than the male guards.

Graciela: Mainly the . . . ones that are assholes in there are the women.

Excessive Use of Force

The verbal abuse of prisoners was frequently accompanied by physical abuse (Kolts 1992).

Graciela: They'd call you names . . . "Asshole, shut the fuck up!" . . . If they catch you talking they take you out of line, throw you up against the wall, tell you, "Put your face on the wall!" . . . And then they'll put the handcuffs on you . . . real tight. They'll twist your arm . . . They would handcuff me and take me to Lockup.

Luisa: They screamed at you . . . And then they'd shove it [your face] up in the . . . wall . . . and they'd just beat you . . . The cops jumped you . . . And not one or two, four and five at a time. Fucking bitches! . . . These were women, white, honey!

Though pintas fought back and frequently stood up for others, prisoners' resistance only led to their being physically abused by guards and sent to Lockup.

Rita: When you walk down the . . . side of the wall to go to meals, you can't be looking around, right . . . But everybody's gonna turn and look around . . . And . . . the cop will come, "What you looking at?" . . . What do they call that shit now? "Reckless eyeballing" and . . . "rubber-necking." . . . "Keep walking!" "Don't . . . shout. I'm not a kid!" . . . And they'll just like put you against the wall and they'll humiliate you, making you face the wall. And I flatly refused . . . "You're not gonna do it?" And then they'll just push you up against the wall and just handcuff you and take you to Lockup.

Rita: A cop would get up in your face. And . . . if you know this person's younger than you and . . . even though you're the one that's in there serving time, you're not gonna let them disrespect you . . . So they used to just fight, even with the men cops.

While not all prisoners who defied guards were beaten by them, all were roughly handled. Physical abuse frequently involved assault on one prisoner by two or more guards. Supervisors seemingly condoned or covered up the abuse.

Graciela: I've been choked . . . by two . . . county sheriffs . . . that worked there . . . This happened like two years ago. I was waiting to go back to the state penitentiary and . . . somebody said that I was selling drugs there. So . . . three officers came in to get me . . . two men, one woman . . . All three of them were white . . . When I walked out of the dorm they had all three of 'em walking from behind me and told me to keep my hands to my side . . . I happened to put my hand in my mouth 'cause I was eating cookies . . . and he said that I was shoving something down my throat. So that's when he grabbed me and choked me . . . They bent me over, choked me, put my hands to my back, and bent my hands all the way up and kept telling me to spit it out! . . . And I kept trying to tell 'em, "I have nothing to spit out." . . . And they noticed that the people from the inside were looking out . . . so they drove me down the hall. And he . . . looked at me, he goes, "You stupid bitch, I knew it! . . . You asshole! I told you to spit it out . . . Are you gonna OD on us? Tell me so we can help you." I said, ". . . I didn't swallow nothing." "Yes, you did." . . . He goes, "Get that bitch and take her out of here!" So he had the female officer take me and strip-search me. They didn't find nothing . . . Nine o'clock that night, right before count time, a . . . white . . . sergeant came down, pulled me out of the dorm and took me upstairs to the infirmary and made me sign a paper saying that I was all right 'cause of the way the officers had grabbed me.

Graciela explained why she signed the form.

Because . . . I know . . . there's no way of winning in the county jail. All them sheriffs are gonna stick together. They're gonna take the sheriff's word before they'll take an inmate's word . . . So it's like . . . they'll listen and it's like they're not listening. It goes in one ear and out the other, just to pacify the person. And I wasn't gonna be looked like . . . no fool.

Guards also used other methods for subduing prisoners.

Rita: They could hold them and . . . they used to . . . choke-hold, you know. And . . . they carry the spray around . . . And then they just . . . put 'em against the wall. They just hold them down . . . And they . . . put all their body weight on you, when they have you down.

Perhaps the most discussed form of physical abuse at SBI was the infamous "elevator ride."

Rita: If a woman fought a woman, another inmate in there, they would just break it up and take them both to Lockup. But if you hit a cop they would . . . take 'em on the elevator, . . . turn off the elevator and just beat 'em up and then take 'em out and take 'em to Lockup . . . They don't let you see them beating up on another inmate . . . because they can get in trouble.

Marta: They . . . give you "elevator rides." There's like seven, eight cops in one elevator with the inmate. And supposedly she's going to Lockup. You get her in the elevator and . . . let's say, between four and three . . . he'll stop the elevator. And all of a sudden one will push you, the other one, if she touches him he'll push her back. All of a sudden they just start fucking her up . . . And then . . . after they beat her up, they take her to the infirmary to find out if she's . . . hurt bad . . . Well, shit, you had seven, eight cops on her, how . . . she's not gonna be hurt bad?

Asked when was the last time she heard anyone had been beaten by guards in the elevator, Marta replied:

Shit, how long ago was that? That still goes on every now and then.

Some guards went out of their way to harass prisoners in other ways.

Rita: They sit there and they let your food get cold until they want to serve it to you . . . just to be jerks . . . And sometimes, they keep you sitting up there . . . and your visitor will be down. And then they'll, "Oh, you got a visit!" . . . And sometimes say, "Oops, your visit's gone now."

Sexual harassment and guard favoritism were also evident at SBI.

Lucy: Sure there were favorites . . . I never went that route . . . but my sister would always get to roam and . . . travel from here and there and make sure I had something. I don't know if she would do sex . . . I worked people, but when it came down I wasn't . . . into it. I manipulated.

Cristina: Or if it was a pretty girl, like the officer I always had conflict with, when there was a pretty real nice one he'd sit there and tried to talk to 'em. If you came on to him he treated you good as gold, you know. But if you . . . didn't want to pay attention to him, he got pissed off.

Gina also felt that guards favored African-American but particularly white prisoners.

At Sybil Brand, there's a lot of prejudice. 'Cause you can tell, favoritism . . . Like we'd get written up or something, they'd just get warned, the whites . . . They get the typing. They get the working up front. But . . . you know what? Even the Blacks get better jobs than the Latinas.

Prisoners who refused to cover up for the actions of peers favored by guards could suffer reprisals. For example, Cristina lost her job in the laundry room and as a result her bed in the Honor Dorm when she refused to cover up for a prisoner favored by her supervisor.

In the 1973 class action suit *Inmates of SBI*, prisoners challenged the "inadequate training of guards and supervisors," and the manner in which disciplinary procedures were enforced. Neither the suit nor the 16-week training guards received in the Sheriff's Academy did much to change guards' behavior toward prisoners or the way disciplinary procedures were enforced throughout the period studied.

Guards and Spanish-Monolingual Prisoners

Pintas interviewed felt that guards tended to treat non-English-speaking women and Latinas in general more harshly.

Rosa: I think they treat them worse. They seemed to be more angry with the Latina women and want to catch them at more things and give them harsher punishment. I noticed that more at SBI.

White male guards were particularly harsh with Spanish monolingual prisoners.

Cristina: The white ones, they didn't care . . . They talk to you like dogs, "Go back . . . to TJ!" . . . They would ignore you totally. I mean, if it was . . . a white girl and you were a Mexican, we'd both come for the same thing. They gonna come to me before they go to you, specially 'cause you can't speak my language, "Well, I don't know what you're saying. I can't understand." You know, a shrug off, a push off.

Gina: Sometimes they . . . couldn't understand what they were trying to tell 'em and they'd say, "Stupid wetback!"

There were times when Spanish monolingual prisoners were not allowed to speak in Spanish by guards who did not understand Spanish (Gina).

While pintas expected Chicana/o guards to be more compassionate with Chicana and other Latina prisoners, that was not always the case. There were a few bilingual Chicana/o guards who took the time to address Latina concerns. However, because guards were rotated among the dorms, Spanish monolingual prisoners did not always have access to them.

Cristina: They had some that were bilingual. Like Ms. Winters, she was bilingual and she would tell 'em in Spanish . . . Pay attention to 'em. Sit there and actually conversate with them and see what they need.

As a result of the haphazard way in which translations were provided, Spanish-monolingual prisoners were more likely than their English-speaking peers to be charged with rule violations (Gina).

Rules and Raids

In addition to the relentless verbal, physical, and sexual abuse perpetrated against prisoners, pintas complained of being psychologically battered by excessive and meaningless rules and regulations. Some of these were spelled out in SBI's rule book:

No personal contact is permitted. This includes playing, wrestling, massaging, plucking eyebrows, etc . . . You are not permitted to give, exchange, borrow, or loan ANY personal items such as clothing, shoes, commissary, money, etc . . . Each letter is limited to four (4) pages written on one side only. Do not write in margins . . . You may work on one (1) needlework project at a time. (Watterson 1996: 364)

Sonia further illustrated the numerous ways staff sought to control women's behavior, few of which had anything to do security concerns.

It's real petty in the . . . county . . . It's a lot of dumb . . . rules . . . Like, for an example, . . . two people can't sit in the same bed . . . So if one person's sitting on the end of the bed and you're sitting on the bed, you . . . had to sit with . . . your legs down. You couldn't just kick back and . . . talk on the bed because right away . . . you are accused of [being] homosexual . . . Okay, you couldn't . . . be combing somebody's hair . . . If somebody had a backache you couldn't massage 'em because right away the . . . mentality is "homosexual, homosexual, homosexual." . . . If too many hung around together they thought it was a gang . . . And . . . even the canteen, you know, the things that they sell. They only sell cotton candy and certain things . . . In SBI . . . you have to visit through a glass . . . In the county . . . we couldn't go outside and . . . when we did it . . . you had to go with the . . . dorm whoever. You had to sign in to go . . . outside. You had to sign in to go to church. And you had to be escorted over there and escorted back . . . And . . . in SBI you try to talk to officers and it's really no conversation . . . And . . . it's county soap . . . You have scissors there and the scissors are . . . broken in the ends . . . so you . . . won't pick nobody . . . Let's say you need a haircut . . . and somebody cuts your hair, you get written up for cutting your . . . own hair.

Pintas also complained about excessive restrictions concerning movement within the facility (*LAT* 2/16/77).

Such rules were accompanied by raids. Jail administrators frequently raided dorms searching for contraband, a painful reminder of the destructive raids on their homes by officers on the outside.

Rita: They have raids in there . . . I've been in a few of 'em. They're just like . . . if they were busting down doors in a house. They just run in there with dogs and everything sniffing around . . . They go in there with all kinds of officers and they strip everybody down . . . They tear your beds apart. They . . . shake your stuff and . . . if they feel something in there, they'll empty it all out. They mix your shit with everybody else's shit. Everything just gets all tossed up, you know . . . They'll keep you sitting up for days and days if they wanted to.

The raids were frequent and took place at any time of the day or night.

Rita: Any time of day . . . There's no grace period between times. Believe me . . . I mean, they happened quite often.

Guards frequently carried out raids based on information obtained from snitches, or they manipulated and coerced prisoners into giving them information.

Rita: Or . . . sometimes they . . . plant people in there. And what I mean is that . . . sometimes they . . . have ways of getting information out of inmates . . . You know, like just talking to them and . . . they get real buddy-buddy . . . And maybe . . . they play favoritism towards them and they get information.

The types of items found by guards during one of the raids carried out in Cell Block 5200, the maximum-security block, in July 1986, clearly illustrated that raids often had more to do with harassing and intimidating women prisoners into submission than security.

"We find altered razors, candy above and beyond what they're permitted and excess linens . . . They hoard towels and blankets." (*LAT* 7/13/86)

an unfinished blanket being knitted by one woman, candy bars and cigarettes, shampoo, letters ('excess mail'), as well as mattresses and uniforms. (*LAT* 7/13/86)

"fire hazards"—photographs and magazine cutouts that the women had put up to personalize their cells—were torn off walls. (*LAT* 7/13/86)

Lockdown, Pending Lockup, and Lockup

Prisoners who broke institutional rules or otherwise defied institutional personnel were often locked down in single cells. Prisoners were frequently denied both notice and hearings prior to placement in disciplinary isolation (*Inmates of SBI* 1982b). As the number of prisoners increased during the late 1980s and early 1990s, so did the number of rule violations filed against them.

Estela: Lockdown is when they put you in your dorm, you can't go out for no reason at all . . . You're still in the same dorm but . . . you can't go nowhere. Nobody could come in . . . They'll bring you sack lunches in . . . You can't watch TV . . . You can't get visits. They take everything from you, all your privileges . . . You can't use the phones . . . That's bad enough right there when you can't use the phones because you can't communicate with the outside world. You wanna call your family or whatever, your kids.

Others who broke institutional rules were "routinely placed in disciplinary isolation" or "pending lockup" until a disciplinary hearing was held (*Inmates of SBI* 1982a). Institutional authorities had 72 hours to proceed with the charges. Once the final decision was made, prisoners were either released into General Population or sent to the Adjustment Center cell block, also known as Lockup or The Hole (*LAT* 7/13/86).

The use of "disciplinary isolation" was frequent, ranging from "45 to 50 prisoners per month" (*Inmates of SBI* 1982b).

Victoria: You'd go to . . . [Pending] Lockup first . . . You'd go in there for like a day or . . . a couple of days, and then you'd get a hearing. Yeah, because you're going to Lockup so they stick you in this dorm until they get room in . . . the Lockup cells. And you'd go before . . . a panel of three, the lieutenant, the sergeant, and then the senior . . . sheriff.

Pintas referred to these hearings as "Kangaroo Court" because they tended to rubber stamp guards' original decisions. Prisoners were, nonetheless, allowed to present witnesses on their behalf. Rita described possible hearing outcomes.

Rita: They have Kangaroo Court. And what I mean by Kangaroo Court is you go into a day room, right, . . . they have a senior deputy, an officer, and a sergeant sitting in front of you. They tell you what your charge was, [say] "tier roaming." And the roamings you get . . . automatically three days in the Hole. So they could give you either one day in the Hole and three days suspended, or they can just give you "suspended days." That means if you get in trouble again they give you those suspended days plus the days that you got in jail that you got caught with again, okay. Usually they just give you the three days. If it's packed, they'll give you suspended days. Or they could give you verbal warnings. It depends on the situation . . . Fighting is 10 days . . . If you're stealing, that's another charge . . . If you're caught with paraphernalia, with the syringe, they take you to court in East L.A. . . . If you're caught with possession, they take you to court and I think that's in East L.A. Then they hand it over to Superior Court, L.A.

Prisoners went to Lockup for additional reasons.

Estela: Lockup's for like if you disobey an order, you're caught doing something . . . you shouldn't be doing, . . . fighting.

Graciela: For talking back or for . . . refusing to go to work . . . Or if you get caught with cigarettes now because there's no smoking. [If] you get caught with excess money.

Deborah: Mostly fighting . . . contraband . . . bringing in drugs into the jail . . . fighting with a police officer . . . If somebody's got like hickeys . . . Or they catch you in bed with somebody there, you know.

Victoria: When you sneak from dorm to dorm it's considered roaming, and you can get into Lockup for roaming because they look at it like you can be delivering drugs to a person or . . . anything.

Guards' obsession with preventing "homosecting," that is, sexual activity between prisoners, meant that pintas were sometimes mistakenly sent to Lockup on that charge.

Rosa: There was a lot of talk about people being together sexually in the tank. And they came down and searched all the prisoners to see if you had any marks on you. And I had gotten a mark from fighting. And they said that it was a "monkey bite." And they checked me with a . . . nurse . . . and the nurse said that it was a monkey bite and I ended up in 5000 for four months,[3] until I was released. There was no charge. They just said . . . I couldn't be in General Population because of homosexual activity.

Lockup was located on one side of a cell block containing 24 cells. Prisoners in Lockup were restricted to the cells.

Rita: Lockup . . . The Hole . . . is where you stayed locked down in your cell . . . You don't go out to meals. The meals come to you . . . You have no visits . . . They let you out 15 minutes . . . a day, period . . . You shower . . . and then you go back . . . You can exercise in your cell . . . You can't have no nurses' line[4] . . . If you're prescribed meds, they bring 'em to you . . . You can't shop . . . You can't have no cosmetics . . . All you can have is your shampoo, your comb, and your soap.

Estela: You don't get to use the phones, no TVs, nothing . . . Once in a great while you get a book, and that's only like if somebody leaves a book in there.

She's not allowed to smoke and can have no reading material, no writing material, no candy, and no cigarettes . . . She does not get dessert (Watterson 1996: 71).

Prisoners in Lockup were housed one or two to a cell depending on how crowded the facility was. Cells contained a metal bed, a sink, and a thin mattress. Although other prisoners were prohibited from speaking with those in Lockup, trusties carried messages back and forth from Lockup to the other dorms (Victoria).

Protective Custody

Prisoners held in protective custody, or PC, were generally snitches and women with child abuse or child murder cases and were separated from the General Population, but they enjoyed privileges not given to other prisoners.

Estela: They had their own little rooms . . . Like they had . . . it better than . . . the girls downstairs in the regular dorms . . . Like they got to use the phones whenever they wanted. They got to watch TV and they got their hygiene . . . Their gates open for them until the nighttime . . . nine o'clock . . . There's two to a cell, sometimes one to a cell . . . I used to work cleaning . . . so I used to go in there, you know. And I knew a few of the girls. I used to talk to them.

Prisoners considered to be mentally disturbed were also held isolated from the General Population.

MOs

Mentally ill prisoners were generally housed in the infirmary or in Lockup (*LAT* 7/13/86), where prisoners considered dangerous or disruptive also were held. One of the scariest experiences for pintas was when guards placed mentally ill prisoners temporarily in their cells or shackled them together while being transported to and from court. Such prisoners were eventually housed by themselves. However, guards were mandated by departmental regulations to check up on them every 20 minutes, something they frequently ignored. Guard carelessness sometimes had dire consequences, as when mentally ill prisoners attempted or committed suicide (*LAT* 4/10/73, 2/16/77, 9/7/90).

Linda: I seen a woman slash her throat from one end to the other . . . We kept telling the officers . . . , "The woman is not okay. There's something wrong with her . . . She's gonna do herself in." . . . But they didn't listen to us . . . And in jail, there's such a thing as a "fish-eye." The fish-eye is a person who's getting writ[5] a lot. I mean, they're spacy. This woman had been spacy and we had been telling them . . . This day when . . . somebody came in in the morning, found her with her sliced throat. She did her jugular.

In another case, a prisoner in SBI's psychiatric ward tried to commit suicide by setting her mattress afire with a cigarette given to her by a guard. The flammable urethane mattress was used in the jail despite the fact that between January and September 1979 there had been 48 mattress fires in California detention facilities and the CDC had banned the use of such mattresses in its facilities two years earlier (*LAT* 1/30/79, 12/4/79). Despite the suicide attempts at SBI, as late as 1977 there were still no psychiatrists available to prisoners (*LAT* 2/16/77).

The stories told above demonstrate that the goals of much of the treatment accorded prisoners at SBI had less to do with genuine security concerns than with hindering prisoners' ability to exercise personal agency. The enforcement of excessive and meaningless rules and regulations along with the rampant use of raids in an institution primarily for low-level, nonviolent offenders seemed clearly designed to limit women's individual and collective efforts on their own behalf.

Pintas nevertheless defied the actions of penal staff, sometimes verbally, sometimes physically, much as they had confronted law enforcement officers in their barrios. The price they paid for such resistance, however, was to be further abused by guards and to be isolated for various periods of time from their main source of support, other pintas.

12

Programs and Services

According to the California Board of Corrections (CBC), the types of services and programs offered to county prisoners throughout the state in 1970 were categorized as "work programs, vocational rehabilitation, academic training, correctional services, medical services, and recreation" (CBC 1970: 3). Academic training programs were those offering a high school diploma or a GED (CBC 1970: 43–44). Vocational rehabilitation programs were intended "to teach vocational skills by classroom and/or on-the-job training" (CBC 1970: 41). Correctional services included those that did not fit into any other category, such as social services provided by probation departments, work furlough programs, pre-release services, probation supervision in the community, job and family counseling, Alcoholics Anonymous (AA) and Narcotics Anonymous (NA) meetings, and religious services (COC 1970: 70–71). While some of these were offered by the county, others were sponsored by outside volunteers. These categories did not change much prior to the closing of SBI in 1997.

Several studies have shown the poor quality of health care services and the lack of adequate educational and vocational programs for women in state prisons throughout the United States.[1] Women in jails have even less access to these than women in state prisons. While the services and programs available to male prisoners have never been adequate to meet their needs, incarcerated women have had even less access or options available to them.

This chapter examines the services and programs available to pintas at SBI. They included medical services and a limited number of religious, drug rehabilitation, work furlough, and educational programs. These were rarely adequate, either in terms of quality, availability, or scope, to meet the needs of prisoners. It was partly in an attempt to remedy these conditions that prisoners at SBI filed *Inmates of SBI*.

Health Care Services

The general consensus among pintas interviewed was that the medical services available to prisoners at SBI left much to be desired. During their first two weeks in jail, prisoners were given some pelvic exams and blood tests.

Estela: They do a pap smear . . . The call it a B&V. They do blood and a vaginal. That's mandatory when you go in. Like the first, like, week you get in there, they do all that.

Beyond the initial tests, prisoners received little or no medical attention while incarcerated. Those who were taking medication when they came in frequently got "the wrong dosage or the wrong prescription" (Watterson 1996: 69). As a result of bureaucratic procedures and overtaxed resources due to overcrowding, those who did had to wait long periods of time for basic care (*LAT* 4/10/73, 2/16/77, 12/28/97). To receive medical care, prisoners had to sign up for "sick call."

Estela: You got to sick call . . . Like when you're in the dorm, the nurse comes in the day room every day . . . And you could go in there and you sign up and . . . tell them what's wrong with you whatever and then they call you. But they don't see you till like a week later or so . . . They're not good with you when you're sick. Say like . . . I have the flu. You gotta go sign up for the doctor. It'll take you a week from the day you sign up to see the doctor . . . You know, if you have high blood pressure, . . . you need medication, it's gonna take you a week to go back and get that medication. Now, in between that time you can have a stroke . . . 'cause they're too slow . . . Like when I went in there and I told them I had asthma . . . They said, "Well how do you know you have asthma?" I said, "I was born with it." . . . But they didn't believe me . . . It took . . . two weeks for them to call me back and take my blood pressure and . . . they finally gave me my medication.

Another major problem with the health care system at SBI concerned the delivery of emergency medical care. Prisoners first had to convince guards on duty, who were not medical personnel, that a medical emergency existed (*LAT* 4/10/73, 12/28/97). The infirmary staff then decided over the phone if it was an emergency.

Estela: Tell the officer . . . and they call up to the infirmary. And then, if they feel it's an emergency they'll send you up right then and there. But if not, well, they'll tell you, "Go to sick call tomorrow." And then you gonna sign up for sick call.

Lucy: Sybil Brand, with it being so full and packed and time-consuming, it takes a couple of days before you're ever pulled out . . . to go to the doctor . . . I've known people that . . . have lost kids. Or were sick and kept telling people and actually where the family . . . did it on behalf of them. People . . . were pregnant and . . . were having pain. They thought they were sniveling . . . so they like miscarried . . . People who have had pneumonia. I mean, you know, just stuff. We'd sit there and laugh and joke around. "You have to be dead!"

Pintas all commented on the harsh treatment prisoners at SBI received from the medical personnel.

Deborah: I can't even see how they called themselves medical staff . . . But . . . they were just cold, cold people . . . There was just nothing you can remember good about them. They weren't . . . like . . . gonna sit you down, "Are you okay?" and "How do you feel?" . . . They just herd you in like cattle and herd you out.

Addicts seldom received medical treatment when they were withdrawing from heroin or other drugs (*LAT* 4/10/73, 2/16/77).

Linda: The first time I hit Sybil Brand was when I was 18 . . . I was coming off the drugs and I was coming off the alcohol. All I remember is laying on a cement floor and that was it . . . I never got the medical attention. The only thing they ever did to me was throw me in a cell . . . They'd throw me by myself.

Rita: Every time it's different . . . If you don't complain and you just kick on your own, you just kick on your own . . . Sometimes . . . they give you this . . . Med-Card . . . for two weeks or for a week . . . and you go up three times a day . . . They just have these pills that they just give you . . . But then, one time 'cause I was kicking methadone, I was kicking so bad I had blackouts so they hospitalized me for like two weeks in the infirmary, and they were giving me medication to help me to eat . . . I couldn't even walk to the meals so I was housed in a bed in the infirmary.

While little attention was given to addicts kicking drugs at SBI, a significant number of prisoners were overmedicated by doctors who prescribed legal drugs. A federal study conducted at SBI during 1975 and 1976 found that doctors prescribed tranquilizers and mood stabilizers to more than 50% of the jail's prisoners (*LAT* 8/11/77; Glick and Moore 1990). Critics claimed that prisoners were being unnecessarily medicated both because they were women and because drugging made them easier to control. Eventually budget cuts and outside criticisms led to a change in drugging practices at the facility.[2]

Other medical irregularities plagued the facility until its closure in 1997. These included the failure to conduct necessary medical tests, misdiagnosis of patients, giving prisoners the wrong dosage of medications, failure to provide follow-up care, contradictory entries made in medical charts, and the loss of medical charts (*LAT* 12/18/97).

In response to medical and dental care conditions and the death of a prisoner, Nancy Elizabeth Douglas, both individual[3] and class action suits were filed against the county in 1973 (*LAT* 4/10/73; *Inmates of SBI* 1982a). The class action suit argued:

As a direct and proximate result of defendants' practices and policies, including the failure to adequately diagnose prisoners at admission, control of access to medical care by non-medical personnel, and failure to provide emergency medical care on weekends, Nancy Elizabeth Douglas died in her cell at the jail on Sunday, Aug. 20, never having received any medical aid. (*Inmates of SBI* 1982a).

HIV and AIDS

A significant number of injecting drug users were sentenced to SBI, where drugs were available and needles frequently shared. This meant that the number of prisoners who were HIV-positive or had AIDS was presumably high. However, the actual numbers were unknown because prisoners were not legally mandated to take HIV tests, and those who wanted one had to submit a written request. Moreover, those who tested positive for HIV were generally not willing to disclose that information to others. In fact, the secrecy around one's HIV status was so high among pintas that not one of those interviewed admitted that she was HIV-positive or had AIDS. Many did say they were HIV-negative.

While those who were HIV-positive or had AIDS were supposed to receive medical attention, Marta exclaimed, "I never heard of anybody getting any." In fact, as late as 1997, when SBI was closed, it was common for prisoners in Los Angeles County jails to be denied HIV and AIDS medication for days at a time (*LAT* 12/28/97). The neglect was so severe that in 1994 a court order was issued mandating the LASD to provide medication to patients with HIV and AIDS. The neglect shown such prisoners characterized the type of medical treatment given to other county prisoners suffering from life-threatening illnesses such as asthma, tuberculosis, and diabetes (ibid.). The lack of adequate health care services was also evident in the jail's infirmary.

The Infirmary

Even prisoners housed in the jail's infirmary received minimal care. Cristina, who was held in the infirmary for 10 days, did not receive the special diet her diabetes required.

And then for me being diabetic I was supposed to get a special plate and never got it . . . You gotta have good hamburger meat, not all this synthetic stuff they give you . . . I call it "blow up food" 'cause you go in there thin and you . . . come out like a fat pig . . . And they gave me regular food, which I couldn't eat . . . This was at the hospital. That they knew I was a diabetic—that's why I was put there . . . All I did was eat the damn prunes.

Pregnant prisoners were not treated much better than diabetics, though they were given vitamins and regular checkups. Prisoners known to have seizures or insulin attacks were frequently assigned to sleep in the top bunks, contrary to institutional regulations.

Cristina: This girl had a seizure during our . . . roll call. She . . . fell from the top bunk, hit her head, and went to the bottom . . . Do you know when they brought her back they put her on the same damn bunk!

Aside from having their food brought to them, prisoners were locked in the infirmary all day receiving little other attention from guards or medical personnel.

Cristina: There's nobody really in there but you and the other inmates. They lock the door. They come in there, check your pulse, temperature, and they're gone. Bring you food, they're gone . . . You're there by yourself in that room all day . . . You had to scream if you wanted attention, yeah, or pound on the window.

Prisoners housed in the mental observation part of the infirmary, called MOs by prisoners, were equally ignored although guards were required to check on them every 20 minutes (*LAT* 9/7/90).

Cristina: The floor above me was where they had the MOs . . . And they had some on our floor too. Mentally OBs, they . . . strapped . . . 'em in four points sometimes. Where they strap your legs and your arms down. Oh, you can hear 'em screaming sometimes.

The treatment of mentally ill prisoners by LASD was so negligent that during the 1990s the U.S. Department of Justice ordered LASD to improve care for mentally ill prisoners or face a federal lawsuit (*LAT* 12/28/97).

In another infirmary incident, staff negligence led a prisoner to have her baby in the ward's hallway when staff members delayed attending to her.

Cristina: That's where we got to see a girl have her baby on the floor in the hallway . . . Then they shipped her to . . . MC, something like that. It's a hospital that they work with . . . Checked it out . . . Stitch her up, whatever they do, and brought her right back.

Prisoners in the infirmary responded to medical emergencies by assisting one another.

Cristina: If someone got sick in there where we couldn't handle it . . . or if . . . someone would fall off the bed . . . , if we couldn't help you, it don't get done. They rarely checked on you 'cause they'd just lock the door and you're there . . . The inmates do more for the inmates than the medical staff. They'd get the toothbrush or a comb and they'd put [it] on . . . the seizure victim's tongue so she don't swallow it.

The support prisoners gave one another in the infirmary showed how prisoners were able to put aside racial, ethnic, and barrio differences to form alliances that would allow them to survive incarceration together.

At SBI, medical malpractice and negligent medical care sometimes led to the death of prisoners. Marta described two incidents during her imprisonment when prisoners died as a result of inadequate medical care.

There was two of 'em in Sybil Brand that have died behind medical problems. One of 'em . . . had high blood pressure and was a diabetic, and the other had those grand mal seizures. Yeah, she would have 'em back to back . . . And they would take 'em to the infirmary. As soon as they come out, they said, "Okay, you're all right. Go back to your dorm." And then she's going back to her dorm she . . . has another one . . . and bit herself to where she bled and choked herself in her blood . . . And that was just leaving the infirmary . . . She was a *gavacha*.

In the second case, a Mexican immigrant died the day after having been sent back to her dorm following a seizure.

The irregularities in health care services continued to plague the facility until its closing in 1997. As late as 1996 a wrongful death suit was filed by the family of Andra J. Reynolds, who died as a result of medical irregularities while at SBI (*LAT* 12/28/97).

Programs

During the early 1960s and 1970s, ceramics, handicrafts, and sewing work rooms were available at the facility (*LAT* 1/26/64; Watterson 1996). By 1986, a few additional programs had become accessible to prisoners. However, due to the limited offerings and scope of the programs plus severe overcrowding, few prisoners had access to them. Such programs included GED classes, parenting classes, arts and crafts (*LAT* 5/15/86), AA, and NA. They were offered by civilian personnel or outside agencies once or twice during the week.

School

Pintas who knew English and had dropped out of high school could study for a GED while at SBI and receive a degree through the Hacienda/La Puente School District (*LAT* 12/6/93). Sometimes classes were also scheduled for Spanish-monolingual prisoners (Graciela). Other classes offered intermittently included cosmetology and office skills.

The importance of educational programs cannot be overestimated, given the fact that almost all of the pintas interviewed had dropped out of school before finishing high school. While some were able to complete high school or acquire their GED while in jail or prison, at the time of the interview 11 out of the 21 pintas interviewed for whom information was available still had not finished high school or gotten a GED.

Pintas were generally concerned about pursuing their education and were aware that without additional schooling it was difficult to secure better-paying and lawful employment. Nonetheless, it was difficult, even for those who did not use drugs while in jail, to focus on continuing their education. Pintas' time in jail was taken up by detoxing from or using drugs, socializing with other prisoners, and working.

The scarcity of educational programs at the facility remained basically unchanged during SBI's existence despite the filing of *Inmates of SBI*, in which prisoners complained of the lack of educational and vocational programs.

Arts and Crafts Classes

During the early 1970s, when Kathryn Watterson (1996) visited SBI prisoners had access to a craft workshop. While in some institutions women prisoners were allowed to sell the products they produced, this was not the case at SBI.

The women don't make money individually for the things they make in craft shop programs. That money theoretically goes into the inmate welfare fund to pay for the various activities and to provide occasional cigarettes, soap, or toothpaste for destitute women who don't have anyone to bring them money from the outside. (Watterson 1996: 231)

During the mid-1980s, arts and crafts classes were still available to prisoners and included a ceramics workshop.

Estela: They have ceramics . . . You're in a certain dorm and you go work out there and you paint the ceramics.

However, access to classes was limited because prisoners had to pay for their supplies. There was also a program for prisoners to learn tile setting (*LAT* 5/15/86).

Parenting Classes

One of the difficulties prisoners faced when entering SBI concerned the regulations regarding child visitors. Until April 1973 children were prohibited from visiting their mothers (*LAT* 4/10/73). While SBI could claim that it did not have adequate facilities for children to visit their mothers, the treatment accorded prisoners by staff clearly demonstrated that many of them did not think women prisoners were or could ever be good mothers. Therefore, it was best for the children not to be exposed to them. Ignored was the psychological harm done to both mother and children who were separated from one another, especially if the children were young and had little understanding of the reasons for the forced separation.

In response to the filing of *Inmates of SBI* in February 1973, jail administrators began to allow children to visit their mothers for the first time. However, the children were processed as adults into the jail. That is, they were searched for contraband and were not allowed contact visits (*LAT* 12/8/78). They spoke to their mothers only through a glass window while using a telephone. This proved scary and painful for both children and mothers who wanted to hold one another at a time when they needed the most support. As a result, some pintas opted not to have their children visit them while they were incarcerated.

It was not until the introduction of parenting classes in 1982 that prisoners were allowed to have contact visits with their children. Parenting classes were run by the Hacienda/La Puente School District. They were available to English-speaking male and female Los Angeles County prisoners. Prisoners registered for classes on a first-come, first-served basis. While some parents participated in the classes voluntarily, others were mandated by the courts to take the classes if they wanted to regain custody of their children upon release.

Although prisoners did not necessarily assume, as criminal justice personnel did, that they were inadequate parents just because they were in jail, they were required to take the classes if they wanted to have contact visits with their children for two hours on Saturday. The classes, however, were available only to a small number of the 2,300 prisoners held at SBI in 1993, nearly 75% of whom were mothers and 10% of whom were pregnant (*LAT* 12/6/93).

Cristina: I was in . . . a program . . . parenting classes . . . You had to keep these classes up so you can see your kids. You were required the first three. So I kept going and it got to where you got to see your kids on a Saturday for two hours. They actually came in the gate. They didn't search 'em or nothing. They couldn't bring in bottles or diapers. We had that on the inside . . . You'd work with them, arts and crafts . . . They would . . . fingerpaint, sing, play, dance, write songs. And we'd give them a book before they leave, you know, a little gift. We give it to 'em and they'd bring it home . . . to remember.

In 1984, the parenting classes were expanded to include in the jail's visiting system a program called Teaching and Loving Kids, or TALK (*LAT* 12/6/1993).

HIV and AIDS Education

In view of the limited services offered to prisoners who were HIV-positive or had AIDS (see also Chapter 16), during the 1990s an HIV and AIDS education course was offered by a Chicano advocate at the facility.

Lucy: I think every other Monday . . . they would have the AIDS guy come in there. And then they would call certain names. If you were a new . . . fish . . . then you would just go ahead and have to sit in there.

Marta: And then they said, ". . . They have a . . . group . . . and you can go in there if you want and . . . you learn about it." . . . And so I did . . . He's a man that comes out from the street. And he has a class for about an hour . . . And . . . it made me think . . . not to share needles with anybody . . . And if you do, bleach 'em . . . , you know.

Such counseling was necessary not only to support prisoners who were HIV-positive or had AIDS, but also to educate their peers, many of whom rejected prisoners with AIDS because of ignorance about the disease.

Marta: They didn't wanna be around them. I used to . . . tell 'em, "Why do you do that to them? You know, you make 'em feel uncomfortable." "Well, I don't want them next to me."

Vocational Programs

During the early 1970s, male prisoners in California county jails had access to a number of vocational programs. These included laundry, maintenance, work furlough, garage, bakery, print shop, carpentry, auto maintenance, toy repair, and academic programs (CBC 1970: 53). Although they were classified as vocational programs, according to CBC, "their primary *effect* is to obtain labor from inmates" (ibid.: 52–53). That is, "the overwhelming majority of vocational and on-the-job training programs currently offered appeared to be for the county government's benefit and *not* for the inmates" (ibid.: 61).

Women at SBI had access to a small number of these programs including laundry, maintenance, auto detailing, sewing, and doll repair for charitable causes. They also performed other major jobs that helped keep the institution running (see Chapter 12). However, the number of women involved in these programs was small. Also, according to CBC, the county's sewing program, which was "almost entirely restricted to female inmates . . . was almost the *only* type of training program available for women in county jails" (CBC 1970: 53).

During the early 1970s, male prisoners had access to a work furlough program as well as college educational furloughs (CBC 1970: 5). While work furlough programs allowed prisoners to work outside the institution during the day and return to the jail after work, college educational furlough allowed prisoners to attend college during the day. Both of these were denied to women prisoners at SBI.

In response, the 1973 *Inmates of SBI* (1982a, 1982b) class action suit alleged that women prisoners were being discriminated against by not being offered the same work opportunities afforded male prisoners. The suit claimed that the only work available to women prisoners was menial jobs that were necessary to the functioning of the institution but did not prepare them for gainful employment. Shortly after the suit was filed, jail administrators instituted a work furlough program at SBI (*LAT* 8/19/72, 3/16/73). Once available, however, the program was accessible to only a small number of prisoners.

In 1989 LASD established a prisoner information program whereby prisoners at SBI answered calls from the general public concerning prisoners' "housing location, charge, bail, and next court date" (LASD 1989). Training for the program was provided by the Hacienda/La Puente School District.

While it is true that pintos, even when skilled laborers, had a difficult time obtaining work after their release from jail due to employer prejudices and competition from other men, pintas who had learned how to sew at SBI, for example, had to compete for intermittent and low-paying jobs in the sewing industry with more experienced and skilled workers. Moreover, those few pintas who had acquired skills in traditional men's work (e.g., maintenance, auto detailing) had to compete with men for the same jobs in male-dominated fields.

Alcohol and Drug Rehabilitation Programs

Two of the most consistent sources of outside support for Chicana addicts in jail were provided by AA and NA. While the meetings were conducted in English, Spanish-monolingual prisoners could attend them and arrange to have one of the bilingual speakers take them to a Spanish-speaking meeting upon their release from SBI. While pintas interviewed were aware of the existence of the meetings, only a handful tried to recover from addiction while in jail.

Rosa: I went to . . . AA but not for recovery. It was just to get out . . . of the dorms or out of the tanks . . . And I think most of us did that.

Sonia: When I started going to NA . . . I used to go in Sybil Brand. But I used to go only to go check out the women or just to get out of the dorm.

During the early 1990s, a drug rehabilitation program called Reach was begun at SBI. Reach was started because jail administrators finally acknowledged the rampant use of drugs at the facility (Deborah). Despite the demand for the program, however, only about 25 prisoners could participate in it at a given time. Prisoner participation was also limited because only sentenced prisoners could participate. At the time, more than 50% of SBI's population was composed of pretrial prisoners.

Religious Groups

In 1988 SBI had full-time Catholic and Protestant chaplains, weekly Christian Science and Islamic services, and a rabbi for occasional services (*LAT* 4/30/88). While most pintas came from families that identified themselves as Catholic or "Christian," only a few spoke about attending religious services while incarcerated. Immigrants from Latin America were more likely than Chicanas to attend such services. This was partly so because it was the only program consistently available in Spanish.

Generally, however, the resistance among pintas to religious groups was partly due to their own sense of guilt and shame about their lifestyles and to the historical condemnation by organized religion of "fallen" women. Many pintas interviewed were also hesitant to attend religious services run by white women chaplains. Prisoners sometimes found them condescending, and at least one chaplain publicly referred to prisoners as "children" (*LAT* 4/30/88).

Estela: We had the Catholic chaplain lady . . . She was a really nice lady . . . That Protestant lady though, ugh, she was . . . terrible . . . Like . . . we're coming out and she'd . . . squeeze your hand . . . and she'd say, "Hurry up and get out!" . . . She was white.

Victory Outreach, an evangelical Christian church, was particularly appealing to Chicana addicts because it had a strong ministry in the Chicana/o community of East Los Angeles. It specifically reached out to addicts, sex workers, prisoners, and former prisoners. A significant number of its members and some of its ministers were former addicts. An additional attraction was that the group offered prisoners limited financial assistance after their released from jail.

Marta: That's a . . . Christian church that they go to, a lot of 'em do, Latinas . . . Once they're ready to get out they . . . put up a pad for them . . . and their rent is paid for maybe two months until they get on their feet . . . Every other Saturday they have a car wash to help people . . . that need help.

Recreation

Aside from the programs discussed above and entertainment events brought in sporadically by outside volunteers, there was little in terms of organized recreation provided to prisoners at SBI. While prisoners who had yard privileges could join some of their friends in the yard for a short time each day, the size of the yard did not allow for all prisoners to be there at the same time.

Prisoners did keep themselves occupied in other ways such as working institutional jobs, playing cards, watching television, reading books, getting high, getting involved in sexual relationships with other prisoners and staff (see subsequent chapters), and, when allowed, using the law library.

In *Inmates of SBI* prisoners sought redress for some of these conditions by challenging the denial of direct access to the general library, limited access to the law library, limited recreation time, and the multiple restrictions placed on the receipt and use of magazines.

In response to the lawsuit, in 1982 pre-trial and sentenced prisoners were allowed two one-hour outdoor recreation periods a week. Male prisoners in county jails, however, were allowed outdoor recreation time on a daily basis.

While some minor changes were made in terms of access to the general library and access to magazines sent in from the outside, overcrowded conditions combined with restrictive jail policies continued to keep prisoners from having adequate access to all of these, but particularly to recreation time and the law library.

Spanish-Monolingual Prisoners, Programs, and Staff

While the number of programs available to prisoners who spoke English was limited, those available to Spanish-monolingual prisoners were even more scarce.

Graciela: Church services were done in English and Spanish at a certain hour. And your school is done in Spanish at a certain hour, English at a certain hour . . . They have NA, AA. But that's . . . if the people that are coming in, if they speak Spanish, they speak Spanish, if they don't they don't. There's nothing really scheduled for Spanish-speaking people to come in.

As late as 1992, only five (2%) of the 260 staff members at SBI spoke Spanish (Kolts 1992: 195). Although not all Chicana/o guards knew Spanish, even those who did sometimes refused to speak it with prisoners.

Deborah: There was Chicana guards in there . . . But they didn't speak Spanish . . . As a matter of fact, Deputy Officer Bolivar I know speaks Spanish, . . . but she speaks English to the inmates.

Spanish-monolinguals were generally ignored by guards.

Gina: The staff don't pay attention to them because they can't speak Spanish, and the ones that can speak Spanish don't wanna speak Spanish.

Although the need for translation services grew as a result of the continuing increase in the number of immigrants from Latin America incarcerated at SBI, at no time did pintas interviewed see institutional rules and regulations translated into Spanish.[4] Nor did they ever see translation provided for non-English-speaking prisoners in the receiving area, where they were first introduced into the facility.

Lucy: They just stood there like they're dumb. Have someone else translate for them, or you just pull them off to the side 'cause you feel sorry for them . . . and then translate . . . the best that you could . . . the best that I could.

Faced with these difficulties, Spanish-monolingual prisoners frequently learned what needed to be done "by seeing what everybody else does" (Deborah).

The lack of bilingual staff extended to personnel in other areas of the facility such as teachers, cooks, counselors, psychiatrists, doctors, and nurses. None of the pintas remembered seeing a doctor speak in Spanish to a prisoner, although for a time there was a bilingual Chicana nurse available during some work shifts (Estela).

Deborah: They have teachers but . . . none of 'em were bilingual . . . There are no bilingual teachers in there . . . right now [1996].

Spanish-monolingual prisoners sought the help of the few bilingual civilian staff and outside volunteers available.

Deborah: They go to the chaplain . . . There's a . . . couple of chaplains in there that speak Spanish . . . They would seek Friends Outside.[5]

The lack of bilingual personnel meant that bilingual Latinas performed most of the translations in the facility. Frequently staff members requested their services. At other times they volunteered to translate.

Monolingual prisoners also sought them out for assistance.

Marta: And . . . if they do need anything they'll come up, *Marta, ¿me haces un favor mi'ja?* . . . *¿Le puedes a preguntar al . . . policía cuando voy pa' corte . . . ?*[6] You know, whatever . . . And to get socks or underpants, bras, you know, how to sign up . . . to see the chaplain. "Can . . . you ask him . . . if they could call the infirmary 'cause I don't feel good."

Victoria: If we'd see someone like in trouble or not understanding and we see a sheriff yelling at 'em . . . we'd go up, *¿Qué es la problema?* . . . *El me dice que . . . no puedo agarrar un jabón de aquí.*[7] . . . I . . . just remember that . . . it used to be really basic stuff that these sheriffs didn't really have a lot of training in . . . regards to . . . telling them things . . . Like where to get the soap, what shower works the best, how to get shoes, . . . where to go to school, how to get to the . . . health office upstairs. You know, real basic . . . needs. Like I said, the . . . washing soap for the machine . . . and soap for their body, and how to fill out . . . the county . . . issue. You know, which . . . back then . . . you would of get a couple of packages of deodorant, that powdered toothpaste, a toothbrush, a comb, and a razor, and maybe like a bar of soap.

13

Jailhouse Economy

SBI administrators were responsible for providing prisoners housing and minimal goods and services including food, clothing, and some toiletries. While some items, such as jail uniforms, were distributed to prisoners upon entering the facility, others, like sanitary napkins, were rationed out on a "need basis." Additional goods were sold in the institution's commissary and in dorms with access to vending machines. The supplies provided by the jail, including food, however, were rarely sufficient to meet prisoners' needs.

Prisoners, on the other hand, wanted access not only to more basic necessities than those provided meagerly by the county but to a host of other items. While some of these items could be mailed or brought to prisoners by third parties, that is, families, friends, partners, and the like, others, such as illegal drugs, had to be smuggled into the facility.

Pintas' access to desired goods, whether sold by the facility or smuggled in, was limited by lack of financial resources to buy them. Those they knew on the outside also had limited resources. This was particularly true of women relatives who generally took in the children of incarcerated Chicanas and therefore had their own incomes strained to the limit by the added responsibilities. Likewise, the partners of pintas interviewed were frequently addicts themselves and could not be counted on for long-term support. As a result, pintas were forced to devise creative ways to meet their own needs and desires just as they had on the outside.

In view of the above, some of the questions explored in this chapter are: What types of goods and services were most desired by pintas? How did they acquire them? Who provided them?

Work Assignments

Prisoners often gained access to goods they could sell and barter in the underground jailhouse market through their work assignments.

Work assignments were generally made by the Classification Committee upon a prisoner's entrance into the facility. In designating work assignments the Classification Committee took into account a prisoner's acquired skills before incarceration, willingness to learn new skills, and preferences of work supervisors for one prisoner or another. While some pintas chose not to, most preferred to work.

Rita: If you don't wanna work then you sit there and you don't do nothing . . . If you're just sitting there doing nothing . . . and waiting to get sentenced or just sitting there killing time, 'cause they just refuse to work for the county, . . . your time's gonna drag and you're gonna get bored and you're gonna get frustrated . . . There are some there like that. You know, "Well, I'm not gonna work. Shit! . . . They ain't paying me for it."

Nonetheless, not all prisoners who wanted to work could do so because of the limited number of jobs available.

With few exceptions, work supervisors were guards, although civilians could be found working in clerical positions, teaching, the laundry room, sewing room, and kitchen. Guards' recommendations generally influenced the decisions of the Classification Committee. Chicanas repeatedly sentenced to SBI were sometimes able to use their previous acquaintance with guards to maneuver themselves into getting preferred assignments.

A large number of prisoners were employed in the laundry and the sewing room. Another large number worked in the prisoner and staff kitchens. Cleaning crews could be seen working throughout the facility. Those working on the docks loaded and unloaded food and other supplies. A few prisoners worked in receiving, where they helped process newly admitted prisoners. While prisoners were not allowed to work in the commissary, a few worked in the closet, distributing clothes to prisoners and cleaning up the state dorms after guard raids. Prisoner clerks performed secretarial duties, while beauticians or barbers cut hair for both staff and prisoners. Some prisoners also repaired dolls for charitable causes, such as children with disabilities (CBC 1970).

According to Captain Helena Ashby, in charge of SBI during the mid-1980s,

[h]ere we make all our clothes, do all the cooking, all the cleaning, all the laundry, all the painting, all the tiling, and run the infirmary. (LAT 7/13/86)

According to pintas interviewed, as of 1996 only three positions, shoe shine, car wash, and laundry for staff, were paid. Prisoners were paid for washing and also for making blouses for guards "through their employee fund" (Watterson 1996: 231).

During the late 1960s and early 1970s, for example, washing and ironing a blouse paid three cents, of which two

were divided between the laundress and the ironer, and one goes to the soap fund, since the officers aren't allowed to use county soap to wash their blouses (ibid.).

While prisoners were otherwise not paid, time was taken off their sentences in exchange for working (Graciela).

Rita: There's no pay . . . If you work you get time, Good Time . . . And what I mean by that is like you get time off [your sentence] . . . There's only two jobs specifically that you could actually get paid in . . . the county facility, and that's auto detailing, that's washing cars, and . . . laundry for press, to iron officers' uniforms.

Cristina: They wash the cops' car, their personal cars. And the shoe shiner goes around any . . . officer that wants his shoes shined.

Work assignments preferred by prisoners included "visiting, reception, and ODR" (Rita). Those jobs allowed them access to visitors, other prisoners, and better food.

Rita: The officers' meal . . . 'cause . . . you could eat good 'cause you could eat what they eat . . . And the reception is because you see everybody coming in and . . . because you see all your friends . . . You know, you see 'em going in and out of court . . . You make [bed] roll-ups for the new bookies. You get court line ready. You feed the people that come in in the morning, . . . people that are getting transferred out . . . Actually, it's kind of hard, though, because you clean up all the holding tanks . . . and it smells bad down there . . . As people be staying down there for hours and hours . . . So . . . it's not like a real kick-back but . . . that was one of the good jobs . . . everybody liked.

The visiting room was considered an easy job, or in the words of prisoners it was a "kick-back job" (Rita).

Rita: Visiting, where you . . . sit there and you . . . call the inmates for their visits . . . You just tell 'em where to sit . . . You just write . . . who got the visit, at what time they came in, what time they left . . . But you see . . . your friends in different dorms and you get to talk to them.

Prisoners could enhance the privileges that accompanied work assignments depending on the type of relationships they had with work supervisors. Guards' favoritism was apparent in the privileges they granted or withheld prisoners working under them.

Rita: Like, okay, if you're working in the ODR, . . . it's up to the officer if they let you eat . . . the officers' food . . . Now, say . . . he lets me but not you, and then if he sees you eating . . . you're gonna Lockup up 'cause that's stealing for them.

Work shifts varied depending on the type of work assignment and whether prisoners were housed in the county or state side.

While some prisoners felt that racial discrimination determined jobs assignments, others felt that prisoners' sentence length was the determining factor.

Runners

One of the most frequent observations made about prisoners is that when a man is incarcerated the women in his life (e.g., partner, mother, sister) provide him and his children emotional and financial support. His partner will visit him, send him money and packages, take care of their children, and take them to see him.

Incarcerated women also receive support from women in their lives, but it is seldom as extensive as that given male prisoners. Sexist societal norms that deem women who break the law to be more immoral than men have meant that women prisoners receive less support from loved ones or others. Further, male partners seldom stick around when women go to jail, especially if the men are addicts themselves.

Nonetheless, some pintas were able to tap into "runners" on the outside who looked out for them. Runners included family members, partners, friends, "sugar daddies," or "tricks." Lucy and Carmen described the roles played by runners.

Lucy: Someone who's out there on the street, who's giving you money, . . . supporting us from the outside . . . Who would . . . just go ahead and put some money on their books or . . . bring them . . . underwear, socks . . . Come and visit them and make sure whatever they need to be done . . . in the outside world, that they would be the one who would see to it getting done.

Carmen: They had pimps out there or sugar daddies who would take care of 'em, you know, . . . or their families or kids.

Few runners, however, were a consistent source of support. This was so because most were poor themselves. Some also had to provide for their own children and those of pintas. Others were themselves in the throes of addiction.

Mercedes: At one point in time [my] boyfriend used to come and see me often, bring me money . . . I remember one time I even told him I was pregnant and I wasn't . . . you know, just to have a . . . runner . . . 'Cause . . . partners that are addicts are never positive support systems. Basically, they continue to use and . . . you get forgotten in there.

Until at least 1991, county prisoners were allowed to have up to $40 in cash in their possession. After that, money was replaced by tokens, and prisoners were sent to Lockup if they were found holding cash. Money or tokens were used to buy a host of products sold in the institution's commissary, including toiletries, books, paper, envelopes, stamps, food, and more:

Rita: Cosmetics, makeup . . . deodorant, shampoo, combs, the newspaper, candies, peanuts, coffee. I don't know if they came up with sugar yet, but I know they used to sell coffee, no sugar . . . Not cigarettes no more but before, cigarettes, soups . . . you know, the soup broth.

Chicanas who were repeatedly incarcerated developed a network of friends and acquaintances inside the jail who looked out for them through the years.

Rita: As soon as they say, "Hey, Rita, what's up?" "Nothing, fix me up, man." Bam! I had it! . . . They'd give you a nice dress, you know . . . Because it's . . . like they knew you were a regular already . . . The other inmates in there. You get to know people going in and out, in and out.

Pintas supplemented the inside and outside support they received by bartering or selling goods and services. "Canteen or shoes, underwear and socks that are allowed to come in" (Graciela).

Mercedes: I didn't like to do your normal things in jail, play cards, have lovers . . . I mean, I was with . . . one woman and, basically, I was an artist . . . To me . . . that was my forte. That was my . . . heart. That was my interest. That was my escape from that institution, from that system . . . I bartered or sold.

Graciela: The . . . girls have jewelry on . . . when they get busted. If they don't come off their fingers they keep 'em. Some of them act like they don't come off so they trade 'em and sell 'em for money. They don't have people on the outside. They sneak their jewelry in when they're getting booked in.

Rita: Somebody would tell you, ". . . why don't you do that and I'll . . . buy you a candy bar or something." You know, ironed their shirts, their pants.

The most coveted goods were food and clothing. While some pintas sold goods stolen from their work assignments, others gave them away.

Rita: If . . . you work in the kitchen you can make up the burritos with the stuff that they have in there, real good, healthy-ass burritos, and take 'em back to the dorm and sell 'em . . . And you sell cookies, cakes . . . They sell the coffee . . . Whatever they have there . . . you're gonna sell it.

Rita: They had a lot of scandalous stuff going on in there, people selling county shoes, county underwear, county bras, the soap . . . They'd sell anything that belongs to the county, socks, dress, towels. If they had extra and they knew you were a new fish coming in and . . . they knew you needed the stuff, they would sell it to you . . . Me, personally, . . . if I wanted to help somebody, I'll just help 'em out . . . I remember this one lady, she knew I was working the kitchen. I've known her for a while, in and out of the system. She said, "Hey, Rita if they have anything extra, why don't you bring it down?" . . . Now, either you could sell it to them and make money off it or you can give it to them. Me, I just gave it to 'em 'cause I felt maybe they were . . . hungry still . . . And . . . it was free stuff to me . . . If I seen a friend of mine going to court and she wanted a . . . nice jacket or a nice dress and I worked in the closet, and she'll say, "Hey, man, I gotta go to court." You don't wanna go to court with your dress all wrinkled and the . . . judge will look at you like . . . you just arrested . . . You wanna look presentable . . . Because . . . that makes a lot of difference when you're in court, and especially if you're on trial.

Mercedes discussed how she established a "store" within the jail.

And I . . . had a store . . . At that time . . . we were allowed . . . money . . . So you got a good price . . . You know, you got charged 50 cents for a candy, you charged a dollar . . . I'd buy shampoo. I'd buy conditioner . . . I had to have lipstick, girl! . . . You know, it was survival. It was being able to be a little bit comfortable in that . . . kind of . . . setting.

Enterprising prisoners also took advantage of the fact that the commissary was closed on the weekends.

Rita: There's no commissary on weekends and you have a lot of new fish coming in during the weekends . . . Friday nights they drug-raid every area that you can think of, and the cops bring 'em all in to . . . Sybil Brand . . . And these people are kicking, going through withdrawal, going through changes, and they want candy. They wanna be eating up all that sugar . . . So you buy a candy for 50 cents. You could . . . sell it for a $1 or for a $1.50, sometimes on Sundays $2 . . . Cigarettes, the roll-ups, five bucks for a roll of cigarettes this big, this thin (showing a small, thin cigarette) . . . There's money to be made in those jails.

Lucy: I was always going out to court because I always had these Mickey Mouse things that I had, and had to clear all of those counties . . . So I . . . always . . . get to have a trip . . . So what you would be able to do would be like take in some cigarettes from the state because no one in the county had cigarettes . . . Keester them and put them up there. And you could . . . break a cigarette down to four . . . You pinner them . . . One cigarette there you'll make . . . anywhere from $20 to $30.

After penal authorities prohibited smoking in jails and prisons throughout California during the 1990s, cigarettes became even more expensive, $10 to $15 each (Graciela).

The underground jailhouse economy also involved the sale of legal drugs prescribed by jail doctors and the trafficking of illegal drugs such as heroin, marijuana, and rock cocaine (Deborah). Drugs were smuggled into SBI by visitors, newly admitted prisoners, guards, and civilian workers.

Estela: The girls that were getting busted or like people getting visits would . . . smuggle it in through the tennis shoes or bras . . . Guards too . . . A lot of them bring in drugs . . .

Rita: Prisoners and county workers, . . . civilians . . . You can keester the drugs up in you when you come in. You know you're going to court and you know they're gonna keep you, you bring in the *clavo* with you, the sack. You either swallow it or you put it up you . . . They have ways to get drugs in there with the tennis shoes or . . . sewn them in the bras.

Sometimes drugs were smuggled in through packages being sent in from the outside.

Graciela: At Sybil Brand . . . they were bringing it to me through the shoes. They have a . . . ticket[1] and they have [it] unsewn. They put the drugs in and take it to a shoe place and have it sewn back in. So when they check the shoes they . . . cut the inside out, they don't check the outside.

According to pintas, drugs most often were brought in by white civilian staff and guards, although some African-American and Latina/o staff and guards also brought them in. Both male and female guards brought drugs and other contraband into the jail, particularly for prisoners they were sexually involved with.

Estela: The guards liked the girls in there and . . . were messing around with them and . . . they would . . . put money on their books . . . They used to bring in heroin for them. They used to bring in cocaine for them . . . Or they'd just bring a pack of cigarettes and throw 'em and they get 'em . . . They do it through the docks . . . I know because two of my friends were seeing . . . two different . . . women . . . guards.

Graciela: They [white prisoners] were involved with the guards there too and the cooks. The . . . white . . . cooks that come in, they're the ones that bring it in also.

While staff brought in drugs to favored prisoners, "The money . . . it makes" was, according to Graciela, their primary motivation.

Though drug trafficking was supposed to be a private affair, frequently other prisoners and guards knew it was taking place.

Graciela: I mean, it's supposed to be kept hush-hush, but everybody knows what's happening.

At SBI, drug dealing was generally an individual enterprise and not a gang-related matter (Graciela). Nonetheless, prisoners who wanted guards to bring them drugs would use middlemen. Chicanas generally used other Chicanas as go-betweens.

Graciela: You don't approach them, there's always a third party. There's always a middleman inside.

While it took some prisoners a while to make the necessary contacts to bring drugs in, others were able to have access to drugs from the moment they arrived at SBI (Graciela). How quickly a prisoner had access to drugs depended on whom she knew and where she was housed. Chicanas generally would ask a Chicana acquaintance who was dealing drugs within the institution (Graciela). While African-American prisoners also used middlemen, according to Graciela, African-Americans tended to get their drugs from visitors and not guards.

The majority of the Blacks are coming off the visits, and their people are bringing it in to them.

Graciela also observed that African Americans brought in powdered cocaine and, on rare occasions, crack. Latinas brought in the heroin. Marijuana also came in, but not frequently (Graciela). Paraphernalia for shooting heroin, mainly needles, could be obtained from other prisoners.

Graciela: Diabetics steal it from the infirmary, and they come out to the yard and sell 'em.

Guards also brought in other types of contraband.

Estela: I knew this one guard that was bringing in cartons of cigarettes. Give them to the girls that pay him so much money to bring them in cartons of cigarettes . . . Like they'd pay him $200 for a carton of cigarettes.

Gender Roles and Economy

Another major way prisoners obtained much-needed and desired goods and services was by exploiting "feminine" or "masculine" gender roles to their advantage. Prisoners who were "studs," or who adopted a stud persona while in jail, that is, a masculine demeanor and appearance, benefited from being catered to by other women who were labeled "femmes." Studs were also called "little boys," "butches," and "daddies."

Lucy: They would do the male role, yes . . . You know, the little stud walking around the house when they come in there. And they're all prepped and everything, looking cute and walk in there. And the woman would just cater to them, candy or whatever. I'm serious, shampoo, deodorant, whatever you want . . . Sex, dope, canteen, whatever they need. I mean, shoot, it's just like being out there. You can work it to get whatever you want to.

Graciela: They'd do everything for you . . . I mean, you don't . . . have to do nothing . . . All you gotta do is, if you want something, "Hey, can you go get this?" . . . And they'll be more than one ready to go do it for you . . . They . . . all used to look up to me and . . . I was always given stuff. I was asked, "Do you want this? Do you want that?" I'd come back to my room, this would be laid out, that would laid out . . . As far as like my clothes being ironed, all that was done. My clothes being washed, that was done . . . They'd come to my job and ask me if I wanted them to help me work on my job.

The irony was, according to Lucy, a former sex worker, that some of the studs "played" other women much like sex workers played their customers on the streets to survive. Ironically, some studs were themselves former sex workers.

Lucy: I think it's still just a form of prostitution to meet their needs . . . And someone's just a ho in there too, you know . . . Go in there and go get them an old lady to get their canteen. I mean, I would sit there and watch them.

The demand for studs was so intense that they did not need to seek out other women to meet their needs. Femmes, in fact, actually competed with one another for the studs' attention.

Prisoners who were femme and/or heterosexual on the inside also used gender roles to obtained much-desired goods and services. For such women their adaptation to jail did not necessarily entail a sharp break with the gender roles they played on the outside. Some, labeled by other prisoners "commissary berries," used their femininity on the inside, playing on the studs' vanity and privileged status, to get what they wanted. "Working" someone entailed several approaches. While some femmes aggressively pursued the people they wanted, others played a more traditional role, waiting to be pursued.

Lucy: I . . . manipulated . . . someone who has connections on the outside, until . . . my money order . . . came through . . . And so I had to work, sure, I'd let someone, you know, "You're cute. You want to sit down?" "All right." . . . I would sit up there and talk . . . with them and just be around them and . . . make sure I get coffee and candy . . . So I was doing the same thing . . . But I knew what was going on . . . It's like when someone is attracted to you and you just like working them like you're doing a trick . . . and you smile and you tell them what you think they want to hear. And then, . . . ultimately, you benefit also. So it's actually doing the same thing, a . . . different form of prostitution. It's a different object.

Once approached, Chicana femmes like Lucy would spend time with the stud, going on "dates," until they got what they wanted.

Like you can go out to the NA meetings. You can go to church. You can go out and watch a movie. You can go out to the yard. And that's just at Sybil Brand . . . I guess you can kind of call it companionship, too, just friendship, just being able to sit there and just bullshit . . . But it . . . could even be a group thing.

While for Lucy the dynamic between a butch and the femme who was working her resembled that of a prostitute working her john, the difference was that in her case there was actually no sex involved.

Lucy: The only thing is . . . that it never got to the point to an actual sexual kind of thing or even to an intimate kind of thing of even us kissing or nothing like that. Where I've had people make me . . . special things, . . . you know, like . . . cute pretty bears that we sold with golden trimming . . . Or someone sends you like candy bars and, "Thinking of you." . . . So I would just trip. Women really go all out there.

The reasons prisoners manipulated one another were simple to understand.

Carmen: Probably a lot of 'em because they didn't have nobody running for 'em . . . So then it's a means of survival, a means of . . . having your needs taken care of.

Lucy: I'd get companionship and also, you know, . . . if there was dope, if there was . . . canteen . . . Friendship, coffee, connections to the out world, a phone call.

Sometimes the butches would give the femmes goods directly without manipulation.

Lucy: I've had people come in and put brand-new Levis when you come out to court from prison . . . Or something . . . so you can have something to wear out in the yard.

At other times the butches would ask their runners to bring goods to another prisoner. Hence, the runner ended up providing for two prisoners instead of one.

Lucy: They would just go ahead and three-way you out to somebody else . . . asked her runner to bring in something . . . You know, someone come and visit you and bring you shoes, brand-new shoes, from the outside.

In summary, the means pintas used to satisfy their needs and wants varied depending on their personalities, the availability of runners, their access to work assignments from which they could steal goods to barter and sell in the underground jailhouse market, and their willingness to exploit gender roles to their advantage. Through these means, pintas demonstrated that, as on the outside, they were willing to use all available resources to provide for themselves and/or their loved ones on the inside.

14

Living Together

Prisoner Alliances and Hostilities

The treatment accorded pintas by guards at SBI exacerbated further the feelings of frustration, fear, anger, and abandonment they carried from years of untreated emotional, physical, and sexual abuse and addiction. Jail, however, was not the best place to recover from these experiences.

Moreover, once imprisoned, pintas were forced to associate more intimately than most had ever done before with African-Americans and whites, both as prisoners and staff. Such exposure, combined with different cultural values, racial/ethnic rivalries brought in from the outside, and emotional conflicts traced to previous abuse, led pintas to respond to those around them in diverse ways. On the one hand they formed groups, generally along ethnic/nationality lines, for mutual support and protection. On the other hand, they sometimes vented their anger at other prisoners and staff.

Some of the questions asked in this chapter are: What types of relationships did pintas have with other prisoners? Did gang affiliations make a difference on the inside? What groups were they most likely to gravitate toward or away from? Were there times when prisoners were able to form alliances across racial and ethnic lines to support one another?

Chicana Cliques

Discriminatory criminal justice policies fueled by the war on drugs had such an extensive and profound impact on Chicana/o barrios that when pintas arrived at SBI they were not surprised to find a significant number of their Chicana homegirls already incarcerated there. Homegirls included friends, relatives, lovers, and barrio acquaintances. It was toward them that pintas gravitated.

Estela: They would subdivide. They'd go in their own little clique. Like they'd say, ". . . Hey, homes, we're meeting over here," and . . . they get all their friends. Like, friends they knew from the streets and . . . did time with . . . Mostly people that they knew from the street . . . clique up together . . . I mean, they . . . associate with all the Chicanas, but they had their own little cliques. We had one bed . . . area where all the Chicanas would be, yeah.

Rita: If you know these people from the streets . . . and . . . you sell drugs to 'em and you hung out with them, got high with them, you say, "Hey, homes, what's up?" . . . Like, for me, okay, I ran with a lot of people from East L.A., Maravilla, . . . La Puente . . . I didn't try to make new friends in there . . . People that I knew I hung with. People that I knew I talked to . . . These people that I knew, yeah, were just mostly Chicanas, people like me.

Pintas also formed new friendships with roommates and dormmates and, as they became regulars at SBI, other women with whom they had shared a previous incarceration. Some of these networks were interracial. Graciela, who did not have any homegirls in her dorm the first time she went to SBI, was fortunate to find compatible roommates of diverse racial and ethnic backgrounds.

[I] kind of got lucky and went into a dorm that there was . . . girls that . . . tried to make you feel at home . . . It was girls that are doing a length of time . . . So they know I was gonna be there for a while 'cause I got sent to that dorm. So they kind of like . . . wanted to let me know that everything was gonna be all right, . . . that . . . we were like a family . . . It was all mixed together, white, Black, and Chicanas . . .

Sometimes pintas found that their own sisters, mothers, daughters, and even their grandmothers were already serving time at the institution.

Rita: I remember this one girl . . . She seen her mother there and she started crying . . . And in back of my mind I would tell myself I . . . don't know what I would do if I'd seen my mom walking through the line. You know, that's just . . . a real sad, sad situation to me.

Pintas spent time with friends during scheduled recreation time in the yard and at meals. They also met friends at church services, in their dorms, at school, and at work. However, opportunities for socializing with friends housed in other areas of the jail were limited by institutional regulations and the fact that the area was not large enough to accommodate all the prisoners at one time.

Prior to incarceration, pintas were divided by barrio loyalties and gang affiliations, type of drugs used, and language groups. Once at SBI and confronted with a predominantly white guard and civilian staff along with African-American and white prisoners, Chicanas tended to set aside most differences in order to survive, cope, and, if possible, thrive within an environment they considered stifling and destructive. While gang divisions within the California Chicano prisoner population were severe, pintas interviewed felt that once in jail, Chicanas "kind of outgrew it" (Estela). According to Sonia, "I think when you come to prison you kind of let it go, I mean, well, in the County anyway." Hence, when fights broke out, they were not generally gang-related.

Deborah: Not unless there was some kind of conflict from the street . . . You could fight . . . but it wasn't normally gang stuff. It was just . . . you burned me or . . . something happened in the street . . . Or . . . maybe it was a rival thing.

Overall, pintas felt that during the 1970s, 1980s, and part of the 1990s, Chicanas supported one another.

Estela: Like if you're a Chicana, you know, if you didn't have shampoo, toothpaste, or something, . . . they would help you out . . . All the Chicanas stuck together. That was one good thing.

Graciela: It was like, you know, you see when your homegirl's coming and she don't have nothing . . . don't have no kind of money . . . You go around and get a care package together and you give it to her . . . They called it a "care package." You know, put stuff together like shampoo, your hygiene stuff, and . . . they'll give it to you.

By the end of the 1990s, however, the degree of solidarity exhibited among Chicanas at SBI had declined. Some pintas blamed the increasing conflict among Chicanas to the growing number of young, gang-affiliated Chicanas who had a more aggressive manner of settling their differences with other prisoners.

Marta: Because the ones before when they gang-banged there was always one-to-one . . . and they never rat-packed anybody . . . Now, when they jump you, six on one, they stick you, you know. And they think they're bad, you know, because there's six of 'em and only you.

Spanish-Monolingual Prisoners

While the number of Spanish-monolingual prisoners, most born in Latin America, was not particularly large at SBI compared to other county jails, their presence was noticeable because of their distinct cultural and linguistic needs. During the 1980s and 1990s, as a result of the intensification of the war on drugs, their numbers increased. Women from Mexico, always the largest number of Spanish-monolingual prisoners in jail, were joined by women from El Salvador, Guatemala, and Colombia. A few came from Ecuador, Peru, Cuba, and Puerto Rico (Marta; Lucy).

Some pintas felt that such women tended to be older than Chicanas.

Victoria: I think the Spanish-speaking women, they were well into their 50s and 60s some of them.

Although pintas interviewed were likely to be incarcerated for drug-related crimes, such as being under the influence and possession, women from Latin America were more likely to be incarcerated for transporting drugs into the United States (Cristina; Victoria). That is, they were mulas, drug couriers.

Deborah: United States Latinas, I see them incarcerated for drug-related charges . . . What I see these other people that are from other countries being incarcerated for are those transporting of drug cases . . . Have never had a record before and are there for these big, big cases . . . Other . . . members of the family are incarcerated with them . . . Or . . . the husband's in Men's Central, . . . she's over here.

Victoria: Which sticks out in my mind so much are the more Spanish-speaking people, maybe like women that weren't even legal here and they were caught . . . working . . . Or they were holding the . . . drugs for their boyfriend.

Some were held for several years in pretrial detention while fighting their cases.

Deborah: I've seen one woman there for three years . . . I got a couple now that have been there already two years. They have not been found guilty [yet] . . . But their cases are very heavy . . . murder, . . . heavy drug charges . . . I'm talking about people that have transported from another country to this country.

Due to language barriers, there were Spanish-monolingual prisoners who had no idea why they had been arrested and imprisoned.

Mercedes: Sometimes they didn't even know why they were arrested . . . In the county facility you always had a pink slip that told you why you were arrested, when you were arrested, and . . . when you went to court. So we would be able to read that to them to let them know . . . And they were just so emotional and always crying. So we tried to . . . be supportive.

If found guilty, those who were undocumented faced deportation.

Graciela: Some of 'em were . . . from El Salvador. Others were from different parts of Mexico. And some of them would be crying 'cause they don't wanna go back 'cause their family is here but they just didn't have papers to be here.

Lack of knowledge of the English language and cultural differences were two reasons Spanish-monolingual prisoners formed their own clique (Díaz-Cotto 1996).

Rita: All the people that spoke Spanish . . . mostly hung out together.

Language barriers and staff prejudices also restricted them to working in certain areas of the facility, such as the kitchen and sewing (Victoria).

The attitudes of Chicanas toward such women varied. Some pintas resented Latin American prisoners for several reasons. The conflicts between them were based on cultural, linguistic, and class differences. Sometimes they were based on the different relationship each group had to the drug-related crimes for which they were arrested.

Lucy: They were total elitists. They just isolated themselves . . . They even considered their selves different from . . . us, the Chicanos that were here. We were considered *pochas* . . . Pocha is someone who's born here and didn't speak Spanish. I take it personally because regardless of what side or what state that I was born, the blood that still pumps from these veins are Mexican.

Sonia: And I didn't like 'em. And I guess that's because . . . although we're supposed to be Mexicans just like them, because we're born here, the people like from Mexico, they don't like us. You know, they don't like the Chicanas here. They think that . . . we're different than they are because we don't speak the Spanish they speak . . . They consider . . . us like a . . . white person 'cause we're born here . . . So . . . we've learned that as a child that they didn't like us so we kind of like dog them . . . or don't like them . . . We didn't hang out with them or nothing. They were like a whole different race like, to a certain extent.

Sonia: If they're not a heroin user or a cocaine user but their . . . crimes is transporting, . . . big money, you know, they think they're better . . . They don't see themselves that they committed a crime, . . . So they think they're better 'cause they're just trying to make some money, while we commit crimes to support this habit that we got a hold of . . . They look down on dope fiends, in other words, . . . "Oh, she's a *tecata.*"

Sonia: And the majority of . . . [Latina] women that were in prison mostly their . . . thing was selling drugs, you know, transporting drugs from Mexico, from Tijuana to this way. So . . . they always had money. Well, we didn't . . . Some . . . still continue to think that they're better . . . And the way they do it is with their clothing . . . or their TVs and the radios, where a lot of us can't afford it.

Given these attitudes, English-speaking pintas did not always provide support to such prisoners.

Marta: A lot of the . . . Chicanas here don't wanna deal with . . . people from Mexico or from any other place . . . They don't wanna be bothered.

Victoria: They get treated like they weren't even there, basically. I mean, they'd have nothing to really talk about so.

A few pintas who didn't speak Spanish went as far as physically assaulting Latin American immigrants and calling them "wetbacks" (Lucy).

Gina: People take advantage of them there, the other inmates . . . By taking their stuff, taking their money . . . They beat them up, you know.

Sonia: We would steal their canteen or . . . threaten them . . . We would get over on them if we could.

According to pintas, African-American prisoners were also more likely to treat Spanish-monolingual prisoners with disdain.

Rosa: Now, the Blacks would look down on the . . . ones that didn't speak English . . . [They were] treated as if they were stupid because they couldn't speak English . . . Like, "Can't you hear me? I'm talking to you. What are you doing?"

Victoria: Sometimes the African-American women would pick on, say, the older generation that didn't speak any English.

Notwithstanding their mutual animosities, however, there were times when bilingual and English-monolingual Chicanas did actively support Latin American Spanish-monolingual prisoners.

Sonia: You're in the county jail and the beds are next to each other. So if . . . I happen to have one that's from Mexico or . . . Salvador or wherever and they slept next to me and . . . the person used to talk to me . . . I would give 'em whatever answer or whatever they want . . . And they became my friend . . . because they were my . . . neighbor on the same bunk . . . I wouldn't hang with them, but they were still my neighbor . . . So if that person was . . . all right to me and I don't feel that they had something coming, . . . and if it was a friend, . . . then I would stick up. But if it were just a strange person I wouldn't.

Chicanas and other women of Latin American descent also came together when conflicts arose with African-Americans and whites.

Lucy: When something goes down it's like . . . that's the one thing that's bonding, not just the dope, but the color of your skin or the language that you speak . . . We're segregated but we're still more like each other than . . . the African American or the . . . white.

One of the ways English- and Spanish-monolingual prisoners were able to cut across language barriers was when the latter taught their English-monolingual peers how to crochet doilies and blankets (Cristina).

It was bilingual prisoners who played a mediating role between Spanish- and English-monolingual prisoners.

Cristina: Like the ones that spoke Spanish did hang out to just Spanish-speaking. And a bilingual would come back and forth and let them know what was going on.

Bilingual prisoners, however, were not allowed to translate for Spanish-monolingual prisoners during disciplinary hearings. As the 1990s drew to a close and their numbers increased, the demeanor of many Spanish-monolingual prisoners changed.

Graciela: Most of 'em stand up for themselves now. Back . . . in the early years when I went, . . . they'd cry because somebody was yelling at them . . . But now it's like . . . they don't let people push 'em around no more . . . If that person wants to fight them, they'll fight. They'll just let the person know that they can't take nothing from them and they can't get over on 'em any more.

Changes in Latina Prisoner Population

During the late 1980s and throughout the 1990s, pintas interviewed noticed a number of changes taking place within the Latina prisoner population. While their observations were largely directed at the felon population, the fact is that those pintas who eventually end up in state prisons have to go through the jails, even if temporarily, while their cases are being decided.

Thus, while pintas were aware of the impact of mandatory and drug-related sentencing laws on Latinas, some, like Graciela, argued that the growth in Latina incarceration reflected the growing use of drugs among the women.

They're doing more . . . I mean, nowadays . . . I get surprised of even seeing the . . . Latinas that I see in jail using drugs . . . 'Cause you got some that are up from . . . like the older Mexican families that are raised . . . real strict. And you're seeing people like that coming in.

Such an increase could be reflected in CDC statistics that show that more Latinas were sent to state prisons in California for drug-related offenses in 1999 (23.6%) than in 1983 (20.0%) (CDC 2000a: 14).

Another change pintas observed was the growth, although small, in the number of young gang-identified Chicanas who were incarcerated for drive-by shootings, a crime previously associated with male gang members.

Graciela: They would talk about the things that their gangs used to run around and do, how they'd get their guns or they'd go gang-banging, you know, just drive-by shootings . . . And I'm surprised to see the girls that are coming in they're very young, 18, 17, 16 years old. They're coming in for drive-by shootings . . . And just doing it for the heck of it.

Other pintas also felt more Latinas were being sentenced for economic crimes as a result of worsening economic conditions in the barrios (Carmen). Some also alluded to the fact that Latinas were increasingly likely to go to jail and prison for joint crimes committed with Latinos, particularly their partners.

Deborah: They're going in for the guys now . . . The guys . . . are taking them down with them, you know . . . Either they take the rap or the guy won't cut 'em loose, you know.

Race, Ethnicity, and Prisoner Conflict

Prisoners at SBI subdivided along the same racial and ethnic lines as on the street.

Sonia: In Sybil Brand . . . they all hang around with their own race. And . . . like the Latinas . . . it didn't matter what . . . neighborhood we were from. We were

Mexican, so the neighborhood kind of stopped to a certain extent, you know. It didn't matter if you were from downtown L.A., if you were from the West Side or . . . 18th Street or . . . Maravilla or Flats. If you were Latina you hang around together, if you were Chicanas . . . Blacks hang around together. Whites hung around together, mostly.

Lucy: Out here you have the Chicanos on one corner. You have the mayatas on the other. It's exactly the same thing [in jail] . . . Here you have like . . . the *manfloras* over here, where they kick it . . . together and everything like that, just like you on the streets.

The racial and ethnic prejudices pintas exhibited before incarceration strongly influenced who became their friends in jail. Chicanas were more likely to socialize with white than African-American prisoners. While a few of the pintas commented on the prejudice pintas frequently felt toward African-American prisoners, all those interviewed made clear distinctions between themselves and whites but particularly African-American prisoners.

Rita: Because I know white people are scared in there all the time . . . And . . . if you intimidate one, believe me, they'll do what you want them to do . . . Hispanic people are people that are real quiet. We got some loud ones, but the majority of them are quiet and they just kick back and observe . . . The Black people are like real loud . . . 'Cause they like to play spades a lot. Bam! Bam! Slap those bones! . . . They're just really obnoxious, really loud people . . . And I'm not like real prejudice but sometimes, you know, you sit there and . . . they're loud and they talk and they talk and, ". . . I'll beat your ass and I'll fuck you up! And I . . ." But the minute you get in their face they run to the cop shop, "She . . . wants me . . . !"

Graciela: Back then, . . . I really didn't associate with Black people . . . just white and . . . Chicanas . . . They're loud. I don't like their attitudes they have. They just think that they're gonna run the whole show . . . And then, . . . if they had something against you they'd come after you with a group of people. They wouldn't come after you one-on-one.

Despite such prejudices, some pintas developed friendships with African-American prisoners while incarcerated.

Sonia: Like I was raised with nothing but my own people . . . I didn't really get to know Blacks until I went to jail . . . But doing time . . . I had a lot of Black friends.

While there were white prisoners who identified with the white supremacist Aryan Nation, none of the pintas interviewed gave examples of fights taking place between themselves and prisoners so affiliated. Other white prisoners sought to associate with women of color.

Rosa: But there's quite a few whites that always want to go into the other ethnic groups and start acting like they're Black or . . . Mexican.

White prisoners were sometimes seen as being both opportunistic and cowardly.

Graciela: Majority of them they all hang with Chicanas so it's like they got to have somebody with them too . . . Or they'll come and they'll says, "Hey, what should I do about this?" They always try to involve somebody instead of taking care of it on their own.

While multiracial political alliances such as the one that led to the filing of *Inmates of SBI* were not common, neither were riots motivated by racial or ethnic hostilities among prisoners. Interestingly, whenever I asked pintas if they had seen riots taking place in the jails or prisons they had been in, pintas would invariably assume that I was referring to racial riots and not to riots aimed at changing jail or prison conditions.

Fights among Prisoners

The lack of privacy, coupled with overcrowded conditions and conflicting personalities, led prisoners to live in a constant state of frustration and anger. Added to these tensions were those created by the craving for drugs, loneliness, missing loved ones, racial and ethnic differences, and the sexual harassment and physical abuse of prisoners by guards. The lack of adequate defense attorneys to represent them and the impact of the Three Strikes Law were also contributing factors. In reaction to these tensions, prisoners argued and fought with one another over diverse issues.

Estela: Stupid things, like somebody stole something from them or somebody looking at their old lady.

Rita: I'd seen people fighting in there . . . over the phone, over, "You looked at me stupid." . . . "Don't be changing the TV." "You cheated . . . !" You know, if you're playing cards or something . . . "It's my turn . . . in the washer." . . . Or if somebody be's with somebody else's woman, they go in there and they fight.

Gina: You get a lot of fights there . . . What's the . . . fighting over? . . . "You're sitting in my bed." Or, "I want your money." . . . Or there's jealousy there behind their other women . . . A lot of the Blacks and Chicanas get into it.

Rita: It's so crowded there's a lot of fights. You wanna sleep and people are just making a lot of noise and you get up and you get up angry. "Can't you keep the noise down?" "Hey, where the fuck you think you're in? Jail! You wanted peace and quiet, go. Keep your ass out. Stay home." You know, I mean, it goes with the flow . . . If you're in there you're gonna be in constant battle, war.

Sometimes fights broke out over issues of respect.

Deborah: One fight I got into . . . there was a girl . . . She's a Chicana . . . She . . . was there, first time there. She . . . had kind of like a . . . big mouth . . . I was on my own . . . bunk minding my own business, reading a book, and she comes over there to rap to me. And when she came over . . . there was . . . a . . . mayata on the top bunk from me. She was cool . . . But she had some people on her bunk and . . . these people were real loud . . . She [the Chicana] . . . tells this other Black girl . . . "Why don't you . . . shut the fuck up! You know, you're so goddamn loud!" . . . And then she sits down on my bed . . . And this girl jumped off of that top bunk . . . and she fires her up . . . And . . . her lip . . . was bleeding . . . and she didn't do nothing! . . . I looked at her like, "Get up!" you know . . . And I just automatically reacted . . . I got up and I start boxing with her [the mayata] . . . just out of principle . . . I was just pissed off . . . that she disrespected where I was at . . . And . . . we fucking really boxed . . . And the . . . other girl said, "Deborah, the cop's coming in!" And I ran and got back to my bed. And . . . the mayata goes . . . "Guard!" She . . . started telling them that she was in this fight . . . And I just sat there and acted like nothing was happening . . . I mean, nobody would say anything. And . . . she pointed me out . . . And . . . my hand was bleeding . . . so we went to the Hole for that . . . I was there for 10 days and she was in there for 10 days.

African-American and Latina prisoners also argued about what television programs to watch.

Cristina: It was being racial because the Blacks would be wanting to watch . . . "Soul Train." And a lot of 'em . . . they . . . don't wanna watch "Soul Train." It's boring. But Sundays it's always boring in any of the dorms. So that would . . . start it right there. 'Cause all the Blacks wanted it and one Mexican would say, "Well, you know what? I'm tired of watching that nigger shit," you know. And someone will, "Well, fuck you! You're nothing but a wetback anyhow. Shit, we gonna watch it anyhow. You don't like it, that's just too damn bad. You can go back to the border." And there it goes. And then . . . sometimes they would fist-fight.

Frequently, pintas objected to the manner in which African-American prisoners, avid domino players, slammed the dominoes on the table. At times fights broke out when prisoners were seen as unfairly supporting others of their same race or ethnicity.

Deborah: Issues of . . . fairness, maybe a . . . Chicana fighting with a Black and another Black jumping in . . . That would fuel it.

Rosa: I was coming out of the tank . . . there was a Black girl coming and she told me to "Move, bitch!" And I told her, "Move me!" And we started to fight. And then my girlfriend tried to separate us and somebody thought that she was jumping into the fight and everybody started getting in to fight.

The tensions between African-American and Latina prisoners made it difficult for the few who had been friends on the outside to actively continue their friendships on the inside.

Cristina: I knew a lot of Black people . . . like I have this one [friend], I call her "my aunt," that's out on the streets. But when I was in there, she knew what time it was. She knew I couldn't really . . . talk to her so . . . she wouldn't really talk to me, you know.

Sometimes veteranas helped reduce tensions.

Cristina: There was this one Black lady in the dorm I was on, she . . . was a spokesperson and calmed everybody down. And there'd be this other Mexican lady that calms everybody down, "You know what? Let's just get along . . . You know, we got to live with each other." And it . . . would fan out.

Luisa tried to avoid conflicts by minding her own business.

And what I used to do was just, I kept it very low, low-key. Low-key means being *calladita*. Talk, bullshit, make jokes, fine, but low-key. Meaning I wasn't the *chismolera*, the *comadre*, "Oh, well did you hear that so-and-so is a rat? Did you hear that so-and-so is no good?" None of that shit was my business . . . I used to see women get their ass kicked behind carrying shit like that . . . I never . . . got into that mode . . . People told on me but I never told on nobody.

Prisoners usually tried to quiet disturbances before guards noticed what was happening and imposed blanket reprisals.

Cristina: They'd go in there and break it up and tell us there ain't gonna be no TV, so we tried to break it up before they noticed.

While guards would break up fights between prisoners, they were also known to fuel interracial tensions, particularly between Chicana and African-American prisoners.

Cristina: Well, . . . more the white-looking cops . . . would sit there and say, "Oh, look at that nigger getting his ass whooped." Or "Let's see who's gonna win, the Mexican or the . . . Black." You know . . . underneath where you can't hear unless you're paying attention to what they're saying. "That Black girl looks scroungy over there . . . That Mexican looks pretty healthy, she'd get her." Or the other way around, you know.

Arguments between Chicana and white prisoners broke out less frequently but sometimes took racial/ethnic overtones.

Cristina: There was this white girl, she talked Mexican. Then when she get around the Mexican she talked like a Black girl . . . And she got smart with me and she goes, "Oh, you ain't nothing but a . . . Mexican." . . . I go, "You ain't nothing but a white bitch. Don't get me started." And everyone says, ". . . Just let her go."

Despite conflicts between prisoners, jail authorities claimed that in mid-1986, when the prisoner population was already over 2,000, "actual physical injuries were infrequent" (*LAT* 7/13/86). Authorities recorded only 30 to 35 "altercations" between prisoners each month, with "incidents involving inmates and deputies" running one or two a month (ibid.). This figure did not include fights between prisoners that never came to the attention of guards or assaults on prisoners by guards.

Victimizing Other Prisoners

Conflicts between prisoners also took the form of the victimization of one or more prisoners by peers.

Graciela: Each visit you went to they used to be able to leave us $40. So if you see somebody that was real weak and you can get over on, they'd be right there ready to take their money from them when they came in from a visit. Whenever they shopped on canteen, they'd take that from 'em. Or they had the person shop for them . . . You know, they'll tell 'em, "Look it, I want you to buy me this and buy me that and you better buy it." And the girl would buy it.

Frequently, prisoners would watch as others were victimized.

Graciela: So when I seen somebody getting abused or getting taken this or taken that from 'em, I just turned the other way 'cause it was none of my business . . . 'Cause I remembered that's what my older people that I hung around with . . . used to tell me.

Graciela did not prey upon others during her initial incarceration. But as she became a regular at SBI and got involved in drug dealing, she did so.

After a few years of being in there . . . if somebody owed me something, instead of taking just what was mine, I would take all of it. Because of the simple fact that I'd give that person a chance to give me what's mine. If you don't give it to me, then if I have to go take it, I'm taking all of it . . . They shop . . . canteen. I would take all of it . . . Or I could have their people wire money . . . And if they weren't on time they would get doubled. If it was $100 and they didn't pay it on time, it was $200 . . . See at that time is when I was involved in . . . dealing drugs.

She went as far as assaulting a prisoner who had not paid her drug debt.

Graciela: I had to do it once, and I guess from that one time they knew that I didn't play around . . . Everything was always paid on time.

Sometimes threats were enforced with homemade weapons.

Diana: In the county, only because you can't get anything better in the county, . . . you can get . . . disposable razors, and you either break or melt . . . part of . . . the razor off. And you can cut one end of the handle and put the razor in that and tape it up or string it up or . . . however . . . you can get that thing to stay on, and there's a shank.

Carmen: Over drugs, over somebody stealing somebody's old lady. It was with weapons, with knives. They were made up in there.

According to Graciela, prisoners might resist the threats and fight with their suppliers over debts. The debts were then settled by the actual fight.

They can do that too. And once . . . you fight with them then the debts are paid.

In a few cases pintas spoke about how other prisoners had tried to rape them or intimidate them into having sexual relationships with them.

Linda: There was one Black woman that wanted to rape me . . . I was in a holding tank. And that one had two bunks, like twin beds and then the toilet bowl. And they opened up the gate in the daytime . . . for awhile. And you know, I'm going through my trip with this drug stuff and most of the time I'm laying in bed . . . Anyway, this woman was supposed to have been running the tank . . . Because everybody else was thrown in bed 'cause they're going through drug withdrawal . . . And she must have weighed about 300 pounds . . . And she had these other two Black women with her. And I was scared to death. I thought she was going to beat the shit out of me . . . And she comes into the cell and she says, "Well, my name is so-and-so . . . and I like me some Mexican." . . . And I says, "Well, I don't play that shit." She says, "Well, I like me some Mexican. I like me a connection." I says, "I still don't play that shit." . . . She says, "I'll be back." And I says, "Hey go for it, you know." . . . Listen, inside of me I'm shaking . . . But, of course, I wouldn't say anything . . . And she came back the next day and one more time, "I want me some Mexican." And she says, "Anyway, you're going to the joint . . . and somebody's gonna get it." And I'm . . . saying, "I already told you, man, I don't play that shit so just get the fuck out of here!" And she's says, "Well, I'll be back tonight." . . . Anyway, what happened is that they stole a white woman's money . . . So once a white woman told on them, boom! they shipped them out and I went, "Whew!"

As in all penal institutions, prisoners went out of their way to shun, harass, humiliate, and/or physically assault snitches and women incarcerated for child cases.

Sonia: If there was a . . . woman there, it didn't matter what race she was, . . . and she had a baby, child case, . . . we didn't accept her. We "dogged her" like we says . . . 'Cause we all have children and a lot of us, . . . we . . . weren't perfect with our kids, but we didn't go beating them up, burning them up, or throwing them over . . . the freeway, like some of these women do. And yet, they got less time than we did sometimes for the crimes that we did. And so we would tell them to put themselves in protective custody or get out of the dorm. Same thing with a . . . person that would rat. The snitch took the stand and snitched on somebody . . . And . . . let's say a Black girl came or a white girl came and . . . was doing something to that person who had . . . like we say, . . . a "snitch jacket" or a child case, we wouldn't interfere . . . Even on ourselves we'd go get them if we . . . knew that. You know, . . . four or five of us would jump over one . . . And people might say, "It's not fair." . . . I goes, "Well, you're . . . sending somebody to prison and you weren't fair about doing that." . . . You were facing so much time so you'd give up that person but yet you were involved somehow. You bought from them or . . . you were there when they did the crime and you were involved but you took a deal . . . So . . . it doesn't matter if two, three, four, five people jump on you or hurt you . . . Same thing with a baby killer . . . "Why should we feel sorry for you? You know, you could defend yourself, that baby couldn't defend himself" . . . And a baby killer that walks the yard, . . . they'll spit at them. A rat that walks the yard, they'll spit on 'em and kick 'em . . . They go to buy their groceries or canteen, they'll take it from them. So mostly they put them in protective custody so they don't walk the population.

Once a woman acquired a reputation for snitching, whether inside or outside jail, the label followed her everywhere she went.

Sonia: Once you snitch, you'll always carry that jacket with you . . . You're never to be trusted . . . man or a woman snitch . . . If you snitched one time they figure you're gonna snitch twice . . . Nobody's gonna want . . . you around . . . If you snitched inside it goes outside with you . . . If you're thinking of committing a crime . . . you gotta make sure you don't say it in front of that . . . person that you think is a snitch because she could go run and tell and you're going right to prison.

Pintas' stories reveal that the types of interactions prisoners had with one another were influenced by both personal and institutional factors. On the one hand were their individual perceptions and personalities, racial, ethnic, and other prejudices acquired prior to their incarceration, and tensions created by their loss of freedom and contact with loved ones. On the other hand were the tensions created by overcrowded and noisy facilities, idleness, the lack of adequate services and programs, and abusive treatment at the hands of staff.

Pintas responded to the conditions they encountered by forming cliques and homegirl networks, taking lovers, forming prison families (see Chapter 15), and becoming friends with roommates and/or women with whom they had been previously incarcerated.

Although the multiple tensions also led Latina, African-American, and white prisoners to vent their anger at one another, rarely did the arguments and fights result in serious physical injuries. Equally important, prisoners were from time to time able to set aside their differences to demand changes in oppressive prison conditions and treatment (see Chapter 17).

15

Gender, Sexuality, and Family Kinship Networks

The previous chapters have illustrated how pintas continually sought to exert their independence from gender role expectations placed on them by their families, their barrios, and society at large. They ran away from home to escape abuse, neglect, or parental authority, cut school partly in response to abusive and racist teachers and staff, and joined Chicana/o gangs seeking power, status, and recognition. They used drugs to escape painful feelings and neglected their children and themselves when their addiction intensified. Moreover, they broke the law, victimized others to support themselves, their families, and their drug habits, and subsequently went to jails and prisons.

Once the women were incarcerated, institutional personnel sought to make them conform to traditional heterosexual gender roles that demanded submission and docility on the part of women, particularly poor and working-class women. Further obedience was demanded from women of color by their white jailers. The fact that their jailers were primarily women themselves underscored the irony of such expectations and the abusive treatment that accompanied it. It also made pintas' defiance of their white jailers all the more significant.

Pintas struggled with demands placed on them simultaneously by their families, their barrios, and the state. Gender roles, sexuality, and sexual identification were arenas within which pintas challenged such expectations. As such, pintas took advantage of the institutional setting to experiment with many different types of relationships with other women, some of which were sexual in nature. They also had both voluntary and involuntary sexual contact with female, but most often, male staff.[1]

This chapter asks questions such as: How did pintas seek to exert their independence from oppressive gender role expectations placed on them by jail administrators and staff? What types of sexual and nonsexual relationships and networks did pintas form while incarcerated?

What were their motivations for participating in such relationships? How did penal staff react to same-sex relationships between women?

Sexual Identification

Sexual identification for most pintas interviewed varied throughout the years. It hinged upon the pressures they received from their families and peers to be heterosexual, whether or not they were incarcerated, and their personal preferences at any one time. While almost all the pintas interviewed had at least one lesbian encounter or relationship in their lives and a number of them identified themselves as lesbians when they were teenagers, not all of them did so at the time of the interview. Some who knew they were lesbians from an early age had married men and had children at some point in their lives to please their families. A few lived only as lesbians or heterosexuals whether they were in or out of institutions. Others became involved in same-sex relationships while they were incarcerated, only to return to heterosexual lives upon release from the institution. Still others identified themselves as bisexual throughout their lives or at the time of the interview.[2] Graciela illustrates how sexual identification could be fluid.

[I was gay] since I was 13. I got married when I was 17 and I separated three years after that, in '81, and I went back to women. And then I've been in and out of prison since '84, and I just messed around with women. And then I . . . decided I wanted to have a baby. So then I got pregnant with my daughter. I had her in '91 and I haven't been with nobody . . . Just this past few months I've had a relationship with a man. [I'm now] bisexual.

Pintas, like other incarcerated women, frequently explored their sexuality for the first time while incarcerated.

Rosa: A lot of times the women would come in straight and end up being homosexual when they got there. And then left straight again . . . It happened within all the races.

Deborah: And they come out into the streets and . . . they're with their . . . old man and their kids again, and they act like they're not like that at all . . . It's like the person that does religion in the jail and then when they get out they're no longer religious.

Mercedes: I had an encounter with a . . . woman . . . at Sybil Brand. Something that I said I was never going to do . . . She was a Chicana . . . I had this homosexual experience and, you know what? I had the greatest time of my life! I lived it for every moment knowing that this was not my life. Knowing that this was not what I wanted . . . We did intimate things. And it might sound crazy, but the intimate thing there was . . . to feel close, . . . to have your socks washed, to . . . get your hair brushed . . . Of course we had sex!

Most of these jail affairs were not long-lasting.

Victoria: A lot of . . . like . . . "fly by night" sort of things. You know, women they . . . meet each other, they hook up, and . . . then they're like with someone else . . . And . . . it's kind of like with a soapish opera sort of . . . ring to it . . . A lot of drama . . . And I think maybe some people like feed off of that.

Pintas gave various reasons why prisoners who did not generally identify as lesbians became involved with other women while incarcerated.

Deborah: I just think that they do that just to fit in. It's a protection thing . . . It's kind of like a backup thing, you know . . . Maybe they can't go without sex . . . (laugh).

Though prisoners did have interracial and inter-ethnic relationships with other prisoners, the tendency at SBI was to stick to "your own kind." When involved in interracial relationships, Chicanas tended to prefer white over African-American prisoners. In fact, relationships with African-American prisoners were discouraged by other Chicanas.

Graciela: You were looked down on. They just didn't like the idea of you going with a Black person . . . They'd call 'em names. Call 'em *mayateras* . . . Or they would use the word "nigger lover." You were just a disgrace.

Cristina: They would walk up and tell you, "You don't hang around with them. You hang with your own kind. If it goes further than this then, yes, I will kick your ass."

While interracial relationships were still frowned upon, by the mid-1990s pintas agreed that the attitudes toward such relationships had changed somewhat.[3]

Graciela: Back then it was very seldom seen. Now . . . you see it more.

Regardless of how women defined themselves sexually, the overwhelming number broke institutional rules to have such relationships.

Guards' reactions to same-sex relationships between prisoners varied. Some guards tolerated such relationships, and a few even went out of their way to support them. They housed lovers together and ignored outright signs of affection between them. Some, while not approving of such relationships, gave prisoners verbal warnings.

Victoria: And . . . there was this one officer [a Chicana] and . . . she hooked it up for us to be in the same dorm. And . . . she just said, "You know what? You guys could stay together, but, yeah, I better not see not one hickey on your neck . . . or else . . . I'll send you straight to Lockup and I'll separate you two . . ." Eventually . . . we both had hickeys on our neck. She'd seen one time and she didn't do nothing about it.

While some prisoners could claim that they got hickeys during sexual encounters with male staff, they did not generally make reference to such incidents. On the one hand, sexual contact between prisoners and staff was also prohibited. On the other hand, the staff in question could always deny it. Rita declared, "Yeah, . . . but they have to catch you in the act and it's your word against theirs."

Most guards frowned on same-sex relationships and enforced institutional regulations that penalized prisoners for having "personal contact," or "homosecting," with other prisoners. Personal contact included sitting on each other's beds, combing each other's hair, "standing too close," hugging, kissing, having hickeys, and making love.

Administrative policies frequently included asking new prisoners if they were "homosexual" and if so, if they were "femme" or "butch." Regardless of how prisoners identified themselves, those deemed to be masculine in appearance and demeanor were automatically labeled "obvious homosexuals." They were also referred to as "butches," "dykes," "daddies," "little boys," and "stud broads" (Díaz-Cotto 2000b). While prisoners also used such labels to refer to other prisoners, they did not generally tend to do so in a pejorative manner.

At times guards sought to discourage prisoners from engaging in same-sex relationships by repeatedly charging at least one of the partners with rule violations. Likewise, they went out of their way to penalize the butches, who were labeled a priori as "troublemakers" because of their demeanor and appearance. Pintas also argued that guards set butches up for further punishment by sexually harassing the butches' lovers in front of them.

Carmen: They would . . . pat 'em down, touch 'em in front of you. And . . . what I experienced is . . . they would like try to play on 'em and . . . flirt with them in front of you and tease you about it . . . Well, we'd get pissed off and we would cuss back and tell 'em things and then we'd get in trouble.

The butches responded in anger not only because they wanted to protect the femmes but also to show guards and other butches that they were willing to stand up for themselves.

Carmen: When you're in that kind of . . . environment, life, it's like you have this pride . . . You will tell back a CO and you will speak up because it's like you got a lot of other little boys listening to you and watching you. So you . . . gotta carry that image . . . 'Cause it's like every little boy's trying to be better than the next little boy. So it's like you gonna say something. You gonna do something . . . If not, . . . you ain't gonna look good in the system.

Prisoners were also routinely ridiculed, threatened, and punished by guards for such relationships.

Carmen: Oh, well, . . . they would say, "Oh, you think you're slick, huh? We caught you!" . . . Some of them would make fun of it . . . Some would say, "You're going to The Hole." Some of them would say, "I . . . hope you thought it was good because you gonna pay a big price for it."

Verbal reprimands and ridicule were accompanied by write-ups, which were placed in prisoners' institutional files. Once a certain number of write-ups accumulated, a prisoner could lose her "good time" and/or be sent to Lockup for a period of time.

Victoria: They'll get locked up for "PC," . . . "personal contact." . . . They'd get sent to Lockup . . . And . . . they try to separate them like for the rest of their stay.

Write-ups, always included in prisoners' files, were accessible to staff and parole board members. On occasion prisoners' families were also informed when their relatives were sent to segregation for "homosecting."

In spite of the many regulations, prisoners found ways to both continue having sexual encounters with one another and reduce their chances of being caught by guards. Regulars would request assignment to those living spaces in the dorms that were the farthest away from the cop shop.

Mercedes: There's certain areas in the dorm where . . . all the regulars would have, and that was always the back of the dorm . . . We never had to fight for that area . . . Since we we're regulars we pretty much requested it.

During those times when at least some pintas were housed in individual cells, it was easier for them to maintain sexual relationships. For those whose roommate was also their lover, it was an almost perfect arrangement. Those pintas who had sex in the dorms took the chance that other prisoners would snitch on them.

Victoria: A lot . . . of women didn't like it, and a couple of times we'd gotten complaints 'cause we were having sex there and . . . doing whatever we wanted to do . . . Like . . . somebody wrote a written complaint . . . and they had said that we were doing "lewd and vulgar acts" and that we were a bunch of "lesbian pigs" and . . . "dykes" . . . You know, just really bashing us.

Such snitching, however, was not that common, as most prisoners were either involved in same-sex affairs themselves, feared retaliation, or decided it was none of their concern. Pintas housed in dorms sought to have some privacy as well as protect themselves from snitches by covering their beds with sheets while having sex (Rita).

Pintas had a number of other places in which to have sexual encounters.

Carmen: We would have sex in the room if people would pin [look out] . . . It could be always anywhere, the showers . . . in the kitchen, in different . . . isolated areas . . . in the library . . . A lot of times the art room and sewing room.

Rita: Well, in the kitchen . . . you can't have sex but you can mess around . . . They catch women in bed together in the dorms, . . . in showers. Or they see hickeys all over and they know you've been there for a long time. They . . . know you have had sexual contact with another female.

Even when lovers were separated in different housing units by guards, pintas found ways to visit one another.

Victoria: It used to be different-color dresses, but over the years that changed and then it was just a different-color wristband. So they'd have like a red wristband and then a yellow wristband, green, purple. Anyway, so, I would . . . just trade the different color wristbands . . . with someone else. You know, give 'em five dollars . . . You know, trade with someone else . . . that's in that dorm.

Such roaming was possible because of overcrowding and guards' lack of interest in getting to know prisoners. Even then, repeat offenders who became known to guards had to be particularly careful.

Showering together was another activity that required much co-ordination between lovers and their "pointers," generally friends who covered or pinned for them. Pointers were also necessary when prisoners were engaging in sex in the dorm or even just sleeping together.

Rosa: Usually there would be people that would be pointers, you know, friends. And you'd put a blanket across . . . the bed area. And some people don't care. They don't even do that. And if the officer was coming, they'd let you know . . . "Stop!"

Spending the night together required more coordination and the cooperation of additional prisoners.

Victoria: Well . . . we would trade like beds with someone . . . else. And . . . just that night for . . . roll call or wristband check, we'd . . . sit down, you know, they'd get us on our . . . rightful bed. And then at night when the lights were out we'd just trade. You know, the girl knew, "Hey, I'm sleeping here. Go to my bed." And then she would go and then me and her were able to sleep together. We would even push our bunks together so we would . . . almost like imagine that we were in our own house sleeping in . . . our full-size bed.

Some prisoners caught homosecting were fortunate enough to avoid being sent to Lockup.

Victoria: What had happened was that we . . . got a . . . verbal warning . . . You know, the lights are out so we were able to finagle. Half . . . of the dorm is gay, supposedly, when they're in jail . . . And . . . we were able to say, "You know, that wasn't us, officer . . . That must have been . . . Joan Doe who sleeps right next to us. Oh, she has all kinds of girls in her bed." "Well, what's her name?" "We don't know," you know, sort of thing.

Mercedes: Yeah, we got caught sleeping together. We got pulled out to the door like 3 A.M. . . . . They kept us there forever . . . standing in the hallway . . . freezing to death in a little . . . nightgown . . . They call them gunnysack nightgowns . . . I don't recall them doing anything about it, just scolding us and telling us we couldn't do that, no homosexual . . . activities . . . They were basically women guards. They were Black and Chicanas.

When one of the partners in a couple was sent to Lockup, it became harder to maintain the relationship.

Victoria: So she got caught stealing sugar . . . into the dorm . . . and . . . they took her to Lockup . . . But I would write to her every single day little notes. And one of the girls that used to go down and clean the bottom floor, she'd like would throw it in there and she'd get my notes . . . Sometimes she couldn't get to 'em or sometimes the sheriff picked it up . . . and wondered, "Where's this from?" sort of thing . . . That's how we kept in contact, writing letters to one another.

Even the most stable relationships, however, were affected by the release from SBI of one of the partners. At times, pintas resumed the relationship once both were released from jail.

Victoria: And she went home. It was the saddest day of my life. We had seen each other for a couple of months . . . When I met her I was like, ". . . This is gonna be a one-night stand. That's cool with me." . . . And it just turned out to just be more . . . We haven't left each other yet.

Lesbianism as Institutionalization?

Some prisoners, like Lucy, believed that over a period of time heterosexual prisoners could evolve into lesbians as a way of adapting to institutional life. She felt that this was easier than getting clean and sober and coping with life on the outside. While Lucy saw becoming a lesbian as a natural extension of institutional life, she did not see it as something "natural" for herself.

For most people, I believe, . . . especially if they'd been institutionalized, it's . . . a form of adaptation, like evolving. Like how they say that fish evolved and so began to walk on the earth from the water into there. I believe actually that for some people that were doing time, that eventually, that they may evolve into being . . . a lesbian . . . It's a lot more acceptable to change that route than actually change every other part of your life to make it outside in the society.

Despite her reservations, Lucy found herself becoming more and more attracted to such relationships with each subsequent incarceration.

Where in the beginning it was, "I like you," because it was out of necessity, . . . after, when . . . I was making money from having my own store and . . . selling cigarettes, . . . it was more of a game . . . I got scared because I'd seen that I was getting real comfortable and I was never comfortable in jail . . . Not until this last time when I was there . . . in '93 . . . You know, where I could see that . . . I was that much closer to even going that route. You know, of . . . being with another woman . . . Not just the lifestyle of being, . . . I would have to say bisexual, but the whole jail environment itself, . . . women, the dope running in there, . . . the scenes . . . I think I was going for . . . the whole . . . enchilada . . . Where I had finally found that I fit in . . . Actually seeing where it could be comfortable, that's what scared me . . . because I always never got loaded, never played in there, was always saying, "Know what? There's a life out there for me. I'm going to be something." And then all of a sudden the life out there was more scary for me . . . And I was starting to lose . . . what . . . was real to me, you know.

Unlike Lucy, the other pintas interviewed saw their sexuality while incarcerated more as a choice than an imposition and did not tend to consider either lesbianism or having lesbian relationships on the inside as a sign of institutionalization.

Little Boys and Femmes

While the sexual identification (i.e., lesbian, heterosexual, bisexual) and gender roles some pintas assumed depended on whether they were in or out of jail, they expressed their sexuality within the confines of traditional male/female gender roles (i.e., butch, femme). This was so even when individual prisoners sometimes changed those roles in midstream. Such as when they were heterosexual and femme when arriving at the jail but "turned" lesbian and butch once in the institution or when a butch "dropped her belt" and adopted a feminine role.

For other pintas their sexual identification did not change when institutionalized. However, the way they felt about it did. For Carmen, who was state-raised and butch-identified throughout her life, SBI became a safe haven in which to express her sexuality because same-sex relationships for her were the norm.

Carmen: Well, in jail . . . it was easy . . . I was so used to doing time, for me it was like home . . . It was comfortable. I felt safe. I felt like I was accepted . . . being a homosexual . . . You know, everybody around me was gay. It was like a little world of gayness . . . And . . . it was easy to compete against people in there . . . compared to out here, you know, it was so hard. It was so bigger and more expanded, and there wasn't so many people that I knew that were gay. All of them I knew that were gay were in . . . jail or far away.

Butches cut their hair short and dressed like working-class men of their own ethnic groups. Carmen, who described herself as a "lesbian," a "homosexual," and a "little boy," described what that meant in her case.

I was masculine . . . all the time . . . through all my homosexuality . . . I dressed like a little boy. You know, I tried to have short hair and dress like . . . a cholo would dress. The khakis or sweatshirts and slingshots, . . . maybe T-shirts . . . That's the way I was in the system.

For some, embracing the role of butch meant finally giving in to an outward physical appearance that reflected how they felt about themselves. In this sense, going to jail was a liberating experience for some Chicana lesbians, not only because they met women with whom they identified, but also because their appearance and "aggressive" (mannish) demeanor, criticized and ridiculed on the outside, was highly valued and respected on the inside.

Graciela: When I was 13, okay, and I was . . . with women, it was always, like, kept in the closet. When I got taken to jail and I seen this is what I was. I seen gay girls that were aggressive, how they dressed like boys and they looked like boys . . . I've always been aggressive . . . That was just the way I was and . . . even when I was younger I used to dress like a boy . . . I didn't like wearing girls' clothes . . . So I decided I was gonna cut my hair off. And I did. And . . . that's when I decided to come out of the closet. My behavior didn't change, just my appearance.

As discussed earlier, butches were granted special treatment by women labeled femmes, much as men are given deference by many women. Although self-identified lesbians who were butches also benefited from such privileges, they ridiculed and resented prisoners who were just playing the role of "little boys" while incarcerated (Carmen).

Asked why the femmes would cater to the butches, Rosa replied:

Because . . . for one thing, there's no men around. And I don't think that you can take sex completely out of a person. And they're gonna find a substitute whether they're straight or not . . . And a lot of those daddies, they acted like men.

Carmen: They would do anything for us. I mean, . . . even to the . . . fact that . . . if we might have had another old lady in another yard, they would still put up with it 'cause . . . there wasn't very many little boys.

Some butches, however, argued that they provided the femmes protection and sex.

Carmen: Well, we took care of them. We protected them . . . It's like nobody would bother them. You know, they had their needs met. It involved sex, yeah.

Asked what the daddies had to offer femmes in jail, however, Rosa responded, "They didn't offer anything." For Rosa, who was a self-identified femme, the daddies did not even offer protection. This was so because she and her butch lover were involved in an abusive relationship.

Most of the time we had such a violent relationship that we were fighting each other. So I don't know who we were gonna protect each other from.

The "Daddy Tank"

Deemed by administrators as "mentally ill" and considered to be a bad influence on other prisoners, during the late 1960s, the harassment of butches at SBI led to the confinement of lesbians in Cell Block 4200, a maximum-security cell block also known as the "Daddy Tank." The policy was supported by a California state law at the time that required the separation or "exclusion" of identified lesbians from other prisoners (*NewsWest* 1976).

The Daddy Tank was a separate housing area for "obvious homosexuals" (Johansen 1996; *LAT* 4/10/73; 7/13/86). There they remained locked down (two to three prisoners in a small cell) unless they had work assignments, went to meals, had visitors, or were let out for brief periods of recreation on Saturdays. Such restrictive housing also meant that prisoners labeled homosexual were excluded from participating in the few programs available to other prisoners (Watterson 1996). Lesbians also felt guards were more likely to harass them than nonlesbians and place them in solitary confinement.

Luisa: They had a Daddy's Tank. Nothing . . . but *lesbiana* women used to be there. But it was for the ones that were . . . the aggressive, the butch.

Rosa: It was a cell block and it was called 4200 and the women worked in the laundry at night.

Carmen: The Daddy Tank . . . it sucks because it was like they kept us separated. We couldn't get to any of the . . . femmes . . . You could get out of the unit to go to . . . where they put you to work. And then, it was a lot of craziness going on in the jobs to where the . . . sheriffs were coming down on you even harder. And you found most of the . . . little boys in discipline. Either in the Daddy Tank or in discipline.

Prisoners interviewed by Watterson (1996) at SBI also said that women held in the Daddy Tank were often mistreated by guards.

In spite of being segregated, the daddies were still popular with prisoners in General Population.

Rosa: They dressed in blue. And I always looked at it as being an "elite" thing, right, because whenever they walked in, the rest of the women would sort of sit up and take notice. 'Cause it was like . . . men coming in . . . It's so hard to put into words. It was like looking at men!

Rosa: They had to wear dresses. At that time there was no pants.[4] And, oh, God, they hated it. You could see they hated it. But they had their hair cut . . . and they walked very boyish and they did the best they could to look boyish, in dresses!

The only time Daddy Tank prisoners were allowed to mix with General Population was during the weekly Saturday recreation period and in the dining room. While the interaction between the daddies and General Population was strictly monitored, prisoners managed to communicate with one another.

Rosa: The only time that they would mix with the other women would be on Saturday. They had a . . . day that you would go out into the yard. Everybody would be able to go out there for about an hour . . . And also in the dining room, you know, you looked, you winked, you talked, you'd throw kites . . . You really can't keep them apart.

Sometimes lovers arranged to have visitors from the outside come at the same time so that they too could visit with one another.

At the end of 1976, SBI moved prisoners housed in the Daddy Tank to a dormitory (*NewsWest* 1976–1977) where lesbians were granted more freedom of movement and the ability to participate in some programs. However, prisoners identified as homosexuals remained housed separately from the rest of the jail population (*NewsWest* 1976–1977). The dorm, however, was opened to include both butches and femmes.

Rosa: There was some kind of thing going on in Sybil Brand where classification was changing. And they were gonna put every homosexual away from General Population. See before that there used to be a tank for homosexuals that were very dominant, stud girls . . . Those girls got put into 4200. The other women were left out in that General Population. And all of a sudden this drive came through because of this classification officer, sergeant, that decided that she was gonna put away all the homosexuals in a tank to themselves. And because I came in with my girlfriend, I was classified with them . . . Everybody went to homosexual tank whether you were femme or a daddy.

The reclassification, however, backfired on administrators.

Luisa: And then they just mixed them all together. A lot of hanky-panky going on. It was more like a casino. (laughs) Everybody be making out or having sex.

A lot of the women they jump from one bed to another, you know. I was too scared . . . to get caught. (laughs)

Rosa: A lot of women were trying to get in there, . . . especially if they had a girlfriend . . . in there . . . I guess they thought it was gonna be fun.

During the 1980s, SBI administrators ended the policy of segregated housing for lesbians. On the one hand, prisoners organized against it. On the other hand, prisoners' demands for an end to segregated housing was complemented by those of prisoners' rights activists on the outside, particularly women's groups and attorneys. These advocates picketed and demonstrated outside of SBI demanding an end to discriminatory policies and a change in the overall conditions at the jail. Advocates also brought media attention to the plight of prisoners at SBI in the media (*LAT* 6/19/72; *NewsWest* 1976–1977). Ultimately, the segregation of lesbians was terminated because, as prisoners alleged in *Inmates of SBI* (1982a, 1982b), it was a violation of their civil rights.

Carmen: Well, they put a committee together . . . to take the Daddy Tank out . . . I think that had a lot to do with it, though . . . They did it from both sides . . . of the jailhouses . . . They did do away with the Daddy Tank I think about 10 years ago or 15. I think they probably got rid of it 'cause it's against the law to keep people segregated like that.

Pseudo-family/Kinship Networks

Pintas also supported one another in SBI by forming pseudo-family/kinship networks, what prisoners referred to as "play families," that is, networks in which prisoners adopted or were assigned the roles of male and female members of a family such as "father," "brother," "mother," "daughter," etc.[5]

Estela: Like the Mexicans[6] . . . like the stud broads . . . say, "Oh, that's my brother . . ." And like the femmes say, "That's my sister." . . . And . . . if somebody was . . . real older, they'd say, "Oh, that's my kid." And they would call that person "Mom."

Prisoners who participated in pseudo-families could identify as lesbian, bisexual, or heterosexual. While the heads of a family could be a lesbian couple, this was not always the case.

The primary purpose of pseudo-families was to help prisoners survive incarceration by providing emotional support and reducing prisoners' fears and sense of isolation. Such networks also helped familiarize prisoners with institutional rules and regulations as well as prisoner codes, thus socializing Chicanas into institutional life. They provided continuity and stability in an environment where the prisoner body was constantly changing and where rules and regulations were enforced arbitrarily by staff members. Most importantly, they provided prisoners protection from their peers.

Deborah: Well, I just think that it . . . was . . . just a group thing. I mean, we stuck together . . . It would keep probably other people, like the Blacks or the whites, to be aware of, you know, "It's not just one person. This is a group that you're messing with. Even if you see this person outside of this group, you're not to mess with that person 'cause they do get along with this whole crowd over here."

Roles were assigned according to how close prisoners felt to one another. Thus, pintas were careful when assigning such labels. The closeness also carried with it gender role expectations as prisoners were labeled butch or femme. "Male" relatives were expected to protect those they took under their wing. Female relatives were expected to be emotionally supportive.

Pintas claimed that Latinas as a whole seemed to engage in pseudo-families more frequently than other racial/ethnic groups (Graciela; Victoria). Some pintas went further by stating that bilingual Chicanas were more likely to participate in pseudo-families than nonbilingual Chicanas and Latin American immigrants (Rita).

While most pintas interviewed said they had not formed part of pseudo-families, they gave examples of times when other pintas either referred to them as "Mom" or assigned them male roles, or when they themselves called other pintas "Mom."

Deborah: I've had people say, "This is my cousin" but I'm not. You know, "This is my sister" . . . but I'm not related to them . . . In '91 I had a youngster call me Mom . . . I never did it.

Sometimes groups of prisoners developed closeness with one another because they had done time together. In such cases, they related like an extended family network.

Graciela: Someone can be from a different town that I met in there. 'Cause to me it's like we have a family reunion. Every year I've seen the same people . . . We're used to being in the system with each other, not out here.

Some social scientists have argued that competition among different pseudo-families kept prisoners from forming coalitions to demand prison reform (Giallombardo 1966). Pintas interviewed for this book as well as other Latinas (Díaz-Cotto 1996) maintain that other factors kept prisoners from forming coalitions. These included fear of guard retaliation, lack of adequate outside sources of support, the length of a prisoner's sentence, and interracial/interethnic hostilities among prisoners. Despite such obstacles to organizing, pintas agreed that if family heads asked family members to join them in reform-oriented activities, they would do so because they would obey their "parents'" wishes.

Graciela: Like if the "mother" or the "father," if they ask the "daughter" or the "kid" what . . . you want them to do, they're gonna do it.[7]

At their best, pseudo-families reproduced the comfort, companionship, love, and acceptance some pintas had received from loved ones on the outside. The emotional and psychological support pintas received from such kinship networks was particularly important because, while all prisoners were scarred by their experiences within penal institutions, not all survived incarceration. Some died in jail as a result of diseases, staff negligence, or suicide.

Others pintas, like Victoria, felt pseudo-families fulfilled only superficial roles, giving members "a false sense of security and a . . . false sense of family." Likewise, sometimes family members reinforced and supported negative behaviors of their members. Such was the case when the members dealt drugs within the institution and victimized other prisoners. Rita went further by stating that members of pseudo-families tended to exploit other family members.

Rita: And I'd also seen people that used other people because they know . . . they got visits every day, and they gonna latch on to them. And they're gonna say, "Oh, yeah, just call me 'Mom'" . . . And if you're dumb and stupid in there, you're gonna . . . give these other people money.

In summary, being forced to live in a women's institution gave pintas the opportunity to experiment with diverse types of gender roles and sexual identification as well as relationships with other women. While some chose to sexualize those relationships, others did not. Nowhere was the mixture of roles and sexual identities more apparent than in the pseudo-family/kinship networks women created to satisfy a host of spiritual, social, and emotional needs.

It is clear that the various types of gender and sexual roles pintas adopted in jail significantly challenged not only society's heterosexual role expectations for women and Chicanas but also institutional rules and regulations. This was true even when pintas adopted a butch role and imitated male behavior or when femmes catered to the butches. The behavior of butches posed a particular threat to male guards who felt their masculinity challenged by prisoners who had the ability to attract other women's attention.

Those pintas who opted to barter sexual favors with staff for desired goods also broke with institutional rules and regulations even when they did not necessarily break free of traditional gender roles or oppressive relationships.

Outside Looking In

Third Parties

One of the ways pintas sought to break their isolation in jail was by cultivating relationships with people on the outside, particularly those who were willing to support them and/or advocate on their behalf. These included friends, family, community groups and individuals, private and religious organizations, members of the media, and prisoners' rights advocates.

However, penal administrators have historically sought to limit the access of outsiders to institutions, frequently arguing that it was through visits that drugs and other contraband were brought into facilities.

Equally important were administrators' fears that prisoners' access to outsiders, especially attorneys, would enable them to seek legal redress for treatment and conditions. With lawsuits came unwanted publicity, public investigations, and, on some rare occasions, a change in conditions and the firing of staff members and/or administrators. Moreover, lawsuits, whether settled in or out of court, were costly and acknowledged the right of prisoners to challenge their keepers.

This chapter explores: Who were pintas' primary outside sources of support? What types of help did they offer? How effective were outsiders in meeting the multiple needs of pintas? Did such support help prisoners change oppressive jail conditions and treatment by staff?

Pintas and Their Families

A number of pintas were able to maintain at least occasional contact with family members through visits, phone conversations, and letters. They offered pintas emotional and sometimes financial support, the latter in the form of money and packages.

Sonia: Once I got busted . . . the hardest thing was for me to call my mother up to let her know I was back in prison . . . 'cause I knew it would hurt her. You know what I mean? . . . My mother's always stood by my side . . . And we . . . still have a good relationship. And . . . my mother's always been in denial of me . . . using drugs because she's never seen me put a needle in my arm . . . She didn't want to accept it . . . And I was her only daughter so it . . . really had hurt her. But she's always been there for me. She's always gone to see me when she could and send me some money when I needed it in there, you know. But in prison I learned to take care of myself. I . . . draw, so I used to draw and make money out of drawings, you know, and . . . I had a job in the industry sewing.

Pintas who had strained their relationships with loved ones to the limit, however, oftentimes had alienated them altogether. Hence, their support was not always forthcoming. This was particularly true once pintas began to go in and out of jail and prisons, especially if they had also abused or taken advantage of their loved ones.

Those pintas whose partners were also addicts soon found that their partners' addiction interfered with their ability to be there for them. Likewise, pintas were deprived of an outside partner's support when they were arrested together.

While pintas tended to care for their own children at the beginning of their using histories, once they were incarcerated many left the care of their children to women relatives, most often their mothers. In a few cases, the children's fathers or paternal grandmothers took over the care of the children. Frequently, if the partner was a male, he did not wait around for his female partner to get out of jail. A few did take care of their mutual children while pintas were in jail, but this was less likely to be the case if pintas were serving long sentences in state prisons.

Some children became wards of the court and were sent to foster care or other placements until their mothers were released from institutions. For a few children such placements led to their adoption by others, generally a woman relative or a friend. Both children and mothers had to contend with the trauma of separation.

Much has been written about the difficulties encountered by incarcerated mothers and their children.[1] There was the emotional trauma created by the sudden disappearance of the mother from the children's lives.

[A] mother who is locked up faces an immediate and constant anxiety about her children—where they are, whether they're safe and are being well fed, whether they will be taken by the county and put in a children's shelter or foster home. A woman also worries about her child's worries, knowing that her child is concerned and traumatized about her disappearance. Children who are kept in the dark about what has happened to their mother—where she is and why—often get no answers to their questions and feel responsible somehow for their separation and loss. (Watterson 1996: 209)

The visiting policies of the LASD, which allowed prisoners only two 20-minute visits per week, also created difficulties for mothers and children (Watterson 1996: 366). Further, restrictions prohibited contact visits at SBI (*LAT* 4/10/73, 2/16/77, 12/2/78) although such visits were allowed in the Men's Central Jail in downtown Los Angeles (*Inmates of SBI* 1982a, 1982b). Such regulations made the interchange between pintas and their visitors highly impersonal.

Visits . . . become sad circuses, with everyone shouting to be heard, talking through telephones to one another. (Watterson 1996: 209)

Long visiting lines at the institution also made it difficult for family members to visit.

Additionally, prisoners' limited access to telephones, particularly when the institution had a large prisoner population, made it difficult for pintas to stay in touch with their families. The fact that prisoners were allowed to make only collect calls made calls expensive. Many pintas, therefore, could call home only occasionally or not at all. In other cases, the children were too young to hold phone conversations. Writing to their children and family members was less costly, but not all children could read or write. In these ways, pintas frequently lost their connections to family members while incarcerated.

Even pintas fortunate enough to have relatives who could and would bring their children to visit them had mixed feelings about letting their children see them in jail or prison.

Sonia: My mom is the one that's always gone to see me . . . She's took my . . . 15-year-old when he was a baby to visit me. But she raised . . . my son as her son, so he didn't know I was his mother really . . . And, so in '93, . . . I think when I was off parole, then that's when my mother and I finally told my son that I was his mother . . . And my . . . 25-five-year-old . . . the one that . . . was addicted to drugs . . . I think . . . the last time I had seen him in prison was when he was 14 years old. He lived with his stepmother, so I didn't see them very often. Mostly, I saw my mom . . . I didn't really see my children . . . I think I didn't . . . want to or . . . it was . . . more easier that they didn't exist. For me to do time it was better that way.

The difficult experience of having their children see them in jail or prison led some pintas to avoid visits from their children while they were incarcerated.

Lucy: So while they were in with my mother she had knew from before, from being arrested that I . . . couldn't handle it. I told her she could bring other kids, you know, my nephews and nieces, but don't bring mine . . . I would call and send them drawing pictures and I'd . . . draw cards . . . saying . . . Mama was gonna change, but it . . . was nothing that was consistent. My daughter . . . my oldest one . . . she was very angry at me.

Even those Chicanas who were able to maintain relationships with their children while incarcerated had to deal with the emotional trauma caused by separation. Children felt hurt and were frequently angry at their mothers for having abandoned them. They felt that if their mothers loved them they should be able to change their lifestyles for the better.

Moreover, some were angry at mothers (and other relatives) who had physically and/or emotionally abused them prior to their incarceration or who had been unable or unwilling to protect them from abuse by others, such as caretakers. Under such tensions children sometimes acted aggressively at home, in school, and in other social settings.

Pintas frequently felt guilty and angry at themselves for having neglected their children. While they might be able to postpone dealing with their children's feelings while in jail, upon their release, they were confronted with them once again (see Chapter 18).

Other Outside Contacts

As discussed earlier, pintas also depended on runners or "tricks" for support. While some of them were relatives, friends, and partners, others were strangers Chicanas met while incarcerated.

Lucy: Tricks, people that people use. They would term them as being a "runner." Just someone who, you know, gives them the visit. Someone who . . . supplies them with their packages and money . . . There's a lot of lonely old men out there. A lot of just lonely people, period, . . . that are looking for love and looking at it from people who are in jail.

Community Organizations

The number of outside groups that provided services to prisoners at SBI was minimal. According to pintas interviewed, there was no consistent source of outside Latina/o community support for pintas at SBI during the institution's history except for the few fundamentalist Christian churches that brought in services.

Those Chicanas/o and bilingual volunteers who came into the institution tended to be members of larger non-Latina/o organizations such as religious groups, AA, NA, Friends Outside, and Liaison League.

Lucy: I had in Sybil Brand . . . went to church and they had two speakers that came in there and, yes, they were Chicanas and they were former inmates . . . People were sharing how they got out and . . . making it out there but that was only through the church . . . But this is through the route of the church.

A few Chicana/o self-help groups offered support to pintas/os upon their release from jails and prisons and Chicana/o-centered research groups helped publicize the plight of pintas/os through their publications (CPRP 1975a, 1976b). Others continually raised issues such as police brutality and the impact of arrests and incarceration on Latina/o communities.

However, with few exceptions, Latina/o community organizations (active in a number of community struggles against discrimination, police brutality, and inadequate housing conditions) were not likely to have the resources, personnel, time, and/or contacts within the penal system needed to adequately support incarcerated Chicanas.

Likewise, while all barrio residents were affected by police brutality, racial and ethnic discrimination, and drug-war policies, some were also the victims of pintas' crimes. As a result, pintas were often seen as contributing to the deterioration of Chicana/o barrios. Thus, not all Chicanas/os sympathized with the plight of pintas.

Friends Outside

Friends Outside was one of the few organizations that offered consistent support to prisoners at SBI. However, because of the large number of prisoners and the limited scope of the programs, many had difficulty accessing their services (Estela). The most common request prisoners made to Friends Outside was to check up on their children (*LAT* 11/18/87). Deborah was one of the Chicanas whom Friends Outside helped to locate her daughter while she was still at SBI.

Deborah: It just happened that when I was incarcerated, . . . I have two children, and my last child I had lost to the system. I didn't know where they had placed her. And I had put in this request to see Friends Outside and they helped me . . .

find out where my daughter was at and had the social worker come out and see me at the jail.

During the mid-1990s Friends Outside also provided services to Spanish-monolingual prisoners.

Graciela: They'll come and visit you . . . If you need clothes or you need somebody contacted from the outside . . . If a girl . . . just speaks fluent Spanish, they will have somebody come out that . . . speaks Spanish.

Upon her release from SBI, Deborah became one of the bilingual Chicanas working for Friends Outside to provide services to prisoners at the jail.

Deborah: It's a small paid staff . . . There's about maybe five . . . of us that are full-time paid staff . . . Three of us . . . Chicanas . . . What I do is supervise the volunteers that visit inside the jail . . . And I also visit inmates . . . I'm working out at Sybil Brand two days a week . . . since '93 . . . A lot of the women that I work with are Spanish-speaking people.

Liaison League and Other Outside Volunteers

Liaison League was founded in 1965 by outside volunteers who wanted to help reduce the recidivism rate of women prisoners. The objective was to pair off one prisoner with one "sponsor." The sponsors would act as mentors to prisoners upon their release.[2] None of the pintas interviewed mentioned having sought out its services.

Others who would visit Chicanas in jail included women volunteers from nearby communities. However, shame sometimes kept pintas from accepting such support.

Linda: This woman tried to go see me and I seen her one time. And the reason . . . 'cause I was too ashamed to go . . . out of that cell . . . You didn't have a toothbrush. You didn't have a toothpaste, *nada.* And then they wanted you to go visit. I . . . don't know if it was my ego or what, but I was too embarrassed to go see anybody with my hair the way it was and not washing up, nada.

Joint Efforts

During the early 1990s, Joint Efforts, a community organization, received CDC funding to send former prisoners such as Luisa and her African-American co-worker Joy to provide various types of counseling services to prisoners at SBI for at least a three-year period.

Luisa: I had a caseload of 200 women at Sybil Brand. And what I used to take to them is resources. Let's say a woman . . . was in the process of getting out, . . . I can provide her service such as maybe a recovery house, maybe an outpatient program, maybe a . . . sober living home.

Luisa's primary responsibility was to work with Latina prisoners. Joy was responsible for a predominantly African-American caseload. Luisa and Joy would get referrals both from staff persons who had been contacted by prisoners and through the "Request Box" in the jail's dining hall.

Luisa: As you're walking into the chow hall, there's a big huge box . . . and it says, "Request Box." You put them in there and they take those every day or every other day . . . This guy . . . working there . . . would . . . give me . . . and another co-worker of mine . . . a bunch of requests . . . We looked through the bags . . . A lot of these women were requesting treatment, outpatient, "Can you give me a Big Book?"[3] "Can you get me a directory?" . . . "Can you find me a recovery house?" . . . And we'd look through all the names and then we put . . . whoever was getting out sooner, you know, whatever services they need [first].

Luisa and Joy met through the regular visiting channels.

Luisa: I had sessions with them through the window, through the phone . . . HIV or AIDS . . . was never written in paper . . . But the women would say, "Is there anything you could do for a person that has HIV?" I says, "I'm a case manager but I also . . . do HIV and AIDS." . . . She said, "Well, you know, I've been HIV." Or "You know, I haven't been taking my medication," Or "Can you help me?" Boom! that was it! That was my primary way to get the women that were HIV . . . And a lot of them would go and call me and I'd come and pick them up. Some would want to go out and get . . . laid or get loaded and then they'd call me a week later. So . . . the bond was there. And I was there. The comfort was there . . . A lot of them were molested. A lot of them were raped. A lot of them sold their body.

HIV and AIDS

With an increase in the prisoner population at SBI came a growth in the number of pintas and other prisoners with HIV and AIDS. Outside volunteers first had a difficult time getting access to provide HIV/AIDS-related services to prisoners at the jail. Eventually jail administrators allowed a Chicano counselor to provide counseling services to prisoners with HIV and AIDS. Also, Deborah and other staff and volunteers at Friends Outside helped place prisoners in rehabilitation programs upon their release.

Deborah: Inside . . . Sybil Brand . . . staggering, staggering numbers. It's incredible . . . It's very sad . . . They're in just General Population . . . The only thing they can do is send them down to the county hospital if that's what they need to do. But it's not great medical stuff there for them, you know . . . They do have an HIV counselor . . . He's a Latino . . . They have like that group for the HIV, they meet there . . . What we do as Friends Outside is that we try to . . . find them beds for drug programs instead of going back out into the street. We do a lot of that.

Media

Rarely did the English- or Spanish-language media take an interest in women prisoners. This neglect was particularly noticeable in the case of SBI, where a review of seven major California English-language newspapers covering 1972–1999 yielded less than 35 news stories concerning events at SBI.

The one-time pintas interviewed remembered media interest in them was when prisoners were interviewed concerning the parenting class offered at the institution.

Marta: There's only one film in there . . . that I seen, of . . . parenting class, about . . . children. And that's 'cause I'm in it, you know. We're talking about babies on drugs, the mothers using drugs, you now. And that was filmed in '80.

While the women's/lesbian media was more likely to concern itself with issues pertaining to incarcerated women, it generally lacked the resources and mass exposure accessible to mainstream publications.

Legal Advocacy

Perhaps the most influential type of outside support pintas and other prisoners at SBI had was from prisoners' rights attorneys. Through their willingness to support prisoners' class action suits, attorneys encouraged prisoners to continue building interracial/inter-ethnic prisoner coalitions in order to challenge oppressive conditions and treatment.

The publicity generated around the lawsuits also allowed prisoners to publicize their grievances publicly, thus forcing penal administrators to justify their actions to non-penal elites. The latter sometimes pressured institutional administrators to make concessions to prisoners.

Moreover, even partially favorable court decisions that recognized the legitimacy of prisoners' grievances and ordered jail personnel to make reforms interfered, even if only temporarily, with the monopoly administrators had over their institutions and the prisoners under their supervision.

The effectiveness of litigation to force penal elites to make changes at the institutional level, however, was limited by the long periods of time it took courts to make their decisions and the ability of administrators to ignore unfavorable court decisions, sometimes indefinitely. Nonetheless, *Inmates of SBI* did lead to the closing of the Daddy Tank, the establishing of a work release program, and contact visits.

To summarize, the few advocates for prisoners' rights made their support for pintas and other prisoners at SBI felt through a combination of methods. Family members, lovers, and friends, but primarily women relatives, provided pintas emotional and financial support and frequently cared for their children while they were incarcerated. Educational and vocational institutions offered courses and work training programs. Religious and community groups provided pintas emotional support and services both while they were incarcerated and once they were released from the institution. Women/lesbian advocates and prisoners' rights attorneys publicly supported prisoners' efforts to change conditions at the facility through the use of demonstrations, educational media campaigns, and litigation.

The access by prisoners' rights advocates to SBI, however, was closely monitored by penal elites. Equally important, the ability of pintas and other prisoners to force institutional administrators to make reforms was limited by the fact that few outside individuals and organizations were willing and/or able to provide women prisoners much-needed support. Spanish-monolingual prisoners, as usual, were less likely to receive the support of third parties.

Prisoner Complaints and Resistance

It is clear from the previous chapters that pintas at SBI rebelled against the treatment and conditions they encountered at the facility in numerous ways. While some chose to isolate, most formed cliques based on ethnicity/race, sexual orientation, language spoken, type of drugs used, and barrio loyalties. And while most pursued sexual relationships with peers, a few became sexually involved with guards.

Pintas also sold or bartered goods stolen from their work assignments, sold and used drugs, and verbally and physically assaulted guards and other prisoners. A few participated in the limited number of programs and services available at the facility.

While these actions are not generally considered by social scientists and male-centered prisoners' rights activists to be significant acts of political resistance or rebellion, they are, nonetheless, significant ways in which women prisoners have challenged the demands by penal authorities for undisputed obedience.

The literature on incarcerated women has rarely documented the multiple ways that women have responded politically to the conditions of their incarceration. One of the difficulties has been the manner in which activism has been defined. Elsewhere I and others have pointed out that women prisoners have been defined as being "apolitical" because they have not rioted or filed class action suits to the extent that male prisoners have (Díaz-Cotto 1996; Kates 1984).

Nonetheless, even if one were to accept traditional definitions of what constitutes political activism for prisoners, it is clear that incarcerated women throughout the United States have rioted, organized sit-ins, stand-outs, and work stoppages to protest intolerable living conditions and abusive treatment at the hands of staff.[1] Likewise, they have filed individual and class action suits when prisoners' rights attorneys have been accessible.[2]

In this chapter, pintas discuss some of their major concerns and the ways they and other women prisoners sought to change jail conditions and end abusive treatment.

Concerns, Grievances, and Institutional Channels

Prisoner concerns and grievances included a range of issues.

Marta: Get clean blankets, get the air conditioning right, get . . . heat during the winter. We bitched about the food, try to keep it warm for us, you know. The curtains, "We need curtains in the . . . bathroom." . . . 'Cause you . . . have to use your sheet to put over the . . . showers to cover your body, you know, so nobody else will see you take a shower.

Deborah: They've complained about a deputy. They've complained about the food . . . About the medical staff there, medical treatment there.

There were few effective institutional outlets for pintas and other prisoners who wanted to change jail conditions for the better.

Graciela: Back then you didn't have no kind of request to complain about nobody or nothing . . . Just get a hold of the sergeant and talk to the sergeant or a senior officer . . . Now they have a . . . "Complaint Box." I think this it went up in either '89 or '90.

Deborah: When I was incarcerated . . . the only course of action that I've ever seen anybody do is . . . an inmate complaint form.

Pintas who had grievances handled them in a variety of ways.

Cristina: They would talk to their chaplain, their priest . . . That's another way. Their schoolteacher if they . . . relate to their schoolteacher.

Rita: Write to the captain, the watch commander, whoever. But then, it's . . . really not much they would do about it. They'll just take the complaint. They'll just say, "Okay, we got it. We investigated and it wasn't that way. We didn't find no fault in this or that."

Marta: We drew petitions for everything, you know . . . "It would be nice to have a dentist at nighttime here in case of emergency, . . . and . . . a . . . doctor to . . . be there at all times for when people [have] seizures."

Once petitions were signed they were turned over to jail staff, who rarely passed them on to jail administrators.

Marta: They write petitions and everything. And the minute the watch commander sees it, it's like it gets lost somewhere and nothing ever gets done . . .

It's supposed to be an officer taking them, the watch commander . . . And . . . that watch commander's supposed to get it to somebody. And . . . if the officer won't take it to . . . the warden or whoever is in charge, then it's on us to get the nearest lieutenant, you know, or . . . a senior . . . And some of them do . . . get it through . . . [But] they get lost after the watch commander sees 'em.

Prisoners also gave letters and petitions directly to the captain in charge of the jail. Top administrators also ignored prisoners' concerns. Captain Helena Ashby was in charge of SBI during the mid-1980s.

During a recent tour of the jail with a reporter, Ashby was handed a long, hand-written letter by an inmate, another slipped a note addressed to her under a guardroom door. One, she said, was a petition from a group of prisoners who wanted to form an inmate advisory committee; Ashby said there is no need for such a group because most of the women are incarcerated for brief periods (*LAT* 7/13/86).

Technically, prisoners also had the right to file complaints with LASD's Internal Affairs Bureau against guards who abused them. However, guards were seldom penalized for assaulting prisoners.

Rita: For instance, if I were to see a cop beat you up, . . . I can call . . . what . . . police called Internal Affairs. And . . . Internal Affairs has to come down and investigate . . . So they would come and investigate and they would see the inmate. And if they seen the inmate beat up . . . the officers that were involved go on suspension . . . All they're supposed to do is hold them and not to lay hands on them, you know . . . Whether they swing at you or whatever, you're not supposed to hit them back.

The Law Library and Jailhouse Lawyers

It was not until the filing of *Inmates of SBI* in 1973 that all prisoners at SBI were allowed to use the jail's law library. Prior to that, only sentenced and pre-trial prisoners "in propia persona status" were allowed to use its services (*Inmates of SBI* 1982a).

The law library was primarily used by prisoners to conduct research pertaining to their cases. Others who had already been sentenced used it to file appeals. A few went to the law library to learn about prisoners' rights. Those well-versed in these areas and/or willing to share their knowledge with other prisoners were generally known as jail-house lawyers.

Jailhouse lawyers were usually sought out by prisoners who could not afford to consult private attorneys.

Rita: To get advice about their cases, about any actions they can take . . . I guess mostly for their court cases . . . if they wanted to go *pro per.* It's when they defend themselves without an attorney. You know, you get advice. You . . . go into the law library. You read up on your case and your charges and . . . the penal codes that they use in court . . . You look up prior cases that had the same kind of criminal activities that you got into.

Deborah: People . . . would get advice from them. People that are facing other charges that are heavy-duty, they look for these people . . . because they know about the law.

Jailhouse lawyers were usually prisoners who had been to state penitentiaries and were knowledgeable about both criminal and penal law. They frequently counseled prisoners not only about their individual cases, but also about prisoners' rights. Their knowledge and their willingness to share it with their peers made them particularly threatening to penal administrators. The latter feared lawsuits filed by prisoners that could both challenge their authority and prove quite costly.

The filing of *Inmates of SBI* had shown penal administrators that women prisoners could bring about changes, however small, if they were informed about their rights, formed alliances with one another, and gained the support of outside advocates. Consequently, jailhouse lawyers were closely monitored by jail personnel and sometimes physically isolated from other prisoners.

Deborah: There was this girl that I was seeing . . . She was Chicana . . . She was really brilliant . . . She was a paralegal and was incarcerated . . . She wasn't trying to organize. She . . . just had a lot of problems with the . . . whole system . . . She was housed in the High Security because she was using the law library . . . They housed these . . . jailhouse lawyers . . . separately because they use the law library . . . I think with the men they're more . . . in Population 'cause there's much more men. But the women, they housed them separately 'cause if they're in the regular population, no telling what they would start . . . You know, . . . they would teach . . . women what their rights are . . . They watch them very closely. I've never seen anybody that was in General Population that had access to the law library.

Some pintas, like Deborah, knew of Chicana jailhouse lawyers but were not motivated to seek their assistance.

I've seen some . . . on the county bus. You know, going to and from court . . . And I've seen them at the court . . . They were people that I talked to. But . . . like

I said, all my charges were drug-related, you know. But . . . when I get arrested with a guy, he would always take the rap and I'd go home . . . after a little bit of county time. I never felt the need. If I felt like I was facing a lot of time . . . I'm sure I would gravitate towards them.

Litigation

Once in a while pintas heard of prisoners who had filed individual lawsuits against SBI concerning medical issues and guard brutality.

Marta: There was only one time that I can remember and that was in '69 . . . When the officer beat this girl up and her hand got caught in the door, chopped her hand off. Yeah. They took her, rushed her to the hospital and . . . the girl had . . . somebody contact her . . . parents. They went to the hospital. First they said they didn't have her . . . there . . . Well, they had her handcuffed to the door her mom said. So when the officer went around they would come near when they seen their daughter. She had the towel around her hand . . . And they asked how it was did and they said the officers closed the . . . gate, and the girl's hand happened to get cut . . . She don't even have a hand . . . She was Chicana.

Rita: There was this one girl that got beat up real bad . . . The officers, . . . they took her on an Elevator Ride and they beat her up real bad. And then . . . her family tried to come and visit her and they told her that . . . she was in The Hole or that they couldn't find her . . . But they . . . just didn't wanna bring her down to see her beaten up . . . And . . . they sent her to prison, though. And they were going out there to see her in state prison . . . Internal Affairs come in and take pictures of this person . . . They investigate the officers.

Sometimes investigations took place when family members insisted on seeing imprisoned relatives whom they knew had been assaulted by guards.

Rita: See, what happens is that . . . like you got beaten up and I knew your mom. You gave me your mom's phone number to call and I call your mom and I tell your mom what happened and where you're at . . . And if she says, "I wanna see my [daughter]. I wanna make sure they're all right." And the captain comes up with this story, "Well, she's gotten in trouble and she's in The Hole. She can't have no visits." Or . . . "They're not here." . . . And then you . . . say, "Well, I'm calling Internal Affairs . . . I need to see my daughter to make sure she's okay." That's how it's done.

Only one of the pintas interviewed, however, had tried to pursue a lawsuit against SBI. It involved injuries she received after falling in a dirty shower. The treatment she received from guards after she was injured showed the lack of concern for prisoners characteristic of guards at SBI.

Estela: The showers are dirty. Matter of fact, one time I was there in '85, I slipped in the shower. They used to have mats, right, and these mats have these suction cups. And the suction cup . . . were so old and dirty, it had that grime on them, that they slip. When I was shampooing my hair and I slipped under 'em. And they didn't do nothing for me . . . My leg was this big . . . I tore every ligament across here and broke three bones across . . . And the L.A. County jail told me nothing was wrong with my foot and my foot was that big and purple . . . When I went to court I was hopping in the court . . . They wouldn't give me crutches . . . And I called my mom . . . So when I went to court my mom . . . was in the courtroom. My mom got up and said, "Your Honor, how can you let this girl . . . come in here with no crutches, no . . . medication?" The judge released me that day from the court. I went in the holding tank. I didn't walk no more in . . . the holding tank, a minute when they called, "Pimentel!" and they gave me a packet of . . . pain killers.

While Estela got attorneys to look at her case, they eventually dropped it. Although she could have hired new attorneys, her addiction to drugs and her subsequent sentence to CIW interfered with her ability to pursue the case.

Even though most pintas did not become involved in litigation, some were willing to provide prisoners' attorneys information on jail conditions if so requested.

Marta: They would tell the person, "You know, if you need me for . . . whatever happened inside the county jail, here is my name," and I'll just tell 'em what I see.

Others pintas who had heard about the lawsuits chose not to get involved, fearing guard retaliation. Some did not pursue changes through legal means because they did not know their rights. Prisoners' ignorance was reinforced by guards who continually told them that they had given up their rights when they were institutionalized.

Rita: I guess 'cause I didn't know lawyers and I didn't know how to go about it. I didn't know really the rights that inmates in there have because they tell you, . . . "If you didn't want to be in here, you shouldn't be getting in trouble . . . If you don't like our conditions in here then you shouldn't be coming to jail."

Most importantly, however, a number of pintas did not litigate because they did not know any attorneys who could work on their behalf. Asked if she would have been willing to file a lawsuit against the facility if she had known any attorneys, Rita replied:

I would of because, I mean, I don't think it's right for them to treat you like that just 'cause you're in jail. Everybody makes mistakes. You know. I see things . . . both aspects, not just from the criminal mind aspect but from also from the correctional aspect of . . . things 'cause there's inmates that act like assholes too. They get up in your face. They do the same bullshit the way the cops do. It's both parties, both ways. But . . . the cops, sometimes they take the authority figure, they take it like they got more power over you, and that ain't right either.

Hunger Strikes and Stand-Outs

In 1986 prisoners at the jail reacted to the indifference of guards and administrators by holding a series of hunger strikes. To publicize their grievances, prisoners wrote to the *Los Angeles Times.*

In the view of inmates who later contacted The Times, the raid was another example of the arbitrary and unreasonable treatment that recently prompted them to stage small scale-hunger strikes and to try to form an inmate advisory committee to handle complaints, settle disputes, and work for better conditions. (*LAT* 7/13/86)

In response to conditions at the jail, the newspaper wrote an exposé about conditions at SBI (*LAT* 7/13/86). Jail administrators, however, continued to dismiss prisoners' demands for reforms and the creation of an advisory committee.

In some instances, prisoners rebelled against jail conditions and the indifference of administrators by refusing to go back into their cells. When they did, their defiance was met with immediate repression. Rita recalled a "stand-out" that took place during the late 1980s at SBI when prisoners housed in 4100, the Permanently Housed segregation unit, refused to go back into their cells, protesting denial of basic services.

Rita: I remember one time . . . in the late 1980s . . . when I was housed in 41 . . . They were keeping us locked down . . . We were housed in cells . . . We weren't having no cosmetics . . . They would send commissary away, the officers . . . Our toilets were backing up. They didn't wanna call a plumber . . . We weren't getting no meds . . . They were . . . sending Nurses' Line away . . . See, Nurses' Line and Med Line is two different things. You have to have a card to get in Med Line.

Nurses' Line is where you felt sick and you wanted to see the nurse you could get out, go to the Nurses' Line. Well, they didn't give it to us so . . . we just said, "Forget it. We're not gonna take it. We're gonna stay out of our cells." Everybody agreed to it, . . . all the girls . . . housed there . . . So that's what we did . . . Not refused to go out, refused to go back in . . . And they said, "Everybody back in the their cell!" And nobody [moved] . . . So they came with all kinds of cops. They said, "We're gonna tell you right now, get back in your cell!" And we said, "No! We're not moving . . . We want a lieutenant down here, now!" . . . "A lieutenant is not gonna come down!" . . . So . . . officers, they came down and they just started grabbing. I seen them . . . white men . . . they dragged some woman . . . out . . . They handcuffed and they just drug her out . . . on the floor out to the hallway . . . And they drug two people out, Mexicans [Chicanas]. But that's all that was there. It was probably all Mexicans.

As guards began to handcuff and take prisoners out, the remaining protesters went back into their cells.

Rita: We stayed out and then it started dying out . . . It just stopped because they were dragging them, they drug them out.

Most prisoners' demands were, nonetheless, ultimately met. Prisoners who were in Permanently Housed were once again allowed access to the Nurses' Line and to cosmetics. The toilets were fixed, and commissary goods were once again sold in the cell block (Rita). Notwithstanding this success, some pintas felt that the victory was a bitter pill to swallow because some prisoners had been harshly penalized.

Rita: It worked in some ways, but then . . . in some ways it didn't. Because these other people, they got . . . hurt. They got drugged out . . . They went to Lockup and they shouldn't of went to Lockup . . . They got added time . . . They got like . . . 10 days . . . into The Hole.

Jail administrators also responded to the rebellion by segregating prisoners who had participated. Initially some were sent to The Hole, while others remained in Permanently Housed. Eventually, those prisoners sent to The Hole were released back into General Population instead of being returned to Permanently Housed. In this manner, jail administrators hoped to disrupt the unity and leadership that had developed among prisoners.

Rita: And then . . . what happened was that they segregated them. They took us apart . . . And then they sent them out to Population. They didn't sent 'em back to the cells. So they got to go back out to Population . . . I mean, . . . the bottom line was . . . people wanted to go back to Population . . . Because the people that were housed there, they were there for a long time. They wanted to go back to Population. They wanted to get out 'cause they were still looking at a long time. They were still going to court on their cases . . . I ended up staying there regardless . . . until I went home.

Despite the victories that prisoners were from time to time able to wrest from jail administrators, they were hesitant to organize to demand changes for several obvious reasons.

Graciela: Like I said . . . I wasn't gonna be looked like no fool. And to me when you're in the system you're not gonna win because they're gonna listen to a cop before they'll listen to an inmate . . . I thought that most women have that attitude.

Rita: Because I think that if they did anything they would mess up their visits or they would send commissary away. And . . . if anybody acted up they would threaten you, . . . "We're not going to let you see your visit." . . . They would . . . threaten you with . . . "If you guys keep . . . fighting or you guys keep doing this or that . . . you're not shopping commissary." . . . Okay, the commissary is something that you necessarily need to have in there . . . And they would send it away or they wouldn't let you out . . . to buy shampoo or buy deodorant . . . 'cause . . . you have to go upstairs to buy it. And they would only call it once. If you're not there in line to go out when the door opens, you don't get it.

Estela: They were always scared they were gonna get locked down if they protested against it. Or, you know . . . "Oh, we can't get it." Yeah, their fears were they were gonna get locked down, they were gonna get . . . their little bit of hygiene taken away, you know. Because the cops would go in there and raid and they take everything. They didn't care . . . Everybody thought . . . they were gonna take their visits from them . . . We weren't gonna get our activities.

Asked which prisoners were more likely to rebel, Carmen responded that it was Chicanas and African Americans.

At Sybil Brand . . . there was a lot of women that came in that were like cholas hard-core. And the . . . Latinas were the most craziest ones. Because you got the gavachas, . . . you know, the white girls that would come in, they wouldn't . . . do nothing. I mean, they did their time and they, "Yes, ma'am." And . . . then you got the mayatas in there that, you know, they were crazy too, just like us . . . They were down for theirs too. You know . . . were ready to do anything. We don't take nothing. You know, we fight. We'd start riots. You know, start things going on . . . In others words . . . we would rebel against authority.

In summary, pintas and other women prisoners sought to change the conditions and treatment they encountered while incarcerated at SBI in numerous ways. The response of jail administrators to the prisoners' stand-out discussed above clearly demonstrates that such collective protests were immediately met with harsh physical repression by mostly white male guards. Confronted with such circumstances, pintas and other women prisoners found alternative ways to demand changes. These included verbal and written complaints, petitions, hunger strikes, using the services of jailhouse lawyers, and asking family members and community organizations to advocate on their behalf.

While only one of the pintas interviewed had tried to file a lawsuit against the facility, some had heard of Latinas who had. Several also indicated their willingness to become involved in class action suits if attorneys made themselves available.

The ability of pintas and other prisoners to win concessions from administrators and staff at SBI depended on their ability to form coalitions with one another, the response of penal staff to their calls for reforms, and the availability of prisoners' rights advocates who supported their calls for support (Díaz-Cotto 1996).

Picking Up the Pieces

When pintas were released from jail (or prison) after their first conviction, they returned to barrios that continued to be heavily surveilled by law enforcement agencies and targeted by war-on-drugs policies. Such conditions, along with untreated addictions, meant that their struggles with the criminal justice system did not end upon their release. All repeatedly returned to penal institutions for economic and drug-related offenses.

Once released, pintas had to obey the conditions imposed upon them by predominantly white male probation and/or parole officers or face being reincarcerated for probation or parole violations. Often they experienced sexual harassment and racism from these same men.

Pintas also had to find ways to support themselves and their children without returning to drug use or breaking the law. Few had received any educational or vocational job training while incarcerated. For the few who had marketable job skills, employment waiting for them upon release, and supportive families, these changes were difficult enough. For those who did not have a job waiting for them, had never been legally employed, and now had the label of "convict," the obstacles seemed almost insurmountable.

Before their first adult arrests, very few pintas had finished high school or received any college education. At the time of the interviews, 11 of 24, almost half, still had less than a high school education (Appendix A). College education was generally begun or completed when pintas began recovering from drug abuse. Regardless of their educational level, Chicanas who had stopped using drugs were more likely to have better-paying jobs than those who had not.

Before and during the early part of their addiction and between incarcerations, most pintas had tried to support themselves and their children through legal employment or a combination of legal and illegal sources of income (see also Moore and Mata 1981). The former included legal employment and income derived from partners and government assistance programs. As their addictions progressed, it became more difficult for pintas to maintain regular work schedules and, hence, cover their expenses. Consequently, they became more dependent on illegal sources of income.

Partly as a result of their limited education, the types of jobs pintas secured were in low-paying, low-status occupations. These did not allow them to support themselves and their children adequately, let alone their addictions. Even when they managed to get clean and sober and/ or get white-collar jobs between incarcerations, the jobs were generally temporary, many coming to an end when active addiction resumed.

Pintas frequently sought to regain custody of their children after their release from institutions. They also sought to reestablish their relationships with other family members. While pintas looked forward to such reunions, their years of active addiction coupled with the separation imposed by imprisonment made it difficult for them to quickly regain the trust and affection of loved ones. This was particularly true if they had abused their own children, taken advantage of family members, or their children had been physically or sexually abused by others when abandoned by their mothers.

Equally important was the fact that pintas had to cope with all these issues and at the same time learn how to stay drug-free. Staying clean and sober was more difficult when loved ones on the outside were still actively using alcohol and other drugs or were still involved in illegal activities. At the time of the interviews, those recovering from alcohol and drug abuse had taken many years to get any measure of recovery from addiction. This chapter reveals ways in which pintas dealt with the multiple demands placed on them once they were released from institutions.[1]

Linda's Story: Parole Blues

Linda's story illustrates the difficulties pintas often encountered when dealing with white parole officers' racism and abuse of power. She was released from a federal penitentiary in 1967 after serving three years and eight months of a five-year sentence on drug charges. Upon release, she reported to her PO in Orange County.

[In 1967] I paroled out to my sister's house . . . in Orange County . . . I didn't have nowhere else [to go] and three of my kids were there . . . And Orange County at that time was very racist . . . And Hispanics in Orange County were called "bandits" and "tamale makers" . . . and "taco vendors." That's what my kids grew up with, at school, neighbors . . . I went to see . . . the parole officer . . . and he said, "I'm your parole officer . . . That could be good and it could be bad . . . It all depends on how you want to work it . . . Or how nice you want to be . . ." I don't say anything 'cause right away I get all defensive with him . . . 'cause I know where he's coming from . . . And since I didn't respond then he got up and started looking outside the window and the first thing he says is, "You know, Orange County is a nice county . . . It smells good. It's green. It's clean . . . We don't need no . . . dirt around here . . . You got 30 days." . . . Either I move out of the area or I'm back in the institution, that's what it means. Don't forget I already did three years and eight months, so the rest of the time I would have to go back and do it . . . So now I'm under a lot of pressure. Now that I've got to get out of Orange County before this man sends me back for nothing 'cause I didn't give him a piece of ass . . . I had to move out.

Sometimes relationships between Chicanas and Chicano POs were not that much better than those with white male parole officers.

Then I moved back in to L.A. County and I was sent to the parole office in downtown L.A. and I had another parole officer . . . I went to see him . . . and I don't know, something happened between him and I that I never went back . . . I just sent the monthly report . . . He was what you call in the Hispanic community a "coconut."

Work

At the time of the interview, two of the 18 pintas for whom information was available worked as building managers, another two worked for community organizations, seven were employed in the substance abuse field, one had been sentenced to community service cleaning city streets, and six were unemployed. While two of the above ran community organizations in Chicana/o-Latina/o barrios, another ran her own recovery home for women. Other types of legal employment performed by pintas during their lives included hairdresser, seamstress, factory worker, kitchen worker, building manager, outreach worker, case manager, counselor, and supervisor for a health insurance company.

Doris: The first time I got out I . . . was a dishwasher at my brother-in-law's restaurant . . . He hired me on part-time . . . The second time I got out I babysat for a while and I . . . worked waitressing . . . in a bar. And then, the third time I got out, that's when I went to . . . Project Dare . . . They cater to . . . job training. They had like janitorial training. They had electronic training . . . I went to Project

Dare as a student and then later on I went back ... to work there doing clerical ... Then ... they told me they would give me the time to go to school ... In 1983 ... I [took] my GED.

Julia: One time I worked at the Mariposa[2] ... I was ... a resident for a year, clean and sober, and they took me on as an employee ... I worked as a ... "detox monitor." ... I worked there for like eight months ... Taking in people to detox. Doing intakes on 'em. And then I worked ... painting cars ... at a body shop ... One time I was working as a psych tech at Agnus Dei Hospital, ... giving various counseling to handicapped children, taking them out to parks and recreations ... Right now ... I was working for [an] employment agency ... doing computer programming for them ... That was just temporary, though.

Once Carmen got clean and sober, she decided to help others do the same.

I've been clean three years now. I had four but I relapsed. Stayed out there a year and did a year in prison and now I've had three years clean. I'm a drug and alcohol counselor now ... [at] Prototypes Women's Center and I'm going to school to get my bachelor's degree.

Victoria, drug-free two years at the time of the interview, also returned to the community to help addicted women.

I'm a case manager. I work for a drug and alcohol program, and I work right now at a drop-in center for the homeless and ... poor, trying to get these women into recovery. Basically, they use me as like a referral service ... And I transport people to Pomona and everywhere. If I can get them there I'll get them there [to programs] because they need to know how good it is, man, to be clean and sober.

Rosa, who had not used alcohol or other drugs for six years at the time of the interview, used her jail and prison time to resume her education and get clean and sober.

I got sober because when I was in prison ... I wanted to go to school and I knew ... that I needed to work with other people, so I decided to be a drug counselor and to go to college.

Once released from prison, Rosa pursued her goals.

I had gotten my GED and I ... knew that there was programs that would help ... The parole officer would ask about ... going to school and things like that. So I decided I was going to take advantage of that. So when I came out I asked my parole officer about that, and she sent me to the Department of Rehabilitation and they ended up sending me to a support group. And it was funny because I . . . thought I should be in NA 'cause of being a heroin addict and I ended up in AA because of that DUI I had . . . My life changed from going to . . . the program . . . I ended up going to school, and there was a lot of people that were very supportive and encouraged me and kept me going, you know.

By the time of the interview, Rosa was a certified drug and alcohol counselor and had opened a recovery home for women.

Linda, like other pintas, tried to juggle legal and illegal work while trying to get clean and sober and support her children.

After I got run out of Orange County with that parole officer I came back in to Pico Rivera with my four kids. No employment skills . . . I have those 30 years pending,[3] and I got those four kids and I got four blankets . . . And I know I need to come up with a following month's rent. And I know I need to come up with beds, food, if nothing else, one plate each. So what do you do, you never worked in your life? . . . I went back into what . . . I called . . . my "hit and runs." Smuggling . . . a couple of times to . . . pick up some money to . . . get some of the stuff I needed . . . I smuggled . . . money . . . from Tijuana to over here . . . just to get enough to move from one place to another and buy some twin beds, you know, some stuff I needed real quick for the kids . . . I moved into El Monte . . . The place was bigger and the rent . . . seemed a little better . . . And . . . I remember this one guy I used to know. He used to be a connection . . . So I went back to what I knew how to do best, I went and fell in love, you know. And I got me a job with a Jewish woman on Brooklyn Avenue 'cause that was my street and . . . it wasn't a sales . . . department so she didn't ask me no questions . . . So she hired me for two bucks an hour. So that was a beginning . . . It wasn't a lot of money, but . . . I didn't want to go back to jail . . . My oldest brother, you know, it's like he wanted to go back into business . . . He wanted to go back to start dealing, . . . telling me, ". . . I'll set you up. I'll buy you a car . . . All you gotta do is run back and forth." . . . My brother-in-law . . . asking me when I started working . . . , "When you going to get to work?" meaning crossing the border . . . They wanted to pull me back into all that bullshit, you know.

Faced with economic difficulties and still using drugs, Linda gave in to her family's pressure, this time, however, combining legal with illegal employment.

I was doing hit and runs . . . I was still snorting coke. I was still snorting *heroina* and I was drinking. And I'd take pills . . . Part of that time . . . I was working with this woman who gave me that job for two bucks an hour, which means I didn't go full-force like I used to . . . I had done some slowing down . . . I wasn't looking for people like I used to look for people . . . It was my family that had a lot of influence with me, you know. And it was tempting and . . . there was times where I was willing . . . There was times where I would think about the kids and think about the 30 years . . . I was like, you can say chipping, chipping here and chipping there. And then I'd fall in love. So then we had two paychecks for a little while . . . So things got a little better. You know, financially I was able to go on weekend trips and go shopping once in a while . . . So, a lot of usage of men . . . And . . . I managed to stay out of jail . . . I became a counselor. I was still getting loaded as a counselor. The women would walk in with their little drugs . . . I'd take it away and . . . then it would go home with me in the evening . . . So then I started getting exposed to the meetings. I was exposed to the meetings since I was in . . . [prison] . . . They had AA meetings.

While the road to recovery was slow, when I met Linda she had managed to stay clean and sober for 17 years and had been working in the alcohol and drug recovery field for years.

Reconstituting Families

Once released from institutions, pintas with children, for the most part, sought to reestablish their relationships with their children. Resuming those ties was difficult enough when the mothers knew the children's whereabouts. However, sometimes the children had been taken out of the area without their mother's knowledge or consent and could not be located. Other pintas had given up legal custody of their children to relatives. Some had their children taken from them by the courts as a result of their addiction (*LAT* 12/6/93). In the latter case, once released, pintas generally sought to challenge the court's decision and regain custody of their children.

Sonia: When I've gotten arrested, you know, . . . they take me into custody and they want to take the child into custody . . . If you find a good . . . police officer . . . that thinks about the children, they'll have you call somebody to come and pick 'em up. But a lot of them right away . . . will . . . take the . . . child into custody. And, of course, once they take 'em to custody, they put 'em in a foster home, they become ward of the courts. So then you have to battle trying to get 'em back.

Few private or state organizations were available to help imprisoned mothers maintain contact with their children during and after incarceration. Even fewer were the organizations dedicated to helping imprisoned mothers deal with legal issues concerning their children.

Organizations such as Legal Services to Prisoners with Children in San Francisco, dedicated to helping imprisoned women with legal issues, were few and far between (Barry 1985a, 1985b, 1987, 1993, 1995a, 2000). Moreover, limited financial and staff resources made their tasks even more difficult. Pintas faced various difficulties when they sought to regain custody of their children.

Marta: My aunt has 'em 'cause I'm still on parole. And I don't want my kids around me because if I ever get stopped and tooken in, I don't want my kids tooken from me.

Lucy: My mother had gave them up and put them in foster homes . . . I wasn't aware that they had been placed . . . until I was finally in Riverside County for the last 60 days of . . . my using, and I had paperwork . . . saying that my kids were like in orphanages . . . and my mother had kept the oldest one . . . They never contacted me or anything. Eventually, I had got a hold of the DCS[4] worker, and the DCS worker finally informed me of what was going on . . . Within the first year of me visiting them . . . my son was beginning to get worse . . . He started running away from [the group] home . . . I was afraid something was going on . . . And the social worker . . . was actually taking my son away from the . . . group home on the days that I would come and visit. And I had to remind her that I had a court order . . . He will talk about how she would take him to . . . her personal home . . . And she straight out told me that . . . my son was the only Mexican kid there with all the Black kids there . . . And then she goes, "We're not used to mothers hanging around." And I go, "Well, this is one Mexican woman that you're gonna get used to seeing here . . ." His grandmother, his dad's mom, finally went and picked him up 'cause I told them, "My son is running away and I don't know what's happening . . . I want my son removed from there . . . I don't care . . . what place you have to put him." . . . So after I told the grandmother that what was going on, she went and picked him up.

Lucy was fortunate that her daughter Marisela had been placed in a setting that encouraged and facilitated mother-child reunions.

Marisela, where she was at, I think it was a place that was really up and up, and they were real open . . . It was like a . . . place where they had . . . children up until 12 years old. And . . . they . . . had counseling there and they had . . . a lot of support like from the community as far as . . . donations . . . And where they . . . did a lot of activities . . . And . . . before she even came home I had like a year of counseling with her and was able to eat with her there on . . . the premises and everything like that.

When pintas gave up or lost custody of their children to someone else, regaining custody was frequently difficult, if not impossible.

Estela: The first son was born in '82 . . . He lives with . . . my kid's father. But he . . . lives around the corner so he's here all the time with me . . . And usually on the weekends he comes. And then, I have another . . . a seven-year-old . . . He's at my mom's house. Like I said, me and her feud. 'Cause when I . . . got busted, she went . . . and got temporary custody . . . She keeps saying I'm on drugs and . . . that I don't have a place to take him . . . But see, . . . I haven't been on drugs since 1989 . . . And I told the judge, . . . "You know what? . . . I work. I have my place. I have my car . . . I gave you your parenting [classes]. I have your NA and your AA papers. Everything you asked for I gave to you. Now you're gonna go by hearsay for what my mom says because me and her are feuding? . . ." But see, my mom . . . was saying that I wasn't visiting my son regularly . . . She was lying . . . because I used to go up there every week and see my son . . . My mom was telling the Child Services . . . and they went by what my mom said.

Sonia lost custody of her four children as a result of her addiction.

I have a 15-year-old that I had in prison, he lives with my mother . . . That became her child . . . She's 70-something years old . . . I see him . . . They're very happy that my life has changed . . . The 32-year-old's married with three children, works, . . . doesn't use drugs . . . I have a 25-year-old that was eight years old when he was taken away from me and went with a stepmother . . . I have a daughter that's . . . 16 years old. And I had left her with a girlfriend that was another heroin addict . . . I got arrested and . . . while I was in prison she . . . contacted the social worker and . . . took my daughter away from me. So she has legal guardianship. I had visiting rights but she took off with my daughter so I don't know her whereabouts . . . I believe one day I'll . . . see her . . . I don't really look for her because I don't know . . . if she thinks this girl's her mother and I wouldn't want to confuse her . . . And my . . . heart desire's to one day to be able to see her to let her know that I didn't abandon her or . . . did not . . . want her because I didn't love her. It's just that I was . . . in darkness, you know, as far as drugs.

Sadly, in spite of or because of their own addictions, Chicanas were not all able to keep their children from repeating their same mistakes. In some cases, they directly contributed to their own children's addiction.

Linda: My sons have been in and out of prisons, yeah . . . It's all been drugs, IV drug users . . . My son went into . . . the service, and when he came back he was a full-blow addict, heroin . . . It just blew me away. I guess I could have handled the booze. I guess I could have handled the pills, the weed, and everything else. But when it came to the IV, that was what just blew me away with him.

Sonia: [My son] . . . became a . . . heroin addict . . . He did everything, you know, . . . rock, PCP . . . I ran into him when he was 20 years old. And he came up to me and told . . . me he knew who I was. I says, "I don't know you." And where my mentality was, "Did I rob his mom? Did I rob his dad? Did I break into their house?" . . . So then he turned around and he says, "No, you're my mother." And then I told him, "What are you doing with your life?" "Oh, putting that needle in my arm like you and my dad did." . . . Well, we got together. We shot drugs for six months together. I worked the streets and he'd send me customers. Or he would wait at the house . . . And then, eventually, . . . I got sick, he took me to the hospital. While I was in the hospital he got arrested, went to prison. And while he was in prison I started serving God. He came home and he serves God today . . . He's clean and sober, married, has his child . . . At first . . . I think it was . . . hard for him to forgive me for what I've done . . . But now . . . with God, it . . . opens his eyes and . . . lets him understand that . . . I didn't know what I was doing really, you know. We're very close now and . . . he is happy that he has his mother back in his life.

Deborah also had a hard time winning back her daughter's trust.

My oldest daughter was raised with her grandmother on her dad's side . . . My oldest daughter was very angry . . . a lot of resentment, anger. She grew up the same way I did with my parents . . . She's doing well, though, now . . . But at first it was hard for her to believe that I was even gonna change . . . In time she had to start realizing that I'm around to stay . . . She's in recovery.

The Long Arm of the Law

At the time of the interviews, pintas who had gotten clean and sober after their last release from jail or prison had not come into direct contact with the criminal justice system again. Some of them, however, continued to be exposed to the criminal justice system through relatives, partners, or the presence in the community of law enforcement.

History repeated itself when police officers tried to convince Linda's son to become an informant just as they had unsuccessfully tried to convince her to do the same. When he resisted, he too was harassed by officers.

Linda: Harassment with the youngest 'cause they wanted to use him as a snitch as . . . a juvenile . . . It was like a cop said he wanted information on the school activities and who was what in the school system. And my son just said no. So they just kept my son in jail . . . It's just picking him off the street . . . I mean, . . . anything that was petty, anything that was not allowable because he wasn't 18 years old . . . So . . . this kid got arrested for buying a pack of cigarettes 'cause he wasn't 18 . . . One of the times . . . I was supposed to pick him up from work . . . It didn't even take me a half an hour and he was gone . . . The Montebello Police Station had taken him.

Officers also threatened Linda to coerce her into convincing her son to inform.

Linda: And then I had been called by the detectives at Montebello, the ones that wanted to turn my son into a snitch, you know, talking about, "We know where you've been. And my snitch said that you this and you that." And . . . by this time . . . I got about six months in [AA/NA] meetings . . . And he's telling me that . . . I better look out . . . And the only way my son . . . doesn't go to jail is if my son gives him the information he wants from the school activities.

In some cases, Chicanas and their families continued to face life-threatening situations at the hands of police officers.

Linda: A lot of times I got guns pointed at me 'cause I was being put under arrest . . . I've seen a shotgun pointed at my son's head . . . I had woken up 'cause there was scuffling right next to my bedroom window. If it wouldn't have woke me up and I wouldn't have opened that window and seen that cop had a shotgun at my son's head, I don't know what would have happened . . . I said, "What the fuck are you doing?" and he snapped. That's when he told my son to get up . . . Yeah, they still do that here in East L.A. I've seen it on the streets. I see it with the kids, the teenagers.

Getting Clean and Sober

For Chicanas addicted to heroin, alcohol, and other drugs, one of the obstacles that prevented them from starting a new life upon release from institutions was returning time and time again to the same friends they used drugs with and to the same barrios where they had used. While some did manage to get clean and sober amidst familiar surroundings, for many, the old lifestyle proved too seductive. The pull of the narcotics was intensified by the pull of familiar people and places.

Carmen: I mean, I always went back to the same old thing. Always went back to the neighborhood. Always went back to where I came from.

Gina: I . . . can't let go of ex-cons, okay . . . That's the only person I can get involved with . . . I just can't communicate with other people . . . And I'm sick because I'm 62 years old and . . . I'd be hanging around with all the homeboys over here, you know. And they're nothing but gang-bangers . . . And I know they'd gonna be shooting dope and everything and I'm still hanging around with them.

Gina, who had been able to give up heroin years earlier but had continued to drink alcohol until four days before the interview, described how she had nonetheless changed for the better since she had stopped shooting dope.

Like my nephew said, "Okay, so you're drinking, so where's the change?" I said, "You wanna know where the change is? . . . Today I'm responsible . . . I . . . pay my bills. With what I get, $600 a month," I said, "that don't even give me money to eat . . . but I . . . survive . . . I'm not out there hitting people upside their fucking head taking their money. I'm not out there selling dope. I'm not going to jail." I said, "So . . . that's a fucking big change for me . . . It takes time for everything so give me credit for the little bit that I've changed . . . 'Cause you know how I was when I was out there. I was vicious. Didn't feel nothing for nobody. If you had the money I was gonna take it . . . I didn't care what I did to you. . . . I don't do those things today . . . If I have, I have. If I don't have, I don't have, you know, 'cause I'm okay."

Those who had stopped using drugs by the time of the interviews had come to a point in their lives when they realized that to stay out of penal institutions and live a healthier life, they had to give up all drugs, including alcohol. Equally important was the realization that they could not stay clean and sober by themselves. Thus, they sought out and used varied support systems and strategies. A few got clean and sober through fundamentalist Christian churches. The overwhelming number, however, recovered through AA and/or NA. Some also participated in various recovery programs such as Prototypes, Tarzana, Mariposa, Casa Maria, and Casa de los Milagros.[5]

Pintas shared the motivations and conditions under which they began their process of recovery.

Mercedes: I got to SBI . . . But you know what was different? That I got the very front bed . . . Here's the . . . cop shop (drawing a diagram) . . . and here's the bed right underneath their window. And I was assigned that bed . . . And there's a pole that was right in front of the bed and it had the round clock on top of it. And on the side to the right was the bathroom area. And being in that bed you can smell all the . . . odor from the bathroom. And then, the clock felt like the London clock. You know, it was like, "Bong!" Women would pass by you and they'd fart in your face. And . . . they [friends] begged me to go back . . . to the regular place where everybody was at. And . . . you know what? For once . . . in my life I said, "No . . . I need to really take a look at what it feels like to be in this institution, really." . . . And I no longer wanted to be comfortable in there anymore.

Deborah: I was a trustee in . . . the visiting room . . . in Sybil Brand . . . Somebody that I ran around with when I was using, . . . she seen me sitting there . . . She was a gavacha but she ran with the Mexicans . . . And she had like four or five years in recovery. And . . . she . . . told the deputy . . . that she needed to talk to me . . . and . . . they pulled me in the attorney room . . . I was about . . . 36 and . . . I was pretty tired at that time, you know. She had talked to me about coming to some program . . . here in Pasadena . . . She was interviewing women for drug programs . . . And I had never had anybody follow through on me like she did . . . And I had four cases at the time . . . She literally called every court . . . and told them, . . . "We have a bed for her." And I was still like . . . "Oh, I don't know . . ." 'Cause . . . I used drugs and alcohol . . . we're talking 14 to 36 . . . You know, . . . when you have lived your life in one way . . . you can't imagine yourself living your life in any other way. I couldn't in a million years have thought my life was the way it is today . . . And so . . . I'm very into working with women.

Luisa: I . . . finally paroled and I had one of the guys from AA pick me up . . . And then I started going to AA and I started using the men. I would go out to dinner and just conversate. You know, I just wanted the people to treat me good all the time, but I didn't have a clue about giving, right? . . . I went in there 'cause I wanted the parole office off my ass. And that's exactly what happened, you know . . . I got loaded like maybe nine months after . . . The next day I said, "You know what, man? I can't get loaded. I'm too scared." So after that I . . . started going to church . . . I relapsed after eight months going to church . . . And then I went to this banquet and . . . I was crying and I was praying to God that . . . it didn't . . . matter what happened that day just as long as I don't use and drink, you know. "Just please protect me in that area." And you know what? I never got loaded again, and that's been a little over 11 years, and I've been to a lot of places.

Dulce's first attempt at recovery came in 1989 after another heroin addict deliberately ran her down with his car when she refused to buy him drugs. Her major ally while she was hospitalized turned out to be her mother. The two had been estranged throughout much of her using.

My mother didn't know that I was in a hospital until about a week or so after I was there 'cause she was looking for me. They always go looking for me if they don't hear from me within three, four months . . . And when I got out I went to my mother's house 'cause she told me, "Well, I want you to come stay with me 'cause . . . I don't want you out there no more and want to see if you can straighten yourself up."

After accumulating six months clean, Dulce was able to get a job doing HIV and AIDS education outreach in the same neighborhood she had used drugs in. Soon after, she relapsed.

I was offered a job in San Mateo County, in the AIDS program, 'cause I had . . . something like six months clean . . . And I . . . look back and I think that was too quick for me to go and do that kind of work. Because that work with the AIDS program, I'd be working on the field and in the field my place was to go back to East Palo Alto and work with the people there. And, of course, I knew everybody there. And it worked for a minute. But then it was like going into shooting galleries and giving them condoms and giving them brochures, giving them water and alcohol so they can clean their outfits out . . . The temptation was too great. I would . . . just see them there just getting loaded and it was like, "Wow!" And before I know it, I said, "Well, they won't know. And the people in the county won't know." And the next thing, and before I know it, I'm fixing again . . . And . . . one more time I went into the system because I got busted on July of . . . '91.

Dulce's desire to change, nonetheless, led her to seek out the support of two recovery programs. At the time of the interview, Dulce had been clean and sober two and a half years.

Yolanda first got clean and sober at the insistence of her family and lover.

I was gonna parole . . . And my brother was building the county jail downtown, and he was working with a bunch of girls from Casa de los Milagros. It's a recovery home for Latino women . . . And he . . . asked me if I would go . . . into this recovery home . . . I went into recovery for all . . . the wrong reasons. I went in for my brother, for my family, for my kids . . . And . . . Paula . . . was my roommate up at Chowchilla . . . And at the same time . . . her . . . brother was fixing her up to go to Casa Milagros . . . She told me before she left, . . . "I'll meet you there. You better go." . . . I went for her too . . . I didn't go for me . . . And it was hard for me at first because I . . . knew I was a drug addict [but] I was scared of . . . changing my life because . . . all I knew was selling drugs, doing drugs, doing crimes . . . And I was scared of being responsible . . . I had to let all that go too. And with the therapy that I got it's like . . . things are different for me now . . . I've come a long way in a year.

For Yolanda, recovery also meant embracing all parts of herself, including her sexual feelings for other women.

I was attracted to women but . . . I wasn't thinking about my feelings . . . I always thought, . . . "Oh, it's wrong because of my kids . . . I don't want to bring my kids up like that." . . . But when I got . . . into a recovery home I got to know myself. It was like . . . I gotta make what Yolanda wants . . . I have to make myself happy.

For Sonia, who had tried to get clean and sober through detoxes, a methadone maintenance program, and attending NA meetings while in prison, recovery came through a sudden religious conversion.

For a whole year I went to NA while I was in prison. Out here . . . I was on methadone . . . I had gone into hospitals to detox . . . Out here I really didn't go to any drug programs . . . Eventually, I . . . didn't even think there was any hope for me. I didn't think I could ever change. I have four children . . . I had a "heroin baby," I had a "methadone baby," I had a child in prison. And . . . I couldn't even stay clean for them . . . And I love them . . . but I was so selfish and wrapped up in my own misery that I couldn't help them . . . I have six strikes against me . . . but that didn't stop me from using drugs . . . I myself thought I was gonna die in prison. I myself thought I was gonna die with a needle in my arm . . . I thought that was my lifestyle and that's the way I was gonna live until I died. You know, until I . . . cried out to God . . . for salvation . . . And . . . the day that I did cry out to God to change my life, . . . he did grant me the gift of salvation and that day he took the desire of drugs from me. I have never gone back to drugs and that was four years ago.

Sonia's recovery began in a hospital.

I was in the hospital . . . In the hospital there's Christians . . . I . . . was paralyzed at the time. So they told me that they were gonna have the chaplain . . . come and pray for me. Well, it turned out to be that [he] was my homeboy, was my connection once upon a time and he was serving God . . . He came to talk to me . . . And . . . a couple of weeks later out of respect I went to go hear him preach the word of God. And that's when I . . . called up to God to forgive me for my sins and to change . . . So I cried out to God and I got salvation. And . . . I knew it was for real 'cause I had cried to God in prison before and nothing ever happened . . . But that time I remember going back to my . . . room and . . .

about a week later . . . somebody that was in the hospital asked me if I wanted to buy some heroin . . . or methadone. And I looked at him, and I had money in my drawer . . . , and I told him, "I don't have no money." And he says, "I'll kick you down. I'll give it free to you . . ." I looked at him and I . . . told him, "No, it's all right." And after he walked out I . . . laid there and I . . . says, "Wow! That's the first time I ever turned drugs down." That's when I knew that I was delivered, that I had no desire for drugs anymore, that God had come in, that God had changed me.

Sonia subsequently joined Victory Outreach and went back to her community to spread the message of sobriety and spiritual salvation.

Lillian, who was clean and sober for four years at the time of the interview, discussed the difficulties confronted by Chicanas/Latinas trying to get clean and sober.

Now working in a detox, . . . I've had a lot of my homegirls and I've lost a lot of 'em . . . Because you're talking about . . . running from the problem but the problem is that you're . . . the problem . . . That anger and that anxiety keeps us back down. And . . . that shame takes us back out to using again . . . And . . . that's why . . . I am so willing to put my story out there . . . You know, to think that we are capable and we are worth it, as women . . . And if we allow somebody to keep us down it's gonna happen . . . And you try getting back up again, it's tiring . . . You know, to think that we don't have education, we don't have a job. The jobs that we do have we can't support ourselves, so we stay in abusive relationships. We stay in all that. That's all part of the package. This is what society has put on women. 'Cause women . . . can't be the dope fiends, they can't be the alcoholic, they can't be the worker because then you're not a good mother. All that comes in too . . . I never . . . knew that I had something inside me that needed something besides . . . the relationship, . . . besides being a mother. That routine gets boring . . . I never knew that I was capable of doing anything because I didn't think I was intelligent enough to do it, because I only went to two months of my freshman year of high school . . . Even though I had a GED . . . I was intimidated. I . . . was ready to go out there and do everything, but down deep inside it was like, "Am I capable of doing it? Can I really do this?" The fear . . . kind of pulls you back a little bit further. And that's why . . . most of my stuff that I've done even for Friends Outside . . . it's been volunteer basis . . . I felt like I wasn't worth being paid for . . . And . . . after I . . . went through this program [AA] I learned that I am okay . . . I was so tired that I was willing to let go of everything, you know. And I told my . . . old man, . . . "You know what? You go ahead and go through with the divorce. Do what you have to do, you know. I can respect that," you know. "For the first time in my life, after all these years, I've been running from what?" . . . And when I told him that it was like just a . . . complete turnaround. He said, "What are you planning on doing?" "I'm going on with my life. I'm gonna stay clean and sober . . . I know that I can't drink today . . . I drink, I hang around with my homegirls. I end up using again. I end up back in the . . . system. And then I'm another number. I'm a statistic." And, you know what? Today I have a clearance . . . for the jails. And I'm gonna go in and I'm gonna share with these women in there and I'm gonna tell them that "We can do this. We can stay clean and sober." I stayed supporting those women up there in that program . . . for almost two years . . . I'm taking psychology courses . . . I'm a detox manager [for] that . . . same work furlough that I went through.

Rosa and Lillian summarized several factors that helped Chicanas stay clean and sober and out of institutions. While Lillian did not feel imprisonment was a solution to addiction, in her case, being in prison allowed her to resume her education.

Rosa: I think for one thing, it's putting them in a training program in order for them to learn a skill in order to get out into the work force. That's real, real important because a lot of times I think the people that go back to jail is 'cause they can't find a job and they can't maintain in society. So then they go back to the same area that they were before making the money the way they knew how to make it before. And they end up going back to jail. Another thing is for them to have some type of a support group like AA, NA, a church, where there's people doing the same things as them, getting sober. Because if they go into an environment that is drinking and using, they're gonna go back to that because you become your environment.

Lillian: I mean, . . . if it wasn't for me going into this recovery home, number one, I would of never had the self-esteem that I have today. Number two, . . . if I wasn't in prison, I probably would have never got my GED. I don't know if I would have had the balls to do it when I was out . . . So I think lack of self-esteem is number one, thinking that we're just worth it just a tiny bit . . . And then, to be able to . . . walk into AA saying that I needed help . . . because I needed some type of support, and it wasn't my homegirls, guarantee you that.

Despite all efforts pintas made to come to terms with their past, change their lives for the better, and make amends to those they had hurt along the way, nothing seemed to be good enough to win the goodwill of their barrios and society at large. This was particularly felt by some who, like Sonia, had given up drugs, joined a church, assumed a heterosexual lifestyle, and married a man.

I've been clean now . . . four years . . . and I've changed. But for society we're still the same, you know, you still got tattoos or you still . . . are an ex-convict . . . So if for some reason they run a make on you or something, if you're in the wrong place at the wrong time . . . If, for example, . . . I be . . . talking to one of the tenants outside or in the office right here . . . and I don't know that person's holding drugs, a police officer comes in for whatever reasons . . . and that person gets scared and throws the drugs near . . . my foot . . . and the police officer sees it . . . He's not gonna believe it's not mine, right. So I'm gonna get a possession right. And because of my record, I'm going back to prison for life, although I'll be clean four years . . . It seems like our past is never forgiven. Our past is never forgotten . . . As far as society . . . I could still go to prison, you know . . . And . . . people even here in this building, they know I'm an . . . ex-addict, and I tell 'em, ". . . I've changed, you know. I have Jesus in my life. I don't use drugs no more. I got my job." And . . . when I don't allow them to run in and out of here like a shooting gallery . . . right away they tell me, "Oh . . . you think you're better now that you have a job." . . . I'm grateful for my job and I like my job . . . And . . . I don't like the drugs no more. I don't like that . . . lifestyle no more. So I try to stop it in the building, you know, trying to do what I'm paid for to be doing . . . You know how we've tried to change? People don't let us. People always want to keep on putting us down . . . And you wanna do something in your life and yet, the background, you know, "Oh, man, that's an . . . ex-homosexual." . . . For an example, there was tenant living here and I had his . . . girlfriend that he was living with help me with some file . . . And I have tattoos . . . with women's names on me, right, and they saw 'em. And they knew I was an ex-pinta, an ex-convict. They knew I was ex-homosexual. And they knew I'm a Christian now, you know . . . And one of guys turned around and told . . . the guy, "You know what? You better be careful with . . . your old lady being down there and helping Sonia. You know she likes women." And . . . yet they haven't seen me with a woman . . . But, yet, my past is never forgiven . . . It's never forgotten . . . We're still labeled no matter what. We try to change . . . Society still labels us, you know . . . so where do you go sometimes?

19

Concluding Remarks and Reflections

For the past three decades, local, state, and federal governments in the United States and Latin America have been implementing criminal justice policies under the auspices of the U.S.-led international war on drugs. These have led to growing governmental corruption, a surge in human rights violations, increasing imprisonment of poor and working-class people but primarily Latinas/os and other people of color, and the construction of more public and private jails and prisons.

It is chiefly as a consequence of such policies that Latinas in the United States and their sisters in Latin America are increasingly imprisoned predominantly for low-level, nonviolent economic and drug-related crimes. While for most of these women the primary motivation for breaking the law was economic, for a significant number of those in the United States, their actions were also motivated by their drug addictions.

The sale of drugs allowed a few pintas interviewed to be better off financially than others in their communities. However, the expense of addiction, the minor roles all but a few played in drug enterprises, and continued police harassment and surveillance prevented even these from permanently escaping poverty.

Calling for the imprisonment and execution of larger and larger numbers of people, the political Right and the mainstream mass media pathologize or demonize as sick or evil those who break the law. The responses of both liberals and the Left have been ambivalent. Liberals pay some attention to the systemic causes of lawbreaking, primarily economic, and support a number of social welfare reforms to reduce social inequalities based on race, class, and gender. Nonetheless, they continue to emphasize individual or collective pathologies as the causes of crime, lobbying for the construction of new and improved penal institutions in which to house diverse types of offenders. Such efforts have contributed to the building of more penal institutions.

The Left has blamed lawbreaking primarily on racism and economic disparities. However, while some have idealized those who break the law in response to social inequalities, others have labeled those arrested for nonpolitical crimes as "lumpen proletariat," that is, human trash corrupted by capitalism. Despite their differences, all sides generally overlook how individual motivations for lawbreaking are intertwined with the larger social and political structure.

The life histories of pintas included in this book reveal that their fundamental and immediate motivation for resorting to drug use as children and adolescents was their desire to medicate the emotional pain they felt in response to early experiences of abuse. Their initial drug use was also influenced by the use of drugs among peers and adults around them. Their motivations for illegal activities, however, were primarily the result of limited economic resources and, once addicted, the need to support their drug habits. Arrest and imprisonment were, in turn, the result of their own actions but primarily discriminatory and misguided criminal justice policies reinforced by the war on drugs.

They are women who, partly as a result of the violence perpetrated against them as children and/or adolescents and partly in response to the lack of support from the adults around them, began to look after themselves from a very young age. Faced with limited economic opportunities, young Chicanas became more and more dependent on their homegirls and homeboys, whether gang-affiliated or not. However, their friends were, for the most part, young people themselves. They were, in fact, groups of children trying to take care of children.

The peer support received by those who joined barrio gangs was undermined by the use of illegal drugs and violent activities in which some of the gangs engaged. Though gang-banging allowed Chicanas to vent years of accumulated anger, such activities only contributed to the continued victimization of Chicanas/os and other youths.

Seeking emotional and financial self-sufficiency and alienated from most adults around them, some Chicanas opted to leave school and move in with friends. They tried to make ends meet by lying about their age and getting jobs in low-level, low-paying service occupations. Some also supported themselves by joining homegirls/boys in illegal activities. Those who as adolescents could get legal employment at times combined legal with illegal sources of income.

A significant number of Chicana youths moved in with Chicanos, frequently older than themselves, who had already been exposed to drugs and the juvenile and/or adult criminal justice systems. The men either supported Chicanas or complemented their incomes through legal or illegal work. While Chicanas who remained at home during their adolescent years were better off materially, they were not necessarily safer or better off emotionally.

Searching for a way out of their emotional turmoil, most had by their late teens become addicts. As their drug addictions progressed and it became more difficult for them to hold legal employment, most began to depend more and more on illegal sources of income.

Mandatory and drug-related sentencing laws soon led drug-addicted Chicanas to suffer multiple arrests for low-level, nonviolent economic and drug-related crimes. Such laws were spurred on by war-on-drugs policies and a media campaign that criminalized poor and working-class people as well as addicts, sex workers, Chicanas/os, their barrios, and their youth groups.

None of the pintas interviewed were able to avoid profiling, harassment, and some form of verbal, physical, and sexual assault at the hands of the overwhelmingly white male law enforcement personnel with whom they came in contact. Some, however, were brutally beaten and denied access to medical treatment, resulting in permanent psychological and/or physical damage and, in at least one case, a miscarriage.

Once arrested, Chicanas faced discriminatory treatment at the hands of predominantly white prosecutors, defense attorneys, and judges. It was clear to pintas interviewed that being able to contract the services of private attorneys gave those who could afford such services an advantage at the point of plea bargaining and sentencing. The inability of all but a few to cover the costs of bail and secure the assistance of competent private attorneys meant that they were held in detention while plea bargaining or awaiting sentencing. Furthermore, most were denied the ability to participate in alternatives-to-incarceration programs, particularly on their first adult charges.

Once institutionalized, pintas were again exposed to discriminatory treatment, harassment, and abuse, this time at the hands of guards. The abuse took the forms of solitary confinement, verbal insults, pat-searches, narco/cavity-searches, sexual coercion, and beatings. This treatment was relentless regardless of whether or not Chicanas had been arrested for drug-related crimes, whether they were coming into or leaving institutions, and whether or not they had been convicted of a crime. Such treatment further humiliated and dehumanized women who had already been subjected to much violence during their lives.

Pintas responded to jail conditions in a number of ways. These included: creating support networks; participating in institutional programs; using and selling drugs; getting clean and sober; stealing, bartering, and selling goods and services; adopting a butch gender role; exploiting their femininity; getting a lover; confronting guards verbally and physically; filing complaints and petitions to challenge unfair treatment; and maintaining contact with family and others on the outside. In the few instances when attorneys were available, a few participated in individual lawsuits and, in at least one case, a class action suit. Sometimes protests took the form of hunger strikes or refusing to return to cells. All these actions were aimed at reforming jail conditions and protecting themselves from and ultimately ending the abusive treatment by staff.

Repeated incarceration and oppressive criminal justice policies, combined with their addictions, however, further cut away at Chicanas' self-esteem and their reasons for living. They became gradually isolated from loved ones and their barrios. Harassment of addicts and former convicts by law enforcement also disrupted their attempts to get clean and sober and get their lives back on track.

Upon release from institutions, pintas were placed on probation and parole under drug-related and other stipulations that ensured their return to institutions, regardless of whether they continued to use drugs or commit new offenses. Moreover, some had to contend with racism and sexual harassment by probation and parole officers.

The social stigma imposed on addicts and convicts, particularly women, made it more difficult for pintas to secure respect and acceptance in society. Employer prejudices also interfered with their ability to secure employment. Added to these were California state regulations that prohibit former prisoners from working in certain occupations, including education, nursing, physical therapy, real estate, and law (Butterfield 2000).

Moreover, by the close of the 20th century, drug felons in California were denied food stamps, cash assistance, and public housing. Local public housing authorities could deny them the ability to live with relatives in public housing facilities. Those with drug convictions and students being held in state and federal prisons were ineligible for Pell grants that would allow them to pursue higher education. Parole violators could also have SSI payments revoked. Moreover, prisoners and parolees in California were denied their voting rights, the latter until they had completed parole (Byrne, Macallair, and Shorter 2002). Under mandatory and drug-related sentencing laws, even those who were clean and sober and completed parole could be returned to jail or prison and forced to serve long prison terms for minor infractions.

The lack of job training, culturally sensitive drug rehabilitation programs, and employment opportunities hinder pintas' efforts to get clean and sober and sometimes led them to sell drugs to support themselves, their families, and their drug habits. Using and selling drugs, in turn, made them susceptible to being arrested. Arrests undoubtedly led to reincarceration.

Although the illegal actions of most pintas interviewed did not always threaten the physical well-being of others, their actions *did threaten* the foundations of a social structure based on the subordination of women, particularly women of color, a society that expects them to act as submissive daughters, wives, mothers, and workers. They were threatening because they were children, adolescents, and women who, when faced with violence and discriminatory treatment, took whatever actions they could to escape from or change oppressive living conditions. That is, they rebelled against socially prescribed subordinate roles that sought to keep them "in their place" as poor and working-class people, as women of color, as Chicanas, and some of them as lesbians. Most importantly, they were determined to end the violence directed at them.

Ironically, for Chicanas, their drug use was fundamentally an attempt to make themselves happy. For although pintas eventually became physical, emotional, and spiritual prisoners of drugs, they originally began to use drugs to numb their emotional pain and provide a measure of joy in their lives. The fact that the decisions they made were not always in their best interests and that a significant number of their illegal actions were committed under the influence of drugs did not under all conditions take away their agency, that is, their ability to act on their own behalf.

Even as drug addiction led them to act against their own moral values, most pintas interviewed clung to their self-image as loving mothers and partners. That is, while their behavior challenged traditional gender roles, many embraced much of what those roles entailed and, hence, the efforts by most to keep their families intact and continue to live with their children and partners, even in the midst of their addictions. For at least one, acceptance of traditional gender-based and culture-based expectations led her to marry and have children by her rapist. For another it led her to marry a man even after she had told her family she was a lesbian.

Ultimately, pintas interviewed realized that in order to survive and thrive, acquire marketable skills, heal broken relationships, and effectively confront discrimination, they had to get clean and sober. They recognized that their addictions could only lead to placements in mental or penal institutions, physical incapacitation, or death.

At the time of the interviews it was apparent that what made it possible for those pintas who were drug-free to stay that way was a spiritual sense of renewal combined with the support they received from others who were clean and sober or who understood both the nature of addiction and the types of reentry services needed by former prisoners. However, it was Chicanas' courage, great sense of humor, resourcefulness, and determination to thrive that allowed them to begin picking up the pieces of their lives and stay on the path of recovery.

It is also apparent from the life histories discussed in this book that tough-on-crime policies are inefficient and punitive ways of handling the violence, racism, addiction, and economic difficulties Chicanas faced all their lives. In fact, under war-on-drugs initiatives, pintas are denied appropriate access to drug rehabilitation programs by the same government agencies that allow drug kingpins and corrupt government personnel to participate in illegal drug ventures.

Federal and other government agencies have acknowledged that one of the most effective ways to reduce the demand for illegal drugs is through education and treatment programs. Furthermore, critics of war-on-drugs policies have shown that these have failed to have a significant impact on both drug use and drug trafficking. Partly in response to these findings, public pressure, and the need to reduce prison overcrowding and government spending, a few states have begun to implement sentencing and penal reforms that reduce the number of those incarcerated for nonviolent, low-level drug offenses (King and Mauer 2002). Such reforms have increased the number of those referred to drug treatment programs. However, the availability of such programs continues to be insufficient, particularly in the case of addicted women and Latinas/os.

Liberal reforms also leave intact the motivations and structures that support the war on drugs. Thus, while some European countries have sought to find creative solutions to drug use, the United States continues to sponsor punitive criminal justice policies. The narrowness of the U.S.-led drug war and U.S. disregard for human rights abroad was demonstrated in May 2001 when the international community expelled the United States from both the U.N. Human Rights Commission and the U.N. International Narcotics Control Board. With the passage of the USA PATRIOT Act in October 2001 and its use to pursue drug-related crimes while violating basic constitutional rights guaranteed in the Bill of Rights, the war on drugs has reached a new level (Leone and Anrig 2003).

As this book goes to press, the United States continues to spend more and more money on the war on drugs, the war on terrorism, and military interventions in previously sovereign Third World countries and less and less on education, health care, housing, and other human services. As the flight of U.S. capital to Third World countries continues, underemployment in the United States becomes entrenched and Latina/o unemployment soars. Equally important, the gap between rich and poor continues to widen.

As the United States continues to promote the drug war, however, there has been a parallel growth in grassroots resistance to these policies both at home and abroad. Such resistance challenges the policies pursued and the political justifications and socioeconomic structures on which they are based.

• • •

It is clear that if a jail and prison moratorium were declared tomorrow, illegal drugs and commercial sex work decriminalized or legalized, mandatory sentencing laws repealed, and all those currently imprisoned for nonviolent, low-level economic and drug-related crimes released, Chicanas would still be subjected to disparate treatment on the basis of gender, sexual orientation, social class, and racial/ethnic factors. Violence in and outside the home would continue to exist, and so would racial profiling and discrimination by criminal justice practices. Some Chicanas would continue to become addicted to drugs, and others would break the law to support themselves, their families, and their addictions. As a result they would continue to be arrested and incarcerated.

It is also clear, however, that if serious widespread systemic reforms were implemented[1] to reverse the conservative criminal justice trend toward mass incarceration and punitive solutions, the number of actions defined as "criminal" would decrease, and so would the "crime rate" and the number of "criminals" arrested and imprisoned. Jail and prison overcrowding would end, and so would much of the political and economic justification for the existence of the prison-industrial-military complex.

Reforms could include the decriminalization and/or legalization of prostitution and illegal drugs (Blumenson and Nilsen 1997; NYCLA 1996), bail reform, and a moratorium on jail and prison construction. The redistribution of society's wealth would further reduce the motivations for economic crimes.

These could be accompanied by a commitment on the part of those in power to end discriminatory criminal justice policies, respect the civil and human rights of all, and institute educational and structural changes to help reduce, among other ills, drug addiction, violence inside and outside the home, racism and heterosexism, and drug addiction.

In the meantime, private and governmental resources could be better spent on improving living conditions for those still incarcerated, providing more access to rehabilitation programs inside and outside the walls, fostering healthier relationships between prisoners and staff, improving prisoners' access to those on the outside, and providing more widespread post-incarceration services and programs.

Moreover, government agencies could focus on regulating formerly illegal drugs and educating the public about the harmful effects of both currently legal and illegal drugs (Blumenson and Nielsen 1997; NYCLA 1996). More funds would be available for rehabilitation programs for those already addicted to drugs and those who become addicted in the future. This would shift the focus from arrest and incarceration to the fields of prevention and recovery.

Because prevention and treatment options have proven to be more cost-effective than punitive criminal justice policies, the shift away from law enforcement and military solutions to drug use would make more money available nationally for improving education, health care, housing, and job training. Likewise, more capital would be available to invest in economic development, community building, and educating people concerning the harmful personal and systemic effects of violence and discrimination.

Another significant consequence of changing the focus away from punitive solutions to crime and addiction would be the reduction in the level of government corruption now encouraged by the huge profits generated by the illegal international drug trade. Criminal justice agencies could then concentrate more on protecting the public from serious violent crimes and government corruption. Law enforcement personnel could be educated to establish healthier and safer community relations.

The erosion of civil liberties in the United States and Latin America engendered by the internationalization and militarization of the war on drugs would also decrease. A change in U.S. policies away from trying to make the rest of the world conform to its priorities would improve the country's relationships with other nations.

Funds and resources the United States now spends to promote military and anti-insurgency efforts abroad could be used to export technical support and economic assistance that promote true and just economic development. This assistance would begin to compensate for the devastation of land and resources, human rights violations, and murders generated by the exportation of the war on drugs. Latin American governments, currently besieged by the imposition of U.S. political and economic agendas, could then opt to concentrate on meeting the needs of their own people.

The reforms proposed here, however, would reduce the income and privileges accorded to those who benefit the most from the international trafficking of illegal drugs, repressive penal policies, and diverse types of disparities in their societies. As a result, a host of individuals, public agencies, and private corporations would stand to lose the huge profits currently made by participation in the prison-industrial-military complex. Such profits are in fact the primary incentive for continuing the drug war. The stakes are indeed high.

While some say it is useless to dream of reforms, much less widespread structural changes, others guide our actions by just such dreams. Only vision guided by grassroots organizing and political action will make possible any change for the better. In the end, however, each one of us has to be willing to change ourselves for the better and join others committed to changing oppressive conditions. There are solutions; the question is, are we willing to work toward them?

Appendix A

Sociodemographic Characteristics of Chicana Pintas Interviewed

Economic Status of Caretakers	
Working poor/working class	21
Middle class	1
Unknown	2
Parents' Place of Birth	
Southwestern United States	15
Mexico	3
Unknown	6
Raised by	
Both parents	9
Parent and stepparent	2
Mother only	5
Combination of relatives	6
State-raised	1
Friends of family	1
Number of Siblings	
Fewer than five	8
Five or more	14
Unknown	2
Family Addiction	
Mother	8
Father	11
Siblings	10
Children	2[a]
Unknown	5
Family Incarceration	
Mother	3
Father	5
Siblings	14
Children	3[b]
Unknown	5
Place of Birth	
Los Angeles	11
Other Southern California cities	7
Northern California	4
Other states	2

Where Raised

 Los Angeles   12[c]

 Other Southern California cities   6

 Northern California   6

Experienced Placement

 Juvenile Home   6[d]

 Other Placements   4

"Runaway"   12

Level of Education at Interview

 Less than 8th grade   1

 Grades 8–11   10

 High school   1

 GED   4

 Some college   5

 Unknown   3

Language Proficiency

 Bilingual   14

 Little Spanish   5

 English-monolingual   2

 Unknown   3

Sexual Abuser as Children/Juveniles[e]

 Father   7

 Other male relatives   7

 Female relatives   1

 Male acquaintances   8

 Strangers   2

 Raped   6[f]

Physical Abuser as Children/Juveniles

 Father   6

 Mother   5

 Siblings   1

Batterer as Adults

 Male partners   9

 Female partners   3

 Both male and female partners   3

Children

 Pintas with children   20

 None   1

 Unknown   3

Age of First Heroin Use

 12–14   2

 15–17   7

 18–21   7

 30   1

 Not used   1

Unknown	6
Recovery Status at Time of Interview	
Not an addict	1
Actively using drugs (including alcohol)	5
Clean and sober	17
Unknown	1
Gang Membership	
Members	10
Non-members	14
First Adult Arrest: Age	
17	1
18–21	16
22–25	5
31	1
Unknown	1
First Adult Arrest: Offense	
Drug-related	15
Economic	6
Violent	1
Unknown	2
Incarceration	
Jail	24
Prison	
Various state prisons for women	19
CRC	9
Camp	5
Federal	3

[a]Minimum number of pintas with drug-addicted children.
[b]Minimum number of Chicanas with children who had been incarcerated.
[c]One also spent time in Mexico as a child.
[d]Another three spent between a few hours to a few days at juvenile hall on one occasion.
[e]Some were abused by a combination of these.
[f]These pintas specifically referred to diverse incidents of sexual abuse as rape.

Appendix B

Most Frequent Offenses Leading to Arrest

This appendix lists the most common offenses leading to the arrest of pintas interviewed. The number on the left indicates the number of pintas who said they had been arrested for that particular offense. That is, 15 out of 24 reported that they had been arrested for being under the influence, 14 for possession, 11 for larceny, etc. (Some had been arrested more than once for the same offense.)

15 Under the Influence
14 Possession (one of which was a federal offense)
11 Larceny
10 Burglary
10 Violation of Parole
7 Prostitution
7 Robbery (one of which was Robbery with Forgery, also a federal offense)
5 Sales (one of which was a federal offense)
4 Possession with Intent to Sell
4 Receiving Stolen Property
4 Grand Theft (three of which were GTAs)
3 DUI (one of which was a DUI with bodily injury)
3 Transporting Drugs (two of which were federal offenses)
3 Assaulting a Police Officer
3 Forgery (one of which was with Robbery, also a federal offense)
3 Violation of Probation
3 Murder (charges later dropped)
2 Public Intoxication
2 Possession of Paraphernalia
2 Weapons Charge
2 Resisting Arrest
2 Child Endangerment
1 Disorderly Conduct
1 Fraud
1 Bribery
1 Transporting People (across the Mexican-U.S. border, a federal offense)
1 Contributing to the Delinquency of a Minor
1 Fake ID

Notes

Preface

1. In order to protect the anonymity of those interviewed, pseudonyms have been used throughout the text for both pintas interviewed and all others they referenced.

2. According to USDOJ, larceny-theft "is the unlawful taking, carrying, leading, or riding away of property from the possession or constructive possession of another . . . in which no use of force, violence, or fraud occurs" (e.g., shoplifting, purse snatching, thefts from motor vehicles); burglary is "the unlawful entry of a structure to commit a felony or theft"; robbery "is the taking or attempting to take anything of value from the care, custody, or control of a person or persons by force or the threat of force or violence and/or putting the victim in fear" (USDOJ 1980: 16, 23, 27).

3. Space limitations prevented me from including the experiences of Chicanas in state prisons.

Introduction

1. While significant historical differences exist with respect to the development of Chicanas/os and other people of Latin American descent in the United States, there are more similarities in their experiences with the U.S. criminal justice system than there are differences. Thus, in order to highlight the commonalities, the term Latinas/os, when used alone, includes both Chicanas/os and other people of Latin American descent, whether born in the United States or Latin America. When significant differences exist with respect to the treatment U.S. citizens and Latin American immigrants receive from the U.S. criminal justice system, such distinctions have been made. Some pintas interviewed, however, used the terms Chicana, Latina, and Mexican interchangeably. Latin America refers to the 19 Spanish-speaking countries located in North, South, and Central America and the Caribbean.

2. See Belknap 2001; Bloom 1996; James 2000; Mann 1993, 1995a, 1995b; Price and Sokoloff 1995, 2004; Rafter 1985; Spencer 1977; Sudbury 2004a, 2004b.

3. Andersen and Collins 2004; Anzaldúa 1999; Baca Zinn and Dill 1994; Castillo 1995; Collins 1990; Davis 1981; Mohanty, Russo, and Torres 1991; Moraga and Anzaldúa 1983.

4. See Acoca and Dedel 1998; Acuña 1988; Aguirre and Baker 1988, 1994, 1997; AI 1992; CPRP 1975a, 1975b; Davidson 1974; de Jesús-Torres 2000; Díaz-Cotto 1996,

2000a, 2004, 2005, 2006; Dominick 1990; Duany and Pitman 1990; Escobar 1993, 1999; Galarza 1972; HINTF 1986; HRW 1995b; LEAA 1980; Lee 1977; MALDEF 1978; Mandel 1981; McDonnell and Rotella 1993; Meeker, Dombrink, and Mallett 2000; Mirandé 1987; Moore 1978; Morales 1972; Morgan 1954; Muñoz 2000; NCLOE 1931; NYCBOC 1973; NYCLA 1985; Pelaez 2001; Santana 1985; Sissons 1979; Sullivan 1990; Thomas 1974; Trujillo 1974, 1980, 1983; Unión del Barrio 1995; USCCR 1970, 1980; USHR 1984.

5. Díaz-Cotto 1996, 2000a, 2004, 2005, 2006; Flores-Ortiz 1995; Olguín 1995.

6. Andrade and Estrada 2003; Anglin and Hser 1987; Maher 2004; Moore 1994; Moore and Mata 1981.

7. Brotherton and Barrios 2004; Harris 1988; Jankowski 1991; Miranda 2003; Moore 1991; Moore and Hagedorn 2001; Moore, Vigil, and Levy 1995; Quicker 1983.

8. Additional data were gathered for other California county jails, state prisons, state prison camps, and federal institutions where Chicanas were held.

9. The impact of the war on drugs and other criminal justice policies in the United States has also been disproportionately felt by African-American communities, whose members compose the majority of those imprisoned in the United States. See Adamson 1983; AI 2001b; Arnold 1995; Bin Wahad et al. 1993; Bloom 1996; Brown, E. 1992, 2002; Brown, J. A. 1990; Churchill and Vander Wall 1988; Collins 1997; Davis 1974, 1998, 2003; Davis et al. 1992; Flateau 1996; French 1977; Helmer 1975; Hutchinson 1990; Isikoff 1991; Jackson 1970; James 2000; Johnson 2003; Lusane 1991; Malcolm X and Haley 1964; Mann 1993, 1995a, 1995b; Mauer 1997; Meddis 1989; NYCLA 1985; O'Reilly 1988; Petersilia 1985; Rafter 1985; Richie 1996; Shakur 1987; Sudbury 2004b; Tonry 1995. For Black women's experience in England see Chigwada-Bailey 1997.

10. Few studies draw parallels between the impact of the war on drugs in the United States and Latin America. For information on the war on drugs and women in Latin America and/or Latin American women in Europe see Agreda, Rodríguez, and Contreras 1996; AI 1996a; Azaola and Yacamán 1996; CEDIB/CJP/RAI 1996; de Achá 1996; del Olmo 1998; Dorado 1998; WCRWC 1995.

Chapter I

1. Although the United States is also interested in the trafficking of synthetic drugs and methamphetamine, these are manufactured primarily in the United States and Europe (EOP 1997; Smith 1992).

2. About 40% of the $1 trillion laundered in drug money worldwide is laundered in the United States (Maingot 1998: 151; see also FNS 1992). For a discussion of governmental corruption and the war on drugs see Bielski and Bernstein 1987; Castillo and Harmon 1994; CEDIB 1994; Chemerinsky 2000; Christopher Commission 1991; Cockburn 1987; Cockburn and Cockburn 1991; Cockburn and St. Clair 1998; Escobar 1993, 1999; Knapp Commission 1973; Kolts 1992; Kwitny 1987; Levine and Kavanau-Levine 1993; McGehee 1983; Melanson 1983; Mollen Commission 1994; Rossi 1996; Stockwell 1978; USHR 1984.

3. Bloom, Chesney-Lind, and Owen 1994; CANY 1985, 1992; HRW 1997a; Joyce and Malamud 1998; Levine and Kavanau-Levine 1993.

4. Cheney 1990; Dorn, Jepsen, and Savona 1996; EOP 1997; Reagan 1985; UN 1977, 1987, 1991; USC 1990; USDOS 1991; USGAO 1988.

5. The International Narcotics Control Board is responsible for monitoring compliance with U.N. treaties on drug trafficking, money laundering, and narcotics control (*Australian Financial Review* 2001; Williams 2001).

6. The motivations behind such policies were to reduce prisoner populations in the face of fiscal constraints, overcrowded facilities, and criticism from opponents of war on drugs policies.

7. Of these, 58.5% were classified as Mexican, 9.6% as Puerto Rican, 3.5% as Cuban, and 28.4% as other (USCB 2001: 3).

8. Hispanic/race status was reported for only 86% of California's confined population (BJS 2001a: 22; percentages calculated by author).

9. In 2002, 30% of California state prisoners were African-American, and 29.2% were white (CDC 2002: 2). At the end of 1999, 23.6% of imprisoned women felons in California were Latinas, up from 20% in 1983, and 35% of imprisoned male felons were Latinos, up from 26.1% in 1983 (CDC 2000a: Table 14). African Americans composed 34% of imprisoned women felons and 31.2% of imprisoned male felons. Whites constituted 37.7% of imprisoned women felons and 28.4% of imprisoned male felons (CDC 2000a: Table 14).

10. BJS 1997a; Boyd 2003; Byrnes, Macallair, and Shorter 2002; CDOJ 2000b.

11. Petersilia 1985; Quinney 2002; Reiman 1990; USCCR 1970; Wright 1973.

12. See CJC 1997; Díaz-Cotto 2000.

13. Pre-trial detention interferes with defendants' ability to prepare their defense and gather the economic resources necessary to pay for competent attorneys. Hence, most are forced to depend on the limited services provided by overworked and sometimes hostile or indifferent public defenders or assigned counsel who have meager budgets at their disposal to pursue the cases adequately.

14. By 1991, more than 100 federal crimes were regulated by mandatory sentencing laws. By 1994, all 50 states had passed at least one such law (Beckett and Sasson 2000: 176; Tonry 1996).

15. Under the 1973 Rockefeller drug laws, "Criminal Possession of a Controlled Substance in the First Degree (4 ounces or more of a narcotic drug)" is a Class A-1 felony, which carries a mandatory prison sentence of 15 to 25 years to life (CANY 1992: 2–3).

16. See Beckett and Sasson 2000; BJS 2001b; Bloom, Chesney-Lind, and Owen 1994; Danner 2000; HRW 1997a; NYSDOCS 1986b.

17. In 1996 the California Court of Appeals declared the state's original Three Strikes Law unconstitutional because prosecutors but not judges were allowed to ignore one or more of the strikes against a defendant. The revised law allowed judges and prosecutors the same discretion (Beckett and Sasson 2000: 181). This change did not necessarily lead to more lenient sentences.

18. In California, "[p]rior to July 1, 1977, all terms imposed by the court were indeterminate—not of fixed duration. Offenses committed on or after July 1, 1977

are for a period specified by the court except for offenses with 'life' penalties" (CDC 2000b: 7).

19. Barak 1994; Beckett and Sasson 2000; Bourgois 2003; Chermak 1995; Cockburn and St. Clair 1998; Reeves and Campbell 1994; Shapiro 1977. For a discussion of how racism combined with economic trends contributes to this increase see Davis 2003 and Gilmore 1998.

20. In 1998 women in the United States made up "21% of those on probation, 11% of those in local jails, just under 6% of those in prisons" (BJS 1999: 6).

21. In New York City, CANY (1992) found, "Of the women charged with A-1 drug felonies in Queens County between 1986 and September 30, 1991, 8% were white, 40% were African-American, and 52% Hispanic . . . Of the Queens women receiving life prison terms as a result of A-1 drug felony arrests, 6% were white, 24% were Black, and 70% were Hispanic" (20).

22. Between 1997 and 2000, 60.8% to 68.4% of new court commitments for African-American women were for drug offenses. New commitments for white women ranged between 26.8% and 43.7% (NYSDOCS 2000: Table 9.10). In 2001, Latinas continued to be overrepresented in New York state prisons, composing 26% of the women's prison population, although this was down from 30% in 1987 (NYSDOCS 2002: 81).

23. In Queens County, New York, the bails can be set at $100,000 or more (CANY 1992: 13).

24. In New York City, many of the airport "drug mule" cases are assigned to the Legal Aid Society of Queens County (CANY 1992: 13).

25. While in New York these women should be able to get lifetime probation, it is rarely granted by the Queens District Attorney's Office (CANY 1992: 15).

26. In New York, foreign consulates seldom answer requests for assistance, claiming that the Rockefeller drug laws tie their hands (CANY 1992).

27. Searches are also conducted of people who seem "nervous" or give "weird" answers to certain questions, passengers in flights coming from a "drug source country," or persons previously arrested for "carrying drugs through an airport" (CANY 1992: 10–11). The typical courier of heroin and cocaine arrested at John F. Kennedy International Airport (JFK) was a male foreign national. Most women couriers arrested at JFK were trafficking marijuana. These women tended to be African-American and U.S. residents (CANY 1992: 12). In 1980 the U.S. Supreme Court upheld the legality of profiling (*SFC* 1980).

28. Women arrested at JFK smuggled drugs for payments ranging from $1,000 to $5,000 (CANY 1992: 20).

29. Deported aliens can be readmitted into the United States five years after their deportation (BJS 1999: 4).

30. At least 75.7% of noncitizens prosecuted in U.S. district courts in 1994 were from Latin America (BJS 1996: 4). At the time, 48.6% of noncitizens convicted in U.S. district courts were from Mexico, 10.2% from Colombia, 5.7% from the Dominican Republic, and 3.9% from Cuba (BJS 1996: 3). Most were charged with offenses related to immigration or drugs. Of the latter, 35.5% concerned cocaine powder, 34.6% marijuana, and 17.7% heroin (BJS 1996: 6).

31. This included those held in federal and state prisons, territorial prisons, local

jails, INS facilities, military facilities, jails in Indian country, and juvenile facilities (BJS 2001c: 1). The federal government attributed changes in its prisoner population during the 1990s primarily to drugs, weapons, and immigration violations (BJS 2001c: 13). In 1999, 57.4% of those in federal prisons were held for drug offenses, 7.3% for property offenses, 11.2% for violent offenses, and 22.2% for public order offenses (BJS 2001c: 12). Of those under state jurisdiction in 1999, 21.1% had been sentenced for drug offenses, 20.6% for property offenses, 47.9% for violent offenses, and 10.1% for public order offenses (BJS 2001c: 11). Of those in state prisons for drug offenses, 10% were women, 20.7% were Hispanic, 20.2% were white, and 57.6% were African-American (some percentages calculated by the author).

32. Between 1983 and 1999, the U.S. jail population grew from 223,551 to 605,943 (BJS 2001a: 1). As of June 30, 1999, this included prisoners held in city, county, and regional jails and those in "community-based programs run by jail authorities (for example, electronic monitoring, house arrest, community service, day reporting, pre-trial supervision, and other alternative work programs" (BJS 2001a: 19). These figures included federal prisoners held in these jails for federal authorities (e.g., FBI, INS, U.S. Marshall Service, Bureau of Indian Affairs) but not prisoners held in 11 jails run by the Bureau of Prisons (BJS 2001a: 7). At year-end 2000, local jails housed 4.6% of state and federal prisoners (BJS 2001c: 1). Of those in jail on June 30, 1999, 11% were women (up from 6.0% in 1983), 41.5% were African-American, 41.3% were white, and 15.5% were Latina/o, up from 13% in 1983 (BJS 2001a: 3). While 1.6% were under the age of 18, 54% of those were unconvicted (BJS 2001a: iii; some percentages calculated by the author).

33. The 1979 Percy Amendment legalized privately operated prisons and prison labor. At year-end 2000, 10.7% of federal and 5.8% of state prisoners were held in private prisons (BJS 2001c: 1).

34. Davey 1995; Quinney 2002; Reiman 1990; Wright 1973.

35. Davis 1998, 2003; Davis, M. 1995; Evans and Goldberg 1997; Flateau 1996; Gilmore 1998; Sudbury 2004a, 2004b.

36. See AI 1998; Arizona, California, New Mexico, and Texas Advisory Committees to the U.S. Commission on Civil Rights 1997; HRW 1995b, 1997b; NCLOE 1931; USCCR 1980; WCRWC 1995.

37. For a discussion of the impact of the war on drugs in Latin America see Aguiló 1992; AIN 1996, 1997; Alonso 1997; Bagley 1996; Call 1991; CEDIB/CJP/RAI 1996; Cockburn 1987; González and Tienda 1989; HRW 1995a; Jelsma and Ronken 1998; Joyce and Malamud 1998; Laserna 1993; Mabry 1989; Margain 1990; Pinto Quintanilla 1999; Scott and Marshall 1991; Smith 1992; USC 1990; USGAO 1996; Walker 1989; WOLA 1991.

Chapter 2

1. Only one of the two pintas whose parents were fieldworkers had parents actually working in the fields during her childhood. Nine of the mothers were housewives while pintas were growing up. Other mothers worked as factory workers (four), packer, nurses' aide, waitress, secretary, clerks (two), cleaning woman, and video store supervisor. Fathers worked as construction workers (three), janitor, pro-

duce man, laborer, welder, mechanic, refinery operator, carpenter, and counselor. Three owned their own businesses. One was in the Army; another was in prison.

2. Technically, CYA is "the state agency which has jurisdiction over juvenile offenders who are wards of the juvenile, municipal, and superior courts" (CDC 2000b: 6).

3. Citizenship.

4. Tijuana, Mexico.

5. For those diagnosed as being mentally ill.

6. Aid to Families with Dependent Children.

7. Downers.

8. "I would fight with her."

9. "That's it!"

Chapter 3

1. Juvenile hall.

2. Uninflated party balloons filled with heroin.

3. For more discussion of juvenile detention facilities and the juvenile justice system in California and elsewhere see Acoca and Dedel 1998; Boyd 2003 (on Los Angeles juvenile halls); Byrnes, Macallair, and Shorter 2002 (on CYA); CTFJC 1996; Duany and Pitman 1990; Duran 1980; USDOJ 1994.

4. "She is not going to die of hunger."

Chapter 4

1. Brotherton and Barrios (2004) suggest that "street organizations" such as the Almighty Latin King and Queen Nation in New York City should be seen as "oppositional social movements" (315).

2. Brotherton and Barrios 2004; Brotherton and Salazar 2003; Campbell 1991; Harris 1988; Miranda 2003; Moore 1991, 1994; Moore and Hagedorn 2001; Moore, Vigil, and Levy 1995; Quicker 1983.

3. Marie "Keta" Miranda (2003) has pointed out that "unlike territorial gangs that claim a neighborhood through landmarks," the independent girl gangs she studied in Oakland, California, as well as the boys' gangs they collaborated with, "took a broader compatriotic identity as Norteñas," northerners, versus Sureñas, southerners (88). Norteñas were identified as being Chicanas and Sureñas as Mexican or Central American (184–185). A variation of the Norteño/Sureño theme is found in the rivalries between Nuestra Familia (north) and the Mexican Mafia (south).

4. EME is the phonetic Spanish pronunciation for the letter "m." None of the Chicanas interviewed claimed to have run with members of La Familia, the other large organized Chicano gang. See also Donovan 1992; Mirandé 1987.

5. For a discussion of the impact of PTSD on Chicano gang members see Tome 1992.

6. For more on Latina lesbians see Anzaldúa 1987; Moraga 1983; Ramos 2004; Romo-Carmona 2001; Trujillo 1991.

7. Big connection.

Chapter 5

1. Only one used LSD.
2. Other drugs used included downers or barbiturates such as yellow jackets, Quaaludes, Dilaudid, and seconal, or F-40s; and uppers or amphetamines such as bennies, black beauties, speed, cross tops, and whites.

Chapter 6

1. Moore and Mata (1981) found that almost half of the Chicana heroin addicts they interviewed "had the bag at some time in their careers" (88).
2. Bourgois (2003) found that in New York City, "[t]he male-dominated ranks of the underground economy exclude females from the more profitable, autonomous entrepreneurial niches such as dealing, mugging, and burglarizing" (279).
3. Few women in Moore and Mata's (1981) study, however, said dealers had refused to sell to them.

Chapter 7

1. "Let's go!" We went.

Chapter 8

1. Acuña 1988; AI 1992; Boyer 2001; Chemerinsky 2000; Christopher Commission 1991; Díaz-Cotto 2000a; Dominick 1990; Escobar 1999; Kolts 1992; MALDEF 1978; Mandel 1981; Mirandé 1987; Morales 1972; NCLOE 1931; USCCR 1970; USDOJ 1997. Several of these reports were actually motivated by cases of police brutality against African Americans.
2. Several researchers have documented the manner in which Latina/o police officers in New York have been subjected to discriminatory treatment and harassment by both their peers and supervisors (De Jesús-Torres 2000; González 2003).
3. These findings contrast with Moore and Mata's (1981) study (conducted before the full impact of war on drugs policies made themselves felt in California), which found that Chicanas were not more likely to be harassed by police officers because they were addicts.
4. While in 1990 Latinas/os comprised 40% of Los Angeles' population, in 1986 only 16.5% of LAPD officers were Latinas/os (AI 1992: 5).
5. Ironically, the fact that law enforcement agencies have traditionally resisted hiring women also meant that there were few female officers available to search women on the streets or at substations (CGW 1998).

Chapter 9

1. AI 2001; Aguirre and Baker 1994; CJC 1997; De Jesús-Torres 2000; HRW 2000; Mann 1995a, 1995b. De Jesús-Torres (2000) also discusses how Latina/o jurors,

potential jurors, defendants, and crime victims are discriminated against by court actors.

2. The California Rehabilitation Center (CRC) is "a facility operated by the CDC to house Civil Narcotic Addicts (CNA) and selected felons" (CDC 2000b: 5). Civil commitment is "a type of commitment in which criminal proceedings are suspended while a defendant undergoes treatment at the California Rehabilitation Center as a Civil Narcotic Addict" (ibid.: 6). During the early 1980s, for Chicanas sentenced to CRC, maxing out on parole could take as long as 10 years (Faith 1981: 113). That is, parole violators could be returned to CRC for up to 10 years on an original offense for which they would have served much less time at a women's penitentiary. Even if prisoners were deemed rehabilitated by prison psychiatrists before their maximum sentences were up, the courts could keep them at CRC for up to 10 years (ibid.). Under these conditions, some Chicanas chose to go to a women's penitentiary rather than CRC.

3. "Good time" credit. State prisoners who committed crimes "on or after July 1, 1977, earn one day off their time to serve for every three days of good behavior or participation, if they are ineligible to earn day for day credits under the Inmate Work Training Incentive Program" (CDC 2000b: 7).

4. She was being held in the San Jose County Jail felony offenders' section.

5. They were DUI, sales, direct sale to a police officer, and disorderly conduct.

6. To be transported to prison.

7. California Institution for Women, at Frontera.

8. A facility where state prisoners are first evaluated and categorized and from which they can be transferred to other state institutions to serve their sentences.

9. Board of Prison Terms.

10. Madera refers to the Central California Women's Facility, which is actually located in Chowchilla, near Madera. Pintas tended to use the two names interchangeably.

11. Luck.

Chapter 10

1. From 1925 until October 1979, the top four floors of the Los Angeles Hall of Justice housed the Los Angeles County jail (*LAT* 10/6/79).

2. This was in addition to the more than 700 women prisoners processed through the Twin Towers Inmate Reception Center during May 1997 (*LAT* 6/9/1997).

3. Mira Loma was closed due to budget cuts (*LAT* 5/18/93).

4. *Inmates of SBI* was filed on February 22, 1973. While the court issued a tentative ruling February 14, 1977 (2 C.T. 438), the court's final decision was issued on December 1, 1978 (3 C.T. 967). The information included in Chapters 10–17 is taken primarily from the appeals filed in 1982 (*Inmates of SBI* 1982a, 1982b).

Chapter 11

1. Díaz-Cotto 1996; Freedman 1981; Rafter 1985; Richie 1996; Ross 1998; Spencer 1977.

2. Percentages calculated by author.

3. Technically, maximum security was Cell Block 5200 (*LAT* 7/13/86).

4. Sign up for medical care.

5. Written up by guards for rule violations.

Chapter 12

1. ACA 1993; Barry 1985a, 1987, 1991a, 1993, 1995a, 1995b; CBC 1970; Díaz-Cotto 1996; Ross 1998; Watterson 1996.

2. During the late 1970s and early 1980s, attention was also brought to bear on the overmedication of and experimentation with prisoners taking place at the California Institution for Women, where 18 of the 24 pintas interviewed eventually served time (Faith 1981).

3. The suit was filed on behalf of the family of Nancy Elizabeth Douglas. Between 1994 and 1997 more than 65 lawsuits related to medical and psychological mistreatment were filed against LASD. At least four of those settled involved Latinos (*LAT* 12/28/97).

4. An African-American former prisoner interviewed claimed to have seen the regulations written in Spanish at one point.

5. Friends Outside is a volunteer nonprofit organization that serves prisoners, former prisoners, and their families.

6. "Will you do me a favor? Could you ask the police when I'm going to court?"

7. "What is the problem? . . . He told me I can't get soap here."

Chapter 13

1. Tag or label.

Chapter 15

1. Brown, J. A. 1990; Díaz-Cotto 1996; Giallombardo 1966; HRW 1996; Owen 1998; Ward and Kassebaum 1965; Watterson 1996.

2. At the time of the interviews, 10 of the 19 pintas for whom information was available identified as lesbians, seven as heterosexual, and two as bisexual. For more on Latina lesbians see Anzaldúa 1987; Anzaldúa and Moraga 1981; Moraga 1981; Ramos 2004; Romo-Carmona 2001; Trujillo 1991.

3. White male guards also frowned upon interracial relationships, particularly between African-American and white prisoners (Carmen).

4. The daddies were subsequently allowed to wear overalls depending on their work assignment (Johansen 1996).

5. Brown, J. A. 1990; Díaz-Cotto 1996; Giallombardo 1966; Owen 1998; Ward and Kassebaum 1965; Watterson 1996.

6. Meaning Chicanas and other women of Latin American descent.

7. In some U.S. women's prisons, heads of households were leading organizers of prisoner coalitions. There were also times when pseudo-families were behind

the creation of formal prisoner groups and were the most active prisoners in these groups (Díaz-Cotto 1996).

Chapter 16

1. Barry 1985a, 1985b, 1987; Baunach 1985; Gabel and Johnston 1995; Henriques 1982; McGowan and Blumental 1976; Pelaez 2001; Pérez 1996; Women's Prison Association 1995.

2. Source: LASD photocopied leaflet.

3. Alcoholics Anonymous (1976) basic text, entitled *Alcoholics Anonymous*.

Chapter 17

1. Brown, J. A. 1990; Baunach and Murton 1973; Díaz-Cotto 1996; Shakur 1987.

2. Aylward and Thomas 1984; Barry 1991a, 1995b; 2000; Díaz-Cotto 1996; HRW 1996; Kates 1984; Ross 1998; Serna 1992; Shakur 1987.

Chapter 18

1. For more on issues confronted by pintas released from penal institutions see Alméstica (1996).

2. Recovery home for women.

3. Federal narcotics agents threatened to send Linda to prison for 30 years.

4. Department of Children's Services.

5. For a discussion of Chicana/o community-based programs serving pintas/os and addicts during the late 1960s and throughout the 1970s see Moore and Mata 1981.

Chapter 19

1. Beckett and Sasson 2000; Bloom 1996; Blumenson and Nilsen 1997; Byrnes, Macallair, and Shorter 2002; CANY 1985, 1992, 1999; Churchill and Vander Wall 1992; CPRP 1975a; CRPC 2000; CSAT 1996; Damuzi 2001; Danner 2000; Davis 2003; EOP 1997; Gerstein et al. 1994; Gilmore 1998; Howe 1994; HRW 1992, 1995b, 1996, 2000; James 2000; Johnson 2003; LEAA 1980; Leone and Anrig 2003; Lusane 1991; Mann 1993; Murphy, Johnson, and Edwards 1992; NYCLA 1985, 1996; Price and Sokoloff 1995, 2004; Rafter 1985; Reiman 1990; Richie 1996; Ross 1998; Shakur 1987; Sudbury 2004a, 2004b; Tome 1992; USCCR 1970, 1980; U.S. Sentencing Commission 1991; Watterson 1996; Whitlock 2001.

Reference List

Written Works

Acoca, Leslie, and Kelly Dedel. 1998. *No Place to Hide: Understanding and Meeting the Needs of Girls in the California Juvenile Justice System.* San Francisco: National Council on Crime and Delinquency.

Acuña, Rodolfo. 2000. *Occupied America: A History of Chicanos.* 4th ed. New York: Longman.

Adamson, C. R. 1983. "Punishment after Slavery: Southern State Penal Systems, 1865–1890." *Social Problems* 3, no. 5 (June): 555–569.

Agreda, Evelin R Norma O. Rodríguez, and Alex B. Contreras. 1996. *Mujeres cocaleras.* Cochabamba, Bolivia: Comité Coordinador de las Cinco Federaciones del Trópico de Cochabamba.

Aguiló S. I., Federico. 1992. *Narcotráfico y violencia.* Cochabamba, Bolivia: Centro de Documentación e Información–Bolivia y Instituto de Estudio Económico y Social.

Aguirre Jr., Adalberto, and David V. Baker. 1988. "A Descriptive Profile of the Hispanic Penal Population: Conceptual and Reliability Limitations in Public Use Data." *Justice Professional* 3, no. 2: 189–200.

———. 1994. *Perspectives on Race and Ethnicity in American Criminal Justice.* St. Paul: West.

———. 1997. "A Descriptive Profile of Mexican-American Execution in the Southwest." *Social Justice Journal* 34, no. 3: 389–402.

Alcoholics Anonymous. 1976. *Alcoholics Anonymous.* 3d ed. New York: Alcoholics Anonymous World Services.

Alméstica, Diana González. 1996. "Making the Transition to Society." *Women and the Criminal Justice System* 4: 221–223.

Alonso, Carlos, ed. 1997. *Guerra antidrogas, democracia, derechos humanos y militarización en América Latina.* Guatemala City, Guatemala: CEDIB, TNI, and Inforpress Centroamericana. April.

American Correctional Association (ACA). 1993. *Female Offenders: Meeting the Needs of a Neglected Population.* Laurel, Md.

Amnesty International (AI). 1992. *United States of America: Police Brutality in Los Angeles, California.* London: AI. June.

———. 1995. *United States of America: Human Rights Violations: A Summary of Amnesty International's Concerns.* March. New York: AI.

————. 1996. *Mexico, Overcoming Fear: Human Rights Violations Against Women in Mexico*. March. New York: AI.

————. 1998. *United States of America: Human Rights Concerns in the Border Region with Mexico*. May. New York: AI.

————. 1999. *"Not Part of My Sentence": Violation of Human Rights of Women in Custody*. New York: AI.

————. 2001a. *Abuse of Women in Custody*. New York: AI.

————. 2001b. *Racism and the Administration of Justice*. New York: AI.

Andean Information Network (AIN), ed. 1996. *The Weight of Law 1008*. Cochabamba, Bolivia.

————. 1997. *Children of Law 1008*. Cochabamba, Bolivia.

Andersen, Margaret L., and Patricia Hill Collins, eds. 2004. *Race, Class, and Gender: An Anthology*. 5th ed. Belmont, Calif.: Wadsworth/Thomson Learning.

Andrade, Rosi, and Antonio L. Estrada. 2003. "Gender, Culture and Substance Abuse: Are Hispana IDUs Tecatas? Reconsidering Gendered Culture in Hispana Injection Drug Use." *Substance Use and Misuse* 38, no. 8.

Anglin, M. Douglas, and Yihing Hser. 1987. "Addicted Women and Crime." *Criminology* 25, no. 2: 359–397.

Anzaldúa, Gloria E. 1987. *Borderlands/La Frontera*. San Francisco: Aunt Lute Books.

Arizona, California, New Mexico, and Texas Advisory Committees to the U.S. Commission on Civil Rights. 1997. *Federal Immigration Law Enforcement in the Southwest: Civil Rights Impact on Border Communities*. March. Washington, D.C.: Government Printing Office (GPO). http://www.law.umaryland.edu/marshall/usccr/titlelist.asp.

Arnold, Regina. 1995. "Processes of Victimization and Criminalization of Black Women." In *The Criminal Justice System and Women*, 2d ed. Ed. Barbara Raffel Price and Natalie J. Sokoloff, 136–146. New York: McGraw-Hill.

Association of the Bar of the City of New York (ABCNY)/The Drug Abuse Council Inc. 1977. *The Nation's Toughest Drug Law: Evaluating the New York Experience*. Final Report of the Joint Committee on New York Drug Law Evaluation. New York: ABCNY.

Austin, James, Juanita Dimas, and David Steinhart. 1992. *The Over-Representation of Minority Youth in the California Juvenile Justice System, Report Summary*. San Francisco: National Council on Crime and Delinquency. April.

Australian Financial Review. 2001. "U.S. Kicked off UN Drug Body." May, 12.

Aylward, Anna, and Jim Thomas. 1984. "Quiescence in Women's Prison Litigation: Some Exploratory Issues." *Justice Quarterly* 1, no. 1 (March): 253–276.

Azaola, Elena, and Cristina José Yacamán. 1996. *Las mujeres olvidadas: Un estudio sobre la situación actual de las cárceles de mujeres en la República Mexicana*. Mexico City: Centro Nacional de Derechos Humanos, Colegio de México.

Baca Zinn, Maxine. 1979. "Chicano Family Research: Conceptual Distortions and Alternative Directions." *Journal of Ethnic Studies* 7, no. 3: 59–71.

Baca Zinn, Maxine, and Bonnie Thorton Dill, eds. 1994. *Women of Color in U.S. Society*. Philadelphia: Temple University Press.

Bagley, Bruce M., ed. 1996. *Drug Trafficking in the Americas: An Annotated Bibliography.* Coral Gables, Fla.: North South Center, University of Miami Press.

Barak, Gregg, ed. 1994. *Media, Process, and the Social Construction of Crime.* New York: Garland.

Barry, Ellen. 1985a. "Quality of Parental Care for Incarcerated Women Challenged." *Youth Law News* (November–December).

———. 1985b. "Reunification Difficult for Incarcerated Parents and Their Children." *Youth Law News* (July–August).

———. 1987. "Imprisoned Mothers Face Extra Hardships." *Journal of the National Prison Project* (winter).

———. 1989. "Pregnant Prisoners." *Harvard Women's Law Journal* 12.

———. 1991a. "Jail Litigation Concerning Women Prisoners." *Prison Journal* 71: 44–50.

———. 1991b. "Pregnant, Addicted, and Sentenced." *ABA Criminal Justice Journal* (winter).

———. 1995a. "Women Prisoners and Health Care: Locked Up and Locked Out." In *Manmade Medicine,* ed., Kary Moss. Durham, NC: Duke University Press.

———. 1995b. See below under Personal Interviews.

———. 2000. "Women Prisoners on the Cutting Edge: Development of the Activist Women's Prisoners' Rights Movement." *Social Justice* 27.

Bass, Ellen, and Laura Davis. 1988. *The Courage to Heal.* New York: Perennial Library.

Bates, E. 1998. "Prisons for Profit." *Nation,* January 5, 1, 11–16, 18.

Baunach, Phyllis Jo. 1985. *Mothers in Prison.* New Brunswick, N.J.: Transaction Books.

Baunach, Phyllis Jo, and Thomas Murton. 1973. "Women in Prison: An Awakening Minority." *Crime and Corrections* (fall): 4–12.

Beckett, Katherine, and Theodore Sasson. 2000. *The Politics of Injustice.* Thousand Oaks, Calif.: Pine Forge.

Belknap, Joanne. 2001. *The Invisible Woman: Gender, Crime, and Justice.* 2d ed. Belmont, Calif.: Wadsworth.

Bielski, Vince, and Dennis Bernstein. 1987. "NSC, CIA, and Drugs: The Cocaine Connection." *Covert Action Information Bulletin* (summer).

Bin Wahad, Dhoruba, Mumia Abu-Jamal, Assata Shakur, Jim Fletcher, Tanaquil Jones, and Silvère Lotringer. 1993. *Still Black, Still Strong.* New York: Semiotext(e).

Bloom, Barbara. 1996. "Triple Jeopardy: Race, Class, and Gender in Women's Imprisonment." Ph.D. diss., University of California at Riverside.

Bloom, Barbara, Meda Chesney-Lind, and Barbara Owen. 1994. *Women in California Prisons.* San Francisco: Center on Juvenile and Criminal Justice.

Blumenson, Eric, and Eva Nilsen. 1997. "Policing for Profit: The Drug War's Hidden Economic Agenda." *University of Chicago Law Review.* http://www.fear.org/chicago.html.

Bourgois, Philippe. 2003. *In Search of Respect: Selling Crack in El Barrio.* 2d ed. Cambridge, England: Cambridge University Press.

Boyd, Ralph F. Jr. 2003. Re: Los Angeles County Juvenile Halls. Letter to Ms.

Yvonne B. Burke. U.S. Attorney General's Office, April 9. www.usdoj.gov/crt/ split/documents/la_county_juvenile_findlet.pdf.

Boyer, Peter J. 2001. "Bad Cops." *New Yorker.* May 21.

Brotherton, David G., and Luis Barrios. 2004. *The Almighty King and Queen Nation: Street Politics and the Transformation of a New York City Gang.* New York: Columbia University Press.

Brotherton, David G., and Camila Salazar. 2003. "Pushes and Pulls in the Resistance Trajectories of the Latin Queens." In *Gangs and Society: Alternative Perspectives.* Ed. L. Kontos, D. Brotherton, and L. Barrios. New York: Columbia University Press.

Brown, Elaine. 1992. *A Taste a Power.* New York: Anchor Books.

———. 2002. *The Condemnation of Little B.* Boston: Beacon.

Brown, Joyce Ann. 1990. *Joyce Ann Brown.* Chicago: Noble Press.

Browning, Rufus P., Dale Rogers Marshall, and David H. Tabb. 1997. *Racial Politics in American Cities.* 2d ed. White Plains, N.Y.: Longman.

Bureau of Justice Statistics (BJS). 1994. *Special Report: Survey of State Prison Inmates, 1991: Women in Prison.* Washington, D.C.: U.S. Department of Justice. March.

———. 1996. *Noncitizens in the Federal Criminal Justice System, 1984–1994.* Washington, D.C.: U.S. Department of Justice. August.

———. 1997a. *Juvenile Delinquents in the Federal Criminal Justice System.* Washington, D.C.: U.S. Department of Justice. February.

———. 1997b. *Police Use of Force: Collection of National Data.* Washington, D.C.: U.S. Department of Justice. November.

———. 1999. *Special Report: Women Offenders.* Washington, D.C.: U.S. Department of Justice. December.

———. 2000. *Sourcebook of Criminal Justice Statistics—1999.* Washington, D.C.: U.S. Department of Justice.

———. 2001a. *Census of Jails, 1999.* Washington, D.C.: U.S. Department of Justice. August.

———. 2001b. *Federal Drug Offenders, 1999, with Trends 1984–99.* Washington, D.C.: U.S. Department of Justice. August.

———. 2001c. *Prisoners in 2000.* Washington, D.C.: U.S. Department of Justice. August.

Butterfield, Fox. 2000. "Often, Parole Is One Stop Back on the Way to Prison." *Parole Revocations Nationwide 2000.* November 29. www.fplao.org/ParoleRevocationsNationwide2000.html.

Byrnes, Michele, Daniel Macallair, and Andrea D. Shorter. 2002. *Aftercare as Afterthought: Reentry and the California Youth Authority.* San Francisco: Center on Juvenile and Criminal Justice. August.

California Board of Corrections (CBC). 1970. *A Study of California County Jails.* Sacramento. April.

California Department of Corrections (CDC). 2002. *CDC Facts, Fourth Quarter.* http://www.corr.ca.gov/communicationsoffice/facts_figures.asp.

California Department of Corrections (CDC). 1992. Administrative Services Division. *Historical Trends Institutions and Parole Population, 1971–1991.* Sacramento: CDC. April.

———. 1998. *Historical Trends Institutions and Parole Population, 1977–1997.* Sacramento: June.

———. 2000a. *California Prisoners and Parolees 2000 Summary Statistics.* Sacramento, CA: June.

———. 2000b. *California Prisoners and Parolees Reference Guide.* Photocopy.

California Department of Justice (CDOJ). 1997. *Female Gang Members—Arrest Records Reviewed.* Sacramento: Office of the Attorney General.

———. 2000. Criminal Justice Statistics Center. *Report on Drug Arrests in California, From 1990 to 1999.* Sacramento.

———. 2001. Criminal Justice Statistics Center. *Crime and Delinquency in California 2000: Arrests, Part 1.* Sacramento: CDOJ.

California Judicial Council (CJC). 1997. *Final Report of the California Judicial Council Advisory Committee on Racial and Ethnic Bias in the Courts.* San Francisco: CJC.

California Task Force on Juvenile Crime and the Juvenile Justice Response (CTFJC). 1996. *Final Report.* Sacramento: California Youth Authority. September.

California Youth Authority (CYA). Information and Parole Research Bureau. 2002. "Characteristics of First Admissions to the California Youth Authority, 1959–2001." Sacramento: CYA. July 16.

Call, Charles. 1991. *Clear and Present Dangers: The U.S. Military and the War on Drugs in Latin America.* Washington, D.C.: Washington Office on Latin America. October.

Campbell, Anne. 1991. *The Girls in the Gang.* 2d ed. Cambridge, Mass.: Blackwell.

Castillo, Ana. 1995. *Massacre of the Dreamers: Essays on Xicanisma.* New York: Plume.

Castillo, Celerino III, and Dave Harmon. 1994. *Powderburns.* Oakville, Ontario, Canada: Mosaic.

Center for Substance Abuse Treatment (CSAT). 1996. National Treatment Improvement Evaluation Study. *Preliminary Report: The Persistent Effects of Substance Abuse Treatment—One Year Later.* Rockville, Md.: U.S. Department of Health and Human Services. September.

Centro de Documentación e Información—Bolivia (CEDIB). 1994. *DEA y Soberanía en Bolivia.* Cochabamba, Bolivia: CEDIB. October.

Centro de Documentación e Información—Bolivia (CEDIB), Consultorio Jurídico Popular (CJP), and Red Andina de Información (RAI), eds. 1996. *Desde la cárcel.* Cochabamba, Bolivia: CEDIB, CJP, and RAI.

Chemerinsky, Erwin. 2000. *An Independent Analysis of the LAPD's Board of Inquiry Report on the Los Angeles Rampart Scandal.* Los Angeles: Los Angeles Police Protective League. September 11. http://lawweb.usc.edu.

Cheney, Richard B. 1990. *Annual Report to the President and the Congress.* Washington, D.C.: GPO. January.

Chermak, Steven. 1995. *Victims in the News.* Boulder, Colo.: Westview.

Chesney-Lind, Meda. 1994 "Girls in Gangs: 'Violent Equality or Media Hype?'" *Extra!*, March/April, 12.

Chesney-Lind, Meda, and Randall G. Shelden. 1998. *Girls, Delinquency, and Juvenile Justice.* Belmont, Calif.: West/Wadsworth.

Chevigny, Paul. 1969. *Police Power: Police Abuses in New York City*. New York: Pantheon.

Chicano Pinto Research Project (CPRP). 1975a. *Community Variations in Chicano Ex-Convict Adaptations*. Final Report. Los Angeles: University of Southern California.

———. 1975b. *The L.A. Pinto Background Papers and Advance Report*. Los Angeles: CPRP.

Chigwada-Bailey, Ruth. 1997. *Black Women's Experience of Criminal Justice: A Discourse on Disadvantage*. Winchester, England: Waterside.

Christensen, Loren W. 1999. *Gangbangers: Understanding the Deadly Minds of America's Street Gangs*. Boulder, Colo.: Paladin Press.

Christopher Commission. 1991. *Report of the Independent Commission on the Los Angeles Police Department*. Los Angeles: Independent Commission on the Los Angeles Police Department. July. http://www.parc.info/reports/index.html.

Churchill, Ward, and Jim Vander Wall. 1988. *Agents of Repression: The FBI's Secret Wars Against the Black Panther Party and the American Indian Movement*. Boston: South End.

———. 1990. *COINTELPRO Papers: Documents from the FBI's Secret Wars Against Dissent in the United States*. Boston: South End.

Churchill, Ward, and J. J. Vander Wall, eds. 1992. *Cages of Steel: The Politics of Imprisonment*. Washington, D.C.: Maisonneuve.

Clark, John, James Austin, and D. Alan Henry. 1997. *"Three Strikes and You're Out": A Review of State Legislation*. Occasional paper. Washington, D.C.: National Institute of Justice (NIJ), U.S. Department of Justice (USDOJ). September.

Cockburn, Alexander, and Jeffrey St. Clair. 1998. *Whiteout*. New York: Verso.

Cockburn, Andrew, and Leslie Cockburn. 1991. *Dangerous Liaisons*. Harper Collins.

Cockburn, Leslie. 1987. *Out of Control*. New York: Atlantic Monthly.

Collins, Catherine Fisher. 1997. *The Imprisonment of African-American Women: Causes, Conditions, and Future Implications*. Jefferson, N.C.: McFarland.

Collins, Patricia Hill. 1990. *Black Feminist Thought: Knowledge, Consciousness, and the Politics of Empowerment*. New York: Routledge.

Coordination Group on Women (CGW). 1998. Office of Justice Programs. *Women in Criminal Justice: A 20 Year Update Special Report*. Washington, D.C.: USDOJ.

Correctional Association of New York (CANY). 1985. *Do They Belong in Prison?: The Impact of New York's Mandatory Sentencing Laws in the Administration of Justice*. New York: CANY.

———. 1992. *Injustice Will Be Done: Women Drug Couriers and the Rockefeller Drug Laws*. New York: CANY. February.

———. 1999. *Mandatory Injustice: Case Histories of Women Convicted Under New York State's Rockefeller Drug Laws*. New York: CANY. April.

Critical Resistance Publications Collective (CRPC). 2000. *Critical Resistance to the Prison Industrial Complex*. Special issue. *Journal of Social Justice* 27, no. 3.

Damuzi, Reverend. 2001. "U.S. Prison Empire." *Cannabis Culture Magazine*, April 19. http://www.youthfederation.com.

Danner, Mona J. E. 2000. "Three Strikes and It's Women Who Are Out: The Hidden

Consequences for Women of Criminal Justice Policy Reforms." In *It's a Crime: Women and Justice*, 2d ed. Ed. Roslyn Muraskin, 215–224. Upper Saddle River, N.J.: Prentice Hall.

Davey, Joseph D. 1995. *The New Social Contract*. Westport, Conn.: Praeger.

Davidson, Theodore R. 1974. *Chicano Prisoners*. New York: Holt, Rinehart, and Winston.

Davis, Angela J. 1996. "Benign Neglect of Racism in the Criminal Justice System." *Michigan Law Review* 94 (May): 1660–1686.

———. 1974. *Angela Davis—An Autobiography*. New York: Random House. Reprint, New York: International Publishers, 1988.

———. 1981. *Women, Race, and Class*. New York: Random House.

———. 1998. "Masked Racism: Reflections on the Prison Industrial Complex." *Colorlines* 1, no. 2 (fall): 12–17.

———. 2003. *Are Prisons Obsolete?*. New York: Seven Stories Press.

Davis, Angela Y., Ruchell Magee, The Soledad Brothers, and Other Political Prisoners. 1992. *If They Come in the Morning*. Lagos, Nigeria: Third Press.

Davis, Mike. 1995. "Hell Factories in the Field: A Prison Industrial Complex." *Nation*, February 20, 229–234.

de Achá, Gloria Rose Marie. 1996. *Violaciones a los derechos humanos civiles durante la investigación policial en casos detenidos bajo la Ley 1008*. Cochabamba, Bolivia: RAI, CEDIB.

de Jesús-Torres, Migdalia. 2000. "Microaggressions in the Criminal Justice System at Discretionary Stages of Its Impact on Latina(o) Hispanics." *Justice Professional* 13, no. 1 (April): 69–89.

del Olmo, Rosa, ed. 1998. *Criminalidad y criminalización de la mujer en la región andina*. Caracas, Venezuela: Nueva Sociedad.

del Pinal, Jorge H. 1973. "The Penal Population of California." In *Voices*. Berkeley: El Grito.

Díaz-Cotto, Juanita. 1991. "Women and Crime in the United States." In *Third World Women and the Politics of Feminism*. Ed. Chandra Talpade Mohanty, Ann Russo, and Lourdes Torres. Bloomington: Indiana University Press.

———. 1996. *Gender, Ethnicity, and the State: Latina and Latino Prison Politics*. Albany: State University of New York Press.

———. 2000a. "The Criminal Justice System and Its Impact on Latinas(os) in the United States." *Justice Professional* 13, no. 1 (April): 49–68.

———. 2000b. "Lesbian Prisoners." In *Encyclopedia of Lesbian Histories and Culture*. Ed. Bonnie Zimmerman. New York: Garland Publishing.

———. 2000c. "Race, Ethnicity, and Gender in Studies of Incarceration." In *States of Confinement*. Ed. Joy James. New York: St. Martin's.

———. 2004. "Latin American Women and the War on Drugs in the U.S. and Latin America." In *Global Lockdown: Race, Gender, and the Prison Industrial Complex*. Ed. Julia Sudbury. New York: Routledge.

———. 2005. "Prisons." In *Encyclopedia of Latinos and Latinas in the United States*. Ed. Deena J. González and Suzanne Oboler. New York: Oxford University Press.

———. 2006. "Latina Imprisonment and the War on Drugs." In *Race, Gender, and*

Punishment. Ed. Mary Bosworth and Jeanne Flavin. New Brunswick, N.J.: Rutgers University Press.

Dominick, Joe. 1990. "Police Power: Why No One Can Control the LAPD." *L.A. Weekly*, February 16–22.

Donovan, John. 1992. "California's Chicano Gang Subculture: The Journey from Pachuco 'Sadistic Clowns' to a Norteño 'Society of Houses.'" *Latino Studies Journal* 3, no. 3 (September): 29–44.

Donziger, Steven A., ed. 1996. *The Real War on Crime: The Report of the National Criminal Justice Commission.* New York: Harper Perennial.

Dorado, María Cristina. 1998. "Mujeres latinoamericanas en Europa: el caso de Colombia." In *Criminalidad y criminalización de la mujer en la región andina.* Ed., Rosa del Olmo, 75–101. Caracas, Venezuela: Nueva Sociedad.

Dorn, Nicholas, Jorgen Jepsen, and Ernesto Savona. 1996. *European Drug Policies and Enforcement.* Basingstoke, England: Macmillan.

Duany, Luis, and Karen Pitman. 1990. *Latino Youths at a Crossroads.* Washington, D.C.: Adolescent Pregnancy Prevention Clearinghouse, Children's Defense Fund. January/March.

Dunn, Timothy. 1996. *The Militarization of the U.S.-Mexico Border 1978–1992.* Austin: University of Texas Press.

Duran, Miguel. 1980. "The Juvenile Justice System—A Research Paper on How It Affects the Hispanic Community." In *National Hispanic Conference On Law Enforcement and Criminal Justice, 1980.* Washington, D.C.: USDOJ, Law Enforcement Assistance Administration (LEAA).

Escobar, Edward J. 1993. "The Dialectics of Repression: The Los Angeles Police Department and the Chicano Movement, 1968–1971." *Journal of American History* 79, no. 4 (3): 1483–1514.

———. 1999. *Race, Police, and the Making of Political Identity: Mexican Americans and the Los Angeles Police Department, 1900–1945.* Berkeley: University of California Press.

Evans, Linda, and Eve Goldberg. 1997. "The Prison Industrial Complex and the Global Economy." Pamphlet. Berkeley: Prison Activist Resource Center.

Executive Office of the President (EOP). 1990. *Budget of the U.S. Government.* Washington, D.C.: GPO.

———. 1997. Office of National Drug Control Policy. *The National Drug Control Strategy, 1997.* Washington, D.C.: GPO.

Faith, Karlene. 1981. "Drug Addiction: From a Study of Women and Criminal Justice." Ph.D. diss., University of California at Santa Cruz.

———. 1993. *Unruly Women: The Politics of Confinement and Resistance.* Vancouver, Canada: Press Gang Publishers.

Federal News Service (FNS). 1992. "Drug Money Laundering." U.S. Congress, Senate Governmental Committee, Permanent Investigations Subcommittee Hearing. February 27. Washington, D.C.: GPO.

Flateau, J. 1996. *The Prison Industrial Complex.* Brooklyn, New York: Medgar Evers College, Dubois Bunche Center for Public Policy.

Flores-Ortiz, Yvette G. 1995. *Pintas.* Report Submitted to the California Policy Seminar. University of California at Davis.

Foucault, Michel. 1989. *Discipline and Punish*. New York: Oxford University Press.

Freedman, Estelle. 1981. *Their Sisters' Keepers: Women's Prison Reform in America, 1830–1930*. Ann Arbor: University of Michigan Press.

French, L. 1977. "An Assessment of the Black Female Prisoner in the South." *Signs* 3, no. 2: 483–488.

Foyt, Sandra M. Beuchert. 1995. *Human Rights of Latinas in the United States*. New York: Puerto Rican Legal Defense and Education Fund.

Gabel, K., and D. Johnston, eds. 1995. *Children of Incarcerated Parents*. New York: Lexington Books.

Galarza, Ernesto. 1972. *Barrio Boy*. New York: Ballantine.

Galindo, Leticia D. 1993. "The Language of Gangs, Drugs, and Prison Life Among Chicanas." *Latino Studies Journal* (September): 23–43.

Garcilazo, Miguel. 1990. "New York's Lewdest: City Cops Give Women Inmates an Earful." *New York Post* (NYP), October 8, p. 3.

Gerstein, D. R., R. A. Johnson, H. J. Harwood, D. Fountain, N. Suter, and K. Malloy. 1994. *Evaluating Recovery Services*. Sacramento: California Department of Alcohol and Drug Programs.

Giallombardo, Rose. 1966. *Society of Women: A Study of a Women's Prison*. New York: John Wiley and Sons.

Gilmore, Ruth Wilson. 1998. "From Military Keynesianism to Post-Keynesian Militarism: Finance Capital, Land, Labor, and Opposition in the Rising California Prison State." Ph.D. diss., State University of New Jersey at Rutgers.

———. 1998–1999. "Globalization and U.S. Prison Growth: From Military Keynesianism to Post-Keynesian Militarism. *Race and Class* 40, no. 2/3: 171–188.

Glick, Ronald, and Joan Moore. 1990. *Drugs in Hispanic Communities*. New Brunswick, N.J.: Rutgers University Press.

González, Juan. 2000. *Harvest of Empire: A History of Latinos in America*. New York: Penguin Books.

———. 2003. "Shades of Bias in Police Academy." *New York Daily News*, July 29, p. 16.

González González, Guadalupe, and Marta Tienda, eds. 1989. *The Drug Connection in U.S.-Mexican Relations*. La Jolla: Center for U.S.-Mexican Studies, University of California at San Diego.

Green, P. 1996. *Drug Couriers: A New Perspective*. London: Quartet Books.

Gregorian, Dareh. 1998. "Latino Cops Say They Got Flak from NYPD." *NYP*, June 15, p. 5.

Gutiérrez, David G. 1995. *Walls and Mirrors: Mexican Americans, Mexican Immigrants, and the Politics of Ethnicity*. Berkeley: University of California Press.

Hames-García, Michael. 2004. *Fugitive Thought: Prison Movements, Race, and the Meaning of Justice*. Minneapolis: University of Minnesota Press.

Harris, Mary G. 1988. *CHOLAS: Latino Girls and Gangs*. New York: AMS.

———. 1994. "Chola, Mexican-American Girls and Gangs." *Sex Roles* 30, no. 3–4: 289–301.

Harris, Ron. 1990. "Blacks Feel Brunt of Drug War." *Los Angeles Times (LAT)*, April 22.

Helmer, John. 1975. *Drugs and Minority Oppression.* New York: Seabury.

Henriques, Zelma W. 1982. *Imprisoned Mothers and Their Children.* Lanham, Md.: University Press of America.

Herman, Judith Lewis. 1992. *Trauma and Recovery.* New York: BasicBooks.

Hispanic Inmate Needs Task Force (HINTF). 1986. *Report, A Meeting of the Minds, An Encounter of Hearts, 1986 (Action Plan).* Albany: New York State Department of Correctional Services (NYSDOCS), Division of Hispanic and Cultural Affairs.

Hornor, Louise L. 1999. *Hispanic Americans: A Statistical Sourcebook.* Palo Alto, Calif.: Information Publication.

Howe, Adrian. 1994. *Punish and Critique: Towards a Feminist Analysis of Penality.* New York: Routledge.

Human Rights Watch (HRW). 1992. *Brutality Unchecked: Human Rights Abuses Along the U.S. Border with Mexico.* New York: HRW. May.

———. 1995a. *Bolivia: Human Rights Violations and the War on Drugs.* New York: HRW. July.

———. 1995b. *Crossing the Line: Human Rights Abuses Along the U.S. Border with Mexico Persist Amid Climate of Impunity.* New York: HRW. April.

———. 1996. Women's Rights Project. *All Too Familiar: Sexual Abuse of Women in U.S. State Prisons.* New York: HRW. December.

———. 1997a. *Cruel and Usual: Disproportionate Sentences for New York Drug Offenders* 9, no. 2(B). New York: HRW. March.

———. 1997b. *Slipping Through the Cracks: Unaccompanied Children Detained by the U.S. Immigration and Naturalization Service.* New York: HRW. April.

———. 2000. *Punishment and Prejudice: Racial Disparities in the War on Drugs.* New York: HRW. June.

Hurtado, Aida. 1995. "Variations, Combinations, and Evolutions: Latino Families in the United States." In *Understanding Latino Families: Scholarship, Policy, and Practice.* Ed. Ruth E. Zambrana, 40–61. Thousand Oaks, Calif.: Sage.

Hutchinson, Earl Ofari. 1990. *The Muggins of Black America.* Chicago: African American Images.

Idelson, Holly. 1995. "Block Grants Replace Prevention, Police Hiring in House Bill." *Congressional Quarterly* (February 18): 530–532.

Inmates of Sybil Brand Institute for Women et al. v. The County of Los Angeles et al. 1982a. App., 181 Cal. Rptr. 599.

Inmates of Sybil Brand Institute for Women et al. v. The County of Los Angeles et al. 1982b. 2d Civil. No. 61642.

Isikoff, Michael. 1991. "Study: White Students More Likely to Use Drugs." *Washington Post,* February 25, p. 4A.

Jackson, George. 1970. *Soledad Brother.* New York: Bantam.

James, Joy, ed. 1998. *The Angela Y. Davis Reader.* Malden, Mass.: Blackwell.

———, ed. 2000. *States of Confinement: Policing, Detention, and Prisons.* New York: St. Martin's.

Jankowski, Martín Sánchez. 1991. *Islands in the Street: Gangs and American Urban Society.* Berkeley: University of California Press.

Jelsma, Martin, and Theo Ronken, eds. 1998. *Democracias Bajo Fuego.* Montevideo, Uruguay: Transnational Institute (TNI), Ediciones Brecha, Acción Andina.

Johansen, Lois. 1996. See below under Personal Interviews.

Johnson, Paula C. 2003. *Inner Lives: Voices of African-American Women in Prison.* New York: New York University Press.

Joseph, Janice, and Dorothy Taylor. 2003. *With Justice for All: Minorities and Women in Criminal Justice.* Upper Saddle River, N.J.: Prentice Hall.

Joyce, Elizabeth, and Carlos Malamud, eds. 1998. *Latin America and the Multinational Drug Trade.* New York: St. Martin's.

Kates, Erika Anne. 1984. "Litigation as a Means of Achieving Social Change: A Case Study of Women in Prison." Ph.D. diss., Brandeis University.

King, Ryan S., and Marc Mauer. 2002. "State Sentencing and Corrections Policy in an Era of Fiscal Restraint." Washington, D.C.: Sentencing Project.

Knapp Commission. 1973. *The Knapp Commission Report on Police Corruption.* New York: George Braziller. March.

Kolts, James G. 1992. *The Los Angeles County Sheriff's Department: A Report.* Los Angeles: Board of Supervisors.

Kratcoski, Peter C., and Donald B. Walker. 1984. *Criminal Justice in America: Process and Issues.* New York: Random House.

Kwitny, Jonathan. 1987. *The Crimes of the Patriots.* New York: Norton.

Laserna, Roberto, ed. 1993. *Economía política de las drogas: Lecturas latinoamericanas.* Cochabamba, Bolivia: Centro de Estudios de la Realidad Económica y Social, Consejo Latinoamericano de Ciencias Sociales.

Law Enforcement Assistance Administration (LEAA). 1975. *The Report of the LEAA Task Force on Women.* Washington, D.C.: USDOJ.

———. 1980. *National Hispanic Conference on Law Enforcement and Criminal Justice, 1980.* Washington, D.C.: U.S. Department of Justice.

Lee, Robert Jose. 1977. "Profile of Puerto Rican Prisoners in New Jersey and Its Implications for the Administration of Criminal Justice." Master's thesis, Rutgers University.

Leone, Richard C., and Greg Anrig Jr., eds. 2003. *The War on Our Freedoms.* New York: Public Affairs.

Lesbian Tide. 1972. "We Mean Business." July.

Levine, Michele, and Laura Kavanau-Levine. 1993. *The Big White Lie.* New York: Thunder's Mouth.

Lewis, Oscar. 1959. *Five Families: Mexican Case Studies in the Culture of Poverty.* New York: Basic Books.

———. 1961. *The Children of Sánchez.* New York: Vintage.

———. 1966. *La Vida: A Puerto Rican Family in the Culture of Poverty—San Juan and New York.* New York: Random House.

Lichtblau, Eric. 2000. "U.S. Crime Decrease Sets Record." *(Binghamton, N.Y.) Press and Sun-Bulletin,* May 8, p. 1A.

———. 2003. "U.S. Uses Terror Law to Pursue Crimes from Drugs to Swindling." *New York Times* (NYT), September 28, p. 1A.

López, Iris. 1977. "Agency and Constraint: Sterilization and Reproductive Rights Among Puerto Rican Women in New York City." In *Situated Lives: Gender and Culture in Everyday Life.* Ed. Louise Lamphere, Helena Ragone, and Patricia Zavella. New York: Routledge.

Los Angeles County Jail Division (LACJD). 1971. *Annual Report of the Los Angeles County Jail Division.* Los Angeles.

Los Angeles County Sheriff's Department (LASD). 1989. "News Release: Sheriff Unveils New Phone System." October 11. Photocopy.

———. 2002. "Sybil Brand Institute for Women." Fax, September 26.

Los Angeles Times (LAT). 1964–1997.

———. 1997. Orange County edition. December 28.

———. 2000. "First Arrests Ordered in L.A. Police Scandal." April 25, p. 12A.

Lusane, Clarence. 1991. *Pipe Dream Blues.* Boston: South End.

Mabry, Donald J., ed. 1989. *The Latin American Narcotics Trade and U.S. National Security.* New York: Greenwood.

Mademoiselle. 1999. "Good Women, Bad Cops." October, 184–187, 212–213.

Maher, Lisa. 2004. "A Reserve Army: Women and the Drug Market." In *The Criminal Justice System and Women: Offenders, Prisoners, Victims, and Workers.* 3d ed. Ed. Barbara Raffel Price and Natalie J. Sokoloff, 127–146. New York: McGraw-Hill.

Maingot, Anthony P. 1998. "Offshore Banking in the Caribbean: The Panamanian Case." In *Latin America and the Multinational Drug Trade.* Ed. Elizabeth Joyce and Carlos Malamud. New York: St. Martin's.

Malcolm X and Alex Haley. 1964. *The Autobiography of Malcolm X.* New York: Ballantine.

Mandel, Jerry. 1981. *Police Use of Deadly Force: Los Angeles.* Washington, D.C.: National Council of La Raza.

Mann, Coramae Richey. 1993. *Unequal Justice.* Bloomington: Indiana University Press.

———. 1995a. "The Contribution of Institutional Racism to Minority Crime." In *Ethnicity, Race, and Crime.* Ed. D. F. Hawkins, 259–280. Albany: State University of New York Press.

———. 1995b. "Women of Color and the Criminal Justice System." In *The Criminal Justice System and Women.* 2d ed. Ed. Barbara Raffel Price and Natalie J. Sokoloff, 118–135. New York: McGraw-Hill.

Margain, Hugo B. 1990. "The War on Drugs: A Mexican Perspective." *Voices of Mexico* 15 (October/December): 3–8.

Marotta, Sylvia, and Jorge García. 2003. "Latinos in the United States in 2000." *Hispanic Journal of Behavioral Sciences* 25: 13–34.

Martin, William G. 2000. "Privatizing Prisons from the USA to SA: Controlling Dangerous Africans Across the Atlantic." *Association of Concerned Africa Scholars Bulletin* 59 (winter): 2–9.

Mathias, Robert A. 1986. *The Road Not Taken: Cost-Effective Alternatives for Non-Violent Felony Offenders in New York State.* New York: CANY. September.

Mauer, Marc. 1997. *Intended and Unintended Consequences: State Racial Disparities in Imprisonment.* Washington, D.C.: Sentencing Project. January.

Mauer, Marc, and Tracy Huling. 1995. *Young Black Americans and the Criminal Justice System: Five Years Later.* Washington, D.C.: Sentencing Project. October.

McDonnell, Patrick J., and Sebastian Rotella. 1993. "When Agents Cross over the Borderline: Law Enforcement Charges of Wrongdoing in Border Patrol Have Forced Even Loyalists To Call for Reforms." *LAT,* April 22–24.

McGehee, Ralph. 1983. *Deadly Deceits: My 25 Years in the CIA.* New York: Sheridan Square.

McGowan, Brenda G., and Karen L. Blumental. 1976. "Children of Women Prisoners: A Forgotten Minority." In *The Female Offender.* Ed. Laura Crites. Lexington, Mass.: D. C. Heath.

Meddis, Sam. 1989. "Whites, Not Blacks, at the Core of the Drug Crisis." *USA Today,* December 20.

Meeker, James W., John Dombrink, and Luis A. Mallett. 2000. "Access to Justice for the Poor and Moderate-Income Populations: Issues for California Latinos." *Justice Professional* 13, no. 1 (April): 91–102.

Melanson, Philip. 1983. "The CIA's Secret Ties to Local Police." *Nation,* March 26.

Mexican American Legal Defense and Education Fund (MALDEF). 1978. "Dallas Brutality Conference Displays Chicano Unity." *MALDEF* 8 (summer): 1–8.

Miranda, Marie "Keta." 2003. *Homegirls in the Public Sphere.* Austin: University of Texas Press.

Miranda v. Arizona. 1966. 384 U.S. 436 at 479.

Mirandé, Alfredo. 1987. *Gringo Justice.* Notre Dame, Indiana: University of Notre Dame Press.

Mirandé, Alfredo, and José López. 1992. "Chicano Urban Youth Gangs: A Critical Analysis of a Social Problem." *Latino Studies Journal* (September): 15–29.

Mitford, Jessica. 1971. "Kind and Usual Punishment in California." *Atlantic Monthly,* March.

Mohanty, Chandra Talpade, Ann Russo, and Lourdes Torres, eds. 1991. *Third-World Women and the Politics of Feminism.* Bloomington: Indiana University Press.

Mollen Commission. 1994. *Commission Report.* Committee to investigate allegations of police corruption and the anti-corruption procedures of the Police Department. New York. July 7.

Moore, Joan W. 1978. *Homeboys: Gangs, Drugs, and Prison in the Barrios of Los Angeles.* Philadelphia: Temple University Press.

———. 1991. *Going Down the Barrio: Homeboys and Homegirls in Change.* Philadelphia: Temple University Press.

———. 1994. "The Chola Life Course: Chicana Heroin Users and the Barrio Gang." *International Journal of the Addictions* 29, no. 9: 1115–1126.

Moore, Joan W., and John Hagedorn. 2001. "Female Gangs: A Focus on Research." *Juvenile Justice Bulletin* (March): 1–12.

Moore, Joan W., and Alberto Mata. 1981. "Women and Heroin in Chicano Communities." Final Report for the National Institute of Justice on Drug Abuse. Los Angeles: CPRP.

Moore, Joan W., and Harry Pachón. 1985. *Hispanics in the United States.* Englewood Cliffs, N.J.: Prentice-Hall.

Moore, Joan W., James Diego Vigil, and Josh Levy. 1995. "Huisas of the Street: Chicana Gang Members." *Latino Studies Journal* 6, no. 1 (January): 27–48.

Mora, Magdalena, and Adelaida R. del Castillo, eds. 1980. *Mexican Women in the United States.* Los Angeles: Chicano Studies Research Center.

Moraga, Cherríe. 1983. *Loving in the War Years: Lo que nunca pasó por sus labios.* Boston: South End.

Moraga, Cherrié, and Gloria Anzaldúa. 1981. *This Bridge Called My Back: Writings by Radical Women of Color.* Boston: Persephone; reprint, New York: Kitchen Table Women of Color Press, 1983.

Morales, Armando. 1972. *Ando Sangrando (I Am Bleeding): A Study of Mexican-American Police Conflict.* La Puente, Calif.: Perspectiva Publications.

Morgan, Patricia. 1954. *Shame of a Nation: A Documented Story of Police-State Terror Against Mexican-Americans in the U.S.A.* Los Angeles: Committee for Protection of Foreign Born.

Moynihan, Daniel P. 1967. "The Negro Family: The Case for National Action." In *The Moynihan Report and the Politics of Controversy.* Ed. Lee Rainwater and W. L. Yancey. Cambridge: MIT Press.

Muñoz, Ed A. 2000. "Latino Sentencing Dispositions, 1987–1991: An Empirical Assessment of 'Gringo Justice.'" *Justice Professional* 13, no. 1 (April): 19–48.

Murphy, Jim, Nancy Johnson, and Wanda Edwards. 1992. *Addicted Mothers: Imprisonment and Alternatives.* Albany, New York: Coalition for Criminal Justice/Center for Justice Education.

Murray, Yxta Maya. 1997. *Locas.* New York: Grove Press.

National Commission on Law Observance and Enforcement (NCLOE), Wickersham Commission. 1931. *Report on Crime and the Foreign Born.* No. 10. Washington, D.C.: GPO.

New York City Board of Correction (NYCBOC). 1973. *Through the Veil of Partial Comprehension.* March 19. New York: NYCBOC.

New York County Lawyers Association (NYCLA). 1985. Special Committee on Penal and Correctional Reform. *How the Criminal Justice System Fails the Spanish-Speaking Community of New York City and What Should be Done About It.* New York: NYCLA. August.

———. 1996. Drug Policy Task Force. *Report and Recommendations of the Drug Policy Task Force.* New York: NYCLA. October.

New York State Department of Correctional Services (NYSDOCS), Division of Program Planning, Research and Evaluation. 1986a. *An Examination of the Trend of Female New Commitments, 1976–1984.* Albany: NYSDOCS. June.

———. 1986b. *Characteristics of Female Inmates Held Under Custody, 1975–1985.* By Kathy Canestrini. Albany: NYSDOCS. September.

———. 1986c. *Selected Characteristics of the Department's Hispanic Inmate Population.* Albany: NYSDOCS. December.

———. 2000. *Characteristics of New Commitments 2000.* Albany: NYSDOCS.

———. 2002. *Men and Women under Custody: 1987–2001.* Albany: NYSDOCS.

NewsWest. 1976. "Law Requires Segregating Lesbians." October 15.

———. 1976–1977. "Lesbian Inmates Gain Freedoms." December 23–January 6.

Olguín, Ben V. 1995. "Testimonios Pintaos: The Political and Symbolic Economy of Pinto/a Discourse." Ph.D. diss. Stanford University.

Omi, Michael, and Howard Winant. 1986. *Racial Formation in the U.S.* New York: Routledge and Kegan Paul.

O'Reilly, Kenneth. 1988. *Racial Matters: The FBI's Secret File on Black America, 1960–1972.* New York: Free Press.

O'Shea, Kathleen A., and Beverly R. Fletcher. 1997. *Female Offenders: An Annotated Bibliography*. Westport, Conn.: Greenwood.

Owen, Barbara. 1998. *In the Mix: Struggle and Survival in a Women's Prison*. Albany: State University of New York Press.

Owen, Barbara, and Barbara Bloom. 1995. "Profiling Women Prisoners: Findings from National Surveys and a California Sample." *Prison Journal* 75, no. 2 (June): 165–185.

Pardo, Mary S. 1998. *Mexican-American Women Activists*. Philadelphia: Temple University Press.

Pelaez, Vicky. 2001. "Cuando una madre es puesta tras las rejas." *(New York) El Diario/La Prensa*, May 13, pp. 2, 3.

Pérez, Judy. 1996. "The Effect of My Incarceration on My Loved Ones." *Women and the Criminal Justice System* 4: 200–201.

Petersilia, Joan. 1985. "Racial Disparities in the Criminal Justice System: A Summary." *Crime and Delinquency* 31: 15–34.

Pettiway, Leon E. 1987. "Participation in Crime Partnerships by Female Drug Users: The Effects of Domestic Arrangements, Drug Use, and Criminal Involvement." *Criminology* 25, no. 3: 741–765.

Pinto Quintanilla, Juan Carlos. 1999. *Cárceles y familia*. Cochabamba, Bolivia: Terre des Hommes.

Price, Barbara Raffel, and Natalie J. Sokoloff, eds. 1995. *The Criminal Justice System and Women: Offenders, Victims, and Workers*. 2d ed. New York: McGraw-Hill.

———. 2004. *The Criminal Justice System and Women: Offenders, Prisoners, Victims, and Workers*. 3d ed. New York: McGraw-Hill.

Quicker, John C. 1983. *Homegirls*. San Pedro, Calif.: International Universities.

Quinney, Richard. 2002. *Critique of Legal Order: Crime Control in Capitalist Society*. Boston: Little, Brown, 1974. Reprint, New Brunswick, N.J.: Transaction.

Rafter, Nicole Hahn. 1985. *Partial Justice*. Boston: Northeastern University Press.

Ramos, Juanita. 2004. *Compañeras: Latina Lesbians (An Anthology), Lesbianas latinoamericanas*. 3d ed. New York: Latina Lesbian History Project, 1987. Reprints, New York: Routledge, 1994; New York: Latina Lesbian History Project.

Reeves, Jimmie, and Richard Campbell. 1994. *Cracked Coverage*. Durham, N.C.: Duke University Press.

Reagan, Ronald. 1985. "Audio Address to the Nation on Proposed Crime Legislation." In *Public Papers of the Presidents 1984*. Vol. 2. Washington, D.C.: Office of the Federal Register.

Reiman, Jeffrey. 1990. *The Rich Get Richer and the Poor Get Prison*. 3d ed. New York: Macmillan.

Reuter, Peter. 1998. "Foreign Demand for Latin American Drugs: The USA and Europe." In *Latin America and the Multinational Drug Trade*. Ed. Elizabeth Joyce and Carlos Malamud, 23–43. New York: St. Martin's.

Richie, Beth E. 1996. *Compelled to Crime: The Gender Entrapment of Battered Black Women*. New York: Routledge.

Romo-Carmona, Mariana, ed. 2001. *Coversaciones: Relatos por padres y madres de hijas lesbianas e hijos gay*. San Francisco: Cleis.

Ross, Luana. 1998. *Inventing the Savage: The Social Construction of Native American Criminality*. Austin: University of Texas Press.

Rossi, Adriana. 1996. *Narcotráfico y Amazonia Ecuatoriana*. Buenos Aires, Argentina: Kohen y Asociados Internacional.

San Francisco Chronicle (SFC). 1980. "Drug Courier Profile Upheld." May 28.

Santana, Luz. 1985. Address before New York Hispanic Inmate Needs Task Force (HINTF) banquet, November 20. Albany, New York.

Schiraldi, Vincent. 1994. "The Undue Influence of California's Guards' Union: California's Correctional-Industrial Complex." San Francisco: Center on Juvenile and Criminal Justice. October.

Scott, Peter Dale, and Jonathan Marshall. 1991. *Cocaine Politics*. Berkeley: University of California Press.

Segura, Denise A., and Beatríz M. Pesquera. 1999. "Chicana Political Consciousness: Re-negotiating Culture, Class, and Gender with Oppositional Practices." *Aztlán* 24, no. 1 (spring): 5–32.

Serna, Idella. 1992. *Locked Down: A Woman's Life in Prison, the Story of Mary (Lee) Dortch*. Norwich, Vt.: New Victoria.

Shakur, Assata. 1987. *Assata: An Autobiography*. Westport, Conn.: Lawrence Hill.

Shapiro, B. 1997. "Victims and Vengeance: Why the Victims' Rights Amendment Is a Bad Idea." *Nation*, February 10, pp. 11–13, 16–19.

Sissons, Peter L. 1979. *The Hispanic Experience of Criminal Justice*. Monograph No. 3. New York: Hispanic Research Center, Fordham University.

Smith, M. H. 1980. "Exploring the Re-Entry and Support Services for Hispanic Offenders." In LEAA, *National Hispanic Conference on Law Enforcement and Criminal Justice, 1980*. Washington, D.C.: U.S. Department of Justice, 131–150.

Smith, P., ed. 1992. *Drug Policy in the Americas*. Boulder, Colo.: Westview.

Spencer, Elouise Junius. 1977. "The Social System of a Medium Security Women's Prison." Ph.D. diss., University of Kansas.

Stockwell, John. 1978. *In Search of Enemies: A CIA Story*. New York: Norton.

Stolen Lives Project (SLP). 1999. *Stolen Lives Killed by Law Enforcement*. 2d ed. New York: SLP.

Sudbury, Julia. 2002. "'If I Die Here, Least I'll be Free': Black Women 'Mules' and the Transnational Prison Industrial Complex." *Harvard Journal of African-American Public Policy* 8 (summer).

———. 2004a. "Women of Color, Globalization, and the Politics of Incarceration." In *The Criminal Justice System and Women*. 3rd ed. Ed. Barbara R. Price and Natalie J. Sokoloff. New York: McGraw-Hill.

———, ed. 2004b. *Global Lockdown: Race, Gender, and the Prison Industrial Complex*. New York: Routledge.

Sullivan, Joseph. 1990. "NJ Police Are Accused of Minority Arrest Campaign." *New York Times*, February 19.

Szalavitz, Maia. 1999. "War on Drugs, War on Women." *On These Issues Magazine* (winter).

Thomas, Piri. 1974. *Seven Long Times*. New York: Praeger.

Tome, Velia. 1992. "Childhood Exposure to Violence and Abuse as It Relates to Development of Post-Traumatic Stress Disorder Among Mexican-American Gang Members in Southern California." *Dissertation Abstracts International* 54 (5–B0 2788), U.S. International University.

Tonry, Michael. 1995. *Malign Neglect: Race, Crime, and Punishment in America.* New York: Oxford University Press.

———. 1996. *Sentencing Matters.* New York: Oxford University Press.

Torres, Dorothy M. 1979. "Chicano Gangs in the East L.A. Barrios." *Youth Authority Quarterly* 32, no. 3 (fall): 5–13.

Trujillo, Carla. 1991. *Chicana Lesbians.* Berkeley, Calif.: Third Woman.

Trujillo, Larry D. 1974. "La evolución del 'Bandido' al 'Pachuco': A Critical Examination and Evaluation of Criminological Literature on Chicanos." *Issues in Criminology* 9 (fall): 43–67.

———. 1983. "Police Crimes in the Barrio." In *History, Culture, and Society: Chicano Studies in the 1980s.* Ed. Mario T. García, Francisco Lomeli, Mario Barrera, Edward Escobar, and John García, 199–242. Ypsilanti, Mich.: Bilingual Press.

Turk, Austin, Barbara Owen, and Barbara Bloom. 1995. "Profiling the Needs of California's Female Prisoners: A Needs Assessment." Washington, D.C.: National Institute of Corrections. February.

Turner, M. G., J. L. Sundt, B. K. Applegate, and F. T. Cullen. 1995. "'Three Strikes and You're Out' Legislation: A National Assessment." *Federal Probation* 59, no. 8 (September): 16–35.

Unión del Barrio. 1995. "The Political Economy of Prisons in Occupied America." *(San Diego, Calif.) ¡La Verdad!,* October–December, 6–7.

United Nations (UN). Department of Public Information. 1977. *Single Convention on Narcotic Drugs.* New York: UN.

———. 1987. *The United Nations and Drug Abuse Control.* Publication No. E.87. I.8. New York: UN.

———. 1989. *Body of Principles for the Protection of All Persons Under Any Form of Detention or Imprisonment.* New York: UN.

———. 1991. *UN Convention Against the Illicit Traffic of Narcotics.* Vienna Convention, 1988. New York: UN.

U.S. Bureau of the Census (USCB). 2001a. *The Hispanic Population.* Washington, D.C. May.

———. 2001b. *Sourcebook of Criminal Justice Statistics: 2000.* Washington, D.C.

———. 2002. *Statistical Abstract of the United States: 2002.* Washington, D.C. December.

U.S. Commission on Civil Rights (USCCR). 1970. *Mexican Americans and the Administration of Justice in the Southwest.* Washington, D.C.: GPO.

———. 1980. *Tarnished Golden Doors: Civil Rights Issues in Immigration.* Washington, D.C.

U.S. Congress (USC). 1990. House Committee on Armed Services. *The Andean Drug Strategy and the Role of the U.S. Military.* 101st Congress, 1st Session. Washington, D.C. January.

U.S. Department of Justice (USDOJ). 1960–2002. *Uniform Crime Reports: Crime in the U.S.* Washington, D.C.

————. 1981. *Report on Youth Gang Violence in California.* Attorney General's Youth Gang Task Force. Washington, D.C. June.

————. 1994. Office of Juvenile Justice and Delinquency Prevention. *Conditions of Confinement, Juvenile Detention and Correctional Facilities Research Report Executive Summary 5.* Washington, D.C.

U.S. Department of State (USDOS). 1991. *International Narcotics Control Strategy.* Washington, D.C.

U.S. General Accounting Office (USGAO). 1988. *Drug Control: Issues Surrounding Increased Use of the Military in Drug Interdiction.* GAO/NSIAD-88–156. Washington, D.C. April.

————. 1996. *Control de Drogas: Esfuerzos Contra Narcóticos en Mexico.* Washington, D.C. June.

U.S. House of Representatives (USHR). 1972. Committee on the Judiciary. "Prisons, Prison Reform, and Prisoners' Rights: California." Hearings before Subcommittee No. 3. *Corrections, Part II.*

————. 1984. *Police Misconduct.* Hearings before the Subcommittee on Criminal Justice. Serial No. 50, parts 1 and 2. 98th Congress, 1st Session.

————. 1990. Committee on Armed Services. *The Andean Drug Strategy and the Role of the U.S. Military,* 101st Congress, 1st Session. January.

U.S. Sentencing Commission. 1991. *Special Report to the Congress: Mandatory Minimum Penalties in the Federal Criminal Justice System.* August. http://www.ussc .gov/r_congress/manmin.pdf.

Vigil, James Diego. 1988. *Barrio Gangs: Street Life and Identity in Southern California.* Austin: University of Texas Press.

Walker, William O. III. 1989. *Drug Control in the Americas.* Albuquerque: University of New Mexico Press.

Ward, David, and Gene Kassebaum. 1965. *Women's Prisons.* Chicago: Aldine-Atherton.

Washington Office of Latin America (WOLA). 1991. *Clear and Present Danger: The U.S. Military and the War on Drugs in the Andes.* Washington, D.C.: WOLA.

Watterson, Kathryn. 1996. *Women in Prison.* Revised edition. Boston: Northeastern University Press.

Welsh, Wayne N. 1992. "The Dynamics of Jail Reform Litigation: A Comparative Analysis of Litigation in California Counties." *Law and Society Review* 26, no. 3.

Whitlock, Katherine. 2001. *In a Time of Broken Bones: A Call to Dialogue on Hate Violence and the Limitations of Hate Crimes Legislation.* Philadelphia: American Friends Services Committee.

Williams, Ian. 2001. "U.S. Lost Seat on U.N. Human Rights Commission Follows Threat to Veto Mideast Resolutions." *Washington Report on Middle East Affairs* 20, no. 5 (July): 32, 72.

Women's Commission for Refugee Women and Children (WCRWC). 1995. *An Uncertain Future, A Cruel Present: Women Seeking Asylum Imprisoned in the United States.* New York: WCRWC. September.

Women's Prison Association (WPA). 1995. *Breaking the Cycle of Despair: Children of Incarcerated Mothers.* New York: WPA. January.

Worthington, Rogers. 1987. "Nicaraguan Woman Gets Three Years in Cocaine Case." *Chicago Tribune*, August 26.

Wright, Erik Olin. 1973. *The Politics of Punishment.* New York: Harper and Row.

Zambrana, Ruth E., ed. 1995. *Understanding Latino Families: Scholarship, Policy, and Practice.* Thousand Oaks, Calif.: Sage.

Personal Interviews

Barry, Ellen. 1995b. April 21.

Carmen. October 20, 1996.

Cristina. May 7, 1995.

Deborah. July 4, 1996.

Diana. January 30, 1999.

Doris. April 19, 1995.

Dulce. April 20, 1995.

Estela. May 7, 1995.

Gina. July 14, 1996.

Graciela. May 8, 1995.

Julia. April 18, 1995.

Johansen, Lois. July 14, 1996.

Lillian. May 2, 1995.

Linda. July 13, 1996.

Lucy. July 6, 1996.

Luisa. March 18, 1999.

Marta. May 8, 1995.

Matilde. May 7, 1995.

Melinda. April 19, 1995.

Mercedes. October 18 and 21, 1996.

Paula. November 19, 1997.

Rita. July 5, 1996.

Rosa. March 19, 1999.

Sonia. March 19, 1999.

Ursula. April 15, 1995.

Victoria. July 11, 1996.

Yolanda. November 19, 1997.

About the Author

Juanita Díaz-Cotto, Ph.D., is an Associate Professor of Sociology, Women's Studies, and Latin American and Caribbean Area Studies at the State University of New York at Binghamton. She is the author of *Gender, Ethnicity, and the State: Latina and Latino Prison Politics* (1996) and the editor, under the pseudonym of Juanita Ramos, of *Compañeras: Latina Lesbians (An Anthology), Lesbianas Latinoamericanas* (third edition 2004). She has been active in various human rights struggles for more than 30 years.